Corporate Governance Essentials

Brian Coyle

PUBLISHING

Published by ICSA Information & Training Ltd
16 Park Crescent
London W1B 1AH

Typeset by Pantek Arts Ltd, Maidstone, Kent and printed in Great Britain by WM Print Ltd, Walsall, West Midlands

British Library Cataloguing in Publication Data
A catalogue record for this book is available from the British Library

ISBN 978-1-86072-399-5

Contents

Acronyms and Abbreviations

ABI	Association of British Insurers
ACCA	Association of Chartered Certified Accountants
ACEVO	Association of Chief Executives of Voluntary Associations
AGM	annual general meeting
AIM	alternative investment market
AQF	Audit Quality Forum
ASB	Accounting Standards Board
ATOL	Association of Travel Operators
CA	Companies Act
CACG	Commonwealth Association of Corporate Governance
CEO	chief executive officer
CFO	chief financial officer
CIMA	Chartered Institute of Management Accountants
CIPFA	Chartered Institute of Public Finance and Accountability
CSR	corporate social responsibility
CTN	Charity Trustee Network
DTI	Department of Trade and Industry
EBITDA	earnings before interest, taxation, depreciation and amortisation
EGM	extraordinary general meeting
ESB	Ethical Standards Board
ESG	environmental, social and governance
EU	European Union
FRC	Financial Reporting Council
FSA	Financial Services Authority
FSMA	Financial Services and Markets Act
GRI	Global Reporting Initiative
HAZOPS	hazard and operability studies
IBE	Institute of Business Ethics
ICAEW	Institute of Chartered Accountants in England and Wales
ICGN	International Corporate Governance Network
IFAC	International Federation of Accountants
IMA	Investment Management Association
IoD	Institute of Directors
IOSCO	International Organisation of Securities Commissions
IPC	investor protection committee
ISC	Institutional Shareholders Committee
ISS	Institutional Shareholder Services Inc

KPI	key performance indicators
LLA	liability limitation agreement
NAPF	National Association of Pension Funds
NCVO	National Council of Voluntary Organisations
NDPB	non-departmental pubic body
NED	non-executive director
NRSRO	nationally recognised statistical ratings organisation
NYSE	New York Stock Exchange
OECD	Organisation for Economic Cooperation and Development
OFR	Operating and Financial Review
OPM	Office for Public Management
PBIT	profit before interest and tax
PIRC	Pensions and Investment Consultants Limited
QCA	Quoted Companies Alliance
RIS	Regulated Information Service
SEC	Securities and Exchange Commission
SEE	social, environmental and ethical
SID	senior independent director
SMEs	small and medium-sized enterprises
SOX	Sarbanes-Oxley Act
SRI	socially responsible investment
TCE	transaction cost economics
TSR	total shareholder return
UKSA	UK Shareholders Association
VFM	value for money

Acknowledgements

The publisher and author acknowledge the following for permission to reproduce the following material in this volume:

Appendix 1 –The Combined Code
© Financial Reporting Council, 2006. Reproduced with permission.

Appendix 2 – OECD Principles of Corporate Governance © OECD, 2004.

Appendix 3 – CACG Principles for Corporate Governance in the Commonwealth
Principles for Corporate Governance in the Commonwealth © Commonwealth Association for Corporate Governance under the aegis of the Commonwealth Business Council, November 1999.

Appendix 4 – King II Report on Corporate Governance: Summary of Code of Corporate Practices and Conduct
Reproduced with permission of ICSA Southern Africa © ICSA Southern Africa, June 2002.

Every effort has been made to locate and acknowledge sources and holders of copyright material in this study text. In the event that any have been overlooked, please contact the publisher.

Chapter 1

Definitions and issues in corporate governance

1. Defining corporate governance
2. Theoretical frameworks for corporate governance
3. Development of corporate governance
4. Stakeholders
5. Key objectives in corporate governance
6. Key issues in corporate governance
7. Approaches to corporate governance

1 Defining corporate governance

'Governance' refers to the way in which something is governed and to the function of governing. The governance of a country, for example, refers to the powers and actions of the legislative assembly, the executive government and the judiciary.

Corporate governance refers to the way in which companies are governed, and to what purpose. It is concerned with practices and procedures for trying to ensure that a company is run in such a way that it achieves its objectives. This could be to maximise the wealth of its owners (the shareholders), subject to various guidelines and constraints and with regard to the other groups with an interest in what the company does. Guidelines and constraints include behaving in an ethical way and in compliance with laws and regulations. From a shareholder's perspective, corporate governance might be defined as a process for monitoring and control, to ensure that management run the company in the interests of the shareholders.

Other groups with an interest in how the company acts include employees, customers and the general public.

Some other definitions that have been provided are as follows:

- 'Corporate governance is the system by which companies are directed and controlled' (Cadbury Report, 1992). The Cadbury Report was a major UK inquiry into corporate governance, and this is a generally accepted definition.
- 'Whilst management processes have been widely explored, relatively little attention has been paid to the processes by which companies are governed. If management is about running businesses, governance is about seeing that it is run properly. All companies need governing as well as managing' (Professor Bob Tricker, 1984).

- Governance might not be an easy concept to understand. In the case of governing a country, it would be concerned with who has the power to rule and what the governors of the country should be trying to achieve. The government of a democratic country presumably sets itself the objective of protecting its people and acting in their best interests, whatever these might be. Powers are shared between the legislative, executive and judiciary, but a matter of debate is how these powers should be shared and exercised. In the UK, for example, there is healthy political debate about the respective powers of Parliament, the Prime Minister and the Cabinet and the law courts in the UK, and the powers of the government bodies and courts of the European Union.

- In a large company, similar issues of governance arise. Corporate governance is concerned with how powers are shared and exercised by different groups, to ensure that the objectives of the company are achieved. Aspects of corporate governance are the rights of shareholders and other interest groups such as the employees, how powers are shared and exercised by the directors, and how the holders of power in a company should be held accountable for what they do.

- A company is a legal entity or 'legal person'. As a person, it is able to enter into contracts and make business transactions. It can own assets and owe money to others, and it can sue and be sued in law. Human beings have to make decisions and arrange transactions in the company's name.

- Just as a country has citizens, a company has members. The members of a company are its owners, the 'equity' shareholders. However, membership changes continually, as investors buy and sell the company's shares.

- The citizens of a country, even in a democracy, have relatively few powers. Power is in the hands of the legislative (Parliament) and the executive (the government). In a similar way, shareholders have relatively few powers, which are restricted mainly to certain voting rights. Power is in the hands of the board of directors, or perhaps just one or two individual directors on the board.

For large companies, the main issue with corporate governance is the relationship between the board of directors and the shareholders, and the way in which the board of directors exercises its powers. The relationship between the shareholders and the board of directors can be described as a 'principal–agent' relationship.

Principles of corporate governance are based on the view that a company should be governed in the interests of the shareholders, and possibly also in the interests of other stakeholder groups. The board of directors ought to use their powers in an appropriate and responsible way, and should be accountable in some ways to the shareholders (and other stakeholders, perhaps).

1.1   Why is corporate governance important?

A company should have objectives. Some of these, such as the reasons for its existence, may be set out in its written constitution. Other objectives may be implied or assumed rather than clearly documented. A company should be governed in a way that moves it towards the achievement of its objectives.

However, although a company exists as a legal person, in reality it is the organised, collective effort of many different individuals. It is controlled by a board of directors in the interests of its owners, the shareholders. The interests of the board and the shareholders ought to coincide, but in practice they may be at odds. The challenge of good corporate governance is to find a way in which the interests of shareholders, directors and other interest groups can all be sufficiently satisfied.

Corporate governance is a matter of far greater importance for large public companies, where the separation of ownership from management is much wider than for small private companies. Public companies raise capital on the stock markets, and institutional investors hold vast portfolios of shares and other invest ments. Investors need to know that their money is reasonably safe. Should there be any doubts about the integrity or intentions of the individuals in charge of a company, the value of the company's shares will be affected and the company will have difficulty raising any new capital should it wish to do so. If there is weak corpo rate governance in a country generally, the country will struggle to attract foreign investment.

It might seem self-evident that good (or adequate) corporate governance supports capital markets. However, the impetus for the development of codes of best practice and stricter regulatory regimes has come largely from scandals and setbacks, where evidence of bad corporate governance has emerged, and company share prices and the stock market generally have suffered as a consequence.

Bad corporate governance is a problem for any country with capital markets that ought to be efficient. Events over the past few decades have shown that it often takes a scandal to focus the attention of the regulators. In recent years, following a number of corporate scandals in the US – Enron perhaps being the most notorious, but by no means the only one – problems of bad governance have emerged in Europe (for example, Ahold in the Netherlands; Parmalat in Italy) and Japan (for example, Livedoor). The problems and challenges of corporate governance are worldwide.

1.2   Governance and management

It is important to recognise the difference between the governance of a company and its management.

Powers to manage the affairs of a company are given to the board of directors, but most of these powers are delegated to the chief executive officer (CEO) or managing director, and are delegated further to executive directors and executive managers. The board of directors should retain some powers and responsibilities, and certain matters should be reserved for board decision-making rather than delegated to the management team (see Chapter 4).

The board of directors should also be responsible for monitoring the performance of the management team.

However, the board of directors is not responsible for day-to-day management. It is responsible for governing the company. Responsibilities for governance go beyond management, and governance should not be confused with management. Even so, it is probably true to say that when a senior executive manager is 'promoted' to the board, he or she may consider the position of an executive director to be a recognition of his or her senior executive position. However, a 'promotion' of an executive manager to the board of directors creates new responsibilities for governance that are not related to management. The executive director ought to think as a member of the board, rather than as a senior executive, in performing his or her duties as a director.

2 Theoretical frameworks for corporate governance

It is useful to consider the theoretical justification for a system of rules or guidelines on corporate governance. There are three different frameworks:

1   Agency theory.
2   Transaction cost theory.
3   Stakeholder theory.

2.1 Agency theory

Agency theory was developed by Michael C. Jensen and William H. Meckling in the 1970s. The theory is based on the separation of the ownership of a company and control over the company's actions. Shareholders own the company, but managers control it. Jensen and Meckling defined the agency relationship as a form of contract between a company's owners and its managers, where the owners (as principal) appoint an agent (the managers) to manage the company on their behalf. As a part of this arrangement, the owners must delegate decision-making authority to the management.

Jensen and Meckling suggested that the governance of a company is based on the conflicts of interest between the company's owners and managers:

- The shareholders want to increase their income and wealth over the long term. The value of their shares depends on the long-term financial prospects for the company. Shareholders are therefore concerned not only about short-term profits and dividends; they are even more concerned about long-term profitability.
- The managers run the company on behalf of the shareholders. If they do not own shares in the company, managers have no direct interest in future returns for shareholders or in the value of the shares. They have an employment contract and earn a salary. Unless they own shares, or unless their remuneration is linked to profits or share values, their main interests are likely to be the size of their remuneration package and their status as company managers.

Ideally, the 'agency contract' between the owners and the managers of as company should ensure that the managers always act in the best interests of the owners. However, it is impossible to arrange the 'perfect' contract, because decisions by the managers affect their own personal welfare as well as the interests of the owners.

Agency conflicts are differences in the interests of owners and managers. They arise in several ways:

- Moral hazard. A manager has an interest in receiving benefits from his or her position in the company. These include all the benefits that come from status, such as a company car, use of a company plane, a company house or flat, attendance at sponsored sporting events, and so on. Jensen and Meckling suggested that a manager's incentive to obtain these benefits is higher when he has no shares, or only a few shares, in the company.

- Level of effort. Managers may work less hard than they would if they were the owners of the company. The effect of this 'lack of effort' could be lower profits and a lower share price.
- Earnings retention. The remuneration of directors and senior managers is often related to the size of the company rather than to its profits. This gives managers an incentive to increase the size of the company, rather than to increase the returns to the company's shareholders. Management are more likely to want to reinvest profits in order to make the company bigger rather than pay out the profits as dividends. When this happens, companies might invest in capital investment projects where the expected profitability is quite small, or propose high-priced takeover bids for other companies.
- Time horizon. Shareholders are concerned about the long-term financial prospects of their company, because the value of their shares depends on expectations for the long-term future. In contrast, managers may only be interested in the short term. This is partly because they may receive annual bonuses based on short-term performance, and partly because they may not expect to be with the company for more than a few years.

Agency costs are the costs of having an agent to make decisions on behalf of a principal. Applying this to corporate governance, agency costs are the costs that shareholders incur by having managers to run the company instead of running the company themselves. They are potentially very high in large companies, where there are many different shareholders and a large professional management.

Agency costs consist of three elements:

- Monitoring. Shareholders need to establish systems for monitoring the actions and performance of management, to try to ensure that management are acting in their best interests. An example of monitoring is the requirement for the directors to present an annual report and accounts to the shareholders, setting out the financial performance and financial position of the company. These accounts are audited, and the auditors present a report to the shareholders. Preparing accounts and having them audited has a cost.
- Bonding. Costs might be incurred to provide incentives to managers to act in the best interests of the shareholders. The remuneration packages for directors and senior managers are therefore an important element of agency costs since they include long-term and short-term incentives.
- Residual loss. Residual loss is the costs to the shareholder that occur when the managers take decisions that are not in the best interests of the shareholders, but are in the interests of the managers themselves. Residual loss occurs, for example, when managers pay too much for a large acquisition. The managers gain personally from the enhanced status of managing a larger group of companies. The cost to the shareholders comes from the fall in share price that results from paying too much for the acquisition.

Agency theory is therefore based on the view that the system of corporate governance should be designed to minimise the agency problem and reduce agency costs. One approach to reducing the agency problem is to make the board of directors more effective at monitoring the decisions of the executive management. Another approach is to design schemes of remuneration for directors and senior managers that bring their interests more into line with those of the shareholders.

Agents should also be accountable to their principals for their decisions and actions. Accountability means reporting back to the principals and giving an account of what has been achieved, and the principal having power to reward (punish) an agent for good (bad) performance. Greater accountability should reduce the agency problem, because it provides management with a greater incentive (obtaining rewards or avoiding punishments) to achieve performance levels that are in the best interests of the shareholders.

Agency theory may therefore be summarised as follows:

- In large companies ownership is separated from control. Professional managers are appointed to act as agents for the owners of the company.
- Individuals are driven by self-interest.
- Conflicts of self-interest arise between shareholders and managers.
- Managers cannot be relied on to act in the best interests of the shareholders because they are driven by self-interest. This creates problems in the agency relationship between shareholders and management.
- These agency problems create costs for the shareholders.
- The aim should be to minimise these costs by improving the monitoring of management and/or providing management with incentives to bring their interests closer to those of the shareholders.

2.2 Transaction cost theory

Transaction cost theory provides a different basis for explaining the relationship between the owners of a company and its management. Although it is an economic theory, it also attempts to explain companies not just as 'economic units', but as an organisation consisting of people with differing views and objectives. The theory of transaction cost economics (TCE) is most closely associated with the work of Oliver Williamson in the 1970s.

The operations of a company can be performed either through market transactions or by doing the work in house. For example, a company can obtain its raw materials from an external supplier or make the materials itself. Similarly, a company can hire self-employed contractors to do work or hire full-time employees. In economic terms, a firm's decision about whether to arrange transactions in the open market or do the work in house (itself) should depend on which is cheaper. When a firm does work in house, it needs a management structure and a hierarchy of authority, with senior management at the top. According to transaction cost theory, the structure of a firm and the relationship between the owners of a firm and its management depend on the extent to which transactions are performed in house.

Total costs are defined as the sum of production costs and transaction costs:

- Production costs are the costs that would be incurred by the company in an ideal economic market. In an ideal economic market, production costs are minimised.
- Transaction costs are additional costs incurred whenever the perfect economic market is not achieved – for example, a company may buy goods from a supplier who

is not the cheapest available because it is not aware that a cheaper supplier exists; or a company may sell goods on credit, not knowing that money owed will become a bad debt.

Transaction costs are sometimes higher when a transaction is arranged in the market, and sometimes higher when the transaction is done in house. Carrying out activities in house rather than arranging contracts externally is referred to as vertical integration. Total costs are minimised when transaction costs are minimised. This should determine both the optimal size of the firm and the size of the management hierarchy. The way in which a company is organised, and the extent to which it is vertically integrated, also affect the control the company has over its transactions. As a general rule, it is in the interests of a company's management to carry out transactions internally, and not in the external market.

Performing transactions internally:

- removes the risks and uncertainties about prices of products and product quality;
- removes all the risks and costs of dealing with external suppliers.

Traditional economic theory is based on the assumption that all behaviour is rational and that profit maximisation is the rational objective of all businesses. TCE changes these assumptions by allowing for human behaviour and acknowledging that individuals do not always act rationally. Williamson based his theory on two assumptions about behaviour:

1   Bounded rationality.
2   Opportunism.

Bounded rationality

Human beings act rationally, but only within certain limits of understanding. This means, for example, that the managers of a company will in theory act rationally in seeking to maximise the value of the company for its shareholders, but their bounded rationality may make them act differently. Business is very complex and large businesses are much more complex than small ones. However, in any business there is a limit to the amount of information that individuals can remember, understand and deal with. No one is capable of assessing all the possible courses of action and no one can anticipate what will happen in the future. In a competitive market, no one can anticipate with certainty what competitors will do.

Playing chess has been used as an example of bounded rationality. The game is very complex and there are many different possible moves. The actions of the opponent in a game of chess cannot be predicted, so it is impossible to predict what he or she will do in response to a particular move. The same problem applies to managing a company: it is impossible to predict with certainty what will happen because there are too many factors and too many possibilities to consider.

Williamson was mainly concerned with what happens when individuals reach the boundaries of their understanding, because a situation is too complex or too uncertain. He wrote: 'Bounds on rationality are interesting ... only to the extent that the limits of rationality are reached – which is to say under conditions of uncertainty and/or complexity.'

When uncertainty is high or when a situation is very complex there is a greater tendency to carry out transactions 'in house' and to have vertical integration.

Opportunism

Williamson also argued that individuals act in a self-interested way and 'with guile'. They are not always honest and truthful about their intentions. Williamson defined opportunism as: 'an effort to realise individual gains through a lack of candour or honesty in transactions'. An individual may take advantage of an opportunity to gain a benefit at the expense of someone else. Managers are opportunistic by nature; given the opportunity, they will take advantage of available ways of improving their own benefits and privileges.

In terms of TCE, a problem with opportunism is that external parties, such as contractors and suppliers of goods, cannot always be trusted to act honestly. As a result, there may be a tendency for a company to carry out transactions itself rather than rely on external suppliers. However, there is also a risk that by taking control of transactions internally, managers will have opportunities to take decisions and actions that are in their personal interests. This self-interested behaviour needs to be controlled. In this respect, transaction cost theory is similar to agency theory. Although they are based on different assumptions, both agency theory and transaction cost theory support the need for controls over corporate governance practices.

2.3 Stakeholder theory

Agency theory is based on the assumption that the main objective of a company should be to maximise the wealth of shareholders. Stakeholder theory takes a different view. The stakeholder view is that the purpose of corporate governance should be to satisfy, as far as possible, the objectives of all key stakeholders – employees, investors, major creditors, customers, major suppliers, the government, local communities and the general public. One role of the company's directors therefore is to consider the interests of all the major stakeholders. However, some stakeholders may be more important than others, so that management should prioritise their interests over those of other stakeholder groups. In the introduction to its principles of corporate governance, the Organisation for Economic Cooperation and Development (OECD) commented that an aim of government policy ('public policy') should be 'to provide firms with the incentives and discipline to minimise divergence between private and social returns and to protect the interest of stakeholders'.

The OECD Principles themselves recognise the role of stakeholders in corporate governance and state that the corporate governance framework should:

- acknowledge the rights of stakeholders that are recognised in law or through mutual agreements; and
- encourage active cooperation between corporations and stakeholders in creating wealth, jobs and the sustainability of financially sound enterprises.

Stakeholder theory states that a company's managers should make decisions that take into consideration the interests of all the stakeholders. This means trying to achieve a range of different objectives, not just the aim of maximising the value of the company for its shareholders. This is because different stakeholders have their own (different) expectations of the company, which the company's management should attempt to satisfy.

Supporters of the stakeholder approach recognise that only the senior managers and directors of a company and the shareholders have any significant power within the framework of corporate governance. A stakeholder approach to corporate governance can therefore be implemented only by:

- negotiation and cooperation between management and employees; and
- legislation giving rights to stakeholders or protecting stakeholder rights.

Stakeholder theory also considers the role of companies in society and the responsibility that they should have towards society as a whole. It might be argued that some companies are so large, and their influence in society is so strong, that they should be accountable to the public for what they do. The general public are taxpayers and as such provide the economic and social infrastructure within which companies are allowed to operate. In return, companies should be expected to act as corporate citizens and act in a way that benefits society as a whole. This aspect of stakeholder theory is consistent with the arguments in favour of corporate social responsibility.

3 Development of corporate governance

Concerns about corporate governance have grown over time. In recent years, the recognition of a need for changes in the way that public companies are governed began with a number of spectacular and well-publicised corporate failures. In the US, many organisations in the savings and thrift industry had to be rescued from financial collapse in the 1980s. In the UK, a number of companies collapsed unexpectedly in the 1980s and 1990s. These included Polly Peck International, the Bank of Credit and Commerce International, British and Commonwealth, the Mirror Group News International and Barings Bank. In each case, there appeared to be serious accounting or financial reporting irregularities and inadequate internal controls and risk management. In some cases 'creative accounting' and inadequate financial regulation were seen as the cause of the corporate failure. In others, such as the collapse of Barings Bank due to the losses of a rogue trader, inadequate controls were a key factor.

When questions were asked about how the corporate collapse could happen to such well-established companies without warning, common themes emerged. Investors were not kept informed about what was going on in the company and the published financial statements were misleading. External auditors were accused of failing to spot the warning signs, but much of the blame was heaped on the self-seeking activities of powerful company chiefs, their apparent lack of personal and business ethics, and the inability of board members to restrain them from acting improperly. In addition, it was recognised that the risk of financial collapse can be prevented by adequate risk management, and that in the case of all the companies concerned, the financial controls had been inadequate or ineffective.

3.1   A brief history of corporate governance

The main impetus for better practices in corporate governance began in the UK in the late 1980s and early 1990s. The Report of the Committee on the Financial Aspects of Corporate Governance (the Cadbury Report) was published in 1992, and was later described as 'a landmark in thinking on corporate governance'. The Report included a Code of Best Practice, and UK listed companies came under pressure from City institutions to comply with the requirements of the Code.

In 1995, a working group was set up to look into the relationship between companies and institutional investors. This was chaired by Mr Paul Myners, who was then chairman of Gartmore plc, and produced the Myners Report, which made a variety of recommendations about how the relationship between institutional investors and company management should be conducted. The Report included suggestions for improving communications between companies and institutional investors and for the conduct of annual general meetings. The significance of the Myners Report is that it urged institutional investors to reassess their role as shareholders and their responsibilities for ensuring good corporate governance and the success of the companies in which they invested. When a company is performing badly, institutional investors should try to do something to put matters right instead of selling their shares and washing their hands of the company. Myners went on to argue that unless institutional investors voluntarily became more active in the governance of companies and exercised their rights more forcibly, they should be compelled to do so by legislation. Representative bodies of the institutional investor organisations (e.g. the Institutional Shareholders Committee, the Association of British Insurers and the National Association of Pension Funds) responded by issuing guidelines for members on corporate governance issues, and principles of corporate governance.

On the recommendation of the Cadbury Committee, another committee was set up to review progress on corporate governance in UK listed companies. This committee issued the Greenbury Report in 1995, which focused mainly on directors' remuneration. At the time, the UK press was condemning 'fat cat' directors, particularly those in newly privatised companies. The Greenbury Report issued a Code of Best Practice on establishing remuneration committees, for disclosures of much more information about the remuneration of directors and remuneration policy, and for more control over notice periods in directors' service contracts and compensation payments in the event of early termination of contracts.

A Committee on Corporate Governance, chaired by Sir Ronald Hampel, was set up in 1995 to review the recommendations of the Cadbury and Greenbury Committees. The final report of the Hampel Committee was published in 1998. This covered a number of governance issues, such as the composition of the board and role of directors, directors' remuneration, the role of shareholders (particularly institutional shareholders), communications between the company and its shareholders, and financial reporting, auditing and internal controls. The Hampel Report also suggested that its recommendations should be combined with those of the Cadbury and Greenbury Committees into a single code of corporate governance. This suggestion led to the publication of the original (1998) Combined Code, which applied to all UK listed companies.

Corporate governance issues remained in the spotlight in the UK, and two influential reports were produced in January 2003. The Higgs Report considered the role and effectiveness of non-executive directors. The Smith Report provided guidance for audit committees. The responsibility for the Combined Code was transferred to the Financial

Reporting Council, and in 2003 a revised Combined Code was issued, which incorporated, as appendices, many of the Higgs and Smith recommendations.

The Combined Code covers most areas of corporate governance, and is made up of:

- Main principles.
- Supporting principles: as their name suggests these supplement and support the main principles. Most main principles have one or more supporting principles.
- Provisions: these are specific measures that companies are expected to take.

The Combined Code is voluntary, but the UK Listing Rules include an obligation on listed companies to disclose the extent of their compliance with it. They must state that they have complied in full with the provisions of the Code, or must explain any non-compliance. This 'comply or explain' rule for listed companies applies to all provisions of the Code.

The Combined Code is now the responsibility of the Financial Reporting Council (FRC), which reviews the Code regularly. A revised Code was issued in 2006.

Some further aspects of corporate governance have been brought into law, with much of the initiative coming from the European Union. New regulations in 2002 were introduced for greater disclosures of directors' remuneration by listed companies, replacing similar regulations that were included in the Listing Rules from 1995. (See Chapter 9 for more details.) The Companies Act 2006 sets out statutory duties of directors (similar to the duties that existed in common law and equity), and contains a requirement for quoted companies to be more accountable to shareholders by publishing a business review in narrative form each year. Amendments to the 4th and 7th EU Company Law Directives approved in 2006 include a requirement for quoted companies to include a corporate governance statement in their annual reports, and a proposed amendment to the 8th Company Law Directive is for 'public interest entities' (which include listed companies) to have an audit committee consisting of independent non-executive directors.

A largely separate, although interconnected, development has been a growing awareness on the part of large companies of the potential risks to their reputation and long-term success from failures to comply with laws and regulations or to act ethically. Many companies have also claimed to recognise the potential long-term benefits from acting in a socially responsible manner.

Although the UK has been at the forefront of the move towards setting up a better corporate governance framework, there have been similar developments in other countries. For many, particularly developing countries, good corporate governance is seen as an essential basic requirement for attracting foreign investment capital. In South Africa, a code of corporate governance was developed by the King Committee. This was revised and strengthened in 2002. On an international basis, recommended principles on corporate governance have been published by the Commonwealth Association and by the OECD.

The USA appeared to show little concern for better corporate governance throughout the 1990s, although there were some activist institutional shareholders such as Calpers. The situation changed dramatically, however, with the collapse of the energy company Enron, followed by a number of other corporate collapses and governance scandals. The major auditing and accountancy firm Arthur Andersen, caught up in the Enron scandal and prosecuted for obstructing the course of justice, collapsed and was broken up. Recommendations for change were proposed by the New York Stock Exchange, and statutory provisions on corporate governance were introduced in 2002 with the Sarbanes–Oxley Act.

3.2   The international aspects of corporate governance

As stated earlier, the need for good corporate governance is a matter of international concern. However, although corporate governance has become a matter of some interest in many countries, the pace of change and the nature of corporate governance vary substantially between countries. The OECD monitors developments in corporate governance in member countries.

Much of the pressure for change has come from institutional investors, particularly in the US, who have invested fairly heavily in companies in other countries. As shareholders in foreign companies, US investors expect to be allowed to exercise their right to vote and to be treated on an equal footing with other equity shareholders. In countries where minority shareholder rights are not always well respected, US investor influence has probably been influential in the corporate governance changes that have happened.

In many developing countries, there have been substantial investments in recent years by multinational companies, such as international banks. It might be expected that US and UK multinationals would establish a system of corporate governance within their subsidiaries along similar lines to the parent company, for example, with non-executive directors on the board representing interest groups in the local country. Some multinationals have become increasingly aware of their reputation in markets in other countries, and alert to the demands of pressure groups as well as governments in the countries where they have operating subsidiaries.

Apart from multinationals, the largest commercial organisations in many developing countries are government-owned or controlled. Government-controlled organisations are not necessarily operated on fully commercial lines and some board membership may reflect political interests within the country. Where the government is heavily involved in commercial activities – water provision, electricity provision, transport, road building, and so on – it should be expected that it will be influential in bringing about improvements in corporate governance.

3.3   Dominant personality and leadership aspects of corporate governance

With some corporate collapses, the failure has been attributed to a dominant individual, acting as chairman and chief executive officer (CEO), running the company as a personal fiefdom and with complete disregard for the interests of shareholders and other stakeholders. After his death, Robert Maxwell was accused of excessive abuse of power in the companies he ran. During his lifetime any such accusations were not made openly and Maxwell enjoyed seemingly dictatorial powers. From a corporate governance perspective, the questions are: How was an individual able to enjoy such power over his companies, and what should have been done by his fellow directors to prevent such a state of affairs?

4   Stakeholders

Stakeholder theory was described earlier. A stakeholder in a company is someone who has an interest (or stake) in it, and is affected by what the company does. A stakeholder in turn has an influence on what companies do. Each stakeholder or stakeholder group can expect the company to behave or act in a particular way, with regard to the stakeholders' interests. A stakeholder can also expect to have some say in some of the decisions a company takes and some of its actions. The balance of power between different stakeholder groups and the way in which power is exercised are key issues in corporate governance.

A public company has a number of different stakeholder groups. They can be divided into:

- financial stakeholders; and
- other stakeholders.

4.1 Financial stakeholders

Financial stakeholders have a financial interest in the company. They consist mainly of shareholders and lenders. Lenders may be banks or investors in bonds.

- A company's members or equity shareholders are the owners. In a small company, the owners may also be directors. In a large public company, the directors may own some shares, but are not usually the largest shareholders. The interests of the shareholders are likely to be focused on the value of their shares and dividend payments. However, the powers of shareholders in large public companies are usually fairly restricted and shareholders have to rely on the board to act in their best interests.
- A different situation arises when there is a majority shareholder or significant shareholder. A shareholder with a controlling interest is able to influence decisions of the company through an ability to control the composition of the board of directors. When there is a majority shareholder, the interests of minority shareholders may be disregarded.
- A distinction can also be made between long-term and short-term institutional investors. Short-term investors buy shares with the expectation of making a short-term profit from an increase in the price before selling the shares in the market. They include hedge funds who buy shares in what they consider to be an under-valued and/or badly managed company, with potential for a significant increase in value if the management problems can be resolved or if the company becomes a takeover bid target. Long-term investors are more interested in the longer-term returns from a company rather than short-term profit.
- Lenders and bondholders provide debt capital to a company, but are not owners. Even so they have a financial interest in the company, and expect payment of interest and repayment of capital on schedule. Excessive borrowing by a company might put lenders as well as shareholders at risk financially; therefore, lenders have an interest in preventing the financial gearing or leverage of the company from getting too high. Loan covenants may set limits on borrowing by the company.

Agency theory provides an interesting insight into the relationship between a company's shareholders, its management and its lenders. A company generates free cash flow, which is cash generated from operations that the directors can use in any way they want, after paying for essential costs such as tax, replacement of worn-out assets and interest costs. Free cash flow can either be paid to shareholders as dividends or reinvested in the business to achieve growth. A concern for shareholders is that managers may reinvest free cash flows in projects and investments that make the company bigger, but do not provide a sufficient return. One way of making managers conscious of the need to make a return from new investments is to finance the investments with debt capital, which must generate a sufficient return to pay the interest costs. Shareholders might therefore have an interest in increasing debt in the company, as a means of reducing the agency problem. In contrast, lenders have an interest in preventing the financial gearing of the company from becoming excessive.

4.2   Other stakeholders

Other stakeholders in a company can also have significant influence. These include the board of directors (some directors may also be large shareholders).

- The board of directors has the responsibility for giving direction to the company. It delegates most executive powers to the executive management, but reserves some decision-making powers to itself, such as decisions about raising finance, paying dividends and making major investments. Executive management is also held accountable to the board for their performance.
- A board of directors is made up of executives and non-executives. Executive directors combine their role as director with their position within the executive management of the company. Non-executive directors perform the functions of director only, without any executive responsibilities. Executive directors combine their stake in the company as a director with their stake as a fully paid employee, and their interests are therefore likely to differ from those of the non-executives.
- The board may take decisions collectively, but it is also a collection of individuals, each with his or her personal interests and ambitions. Some individuals are more likely to dominate the decisions by a board and to exert strong influence over their colleagues. The most influential individuals are likely to be the chairman, who can be a non-executive or have some executive responsibilities, and the CEO (the term CEO derives from the US, but is now widely used in the UK, where the term 'managing director' is also used). The chairman is responsible for the functioning of the board. The CEO is the senior executive director, and is accountable to the board for the executive management of the company. The main interest of individual executive directors is likely to be power and authority, a high remuneration package and a wealthy lifestyle.
- Management is responsible for running the business operations and is accountable to the board of directors (particularly to the CEO). Individual managers, like executive directors, may seek power, status and a high remuneration. As employees, they may see their stake in the company in terms of the need for a career and an income.
- Employees have a stake in their company because it provides them with a job and an income. They too have expectations about what their company should do for them – e.g. security of employment, good pay and suitable working conditions. Some employee rights are protected by employment law, but the powers of employees are generally limited.

- Major suppliers have an indirect interest in a company, because they expect to be paid what they are owed. If they deal with the company regularly, or over a long period, they will expect the company to do business with them in accordance with their contractual agreements. If the company becomes insolvent, unpaid creditors will take a more significant role in its governance, depending on the insolvency laws in the country – for example, by taking legal action to take control of the business or its assets.
- Representatives of investment institutions have some influence over public companies whose shares are traded on a stock market. Representative bodies include the Association of British Insurers (ABI) and National Association of Pension Funds (NAPF) in the UK, and the International Corporate Governance Network, an association of 'activist' institutional investors around the world. These bodies may try to coordinate the activities of their members by encouraging them to vote in a particular way on resolutions at the annual general meetings of companies in which they are shareholders. They represent the opinions of the investment community generally.
- The general public are also stakeholders in large companies, often because they rely on the goods or services provided by a company to carry on their life. For example, households expect utility companies to provide an uninterrupted supply of water, electricity or gas to their homes, or a reliable telephone connection. Commuters expect a rail company to be under an obligation to provide a convenient, reliable and safe transport service to and from work, and at a reasonable price. Pressure groups, such as environment protection groups, sometimes try to influence the decisions of companies.

5 Key objectives in corporate governance

The key objectives in corporate governance have already been introduced in the context of the theoretical frameworks.

A large company has many stakeholders and has to balance the demands and needs of each of them. Although some stakeholder groups have power to decide or influence actions taken by the company, others have little influence and rely on the 'enlightenment' of the company's managers (primarily the directors) to take decisions that are in their interests and beneficial for them.

Often, there will be a conflict of interests between different stakeholder groups. For example, employees may want higher salaries, which their company cannot afford without cutting dividends paid to shareholders.

A major concern with corporate governance is the conflict of interests between the board of directors (and its individual directors) and other stakeholder groups, particularly the shareholders and employees. When the directors take decisions that are in their personal best interests, and regardless of the interests of other stakeholders, should this be allowed; alternatively, how can it be prevented? The directors, particularly executive directors, have greater access to the information systems of their company and so know more about what is going on. They are also often in a position to control or manipulate the information that is released to the shareholders or employees.

Shareholders have to rely on the board to govern their company competently and in their best interests. They are able to monitor the performance of the company (and, by implication, its directors) primarily through the company's annual report and accounts. They make their decisions to invest in the company's shares, and hold on to them, largely on the basis of information supplied by the directors in the company's name. Their only reassurance that the information they are supplied is correct is the honesty of the directors and the assertion by the company's auditors that the published accounts give a true and fair view of the company's profitability and financial position.

The problem has been well expressed by the OECD, the international organisation established to help governments deal with global economic, social and governance:

> 'What makes corporate governance necessary? Put simply, the interests of those who have effective control over a firm can differ from the interests of those who supply the firm with external finance. The problem, commonly referred to as a principal–agent problem, grows out of the separation of ownership and control and of corporate outsiders and insiders. In the absence of the protections that good governance supplies, asymmetries of information and difficulties of monitoring mean that capital providers who lack control over the corporation will find it risky and costly to protect themselves from the opportunistic behaviour of managers and controlling shareholders.'

The relationship between the shareholders and the board of directors is at the heart of many of the problems that arise in corporate governance. Many of the guidelines in the codes of conduct for corporate governance and codes of best practice are directed towards reducing the potential for conflict, by seeking to put some restraints on individual directors, particularly the CEO and other executive directors, and by trying to reconcile the interests of the two stakeholder groups.

6 Key issues in corporate governance

At the heart of the debate about corporate governance lie the conflicts of interest, or potential conflicts of interest, between shareholders, the board of directors as a whole and individual board members, and possibly also a number of other stakeholder groups. The directors may be tempted to take risks and make decisions aimed at boosting short-term performance. Many shareholders are more concerned about the longer term, the continuing survival of their company and the value of their investment. If a company gets into financial difficulties, professional managers can move on to another company to start again, whereas shareholders suffer a financial loss.

Issues in corporate governance where a conflict of interests may be apparent include:

- financial reporting and auditing;
- directors' remuneration;
- company–stakeholder relations;
- risk-taking;

- effective communication between the directors and shareholders;
- ethical conduct and corporate social responsibility.

These issues will be considered in more detail in the chapters that follow.

6.1   Financial reporting and auditing

The directors may try to disguise the true financial performance of their company by 'dressing up' the published accounts and giving less than honest statements. Window-dressed accounts make it difficult for investors to reach a reasoned judgement about the financial position of the company. Concerns about misleading published accounts provided an early impetus in the 1980s and early 1990s to the movement for better corporate governance in the UK. Accounting irregularities in a number of companies led to a tightening of accounting standards, although the problems of window-dressing are unlikely ever to disappear completely.

Concerns about financial reporting in the US emerged with the collapse of Enron in 2001, which filed for bankruptcy after 'adjusting' its accounts. This was followed by similar problems in other US companies, such as WorldCom (which admitted to fraud in its accounting), Global Crossing and Rank Xerox. Problems have emerged in some European companies, most notably at the Italian group Parmalat at the end of 2003. A corporate governance issue is the question of the extent to which the directors were aware in each case of the impending collapse of their company, and, if they knew the problems, why shareholders were not informed much sooner.

CASE EXAMPLE 1.1

Keeping information away from shareholders could be prompted by greed or self-interest. In the wake of the WorldCom scandal in 2002, it was reported that prior to the company's financial collapse (but at a time the share price had already begun to fall) the board of WorldCom lent its chief executive $350 million to persuade him not to sell his shares in the company. Some of this money was invested by the CEO in an online bank owned by a trust whose board of directors included one of the non-executives of WorldCom.

It was also reported in 2001 that prior to the collapse of Enron some of its directors and senior managers had sold shares in the company, giving rise to suspicions that they might have been using insider information to protect their interests.

The implications of false or misleading financial reporting for the relationship between investors and companies was well expressed by Arthur Levitt, former chairman of the Securities and Exchange Commission in a speech in 2001:

> 'If a country does not have a reputation for strong corporate governance practice, capital will flow elsewhere. If investors are not confident with the level of disclosure, capital will flow elsewhere. If a country opts for lax accounting and reporting standards, capital will flow elsewhere. All enterprises in that country, regardless of how steadfast a particular company's practices, may suffer the con-

sequences. Markets must now honour what they perhaps too often have failed to recognise. Markets exist by the grace of investors. And it is today's more empowered investors who will determine which companies and which markets will stand the test of time and endure the weight of greater competition. It serves us well to remember that no market has a divine right to investors' capital.'

When the annual financial statements of a company are shown to have been misleading, questions are inevitably raised about the effectiveness of the external auditors. There are two main issues relating to the external audit of a company. One is whether it should be the job of the auditors to discover financial fraud and material errors. The other is the problem of the relationship between a client company and its auditors, and the extent to which the auditors are independent and free from the influence of the company's management. If auditors are subject to influence from a client company, they might be persuaded to agree with a controversial method of accounting for particular transactions, which shows the company's performance or financial position in a better light. Arthur Andersen, which collapsed in 2002, appears to have lacked independence from major clients such as Enron.

6.2   Directors' remuneration

Directors may reward themselves with vast salaries and other rewards, such as bonuses, a generous pension scheme, share options and other benefits. Institutional shareholders do not object to high remuneration for directors. However, they take the view that rewards should depend largely on company performance and the benefits obtained for the shareholders. The main complaint about 'fat cat' directors' remuneration is that when the company does well the directors are rewarded well, which is fair enough, but when the company does badly the directors continue to be paid just as well.

Interest in arguments about directors' pay has varied in the past among different countries. In the UK, concerns led to the establishment of the Greenbury Committee in the 1990s and the publication of the Greenbury Report. Directors' remuneration has remained a contentious issue ever since. In 2002 company law was changed by the Directors' Remuneration Report Regulations, requiring listed companies to produce a directors' remuneration report annually and to invite shareholders to vote on the report at the company's AGM.

6.3   Company–stakeholder relations

Most decision-making powers in a company are held by the board of directors. The corporate governance debate has been about the extent to which professional managers, acting as directors, exercise those powers in the interests of their shareholders and other stakeholders in the company, and whether the powers of directors should be restricted.

This aspect of corporate governance is about:

- the structure of the board of directors and the role of independent non-executive directors;
- the powers of shareholders under company law and whether these should be extended by corporate law reform – for example, by giving shareholders the right

to approve the company's remuneration policy or its remuneration packages for board members (see Chapter 9 for more details);

• whether shareholders actually make full use of the powers they already have, for example by voting not to re-elect directors.

6.4 Corporate governance and risk management

As a rule, investors expect higher rewards to compensate them for taking higher business risks. If a company makes decisions that increase the scale of the risks it faces, profits and dividends should be expected to rise. Another issue in corporate governance is that the directors of companies might take decisions intended to increase profits without giving due regard to the risks. In some cases, companies may continue to operate without regard to the changing risk profile of their existing businesses.

When investors buy shares, they have an idea of the type of company they are buying into, the nature of its business, the probable returns it will provide for shareholders and possible financial risks. To shareholders, investment risk is as important as high returns. Directors, on the other hand, are rewarded on the basis of the returns the company achieves, linked to profits or dividend growth. Their remuneration is not linked in any direct way to the risk aspects of their business. Risk management is now recognised, particularly in the UK, as a component of sound corporate governance.

Takeovers can also be contentious. A company's board may try to grow their company by buying up target companies, almost regardless of the price they have to pay. The results of a successful large takeover bid at an excessive price are likely to be:

• more power and higher status for the company's board and individual directors (justifying higher salaries);
• a good deal for the shareholders in the target company;
• a loss of wealth for the company's own shareholders when the takeover fails to achieve the expected effect on the company's profits and the share price eventually falls.

A common feature in past corporate failures has been a lack of effective control over the company and the absence of risk management procedures and systems. Corporate collapse may occasionally result from dishonest management finally being exposed, but is much more likely to be the consequence of a well-intentioned board failing to carry out its duties adequately. The duties of the board must include ensuring that there is an operative and effective system of risk management. Shareholders should feel confident that the board is aware of the risks faced by the company, and that a system for monitoring and controlling them is in place.

6.5 Information and communication

Another issue in corporate governance is communication between the board of directors and the company's shareholders. Shareholders, particularly those with a large financial investment in the company, should be able to voice their concerns to the directors and expect to have their opinions listened to. Small shareholders should at least be informed about the company, its financial position and its intentions for the future, even if their opinions carry comparatively little weight.

The responsibility for improving communications rests with the companies themselves and their main institutional shareholders. Companies can make better use of the annual report and accounts to report to shareholders on a range of issues and the policies of the company for dealing with them. The annual report and accounts should not be simply a brief directors' report and a set of financial statements. The company should explain its operations and financial position and report on a range of governance issues such as directors' remuneration, internal controls and risk management and policies on health, safety and the environment. Many companies now use their website to report on such matters. A company can also try to encourage greater shareholder attendance and participation at annual general meetings as a method of improving communications and dialogue. Electronic communications, including electronic voting, should also be considered. For their part, institutional investors should develop voting policies and apply these in general meetings. Where necessary, they can vote against the board to alert the directors to the strength of their views.

6.6   Ethical conduct and corporate social responsibility

Ethical considerations are at the root of many perceived problems with corporate governance. Individuals are expected to behave ethically. Companies may be aware of the need to maintain a culture of corporate ethics, providing a code of conduct that all directors and employees are expected to follow.

In addition, the perception of ethical issues by external pressure groups may affect the reputation of a company or the way it is run. An activist external group may regard itself as having a vested interest in the activities and operations of a company, particularly those involved in areas of advanced scientific research.

CASE EXAMPLE 1.2

An extreme example of external influence was the pressure directed by animal rights activists towards UK-based scientific research company Huntingdon Life Sciences.

The activists, who included a specially formed group, Stop Huntingdon Animal Cruelty (SHAC), wanted the company to halt its experiments on live animals. The pressure included physical intimidation of Huntingdon employees and threats against lenders to the company. In January 2001, the Royal Bank of Scotland cancelled the company's credit facilities of £10 million (although these were replaced by facilities from a US firm), and the company felt obliged to take on a new name, Life Sciences Research Inc., and list itself as a US company in 2001. Whatever the rights and wrongs of the arguments, the Huntingdon case demonstrates the extent to which companies are unable to act with disregard for the views of groups and individuals other than their shareholders.

There is also a growing recognition that many companies need to consider social and environmental issues, for commercial and governance reasons, as well as ethical reasons. Many shareholders, including institutional shareholders, and many customers expect companies to show concern for social issues and environmental issues. Furthermore, the financial risks from government regulation to protect the environment continue to grow. Social and environmental issues can therefore affect reputation, sales, profits and share price.

6.7   The extent of corporate governance legislation

Companies are constrained or limited by law in what they can do. For example, laws regulate the way in which companies deal with people, give rights to creditors and customers, and provide some protection for employees and for society at large. They are also subject to regulations and codes of practice from external bodies, such as the UK Listing Authority.

Issues to consider therefore are:

- the extent to which corporate governance practices should be forced on companies by legislation;
- how much should be left to regulation by the stock market regulators; and
- how much corporate governance should be a matter for companies to decide for themselves, perhaps within a published framework of best practice guidelines.

In the UK, for example:

- Company law provides some framework for corporate governance, but arguably not enough.
- The law is reinforced for listed companies (i.e. companies whose shares are on the UK Official List and are traded on the main market of the London Stock Exchange) by regulations in the Financial Services Handbook, such as the Listing Rules. These rules require companies to comply with certain aspects of corporate governance, but do not provide a comprehensive statutory regime.
- The Listing Rules give support to a code of principles and best practice for corporate governance: the Combined Code. Although pressure is brought to bear on companies to persuade them to apply the best practice measures that are recommended, the Combined Code is voluntary.

In practice, however, although corporate governance is voluntary, the risk of disrupting relations with shareholders is usually enough to persuade companies to comply with guidelines and codes of practice.

The US has taken a statutory rather than a voluntary approach to corporate governance. Following the financial scandals at Enron and WorldCom, statutory rules on corporate governance were introduced by the Sarbanes–Oxley Act.

7 Approaches to corporate governance

There has been considerable debate about what the objectives of sound corporate governance should be. The different views can be divided into three broad approaches which can be related to the agency theory or the stakeholder theory of governance:

1   The shareholder value approach.
2   The enlightened shareholder approach.
3   The stakeholder or pluralist approach.

7.1   The shareholder value approach

This is the well-established view, supported by company law in advanced economies, that the board of directors should govern the company in the best interests of its owners, the shareholders. This could mean that the main objective of a company is to maximise the wealth of its shareholders, in the form of share price growth and dividend payments, subject to conforming to the rules of society as embodied in laws and customs. The directors should be accountable to the shareholders, who should have the power to remove them from office if their performance is inadequate. The shareholder view is closely linked to agency theory or transaction cost theory.

The OECD, in the introduction to its principles of corporate governance, states that from a company's perspective, corporate governance is about:

> 'Maximising value subject to meeting the corporation's financial and other legal and contractual obligations. This inclusive definition stresses the need for boards of directors to balance the interests of shareholders with those of other stake-holders – employees, customers, suppliers, investors, communities – in order to achieve long-term sustained value.'

The International Corporate Governance Network (ICGN) was established to promote corporate governance practices worldwide. In 2005 it issued a revised statement on corporate governance principles. This includes the view that 'the overriding objective of the corporation should be to optimise over time the returns to its shareholders. Corporate governance practices should focus board attention on this objective.'

The strength of this approach to corporate governance is its general acceptance. Many people hold the view that public companies are in business to earn profits for the benefit of their shareholders. Successful companies are perceived as those paying dividends to shareholders and whose share price goes up. Within the broad objective of maximising shareholder values, the board of directors will also act fairly in the interests of employees, customers, suppliers and others with an interest in the company's affairs.

7.2   The stakeholder approach

An alternative view is based on stakeholder theory. The aim of sound corporate governance is not just to meet the objectives of shareholders, but also to have regard for the interests of other individuals and groups with a stake in the company, including the public at large. The OECD argues that there is a public policy perspective towards corporate governance, as well as a corporate perspective:

'From a public policy perspective, corporate governance is about nurturing enterprise while ensuring accountability in the exercise of power and patronage by firms. The role of public policy is to provide firms with the incentives and discipline to minimize the divergence between private and social returns and to protect the interests of stakeholders.'

From a stakeholder view, corporate governance is concerned with achieving a balance between economic and social goals and between individual and communal goals. Sound corporate governance should recognise the economic imperatives companies face in competitive markets and should encourage the efficient use of resources through sound investment. It should also require accountability from the board of directors to the shareholders for the stewardship of those resources. Within this framework, the aim should be to recognise the interests of other individuals, companies and society at large in the decisions and activities of the company.

A problem with the stakeholder approach is that company law gives certain rights to shareholders, and there are some legal duties on the board of directors towards their company. The interests of other stakeholders, however, are not reinforced by company law.

Supporters of a stakeholder (or pluralist) approach to corporate governance argue that there would have to be company legislation giving it support. A pluralist approach is that cooperative and productive relationships will be optimised only if the directors are permitted or required to balance shareholder interests with the interests of other stakeholders who are committed to the company. Changes in company law would be required to introduce such an approach. If the law were to be changed in this way, it is much more likely that directors would be permitted to have regard for the interests of stakeholders other than the shareholders in particular circumstances, but would not be required to do so.

It is important to remember that although shareholder interests are not well protected by company law, extensive protection is provided by other aspects of law such as employment law, health and safety legislation and environmental law.

7.3   The enlightened shareholder approach

The enlightened shareholder approach to corporate governance is that the directors of a company should pursue the interests of their shareholders in an enlightened and inclusive way. It is a form of compromise between the agency view and the stakeholder view. The directors should look to the long term, not just the short term, and should also have regard to the interests of other stakeholders in the company, not just the shareholders. Managers should be aware of the need to create and maintain productive relationships with a range of stakeholders having an interest in their company.

A criticism of the enlightened shareholder view is that most shareholders do not fit the image of enlightened investors. Most shares in public companies are owned by institutional investors, who are themselves relatively unaccountable to their beneficiaries. However, the role of institutional investors in corporate governance is likely to evolve, with institutions expected to be more proactive in promoting the rights and interests of shareholders.

Chapter summary

- Corporate governance is concerned with the way companies are governed. Fundamentally, it is about what the objectives of a company should be. In the case of large public companies, it is also concerned with how powers are exercised by the directors and the accountability of the directors to the company's owners, the equity shareholders.

- Concerns about governance practices arose partly out of corporate scandals and financial collapses and partly from the growing awareness of the need for good practice to attract investment capital.

- There are three theoretical frameworks to justify the need for corporate governance structures and systems. 1) Agency theory is based on the view that managers and shareholders have conflicting interests; therefore, the owners need to have some form of monitoring or incentivising for managers. 2) Transaction cost theory is based on the view that managers act with bounded rationality and opportunism, and their actions need to be monitored and controlled. 3) Stakeholder theory takes the view that the company's management should have regard to the interests of all major stakeholders. One view is that this includes acting responsibly in the best interests of society, as a corporate citizen.

- An issue in corporate governance is the relationship between stakeholders in the company, and their different interests, rights and powers. Stakeholders include the shareholders, board of directors, management, other employees, suppliers, customers, government and the general public (including pressure groups).

- Major developments in corporate governance have included, in the UK, the Cadbury Report, Myners Report, Greenbury Report, Hampel Report the 1998 Combined Code, the Higgs Report, the Smith Report and the 2003 Combined Code (revised 2006).

- On an international level there have been the Commonwealth Association Principles and the OECD Principles. At a national level, major developments outside the UK have included the King Report (South Africa) and the Sarbanes–Oxley Act (US). Some countries rely mainly on voluntary codes of practice, whereas others rely more on legislation and compulsion.

- Key issues in corporate governance, for which codes of best practice have been developed, are financial reporting and auditing, directors' remuneration, the balance of power on the board of directors, risk management and communications between company and shareholders. Personal and business ethics underlie all these key issues.

- The best-established approach to corporate governance is the shareholder value concept. A move to an enlightened shareholder approach or a stakeholder approach would require changes in the law to be effective. However, there is growing awareness of the need for companies to act in a socially responsible way.

Chapter 2

Concepts in governance and the role of the company secretary

1. Concepts in corporate governance
2. The value of corporate governance
3. The relevance of corporate governance to other organisations
4. The company lawyer and corporate governance
5. The company secretary and corporate governance

1 Concepts in corporate governance

There are several concepts that apply to sound corporate governance in all countries where international investors invest their money:

- openness, honesty and transparency;
- independence;
- accountability;
- responsibility;
- fairness;
- reputation and reputational risk;
- ethical conduct.

Ethical conduct is considered in Chapter 11 on corporate social responsibility. The other concepts in the list are considered briefly here.

It is generally recognised that well-governed companies should demonstrate these qualities because:

- demonstrating these qualities will improve the relationship between the company and its shareholders and other stakeholders, and uphold the reputation of the company with customers and the public in general;
- demonstration of these qualities is evidence of good management and a well-run company.

1.1   Openness, honesty and transparency

Openness means a willingness to provide information to individuals and groups about the company, though without giving away commercially sensitive information. It is useful to think of openness in terms of its opposite, which is to be a 'closed book' and refuse to divulge any information whatsoever.

Shareholders and investors in a company need to know what the position of the company is, and will benefit from timely information, delivered via the company's website on a regular basis, about current developments in the company's affairs.

Honesty might seem an obvious quality for companies to have, but in an age of 'spin' and the manipulation of facts, honest information is by no means as prevalent as it should be. A test of a company's honesty is easily checked. Look for reports and announcements by any major company in the press and check the press comment and reactions to the announcement. A sign of honesty is that the company's statement is believed. A sign of questionable honesty is some measure of scepticism and disbelief.

Transparency refers to the ease with which an outsider is able to make a meaningful analysis of a company and its actions. Transparency refers to both information about the financial position of the company and to non-financial issues, such as the direction the company is taking, its strategic objectives, and so on. A transparent company is, therefore, one that investors understand. If investors can understand a company from the information it provides, and if they believe that information, the necessary trust between investors and company should be established.

Transparency also refers to a lack of clarity about the way that decisions are reached or processes carried out. It is useful to contrast a company that reaches its major decisions though a clear process and one that reaches its decisions behind closed doors (in 'smoke-filled rooms').

1.2   Independence

Independence refers to the extent to which procedures and structures are in place so as to minimise, or avoid completely, potential conflicts of interest that could arise, such as the domination of a company by an all-powerful chairman-cum-CEO, or a major shareholder.

The term 'independence' is of particular relevance to a company's non-executive directors and its professional advisers. They are considered independent when they can be expected to express their honest and/or professional opinion in the best interests of the company. Independence can be threatened by having a connection to the company or dependence on the goodwill of the company or its management, so that personal interests can skew the individual's opinions. A non-executive director will not be independent, for example, if he or she has recently been a senior executive of the company or if he or she represents a major shareholder. An auditor may not be independent if the audit firm relies on the company for a large percentage of its annual income.

Independence can also be undermined by familiarity: if a non-executive director or auditor has known the company's management for a long time, he or she may develop personal friendships that blind them to management failings and shortcomings.

1.3   Accountability

Individuals who make decisions in a company and take actions on its behalf on specific issues should be accountable for the decisions they make and the actions they take. Shareholders should be able to assess the actions of the board and the committees of the board, and have the opportunity to query them.

A problem with accountability is deciding how the directors should be accountable, and in particular over what period of time. According to financial theory, if the objective of a company is to maximise the wealth of its shareholders, this will be achieved by maximising the financial returns to shareholders through increases in profits, dividends, prospects for profit growth and a rising share price. It might therefore follow that directors should be held accountable to shareholders on the basis of the returns on shareholder capital that the company has achieved.

However, there is no consensus about the period over which returns to shareholders and increases in share value should be measured. Performance can be measured over a short term of one year at a time, or over a long term – five or ten years, or even longer. In practice, it is usual to measure returns over the short term and assess performance in terms of profitability over a twelve-month period. In the short term, however, a company's share price may be affected by factors unrelated to the company's underlying performance, such as excessive optimism or pessimism in the stock markets generally. In the short term, it is also easier to soothe investors with promises for the future, even though current performance is not good. It is only when a company fails consistently to deliver on its promises that investor confidence ebbs.

If company performance were to be judged by the return to shareholders over a twelve-month period, the directors would focus on short-term results and short-term movements in the stock market price. Short-termism is easy to criticise, but difficult to disregard if performance targets ignore the long term. They should really be looking after the underlying business of the company and its profitability over the longer term.

In an article in the Financial Times (29 January 2002) John Kay, reflecting on the reasons given by the former finance director of Marconi for the company's financial collapse in 2000, made the following comment:

> '[A director's] job is to run a business that adds value by means of the services it provides to customers. If he succeeds, it will generate returns to investors in the long term. And this is the only mechanism that can generate returns to investors. The problem is that the equivalence between value added in operations and stock market returns holds in the long run but not the short. Share prices may, for a time, become divorced from the fundamental value of a business. This has been true of most share prices in recent years. . . . In these conditions, attention to total shareholder returns distracts executives from their real function of managing businesses.'

The problem of accountability remains, however. Even if it is accepted that company performance should not be judged by short-term financial results and share price movements, how can the board be made accountable for its contribution to longer-term success?

The problems of the telecommunications industry provide an interesting example. In 2001, share prices of companies in the telecommunications industry fell sharply. Some directors were accused of taking excessive bonuses, which was unjustified in view of corporate losses and falling share prices. The counter-argument was that the directors were being rewarded for their contribution to the longer-term success of their company and that short-term difficulties should not obscure the longer-term picture.

1.4   Responsibility

A manager who is responsible for his or her decisions and actions should be subject to corrective measures. Mismanagement should be penalised. An issue in corporate governance is therefore whether directors should be liable for their performance to stakeholders, and their shareholders in particular. For example, should shareholders have the right to re-elect all the board directors each year?

A key issue in corporate governance is to decide who should have responsibility. Executive managers are responsible for the operations of the business, and the ultimate responsibility rests with the CEO. The board also has responsibilities, and it is a principle of good corporate governance that the board should establish a list of matters for which it should take the decisions itself, without delegation to management or the CEO. Similarly, when a board establishes committees with delegated responsibilities (for example, an audit committee and a remuneration committee), the terms of reference and responsibilities of those committees should be clearly established.

Accountability goes hand in hand with responsibility. Any individual or group with authority and responsibilities should be held accountable for their achievements and performance.

1.5   Fairness

Fairness refers to the principle that all shareholders should receive equal consider ation. Minority shareholders, for example, should be treated in the same way as majority shareholders. This concept might seem fairly straightforward in the UK, where the rights of minority shareholders are protected to a large extent by company law. But in continental Europe, for example, minority shareholder rights are often disregarded by the larger shareholders and the board of directors.

1.6   Reputation and reputational risk

A company or business, like an individual, will be known widely by its reputation, defined as the character generally ascribed to that entity. A reputation may be good or bad and may be an asset or a hindrance. For any company that has shares traded on a market, a good reputation is a key asset. A strong share price facilitates the raising of extra cash from existing and new members. It also makes the company's shares acceptable as a way of paying for acquisitions, remunerating staff and generally enhancing the way the business is viewed by the financial community. Damage to a company's reputation is very quickly reflected by a drop in its share price, reducing all these advantages.

A good reputation needs to be built up over many years and encompasses many facets of business activity. It will reflect the way in which the company is perceived by the markets and in the wider community. Reputation cannot rely solely on a code of ethics, corporate social responsibility, fair treatment of staff, attitudes to customers, community involvement or willingness to obey the spirit as well as the letter of the law. It is, however, influenced by all of these.

Although it takes years to build a good reputation, this can be destroyed overnight by a badly handled catastrophe or bad publicity. Recovery of a damaged reputation takes even more work than is required to acquire the good reputation in the first place. The loss of reputation can even destroy a company completely. Shell took much time and effort to recover from the damage of its actions in Nigeria and over Brent Spar. The accounting firm Anderson was destroyed by the damage of its involvement in the Enron affair.

2 The value of corporate governance

Before looking in detail at the issues involved in corporate governance, it is useful to consider just what the benefits of good corporate governance might be for public companies.

There are strong differences of opinion about the benefits of corporate governance, and whether these justify the costs of compliance with corporate governance regulations and best practice.

The main arguments in favour of having a strong corporate governance regime for listed companies are as follows:

- Good governance will eliminate the risk of misleading or false financial reporting, and will prevent companies from being dominated by self-serving chief executives or chairmen. By reducing the risks of corporate scandals, investors will be better protected. This should add generally to confidence in the capital markets, and help to sustain share prices.
- Companies that comply with best practice in corporate governance are also more likely to achieve commercial success. Good governance and good leadership and management often go hand in hand.
- Well-governed companies will often develop a strong reputation and so will be less exposed to reputational risk than companies that are not so well governed.
- Good governance encourages investors to hold shares in companies for the longer term, instead of treating shares as short-term investments to be sold for a quick profit. Companies benefit from having shareholders who have an interest in their longer-term prospects.
- Perhaps the key issue is whether good corporate governance reduces investment risks to shareholders, or even improves company performance and share values.
- The main arguments against having a strong corporate governance regime for listed companies focus on costs, benefits and value:
- It is argued that, for many companies and institutional investors, compliance with a code of corporate governance is a box-ticking exercise. Companies adopt the required procedures and systems, without considering what the potential benefits might be. The only requirement is to comply with the 'rules' and put a tick in a box when this is done. Corporate governance requirements therefore create a time- and resource-consuming bureaucracy, and divert the attention of the board from more important matters.
- Good corporate governance is likely to reduce the risk of scandals and unexpected corporate failures. However, the current regulations or best practice guidelines are far too extensive and burdensome.

- The connection between good corporate governance and good financial results (due to good leadership and management) has been claimed by some people, but denied by others.
- Less regulation and fewer requirements for compliance would reduce the costs of corporate governance. At the moment, the costs far outweigh the benefits. To make matters worse, companies that are obliged to comply with corporate governance regulations or best practice are at a competitive disadvantage to rival companies from countries where corporate governance regulation is much less stringent.

3 The relevance of corporate governance to other organisations

The issues in corporate governance that will be considered in detail in the following chapters apply mainly to listed companies. It has been argued that similar principles of good governance should apply to other organisations, such as private companies, state-owned corporations and not-for-profit organisations. There are differences of opinion about this, but the case for a more extensive application of corporate governance deserves careful consideration.

3.1 Non-UK companies with a UK listing

A debate has arisen on the question as to whether corporate governance standards in the UK will come under threat as more foreign companies join the London market. Non-UK companies may have difficulty in meeting UK standards of corporate governance. Index-tracking funds will have to buy shares in these companies, even if their corporate governance regimes do not meet Combined Code standards.

CASE EXAMPLE 2.1

The Kazhakstan mining company Kazakhmys attracted attention by becoming a FTSE 100 company. The company obtained its UK listing in October 2005.

Although the company had taken steps to strengthen its corporate governance, it still fell well short of normal UK listed company practice. Its chairman was not independent, and there were some doubts about the independence of the non-executives, in view of the requirement of the Combined Code that independence means being free from relationships that affect, or could appear to affect, the judgement of the director.

One Non-executive Director (NED) was a director of a company that had a large, secured, interest-free loan from Kazakhmys. Another NED had received payment for services to the company in relation to its London listing. A third NED was vice-chairman of investment banking at J P Morgan Cazenove, financial advisers to Kazakhmys.

F&C Asset Management sent a representative to the inaugural London annual general meeting of the company in December 2005 and raised a question about the company's policy of investing the assets of its employee pension scheme in its own shares. The reply from the board was that such a policy was normal practice in Kazakhstan.

3.2   Corporate governance and AIM companies

The Combined Code does not apply to companies whose shares are traded on the alternative investment market (AIM). However, there are many similarities between listed companies and AIM companies. They are all public companies whose shares are traded on a stock exchange. In most cases, there is a separation of ownership from control: some AIM companies are run by directors with a substantial shareholding, but as a general rule there is a substantial number of shareholders who are not involved in the running of the company.

The strongest argument against a corporate governance code for AIM companies is probably one of cost and benefit. The costs of a corporate governance regime would possibly not be justified by the benefits it would provide.

However, in 2005 the Quoted Companies Alliance (QCA), a body representing smaller quoted companies, issued Corporate Governance Guidelines for AIM companies. The Guidelines are intended to help companies whose shares are traded on AIM to develop good corporate governance practices, which the QCA argues is in the interests of smaller companies.

The Guidelines, which were developed in consultation with institutional smaller company investors, are consistent with the Combined Code for listed companies. However, they are not as detailed or rigorous. Although the Combined Code does not apply to AIM companies, the QCA comments that: 'Compliance with the Combined Code should continue to be an aspiration for AIM companies as they grow'.

3.3   Corporate governance and private companies

In theory, good principles of corporate governance should also apply to private companies, especially companies where a significant proportion of shares are held by members who are not involved in the running of the company. However, in practice it may be difficult to argue in favour of a formal corporate governance regime for private companies, beyond the minimum requirements set out in the law. The relationship between directors and shareholders in a private company is usually quite close and strong. This is the crucial relationship in the governance of companies. Some private companies are run by their major shareholders. Where companies are owned by private equity firms, the shareholders exercise strong influence on the companies through their representation in the management or the board of directors.

There is an argument that private companies should be required to consider the interests of minority shareholders, but minority protection is available by law and should not require a corporate governance regime to reinforce it.

3.4 Corporate governance in non-commercial sectors

Whilst the focus on corporate governance has been primarily on the commercial sector, it is also of importance for the public and voluntary sectors. Many of the issues are the same, but there are some that are of specific importance to these sectors:

- Accountability. This is fundamental to the corporate governance of public bodies, and in recent years the voluntary sector, in regard to both the proper steward-ship of public and donated funds and the increasing demand for service users to be involved in decision-making.
- Stakeholders. Whilst commercial companies are primarily accountable to the share-holders, organisations in the public and voluntary sectors are accountable to a wide range of stakeholders, including service users, the general public, funders and national government. Issues of accountability are not clear-cut and conflicts can arise, for example charity trustees have a legal duty to act in the interests of their beneficiaries, but if the charity is a membership body, this may conflict with the wishes of members.
- Openness and transparency. There is a demand for open government and a distrust of decisions taken behind closed doors. Voluntary organisations also face calls for transparency.
- Governance/board structures. The unitary board is not common in these sectors. Boards, or their equivalent, may be directly elected or appointed, and are often volunteer-based.
- Monitoring performance: In recent years a major emphasis in the public sector has been on performance measurement and evaluation. Increasingly, voluntary organis-ations are beginning to look at ways of measuring outcomes.

A major difference between corporate governance and governance in the non-com-mercial sector is the nature of the governance arrangements.

- There is a senior management group, or a board of trustees, but these are not accountable to shareholders.
- In the case of government departments, the management is accountable to the government of the day, but is expected to retain independence from political bias. Managers of government departments are therefore accountable to the minister in charge of the department and hence to the government itself, but there is also an argument that they are accountable to the general public.
- In the case of charitable organisations, good governance should involve major stakeholders – beneficiaries and contributors of charitable donations – in a way that does not apply to companies or government organisations.

3.5 Corporate governance in the public sector

A key development for the corporate governance of the UK public sector was the Nolan Committee on Standards in Public Life. This committee was set up in 1995 in response to concerns that the conduct of some politicians was unethical and, in particular, allegations of MPs taking cash for putting parliamentary questions. Whilst the committee focused on MPs, its remit included the civil service, non-departmental public bodies (NDPBs) and the NHS. Its early recommendations also had a wider impact on the public and voluntary sectors, and its seven principles of public life have been widely adopted.

THE NOLAN SEVEN PRINCIPLES OF PUBLIC LIFE

Selflessness: Holders of public office should take decisions solely in terms of the public interest. They should not do so to gain financial or other material benefits for themselves, their family or their friends.

Integrity: Holders of public office should not place themselves under any financial or other obligation to outside individuals or organisations that might influence them in the performance of their duties.

Objectivity: In carrying out public business, including making public appointments, awarding contracts or recommending individuals for rewards and benefits, holders of public office should make choices on merit.

Accountability: Holders of public office are accountable for their decisions and actions to the public and must submit themselves to whatever scrutiny is appropriate to their office.

Openness: Holders of public office should be as open as possible about the decisions and actions that they take. They should give reasons for their decisions and restrict information only when the wider public interest clearly demands.

Honesty: Holders of public office have a duty to declare any private interests relating to their public duties and to take steps to resolve any conflicts arising in a way that protects the public interest.

Leadership: Holders of public office should promote and support these principles by leadership and example.

Many functions in the public sector are managed by public bodies. Examples include public corporations, NHS bodies, NDPBs or Quangos and nationalised industries. They operate at arm's length from government departments, although ministers remain accountable for their performance and actions, and are responsible for appointments to them.

The 1980s and 1990s saw a large increase in the number of NDPBs. This led to concerns about the unelected nature of such bodies, and accusations that they were secretive and could not be called to account. In 1998 the government published Quangos – Opening the Doors, which recommended that NDPBs should hold open meetings, publish annual reports and consult users.

In contrast to such public bodies, UK local government is founded on the system of representatives elected by and of the public. Elected members set policy and are accountable for actions taken on their behalf. Traditionally, local authorities were managed via committees, but the Local Government Act 2000 heralded new forms of governance. The cabinet system has now become more common, with councillors acting as part of the executive or sitting on scrutiny committees. Many local authorities now have directly elected mayors with executive powers.

This shift away from traditional methods of public governance has also occurred in the NHS, with a move towards the private sector unitary board model. NHS Trust boards comprise both executive and non-executive directors.

There has also been a gradual erosion of the boundary between the public, voluntary and commercial sectors. There now is a large number of charities and private companies that perform public functions and receive government funding. As they are not technically part of the public sector they often sit outside the mechanisms for accountability and control.

Good Governance Standard for Public Service

In 2004 The Independent Commission for Good Governance in Public Service was established by the Office for Public Management (OPM) and the Chartered Institute of Public Finance and Accountability (CIPFA), in partnership with the Joseph Rowntree Foundation. The role of the Commission was to develop a common code and set of principles for good corporate governance across all public services.

In January 2005 it published Good Governance Standard for Public Service. This is a guide to corporate governance for everyone concerned with governance in the public services and applies to all organisations that work for the public using public monies. Its application therefore extends from public sector bodies to all private sector organisations that use public money to work for the public.

In justifying the need for the application of good corporate governance principles and practice in the public service sector, the Commission has commented that:

- good governance encourages public trust and participation; whereas
- bad governance fosters low morale and adversarial relationships.

The Commission's Good Governance Standard, which builds on the Nolan Principles, consists of six main principles, each with supporting principles, together with guidelines on how these can be applied in practice. It is useful to look at these and compare them with the principles (to be described later in the text) that apply to good corporate governance in the commercial (profit-making) sector. There are many similarities.

The six main principles and their supporting principles are:

1   Focusing on the organisation's purpose and on its outcome for citizens and users of the organisation's services:
    1.1   Being clear about the purpose of the organisation and its intended outcomes for citizens and service users.
    1.2   Making sure that users receive a high-quality service.
    1.3   Making sure that taxpayers get value for money.
2   Performing effectively in clearly defined functions and roles:
    2.1   Being clear about the functions of the organisation's governing body.
    2.2   Being clear about the responsibilities of the non-executive and the executive governors.

2.3 Making sure that these responsibilities are properly carried out.

2.4 Being clear about the relationship between the governors and the public.

3 Promoting values for the whole organisation and demonstrating good governance through behaviour.

3.1 Putting the values of the organisation into practice.

3.2 Individual governors behaving in ways that uphold and exemplify effective governance.

4 Taking informed and transparent decisions and managing risk.

4.1 Being rigorous and transparent in the way that decisions are taken by the governing body.

4.2 Using good quality information, advice and support.

4.3 Making sure that an effective risk management system is in operation.

5 Developing the capacity and capability of the governing body to be effective.

5.1 Making sure that the governors have the skills, knowledge and experience to perform well.

5.2 Developing the capabilities of individuals with governance responsibilities.

5.3 Striking a balance in the membership of the governing body between continuity and renewal.

6 Engaging stakeholders and making accountability real.

6.1 Understanding formal and informal accountability relationships.

6.2 Taking an active and planned approach to dialogue with and accountability to the public.

6.3 Taking an effective and planned approach to accountability to staff.

6.4 Engaging effectively with institutional stakeholders.

3.6 Corporate governance and the UK voluntary sector

The voluntary sector includes a wide range of organisations, from charities to not-for-profit bodies and mutual self-help groups. It is characterised by its variety of legal forms. For example, charities can take the form of trusts, unincorporated associations, charitable companies limited by guarantee, chartered bodies or Industrial and Provident Societies.

Corporate governance developments in other sectors have impacted on voluntary organisations, with many of the recommendations of Cadbury, Nolan and Turnbull being adapted for the sector. For example, the National Council of Voluntary Organisations (NCVO) adapted Nolan's seven principles of public life into a code of conduct for charity trustees; the Charity Commission's Statement of Recommended Practice requires larger charities to include a statement on risks in their annual report.

Corporate governance also developed in response to sector-specific issues, including:

- the increase in size and importance of the sector, particularly as a result of the contracting out of public service to voluntary organisations;
- a perception of a decline in public confidence in charities;
- greater competition for funding;
- a lack of clarity about the duties of voluntary board members, and in particular concerns about the liabilities of charity trustees;

- a growing demand for accountability to service users and beneficiaries;
- demands for greater transparency on how charities spend donated income, and in particular the proportion spent on administration.

This has resulted in:

- A change in the methods of recruitment and selection of board members. Whilst this is still predominately by word of mouth, the use of advertisements and open recruitment procedures has increased.
- Greater clarity about governance structures, with more organisations having documented policies, procedures and control mechanisms.
- The tightening of regulatory regimes and more stringent reporting requirements.
- Since the 1990s, there have been initiatives to improve governance across the sector. In 2005, a code on governance in the voluntary and community sector was published. It was developed and endorsed by the Charity Commission and the National Council for Voluntary Organisations (NCVO), the Association of Chief Executives of Voluntary Associations (ACEVO), the Charity Trustee Network (CTN) and the Institute of Chartered Secretaries and Administrators.

The Code was also endorsed by The National Hub of Expertise in Governance ('The Governance Hub'), which has taken on the responsibility for future work on the Code.

The Code contains seven key principles, and underlying each of these is an additional principle of equality.

1   Board leadership. Every organisation should be led and controlled by an effective board of trustees that collectively ensures the delivery of its objects, sets its strategic direction and upholds its values.
2   The board in control. The trustees as a board should be collectively responsible and accountable for ensuring that the organisation performs well, is solvent and complies with all its obligations.
3   The high-performance board. The board should have clear responsibilities and functions, and should compose and organise itself to make sure that it discharges them effectively.
4   Board review and renewal. The board should periodically review its own effectiveness and the effectiveness of the organisation, and take any necessary steps to ensure that both continue to work well.
5   Board delegation. The board should set out the functions of sub-committees, officers, the chief executive and other staff and agents in clear, delegated authorities, and should monitor their performance.
6   Board and trustee integrity. The board and individual trustees should act according to high ethical standards and ensure that conflicts of interest are properly dealt with.
7   The open board. The board should be open, responsive and accountable to its users, beneficiaries, members, partners and others with an interest in its work.

These seven key principles each have two or more supporting principles, and for each supporting principle the Code suggests ways of applying it in practice.

The Code sets out best practice, but is not mandatory. Like the Combined Code, it will operate on a 'comply or explain' basis. Organisations that comply are invited to say so in their annual report. Smaller organisations with limited resources are encouraged to focus on compliance with the principles in the Code rather than the detailed guidance.

CASE EXAMPLE 2.2

The National Housing Federation represents the independent social housing sector and has approximately 1,400 non-profit housing organisations in its membership.

The Federation provides a code of governance for its members. This was first drafted in 1995. It was one of the first of such models in the not-for-profit sector, and incorporated Nolan's seven Principles. Compliance with the Code is not mandatory for members, but the Federation expects members to consider the issues raised, disclose in their annual reports the extent to which they comply, and give reasons for any non-compliance. The Code covers matters such as board recruitment, the responsibilities of the Chair and the CEO, the conduct of Board business, openness and transparency, accountability, audit, and conduct and probity.

The Code has been updated on a number of occasions to reflect best practice from both the commercial and public sectors. The latest version incorporates elements of the Combined Code for listed companies, and principles arising from the Higgs Report on the effectiveness of non-executive directors.

3.7 The state as shareholder

A company may be partly owned by the government. When this is the case, a question arises about what the interests of the state as shareholder are. A government may act like any other shareholder and simply look for maximum long-term returns from its investment. On the other hand, the government may recognise more openly the interest of other stakeholder groups, such as the company's employees or the public as a whole:

- Shareholders other than the government need to know what the government's interest are, and how these might affect decision-making by the board, in order to put a value to their own investment.
- The board of directors may also take decisions in the belief that should they make mistakes, and should the company get into financial difficulties, the government will be likely to provide further financial support, to prevent job losses.

In some cases, a government that privatises a nationalised industry retains a golden share, giving it the right to veto decisions taken by the company if these appear to be against the national interest, for example, giving it the right of veto over any sale of the company to a foreign buyer.

4 The company lawyer and corporate governance

The in-house company solicitor is an alternative to the company secretary as a source of knowledge on corporate governance. In-house solicitors are able to offer advice to the board on legal risk generally. Legal risk may be defined as the risk to the company from the consequences of breaching the law or any other regulations. These include the risks from shareholder activism as a result of breaching codes of good corporate governance.

When the board suspects that the company has a potential liability from a breach of the law or regulations, it should:

- find out more about the nature of the breach;
- obtain an opinion about whether a breach has occurred, or the probability that a breach has occurred;
- obtain an estimate of the potential liability.

Businesses appear to be increasingly aware of legal risks, perhaps because they are more common than in the past and reported examples now frequently occur. As just one example, in the UK the Law Lords held (in 2002) that the boards of directors of the life assurance organisation Equitable Life had breached their Articles of Association by giving differential terminal bonuses to holders of guaranteed annuity policies. As a consequence of this decision, the liabilities of the struggling Equitable Life were increased by a further £1.5 billion.

However, it is doubtful whether in-house lawyers will play a significant role in corporate governance. This was recognised in Best Practice Guidelines for In-House Lawyers in England and Wales, a document published by the Law Society Industry and Commerce Group in 2005. This suggests that although in-house lawyers will inevitably become involved in corporate governance matters, corporate governance is not their unique responsibility. In-house lawyers should be cautious of taking on a self-appointed role, for example as the 'conscience of the company'.

The Best Practice Guidelines further suggest that there might be some situations where it would be a disadvantage for in-house lawyers to be seen as the champions of corporate governance because it might prevent colleagues and others from talking to them openly about certain issues.

The Best Practice Guidelines also suggest that unless in-house lawyers attend board meetings, it will be difficult for them to exercise a valuable role in enforcing good corporate governance practice, because they will not be properly aware of what the board is thinking and doing. However, a different situation applies if the in-house lawyer is also the company secretary. Circumstances clearly differ between organisations.

5 The company secretary and corporate governance

There is a need for ethical, open, honest and transparent behaviour by a company in line with established best practices and procedures. The application of best practices should be encouraged and monitored. In this respect, the company secretary is in a unique position and could have a major role to play in a company.

The Combined Code makes particular reference to the responsibilities of the company secretary with regard to corporate governance matters. The Code states that, under the direction of the company chairman, the company secretary is responsible for:

- ensuring good information flows within the board and its committees, and between executive management and non-executive directors;
- facilitating induction and assisting with the professional development of board members as required;
- advising the board (through the chairman) on all corporate governance matters;
- being available to give advice and support to individual directors.

The Code also makes a provision that the appointment and removal of the company secretary should be a matter for the board as a whole. The King II Report also identifies that the company secretary has a 'pivotal role' to play and is uniquely placed to observe corporate governance in practice (see Chapter 13).

A brief list of some of the tasks and responsibilities of the company secretary should make this clear:

- The company secretary assists the chairman with preparing for, conducting and reporting the outcome of board meetings and general meetings of the company. He or she attends those meetings and takes the minutes.
- The company secretary will have some involvement in the counting of proxy votes from shareholders for a general meeting. Although the detailed counting is likely to be done by the company's registrars, the results should be sent to the company secretary. The company secretary is therefore well informed about shareholder voting intentions.
- In the UK, major shareholders are required by law to notify the company of changes in their shareholdings above 3 per cent, when the change takes the shareholding up or down by a percentage point or more. These notifications come to the company secretary, who (in the case of listed companies) must then notify an official news channel.
- Directors are required to notify the company of their transactions in shares of the company, by themselves or by related parties. This information should be notified to the company secretary, who (in the case of listed companies) must then notify an official news channel. The company secretary needs to be aware whether the share dealings breach any code (in the UK, the company's code for directors' share dealings, which might be the same as the Model Code in the UK Listing Rules).
- The company secretary is likely to have the responsibility for assisting the chairmen of the committees of the board, i.e. the audit committee, remuneration committee and nomination committee. For example, the company secretary's office is likely to assist a chairman by checking the availability of the other committee members for a meeting and arranging the venue. He or she may also attend the meetings and take minutes.
- If he or she attends the meetings of the audit committee, the company secretary will have some involvement with the external auditors and internal auditors of the company and should be able to offer advice on matters of risk management.

- In some companies, the company secretary has the responsibility for arranging insurance cover for the group. In such cases, the company secretary is directly involved in an aspect of risk management.

The company secretary is close to the board of directors, without necessarily being a director. He or she is in a position to advise and assist the board chairman and NEDs. To provide this advice, he or she should have a proper understanding of corporate governance rules and practice. The FSA has suggested that the company secretary should be involved in handling allegations by whistleblowers. He or she might also be asked to investigate cases of illicit share dealings by directors, potential conflicts of interest of individual directors or the independence of a particular non-executive.

5.1   ICSA Guidance Note on the company secretary's corporate governance role

The ICSA Guidance Note on the corporate governance role of the company secretary provides a specimen job description which includes the following key elements:

- ensuring the smooth running of the activities of the board of directors and the board committees, for example by helping with planning the agendas for meetings and preparing papers for and presenting papers to the meetings;
- keeping under review all legal and regulatory developments affecting the company's operations, and making sure that the directors are properly briefed about them;
- ensuring that the interests of stakeholders are borne in mind when important business decisions are made, particularly those affecting employees. Keeping in touch with the debate on corporate social responsibility and advising the board about its policies and practice with regard to corporate social responsibility (CSR);
- acting as a 'confidential sounding board' to the chairman, NEDs and executive directors on matters that concern them, and taking a lead in dealing with difficult interpersonal issues, such as when a director is removed from the board;
- acting as a primary point of contact and source of advice and guidance for NEDs, with regard to the company and its activities, in order to help NEDs in their decision-making process;
- acting as the 'conscience of the company', by providing an additional enquiring voice in relation to board decisions;
- ensuring compliance with the continuing obligations of the UK Listing Rules. The Listing Rules require listed companies in the UK to comply with the provisions of the Combined Code or to explain their non-compliance. The company secretary should therefore be involved in ensuring either compliance with the Combined Code or that the board of directors provide satisfactory reasons for non-compliance;
- ensuring that the disclosures required by the Combined Code are observed;
- ensuring the dissemination of regulatory news announcements to the stock market, such as trading statements and information about share dealings by directors;
- managing relations with investors, particularly institutional investors, with regard to corporate governance matters;

- responsibility for the induction of new directors;
- making sure that the company avoids committing offences under the Financial Services and Markets Act 2000 (FSMA) and does not put out misleading information about its financial performance or trading condition (see section 395 of FSMA);
- ensuring compliance with the statutory requirements to file returns, such as the annual return and notification of changes in directors;
- arranging and managing the process of calling and holding the Annual General Meeting, and advising on matters to be raised at the meeting and put to the shareholders for a vote.

The company secretary will often have additional responsibilities, relating perhaps to risk management, compliance with trading standards or other executive issues. These will vary from one company to another.

5.2   Independence of the company secretary

The role of the company secretary in corporate governance is such that it is essential to ensure his or her independence from undue influence and pressure from a senior board member. An ICSA Guidance Note on Reporting Lines for the Company Secretary comments:

'Boards of directors have a right to expect the company secretary to give impartial advice and to act in the best interests of the company. However, it is incumbent on boards of directors to ensure that company secretaries are in a position to do so, for example by ensuring that they are not subject to undue influence of one or more of the board of directors. If the board fails to protect the integrity of the company secretary's position, one of the most effective in-built internal controls available to the company is likely to be seriously undermined. The establishment of appropriate reporting lines for the company secretary will normally be a crucial factor in establishing that protection.'

The guidelines recommend that:

- In matters relating to his or her duties as an officer of the company, the company secretary should, through the chairman, be accountable to the board as a whole.
- If the company secretary has additional executive responsibilities on top of his or her core role, he or she should report to the CEO or appropriate executive director on such matters.
- The company secretary's remuneration should be settled (or at least noted) by the board as a whole, or by the remuneration committee of the board on the recommendation of the chairman or CEO. The role of the company secretary should be kept in mind as you read the following chapters on the various major issues in corporate governance.

Chapter summary

- Several concepts apply to sound corporate governance. Best practice will not be achieved unless there is openness, honesty, transparency and fairness. In companies, fairness means giving equal treatment to all shareholders and not oppressing a minority.

- In addition, decision-makers and advisers should avoid potential conflicts of interest that might affect their judgement; and the independence of the external auditors and at least some of the non-executive directors is essential.

- Individuals in positions of responsibility and power should be accountable for their performance and actions. In particular, the board of directors should be accountable to the shareholders.

- There are differences of opinion about the value of corporate governance for listed companies.

- There are also differing views about the extent to which best practice in corporate governance is relevant to AIM companies and private companies.

- Principles of good governance have been introduced into the public sector and not-for-profit voluntary sector.

- Different issues in corporate governance may apply to state-owned companies and nationalised industries.

- Ethical issues in corporate governance are of particular relevance to state-owned and state-managed enterprises (e.g. a national health service), and in some countries there are concerns about corruption and political influence in such organisations.

- The company lawyer might be an important adviser to the board on matters of corporate governance, where the company is at risk of non-compliance with laws or regulations.

- The company secretary is a key individual for the application of best practice in corporate governance. He or she is close to the board, should have a thorough knowledge of best practice in corporate governance, and should be in a position to give suitable advice and guidance. This is emphasised by corporate governance guidelines such as the Combined Code and the King II Report. ICSA has produced a specimen job description for the corporate governance role of the company secretary.

Chapter 3

Directors and shareholders: powers and rights

Introduction

Company law does not provide a comprehensive framework for corporate governance, although elements of company law are relevant. This chapter considers the legal and regulatory aspects of corporate governance in UK law and regulation. In particular, it considers the powers of the board of directors and the extent to which the legal duties of directors can act as a restraint on those powers. It also considers the rights of shareholders and how shareholders can use their rights in the event of disagreement or disillusionment with the directors. It also looks at the regulatory restrictions on the directors of public companies arising from listing rules or stock market rules.

1 The powers of directors

The powers of the board of directors are set out in a company's constitution. Company legislation provides a standard form of Articles of Association (the Model Articles). For companies formed under the Companies Act 1985 this means the 1985 Table A Articles. For companies formed under the Companies Act 2006, there are different Model Articles and these are different for public and private companies. The powers of directors are broadly comparable, however, in all the Model Articles.

Article 70 of Table A states that the directors 'may exercise all the powers of the company'. However, these absolute powers are subject to the following:

- The provisions of company law.
- Additionally, any directions given to them by a special resolution of the shareholders, voting in general meeting of the company, to the extent that the shareholders have the right to make any such resolutions.
- The powers are given to the board of directors as a whole, but Table A (Article 72) states that these powers may be delegated.
- The board may delegate powers to a committee consisting of one or more directors. For example, public companies might establish a remuneration committee, a nomination committee and an audit committee.
- The board may also delegate to any executive director, such as a managing director, such of its powers that it considers desirable for that director to exercise.

Standard Articles of Association therefore provide for the board collectively to be the main power centre in the company, but with delegation of powers to board committees and executive directors.

A distinction should be made between the powers and duties of executive directors as members of the board and their responsibilities as managers of the company. Under the Articles of Association, managers have neither powers nor duties. The relationship they have with the company, including their authority and responsibilities, is established by their contract of employment and by the law of agency.

1.1   Borrowing powers

There is no restriction in law on how much the directors can borrow on behalf of their company. As far as the law is concerned, the borrowing powers of companies are limited only by what lenders are prepared to allow them. Conceivably, the directors could therefore put the investment of their shareholders at risk by borrowing more than the company can safely afford.

The National Association of Pension Funds (NAPF) recommends that, to reduce this risk, there should be a reasonable limit in the company's Articles on the directors' powers to borrow, which should relate to the borrowings of the entire group of companies, not just individual companies within the group.

2   The duties of directors to their company

The directors act as agents of their company. They have certain duties, which are to the company itself, but not to its shareholders, its employees or any person external to the company (e.g. the general public). Although a company is a legal person in law, it is not human. Since the relationship between directors and the company is by its very nature impersonal, it might be wondered just what 'duty' means.

The concept of duty is not easy to understand, and it will be helpful to make a comparison with the duties owed by other individuals or groups.

Examples of individuals owing a duty to something inanimate are not common, although personnel in the armed forces have a duty to their country. It is more usual to show loyalty to something inanimate rather than to have a duty. For example, individuals might be expected to show loyalty to their country, and they might voluntarily show loyalty to their sports team, friends or work colleagues. Arguably, solicitors have a duty to their profession to act ethically, although the solicitors' practice rules in the UK specify that solicitors owe a duty of care to their clients. Similarly, doctors have a duty to act ethically, but their duty is to their patients. Duty is normally owed to individuals or a group of people. It might therefore be supposed that directors should owe a duty to their shareholders and possibly to the company's employees, but this is not the case. Accountability and responsibility should not be confused with duty.

- Directors have a responsibility to use their powers in ways that seem best for the company and its shareholders.
- They should be accountable to the owners of the company, the shareholders, for the ways in which they have exercised their powers and/or the performance of the company.
- They have duties to the company.

Anyone guilty of a breach of duty, should be subject to a process calling him or her to account. There might be an established disciplinary procedure, for example in a court or before a judicial panel, with a recognised set of punishments for misbehaviour. With companies, however, disciplinary mechanisms are difficult to apply in practice, except in extreme cases of misbehaviour. Where measures are taken, they are likely to be initiated by shareholders seeking legal remedies on behalf of the company.

2.1   Common law duties and statutory duties of directors

Companies have many duties and obligations in law, but in the past the directors themselves did not. However, they could be personally liable in some circumstances. For example, directors could be liable to a fine for a failure to take minutes of their meetings or to deliver a copy of the company's report and accounts to the Registrar of Companies.

Until the introduction of the provisions of the Companies Act 2006, the main duties of directors were duties in common law – a fiduciary duty and duty of skill and care to the company. This duty is to the company, not its shareholders. The Companies Act 2006 has now written the common law duties of directors into statute law. It states that these general duties 'are based on certain common law rules and equitable principles as they apply to directors, and have effect in place of those rules and principles as regards the duties owed to a company by a director' (Companies Act 2006, s. 170). The Act goes on to state that the statutory general duties should be interpreted in the same way as the common law rules and equitable principles.

It is therefore useful to begin by looking at the nature of the common law duties and what they have meant.

3 Fiduciary duties of directors

In UK law, the directors have a fiduciary duty to their company. 'Fiduciary' means given in trust, and the concept of a trustee (as established in US and UK law) is applicable. The directors hold a position of trust because they make contracts on behalf of the company and also control the company's property. Since this is similar to being a trustee of the company, a director has fiduciary duties. However, these are duties to the company, not to its shareholders.

If a director were to act in breach of his or her fiduciary duties, legal action could be brought against him or her by the company. In such a situation, the 'company' might be represented by a majority of the board of directors, a majority of the shareholders or a single controlling shareholder.

Presumably, an accusation of breach of fiduciary duty would focus on a particular action or series of actions by the director concerned. If the court were to find a director in breach of his or her fiduciary duties, it might order him or her to compensate the company for any loss it has suffered and account to the company for any personal profit made.

3.1 Tests for breach of fiduciary duty

There are three key tests of whether a director is in breach of his or her fiduciary duties in carrying out a particular transaction or series of transactions:

1 The transaction should be reasonably incidental to the business of the company. If it is not related to the business of the company in any way, it would be a breach of fiduciary duty. For example, the CEO of a building construction company might decide to trade in diamonds and lose large amounts of money in these diamond trading transactions.

2 The transaction carried out should have been bona fide (i.e. in good faith), with honesty and sincerity. If it is not, it would be a breach of fiduciary duty.

3 The transaction should also have been made for the benefit of the company, and not for the personal benefit of the director. Directors have a fiduciary duty to avoid a conflict of interest between themselves personally and the company, and must not obtain any personal benefit or profit from a transaction without the consent of the company. In other words, it would be a breach of fiduciary duty for a director to make a secret profit from a transaction by the company in which he or she has a personal interest.

Suppose, for example, that a company wishes to buy some land and has identified a property for which it would be prepared to pay a large sum of money. The CEO might secretly set up a private company to buy the property, and then sell this on to the company of which he or she is CEO, making a large profit in the process. The actions of the CEO would be a breach of fiduciary duty, because the actions would not have been bona fide, and the CEO would have made a secret profit at the expense of the company.

CASE EXAMPLE 3.1

Development Consultants Ltd v Cooley [1972]

An example of breach of fiduciary duty arose in the case of Industrial Development Consultants Ltd v Cooley [1972]. Cooley, a highly regarded architect, was the managing director of a firm of consultants. The firm advised clients on construction projects in the gas industry. A potential client was planning a new construction project, but had made it clear that it would not use the consultancy services of the firm. Cooley was aware, however, that although the client had objections to using his firm, it might award the work to him personally. He therefore told the board of his company that he was seriously ill and persuaded the directors to release him from his contract of employment. Having been released from his contract of employment, he then succeeded in negotiating a contract with the client to provide his personal consultancy service. His former company found out and took him to court, claiming that he was in breach of his fiduciary duty and must account for his profits. The court agreed, even though the company would not have been awarded the work, and ordered Cooley to account to the company for the profits he had made from the work.

CASE EXAMPLE 3.2

Bairstow and others v Queen's Moat Houses plc [1994]

Queen's Moat Houses plc (QMH) paid dividends to its shareholders on the basis of its accounts in 1990 and 1991. However, the dividend payments exceeded the company's distributable reserves, and so were in breach of ss. 263 and 264 of the Companies Act 1985, which make it unlawful for dividends to be paid except out of profits available for that purpose. The directors did not benefit from the dividend payments themselves.

It was claimed that the 1991 accounts were misleading, because they included some unlawful transactions, adopted some inappropriate accounting treatments and involved significant non-disclosure of information.

QMH brought an action seeking repayment of the unlawful dividends from the directors, claiming that they were in breach of their duties by authorising the dividend payments when they should have known that there were insufficient distributable reserves.

The directors argued that the breach was only technical, because there were sufficient distributable reserves within the group even if not within QMH itself, so no loss was suffered. They also asked the court to use discretionary powers available under s. 727 of the Companies Act 1985 to relieve them from liability, on the grounds that they had acted honestly and reasonably.

The judgement had three main aspects, and the court ruled as follows:

- A reasonably diligent director should know that dividends cannot be paid from capital, and so should know that any dividend paid on the basis of accounts showing insufficient distributable reserves would be unlawful. Any director not aware of this would be in beach of his or her duty of skill and care.
- *The 1990 accounts.* The directors had placed too much reliance on their auditors, and had overlooked their responsibilities to ensure that the distributable reserves were sufficient. However, they had acted honestly and reasonably, therefore the court relieved them of liability (under s. 727 of the Companies Act 1985).
- *The 1991 accounts.* The directors had knowledge that the 1991 accounts did not give a true and fair view. Dividends paid on the basis of inaccurate accounts are unlawful, because the distributable profits cannot be properly established. The authorisation of the dividend payments by the directors, on the basis of accounts they knew to be misleading, amounted to a breach of trust and fiduciary duty, because it was not in the best interests of the company. The conduct of the directors was not honest; therefore they were not entitled to relief under ss. 727 and were liable to repay the dividends (of £26.7 million).

(Note: This case went to the Court of Appeal in 2000, but the breach of fiduciary duty was not an issue in the appeal. The case is now expected to go to the House of Lords.)

---

4   A director's duty of skill and care

In addition to having a fiduciary duty, directors have also been subject to a common law duty of skill and care to the company. A director should not act negligently in carrying out his or her duties, and could be personally liable for losses suffered by the company as a consequence of such negligence.

The standard of skill and care expected of a director is the higher of the skill that he or she has or the skill that would objectively be expected of a director of the particular company. In the case Re D'Jan of London [1993], the judge ruled that the common law duty of care was the equivalent to the statutory test applied by the Insolvency Act 1986, s. 214. This statutory test refers to what would be expected of: 'a reasonably diligent person having both:

- the general knowledge, skill and experience that may reasonably be expected of a person carrying out the same functions as are carried out by that director in relation to the company, and
- the general knowledge, skill and experience that that director has.'

A director is expected to show the technical skills that would reasonably be expected from someone of his or her experience and expertise. If the finance director of a scientific research company is a qualified accountant, he or she would not be expected to possess the technical skills of a scientist, but would be expected to possess some technical skill as an accountant.

The duty of skill and care does not extend to spending time in the company. A director should attend board meetings if possible, but at other times is not required to be concerned with the affairs of the company. This requirement is perhaps best understood with NEDs, who might visit the company only for board or committee meetings. The duties of a director are intermittent and arise from time to time only, such as when the board meets. If a director holds an executive position in the company, a different situation arises, because he or she is an employee of the company with a contract of service. This contract might call for full-time attendance at the company or on its business. However, this requirement arises out of his or her job as a manager, not out of his or her position as a director.

It is also not a part of the duty of skill and care to watch closely over the activities of the company's management. Unless there are particular grounds for suspecting dishonesty or incompetence, a director is entitled to leave the routine conduct of the company's affairs to the management. If the management appears honest, the directors may rely on the information they provide. It is not part of their duty of skill and care to question whether the information is reliable, or whether important information is being withheld.

A board of directors might make a decision that appears ill-judged or careless. However, UK courts are generally reluctant to condemn business decisions made by the board that appear, in hindsight, to show errors of judgement. Directors can exercise reasonable skill and care, but still make bad decisions.

For a legal action against a director to succeed a company would have to prove that serious negligence had occurred. It would not be enough to demonstrate that a loss could have been avoided if the director had been a bit more careful.

CASE EXAMPLE 3.3

Finance Co. Ltd v Stebbing [1989] BCLC 498

In the case of Dorchester Finance Co. Ltd v Stebbing [1989] BCLC 498, a company brought an action against its three directors for alleged negligence and misappropriation of the company's property. The company (Dorchester Finance) was in the money-lending business and it had three directors, S, H and P. Only S was involved full time with the company; H and P were non-executives who made only rare appearances. There were no board meetings. S and P were qualified accountants and H, although not an accountant, had considerable accountancy experience. S arranged for the company to make some loans to persons with whom he appears to have had dealings. In the loan-making process he had persuaded P and H to sign blank cheques that were subsequently used to make the loans. The loans did not comply with the Moneylenders Acts and they were inadequately secured. When the loans turned out to be irrecoverable, the company brought its action against the directors.

It was held that all three directors were liable to damages. S, as an executive director, was held to be grossly negligent. P and H, as non-executives, were held to have failed to show the necessary level of skill and care in performing their duties as non-executives, even though it was accepted that they had acted in good faith at all times.

CASE EXAMPLE 3.4

Re D'Jan of London [1993]

An insurance broker completed an insurance proposal form with an incorrect answer, but a director of the company applying for the insurance signed the form. The company premises burned down, and the insurance company, on discovering the mistake on the proposal form, repudiated all liability under the policy. The company went into insolvent liquidation. The liquidator brought an action against the director who had signed the proposal form, alleging a failure to exercise reasonable care to the company. The court found that although it would be unreasonable to expect a director to read every word of every document that he signed, in this case the form consisted of a few simple questions that the director was the best person to answer. The director was therefore guilty of a breach of duty of care, although, in this case, the director was exonerated on other grounds.

4.1 Wrongful trading and the standard of duty and care

The standard of duty and care required from a director has been partly defined in a number of legal cases relating to wrongful trading. Under the Insolvency Act 1986, directors may be liable for wrongful trading by the company, if they allow the company to continue trading, but know (or should know) that it is unable to avoid an insolvent liquidation. When such a situation arises and a company goes into liquidation, the liquidator can apply to the court for the director to be held personally liable for negligence. The duty of a director under the Insolvency Act was used in the case of Re D'Jan of London [1993] to illustrate a director's general duty of skill and care.

4.2 Duties of directors and delegation

Since directors owe a duty of skill and care to their company, it could be asked how much time and attention a director should give to the company's affairs, and to what extent a director can delegate responsibilities to another person without being in breach of his or her duty.

In a case concerning the disqualification of Andrew Tuckey, a former deputy chairman of Barings plc, the duties of a director with regard to functions he or she has delegated were summarised as follows by Mr Justice Parker:

- Directors, both individually and collectively, have a duty to acquire and maintain sufficient understanding of the company's business to enable them to discharge their duties properly.
- Subject to the Articles of Association, directors are allowed to delegate particular functions to individuals beneath them in the management chain. Within reason, they are also entitled to have trust in the competence and integrity of these individuals. However, delegation of authority does not remove from the director a duty to supervise the exercise of that delegated authority by the subordinate.

- There is no universal rule for establishing whether a director is in breach of his or her duty to supervise the discharge of delegated functions by subordinates. The extent of the duty, and whether it has been properly discharged, should be decided on the facts of each case.

Matters that could be an issue in any particular case include:

- whether the authority was delegated to the appropriate person;
- whether the individual should have checked how the subordinate was discharging the delegated functions;
- whether the system itself, within which the failure occurred, was itself inadequate (for which the person with overall responsibility must accept criticism);
- the extent of the director's duties and responsibilities in this case.

When there is a question about the extent of the director's duties and responsibilities, a significant factor could be the level of reward that the director was entitled to receive from the company. Prima facie, the higher the rewards, the greater the responsibilities that should be expected.

In the Barings case, Mr Justice Parker concluded that Mr Tuckey had failed in his duties because he did not have a sufficient knowledge and understanding of the nature of the derivatives markets and the risks involved in derivatives dealing (which led to the collapse of Barings). He was therefore unable to consider properly matters referred to the committee of which he was chairman.

4.3 Duty of skill and care for non-executive directors

A unitary board consists of both non-executive directors and executive directors, and all board members have the same duty of skill and care to the company. However, non-executive directors are likely to spend significantly less time on the affairs of the company than their executive director colleagues. The knowledge and experience they have of the company's affairs will therefore be much less.

The Combined Code includes a supporting Schedule that gives some guidance on what might be required from a non-executive director to comply with the requirement to exercise skill, care and diligence. It comments:

'It is up to each non-executive director to reach a view as to what is necessary in particular circumstances to comply with the duty of skill, care and diligence they owe as a director of the company. In considering whether or not a person is in breach of that duty, a court would take into account all relevant circumstances.'

In its guidance, the Code suggests that relevant considerations might be as follows:

- The letter of appointment for a NED should set out the expected time commitment for the role. This can be compared with the actual time commitment the director has given.
- The Combined Code requires that directors should be supplied in a timely manner with all the information they need to discharge their duties, and the information

should be in a suitable form and of an appropriate quality. A check can be made to establish whether the information provided to the director met these requirements.

- NEDs are expected to seek clarification of information from management, and additional information if required, and also to take and follow professional advice where appropriate.
- NEDs are required by the Code to undertake an induction on first becoming a director, and to update and refresh their skills, knowledge and familiarity with the company.
- Where a director has concerns about a particular matter, he or she must ensure that these are considered by the board, and to the extent that the matter is not resolved, make sure that the concerns are minuted in the board meeting at which they are discussed.
- On resignation, a director should give a written statement to the chairman if there are any unresolved concerns.

5 General duties of directors: Companies Act 2006

The duties of directors in common law and equity to their company have now been introduced into statute law by the Companies Act 2006, ss. 171–7). These consist of a duty to:

- act within their powers;
- promote the success of the company;
- exercise independent judgement;
- exercise reasonable care, skill and diligence;
- avoid conflicts of interest;
- not accept benefits from third parties;
- declare any interest in a proposed transaction or arrangement.

It is worth remembering that these duties (as in common law) apply to non-executive directors as well as to executive directors.

Duty to act within powers

A director must act within his or her powers in accordance with the company's constitution, and should only exercise these powers for the purpose for which they were granted. If a director acts outside his or her powers to make a contractual agreement with a third party, the company is liable for any obligation to the third party, provided that the third party has acted in good faith.

Duty to promote the success of the company

A director, in good faith, must act in the way he or she considers would be most likely to 'promote the success of the company for the benefit of its members as a whole'. The Act does not define 'success', but the term is likely to be interpreted as meaning 'increasing value for shareholders'. However, in doing so, a director must also have regard, amongst other matters, to:

- the likely long-term consequences of any decision;
- the interests of the company's employees;
- the need to foster the company's relationships with its customers, suppliers and others;
- the impact of the company's operations on the community and the environment;
- the desirability of the company maintaining its reputation for high standards of business conduct; and
- the need to act fairly between members of the company.

The Act does not create a duty of directors to any stakeholders other than the shareholders (members), but it requires directors to give consideration to interests of other stakeholders in reaching their decisions. The Act specifically mentions employees, customers, suppliers and the community. It therefore appears to promote a form of enlightened shareholder approach to corporate governance.

This aspect of directors' duties has given rise to some concerns that directors will need to create a 'paper trail' to provide evidence if required in a court of law to show that they have given due consideration to the interests of other stakeholders in their decision-making, although the government has denied that this is intended by the Act.

It has also been suggested that this statutory duty may be fulfilled for quoted companies by the legal requirement to include a narrative business review in the annual report and accounts, which should discuss the company's policies, and their effectiveness, with regard to employees, the environment and social and community issues. The business review is described in a later chapter (see Chapter 8).

Duty to exercise independent judgement

A director must exercise independent judgement. However, this requirement does not prevent a director from acting in a way authorised by the company's constitution (for example, accepting resolutions passed by the shareholders in general meeting) or from acting in accordance with an agreement already entered into by the company that prevents the director from using discretion. The requirement for independent judgement does not prevent a director from taking advice and acting on it.

Duty to exercise reasonable care, skill and diligence

This is similar to the common law duty of care.

Duty to avoid conflicts of interest

A director has a duty to avoid conflicts of interest with the interests of the company. However, this duty is not breached if the director declares the interest to the board of directors and the interest is authorised by the rest of the board.

In the commercial world, it is inevitable that many directors will have a potential conflict of interest, whether direct or indirect, with their company. For example, a company might be planning to trade with another company in which one of its directors is a shareholder. In such a situation, the director concerned is required to declare his or her interest in the proposed contract to the other directors and must not make a secret profit.

A director or a connected person might have a material interest in a transaction under-taken by the company. For example, the company might award a contract to a firm of building contractors to rebuild or develop a property owned by the company, and the director or his/her spouse might own the building company.

A director might also have a direct or indirect interest in a contract (or proposed contract) with the company. For example, the director might be a member of another organisation with which the company is planning to sign a business contract. Such a contract is not illegal, although the company can choose to rescind it should it wish to do so.

If a director has an interest in a contract with the company and has failed to disclose it, and has received a payment under the contract, he or she will be regarded as holding the money in the capacity of constructive trustee for the company and so is bound to repay the money.

The 2006 Act recognises three situations in which an actual or potential conflict of interest may arise:

1   A conflict of interest may arise in a situation where the company is not a party to an arrangement or transaction, but where the director might be able to gain personally from 'the exploitation of any property, information or opportunity'. For example, a director might pursue an opportunity for his or her personal benefit that the company might have pursued itself.

2   A conflict of interest may arise in connection with a proposed transaction or arrangement to which the company will be a party. If a director has a direct or indirect personal interest in any such transaction or arrangement, he or she must disclose this interest to the board before it is entered into by the company. An example would be a proposal to acquire a target company in which a director owns shares. (Note: the Table A Articles of Association provide that when a director has disclosed an interest in a contract with the company, he or she cannot count towards the quorum of the board that makes a decision about the contract. In practice, the director might be asked to leave the meeting whilst the matter is being discussed.)

3   A conflict of interest arises in relation to existing transactions or arrangements in which the company is already a party. It can be a criminal offence for a director not to make or update a declaration of interest in an arrangement or transaction to which the company is a party.

Duty not to accept benefits from third parties

A director must not accept benefits from a third party unless they have been authorised by the shareholders or unless they cannot reasonably be regarded as giving rise to a potential conflict of interest. In practice many listed companies already have strict internal policies on accepting gifts and corporate hospitality, especially from other companies that are tendering or about to tender for business with the company. An internal policy might include a requirement for a director to obtain clearance from another director before accepting any such benefits.

Duty to declare interests in proposed transactions with the company

This duty is linked to the duty relating to conflicts of interest. A director must declare the nature and extent of his or her interest to the other directors, who may then authorise it.

5.1 Consequences of a breach of the general duties

A director owes his or her duties to the company, and if the director is in breach of those duties only the company can bring a legal claim against the director. In practice, this has usually meant that the rest of the board of directors might bring an action against a fellow director in the name of the company.

The 2006 Act states that the consequences of a breach of a director's general duties are the same as if the corresponding common law rule or equitable principle applied, but it does not set out in detail what these consequences should be.

In addition, the Act introduces a procedure whereby individual members of the company can bring a legal action for a derivative claim against a director. A derivative action may be brought in respect of 'an actual or proposed act or mission involving negligence, default, breach of duty or breach of trust by a director of the company'. A shareholder would have to bring the action against a director in the name of the company, and if the action were successful the company and not the individual shareholder would benefit.

The procedures for bringing a derivative action are set out in ss. 260–9 of the Act. They include safeguards designed to prevent individual shareholders from bringing actions that are not reasonable on the basis of the prima facie evidence. Even so, there is a possibility that in future legal actions against directors will be brought by shareholders under the derivatives claims procedure for breach of their general duties.

5.2 Directors' responsibilities to company outsiders

Although the duty of directors is to their company, a breach of that duty could affect outsiders. When the directors make a contract with an outsider, the contract is binding on the company when it is in accordance with its constitution. However, the directors might exceed their powers in making the contract, for example, because they should have obtained shareholder approval first, but failed to do so. Contracts entered into without proper authority are known as 'irregular contracts', and might seem to be void.

An outsider making a contract in good faith with the directors, when the contract is irregular, would be unable to enforce the contract if it were void. On the other hand, if an irregular contract is not void and is enforceable, a company has no protection against the consequences of unauthorised actions by its directors. So should irregular contracts be void or enforceable by an outsider?

The main provision of UK company law is that an irregular contract is binding on a company when an outsider, acting in good faith, enters into the contract and the contract has been approved by the board of directors. The directors will be liable to the company for any loss suffered. This rule means that irregular contracts do not affect third parties (outsiders). Instead, when they occur, they are a corporate governance problem.

6 Directors' liability insurance

Directors can be made liable for negligence or for a breach of duty or trust in relation to their company. The risk of facing legal action or incurring large personal liabilities might therefore be sufficient to deter individuals from becoming directors. This is particularly the case with

NEDs, who cannot usually be expected to know as much about the company and its business as their executive director colleagues. A NED could potentially be accused of negligence or breach of duty for reasons he or she might not have been fully aware of at the time.

The risk of personal liability for directors leads on to the question of insurance and whether a company can or should take out directors' and officers' liability insurance to protect them against the risk of personal liability.

In the UK, the Companies Act 2006, s. 233 allows companies to purchase liability insurance for directors and officers:

- Any provision in the company's Articles or a contract with the individual director is void if it indemnifies the individual from liability in respect of negligence, default, breach of duty or breach of trust.
- However, this does not prevent the company from purchasing insurance against such liability for its directors and officers (and auditors). Directors can also be indemnified against legal costs incurred in defending an action (civil or criminal) for alleged negligence, default, breach of duty or breach of trust in relation to the company.

The provisions of UK law mean that directors should expect their company to take out and maintain directors' and officers' liability insurance. Any individual invited to become a director should first check that this insurance exists and that the amount of cover provided by the insurance policy is adequate (i.e. sufficient to cover the potential liabilities the director might incur).

The 2003 Combined Code reinforced the legal position with a provision which states:

'The company should arrange appropriate insurance cover in respect of legal action against its directors.'

7 Fair dealing by directors

Certain responsibilities are placed on directors by statute to restrict the extent to which directors could seek to gain unfairly at the expense of the company or its shareholders.

7.1 Prohibition on loans to directors and connected persons

The Companies Act 2006, ss. 197–214 prohibits loans, quasi-loans and credit transactions by a company to any of its directors, unless they have been approved by the shareholders. (For shareholders to give their approval, disclosure of the proposed transaction should be made in advance.) The rules on loans apply to all companies and the rules on quasi loans and credit transactions apply to public companies.

In the case of public limited companies, this prohibition extends to connected persons of a director. The spouse of a director, child or stepchild under the age of 18 and companies in which the director has an equity interest of 20 per cent or more are all classified as connected persons. The prohibition extends to shadow directors and connected persons of shadow directors.

There are some exceptions to the prohibition on loans. Under the terms of the Companies Act 2006, these exceptions apply in cases where shareholder approval is not obtained:

- A company can make a loan or quasi-loan to a director provided it does not exceed £10,000.
- A company may lend money to a director to assist him or her in the performance of his or her duties. For example, if the director has to move from one part of the country to another, the company can assist with a bridging loan. However, such financial assistance cannot exceed a certain limit (£50,000 under the Companies Act 2006).
- Loans may be made by the company on proper commercial terms in the ordinary course of its business. For example, a bank can lend money to a director in a normal lending transaction. (There is no ceiling on the size of such loans.)

CASE EXAMPLE 3.5

Consibee (Oxford) Limited v Tait (1997)

In the case of Tait Consibee (Oxford) Limited v Tait (1997), a company made a loan of £10,000 to the defendant, Tait, who was at the time a director. Later in the same year (1994), Tait left the company and ceased to be a director. In January 1995, the company demanded repayment of the loan. Tait refused, arguing that it had been agreed that the loan would be repaid out of dividends, and the company had not made any dividend payments since the loan was made. The company disputed this. However, it also argued that the loan was illegal, having been made to a director (and exceeding the limit of £5,000 that applied under the Companies Act 1985) and so was recoverable immediately. The court agreed, and ordered Tait to pay back the loan with interest.

7.2 Substantial property transactions

Shareholder approval is required for any transaction between a director and the company in which the director receives from or transfers to the company any non-cash asset (e.g. land and buildings) worth the lesser of £100,000 and 10 per cent of the company's net assets. This is to prevent a director from selling non-cash assets to the company for more than they are worth, or buying non-cash assets at less than their market value, without the shareholders having the opportunity to say no.

Shareholder approval is not required for a transaction of less than £5,000 (when this is more than 10 per cent of the company's assets.)

7.3   Related party transactions and the UK Listing Rules

For companies whose shares are listed and traded on the London Stock Exchange, the requirements of UK law are further reinforced by the UK Listing Rules. These are rules that listed companies must comply with and include a section on 'related party transactions'. In broad terms, a related party means a substantial shareholder of the company, a director of the company, a member of a director's family or a company in which a director or family member holds 30 per cent or more of the shares. A related party transaction is a transaction between a company and a related party, other than in the normal course of business.

For most related party transactions above a minimum size, a listed company is required to:

- make an announcement to the stock market giving details of the transaction;
- send a circular to shareholders giving more details; and
- obtain the prior approval of the shareholders for the transaction.

The effect of the Listing Rules should be to prevent directors or major shareholders of UK listed companies from obtaining a personal benefit from any non-business transaction with their company, unless the shareholders have given their approval.

8   Shareholders' powers and rights

8.1   Shareholders' powers

Shareholders' powers are fairly restricted in UK law, although there is some debate as to how extensive these powers are. In the context of corporate governance, shareholders' powers relate to the actions that shareholders can take to make decisions for the company, or to affect decisions taken by the directors with which they disagree.

The most significant powers of the shareholders relate to their voting powers in general meeting, although the matters on which they can make decisions are clearly delineated. These include electing or re-electing directors, appointing or reappointing the external auditors, decisions on authorised share capital and approving or reducing the proposed final dividend.

Shareholder powers in company law include the following:

- Under the Companies Act 2006, s. 188 a provision in a director's service contract is void if it guarantees that the term of the director's employment will be more than two years, unless the provision has been approved by ordinary resolution of the members. Shareholders also have the right to approve loans, quasi-loans and credit transactions to directors.
- Under the Companies Act 2006, s. 994 a shareholder can petition the court for an order on the grounds that the company's affairs are being conducted in a way that is unfairly prejudicial to some or all of its members. The court may then issue an order, for example to regulate the company's affairs or to prevent the company from doing something.

- Under the Companies Act 2006, s. 303 shareholders representing at least 10 per cent of the voting shares can call an extraordinary general meeting of the company.
- Under the Companies Act 2006, s. 338 shareholders representing at least 5 per cent of the voting shares of a public company can arrange for a resolution to be put to the annual general meeting. The company then has a duty to give notice of the resolution to all the other members.

8.2 Shareholders' rights

Shareholders also have rights. For example, they have a right to receive a copy of the company's annual report and accounts, and the right to attend and vote at general meetings of the company. The rights of shareholders relate mainly to the issues on which they may vote in general meetings of the company.

Company law requires some proposals to be approved by the shareholders voting in a general meeting and specifies the size of majority needed for a resolution to be passed. In the UK, most shareholder voting requires a simple majority (an ordinary resolution) or a 75 per cent majority vote (a special resolution).

In the past, it has been common for shareholders to 'rubber stamp' proposals by the directors at general meetings and to support the directors, with very few questions asked. Most general meetings of a company are attended by very few shareholders and most shareholders vote by proxy. With a proxy vote, the shareholder authorises another person to vote in the general meeting on his or her behalf, normally having indicated how the proxy should vote (for or against each resolution). Institutional investors with large shareholdings in a company might simply indicate how they want to vote on each resolution (normally in favour) and appoint the chairman of the board to cast the votes on their behalf.

Some investors believe that shareholders should use their voting rights more actively, voting against proposed resolutions where appropriate. As mentioned earlier, 'activist' shareholder groups might try to encourage shareholders to vote against the re-election of directors at the annual general meeting to show their disapproval of certain policies of the board.

There appears to be a growing interest in shareholders' voting rights among some institutional investment organisations, and there have been some calls for company meetings to take advantage of current technology with electronic voting.

There are several reasons for the growing interest in electronic voting:

- The technology and software are available to make it possible.
- Electronic voting is more convenient for institutional investors, who hold shares in many different companies, and might encourage them to give more thought to how they should vote.
- Institutional investors would be able to vote more easily at general meetings of companies in other countries, provided that companies in the countries concerned have electronic voting arrangements. US institutional investors are major holders of shares in other countries and could bring pressure to bear on foreign companies to move towards US systems of governance, including shareholder voting arrangements.

Electronic voting and electronic communications with shareholders are considered in more detail in Chapter 6.

8.3 New share issues: rights and authority to issue

An important aspect of the balance of power between directors and shareholders is the authority of directors to issue new shares and the rights of shareholders in any new share issue. Company law in this area varies between countries. In the UK, the major elements in the legislation are as follows:

- The directors cannot increase the issued share capital without prior approval from the shareholders. In theory, this could mean that the directors must always go to the shareholders for approval when they want to issue new shares. In practice, however, this would be too restricting. It would mean, for example, that the directors would have to ask for shareholder approval whenever an employee wished to exercise stock options (share options) to buy new shares in the company. On the other hand, the directors should not be given unrestricted authority to issue new shares whenever they choose to do so.

- In the UK, a compromise arrangement is usually reached by listed public companies, whereby the shareholders grant authority to the directors to issue new shares up to a certain maximum amount. This authority is usually given to the directors by a vote at the annual general meeting, and the authority typically lasts for one year, until the next annual general meeting (when another resolution is put forward to renew the authority for a further twelve months).

- In UK company law, shareholders have pre-emption rights. These are rights to buy new shares in the company ahead of the shares being offered to anyone else. When a company issues new shares for cash, the shareholders have the right to be offered those shares, in proportion to their existing shareholding. For example, if the directors of a company wanted to issue new shares for cash, equivalent to 10 per cent of the company's current issued share capital, it would normally be required to offer those new shares to the existing shareholders, in the ratio of one new share for every ten shares currently held. In this way, shareholders are protected against an erosion of their stake in the company, whereby the directors continue to issue new shares, but sell them to other investors.

- Shareholders can vote to disapply their pre-emption rights. In other words, the directors can ask the shareholders to vote on a resolution permitting them to issue new shares for cash to other investors, without having to offer them to existing shareholders first. Within certain limits, this might be a reasonable requirement of the directors. For example, new shares cannot be issued under share option schemes unless the pre-emption rights of the existing shareholders are disapplied. It is important, however, that a limit should be placed on the number of new shares that can be issued in this way.

- It is, therefore, usual at the annual general meeting of a UK listed company for a resolution to be voted on, proposing that the shareholders should disapply their pre-emption rights and allow the directors to issue new shares to other investors, but only up to a specified limit in the number of new shares. The disapplication of pre-emption rights is a matter of some concern to institutional investors, and the major associations of investment institutions have issued 'pre-emption guidelines' to their members, which they expect listed public companies to follow.

The main representative bodies of investment institutions in the UK are the Association of British Insurers (ABI) and the National Association of Pension Funds (NAPF). These have established Investment Committees (known as investor protection committees – IPCs) who have approved and issued guidelines on pre-emption rights. They recommend to their members that resolutions to disapply pre-emption rights at an annual general meeting should be approved, provided that:

- the total number of 'non pre-emptive' shares issued in any year does not exceed 5 per cent of the company's issued share capital; and
- the total number of 'non pre-emptive' shares issued in any rolling three-year period should not exceed 7.5 per cent of the company's issued share capital.

Proposals by a board of directors to disapply pre-emption rights for more shares should not be approved by the shareholders, the guidelines recommend, unless the board of directors has explained its reasons to the shareholders, and the shareholders have accepted them. In addition, the guidelines recommend that the price of any such shares issued by the directors should normally not be at a discount of more than 5 per cent to the current share price at the time of the issue.

Under the provisions of the Companies Act 2006, pre-emption rights for shareholders may be excluded by a private company (by a provision contained in its Articles of Association).

8.4 Rights to remove a director from office

The shareholders of a company should have rights under the constitution of the company to remove a director from office. If the shareholders are dissatisfied with a director, they have the right under the Companies Act 2006, s. 168 to remove a director from office by an ordinary resolution in general meeting.

A group of shareholders proposing to remove a director from office have the right to call for a resolution on the matter at a general meeting of the company, provided they represent the required minimum of the total voting rights. The board of directors might be hostile to any move to remove a colleague from the board. However, when a group of shareholders puts forward a proposal to remove a director, the board cannot refuse to put the issue to a general meeting for a vote. In practice, however, shareholder initiatives of this sort are most unlikely to happen.

8.5 Election and re-election of directors

Shareholders can hold individual directors to account for their actions by voting against their re-election. The constitution of a public company should provide for the directors to retire by rotation, and, if they wish, submit themselves for re-election at the annual general meeting of the company. For companies formed under the Companies Act 1985 the Table A Articles of Association provide for one third of the directors to retire by rotation. A similar provision for the retirement by rotation of directors is included in the Model Articles for public companies formed under the Companies Act 2006.

The Combined Code on Corporate Governance includes a provision that all directors should be subject to election by the shareholders at the first annual general meeting after their appointment and to re-election after that at intervals of no more than three years.

The retirement of directors by rotation and standing for re-election offers the shareholders an opportunity to vote a director out of office. Some activist shareholder groups have occasionally encouraged investment institutions to vote against particular directors. However, most shareholders vote in support of the directors, and it is still difficult for activist shareholders to vote successfully against the re-election of any director. Even so, shareholder activism or engagement means that shareholder leverage over changes to the board of directors is greater now than it has been in the past.

In theory, therefore, shareholders have an opportunity to overturn the board's decision to appoint a new board member. In practice, it would be very difficult to obtain a majority vote for such a decision.

CASE EXAMPLE 3.6

In September 2002, the finance director of Anite plc, a UK IT software and services company, resigned in the face of strong criticism from investors who were angry at the company's remuneration policy and acquisition strategy.

— The individual concerned was one of the highest paid finance directors among UK technology companies, and his remuneration for the year to 30 April 2002 had risen 10 per cent, despite a collapse in the company's performance compared with the previous year.
— Bonuses for the chief executive and the finance director were based on the profits before tax, exceptional items and goodwill, rather than earnings (profits after tax).
— The company had a policy of growth through acquisitions, and had made 17 acquisitions since April 2000. These resulted in large amounts of purchased goodwill, and the amortisation of this goodwill reduced earnings, but not profits before goodwill.

   The acquisitions were made with an open-ended purchase price. The final purchase price depended on the performance of the purchased assets, with an 'earn-out' for the sellers of the acquired companies. All the purchases were paid for with new Anite shares.
— The Anite share price fell by about 80 per cent in the year to 30 April 2002, which meant that more shares had to be issued to pay for new acquisitions. The result was a big dilution in earnings per share.
— The dilution in earnings per share had no effect, however, on the bonuses of the CEO and finance director. On the contrary, the new acquisitions added to profits before tax, exceptional items and goodwill, even though profits after exceptional items and goodwill fell.
— The finance director, who was closely associated with the funding of the acquisitions, was therefore put under pressure to resign by shareholders. However, questions remained about the responsibility of the whole board for both the directors' remuneration policy and the acquisition funding policy.

Although the finance director was not removed from office by a vote of the shareholders at an annual general meeting, the threat that shareholders would exercise this right was sufficient in this case to achieve the desired result.

8.6   Rights to receive information

An important aspect of shareholder rights is the right to receive information about the performance of the company. This information is needed to enable shareholders to use their other rights and powers – such as voting powers – in an informed and constructive way.

The shareholders in a company have a right to information about the financial performance and financial situation of the company and about the company's business. Much of this information is provided by the annual report and accounts and, in the case of listed companies, by interim accounts for the first half of each financial year. Shareholders use this information to make judgements about how well (badly) the company has been run.

All companies, except small companies, must also include a business review in their directors' report. For quoted companies, the business review should provide an extensive narrative report about the company's performance and position.

Information for shareholders about their company, and transparency and clarity in the information provided, are critically important issues in corporate governance. Financial reporting and narrative reporting are dealt with in more detail in later chapters.

Information rights of indirect investors

Provisions in the Companies Act 2006, ss. 146–53 give rights to indirect shareholders in companies whose shares are traded on a regulated market. Indirect investors, such as individuals whose shares are held in a nominee account and managed by a broker, have the right to receive information from the company, such as the annual report and accounts.

The indirect investor must ask the person holding the shares as the registered shareholder to submit a request to the company that information should be sent to the 'nominated person'. The company is then required to send information to the nominated person as well as the registered shareholder, although the rules relating to communications in electronic form also apply.

8.7   Other voting rights of shareholders

In the past, shareholder voting rights have not been effective in restraining the directors of the company, although they could be effective in some situations. In addition to preemption rights and the right to vote for the election or re-election of directors, shareholders also have some other rights under company law or (in the case of listed companies) that are given by the Listing Rules regulations:

- Shareholders in larger companies vote each year to re-elect the external auditors. In practice, however, it is very unusual for a group of shareholders to try to prevent the re-election of auditors, against the wishes of the board of directors. (The relationship between a company and its external auditors is described in Chapter 7.)

- Similarly, shareholders vote each year at the annual general meeting to approve the final dividend payment out of profits for the previous year. (The directors are able to decide on any interim dividend without shareholder approval.) However, the shareholders can vote only to reduce the final dividend proposed by the directors, they cannot vote to increase the dividend. Votes against the final proposed dividend are uncommon.
- The shareholders of listed companies should vote on the directors' remuneration report each year at the annual general meeting, although the vote is advisory only and is not binding on the board.

The UK Listing Rules for listed companies give shareholders some additional rights. In the case of significant 'transactions' (typically an acquisition or the sale of a business of the company), the company must notify the stock market, send a circular to the shareholders giving information about the transaction, and obtain the prior approval of the shareholders before the transaction can go ahead. This rule applies only to significant transactions. A major public company is therefore able to enter into a number of small transactions. Provided they are for cash or have the authority of the shareholders to allot any extra shares that might be needed to finance the transactions, the board of directors can therefore go on an acquisition spree, buying up a large number of small companies, without the shareholders having any say in the matter.

9   Other restraining measures against directors

The legal duties of directors do not provide a strong defence for the interests of shareholders and other stakeholders in a company. Shareholders can exercise their rights to influence the way in which a company is governed, but these rights are of restricted value. Other regulations and legislation provide some additional protection for shareholders' rights, in the form of:

- Placing restrictions on the ability of directors to deal in the shares of their company when they might have access to price-sensitive information that other shareholders do not have. These restrictions are provided by the UK Listing Rules for listed companies. (It can be argued that legislative measures against insider dealing are of limited practical value, since it is difficult in practice to obtain successful prosecutions.)
- In some extreme cases, to obtain the disqualification from office of individual directors.

9.1   *Restrictions on dealings in shares by directors*

Directors usually own some shares in their company. Even if an executive director is not a long-term holder of the company's shares, he or she is likely to acquire shares at some time or another, through exercising share options that have been awarded as part of his or her remuneration package.

A governance issue that arises with share-dealing by directors is that the directors of a public company are likely to know more about the financial position of the company than other investors. They are also likely to hear about any takeover bid involving the company before it is announced to the stock market. It is therefore conceivable that some directors might take advantage of their inside knowledge to buy or sell shares in the company before information affecting the share price is released to the stock market. For example, a director might buy shares in the company if he or she knows that financial results shortly to be announced to the market will be very good and likely to give a boost to the share price. Similarly, directors might sell shares when they know the company is in trouble, and before the bad news is announced, in order to sell at a higher price than they would otherwise be able to obtain.

9.2   Market abuse and insider dealing

Part V of the Criminal Justice Act 1993 made it a criminal offence for anyone to make use of 'inside information' to buy or sell shares in a company in a regulated stock market. Inside information is defined as information that is specific or precise, has not yet been made public and, if it were made public, would be likely to have a significant effect on the price of the company's shares. It would usually be expected that a director is an 'insider' and so would be subject to the prohibitions against insider dealing. This is hardly surprising. If a director made a personal profit from dealing in the company's shares by making use of inside information, the profit would be obtained at the expense of other investors – shareholders or former shareholders in the company.

In practice, there have been relatively few successful prosecutions of individuals for insider dealing, because the guilt of an alleged insider dealer has been difficult to prove in specific cases. Insider dealing is a criminal offence, with offenders liable to a fine, imprisonment or both.

The Financial Services and Markets Act 2000 introduced a civil offence of market abuse. This was regarded as a civil offence, and not a crime, so the burden of proof was less than for insider dealing.

Market Abuse Directive and FSA Disclosure Rules

The legal position has been changed as a result of the EU Market Abuse Directive, which imposes a common EU position on insider trading and market abuse. The Market Abuse Directive identifies two broad types of behaviour that should be regarded as market abuse:

- insider dealing;
- market manipulation.

The Directive requires member states of the EU to prohibit both types of abuse.

In the UK, the definition of market abuse in the Financial Services and Markets Act 2000 (FSMA) was amended in 2003 by the Market Abuse Regulations, which were issued in response to the EU Market Abuse Directive. The FSMA now identifies seven categories of market abuse, all of which are considered by the Act to be civil misdemeanours, not crimes:

1   Insider dealing. An insider deal is an investment on the basis of inside information.

2   Improper disclosure. The disclosure of inside information to another person otherwise than in the proper course of carrying out a job or professional duties.

3   Misuse of information. This happens when the behaviour of a person is based on information that is not generally available to those using the market, but if it were available to the regular user of the market, it would be regarded by him or her as relevant in deciding the terms on which transactions in the investment should be made.

4   Manipulating transactions. Making transactions that give false or misleading signals about the supply of, demand for or price of financial instruments.

5   Manipulating devices. Transactions that 'employ fictitious devices or any other form of deception or contrivance'.

6   Dissemination. Providing information 'by any means' that is likely to give a false or misleading impression about an investment, where the information is disseminated by a person who should have known that the information was false or misleading.

7   Distortion and misleading behaviour. Behaviour that gives false or misleading impressions about the supply of, demand for or price of financial instruments, that a regular user of the market would consider likely to distort the market in the investment. Market abuse occurs if a regular user of the market would regard the behaviour as a 'failure on the part of the person concerned to observe the standard of behaviour reasonably expected of a person in his position.'

However, although insider dealing is not a crime under the provisions of the FSMA, it remains a crime under the provisions of the Criminal Justice Act 1993.

The Financial Services Authority (FSA) has also published rules and guidance for the implementation of the Market Abuse Directive, in the form of Disclosure Rules.

Insider lists

A requirement in the Disclosure Rules is that issuers and their advisers are required to keep lists of persons who have access to inside information.

The insider list should contain the identity of each person having access to inside information, the reason why the person is on the list and the date that the list was last updated. The FSA has indicated that although the definition of an 'insider' is not the same as a 'relevant employee' for the purpose of the Model Code, both lists will consist largely of the same employees.

9.3   The Model Code and directors' dealings

The law on dealing in shares by directors may be supplemented, in the case of stock market companies, by stock market regulations. In the UK, the Listing Rules (which are a part of the FSA Handbook) require listed companies to have rules for share dealings by their directors that are no less stringent than the rules in a Model Code. The purpose of the restrictions is to ensure that directors 'do not abuse, and do not place themselves under suspicion of abusing, inside information that they may have or be thought to have, especially in periods leading up to an announcement of the company's results'.

The rules in the UK are more stringent than in some other countries, where dealing in shares of their company whilst in possession of price-sensitive information might be quite prevalent. Certainly, when a company gets into financial difficulties, suspicion is certain to fall on any directors selling shares in the period before the company's problems become public knowledge.

The Listing Rules include a Model Code for share dealing by directors and 'relevant employees'. Compliance with the Code should ensure that directors (and other individuals with access to key unpublished financial information about the company) do not breach:

- the laws on market abuse (a civil offence); or
- the rules in the Criminal Justice Act 1993 against insider dealing (a criminal offence).

The main provisions within the Model Code are:

- Directors must not deal in shares of their company during the two months before the announcement of the company's interim and final results, or between the end of the financial year and the announcement of the annual results. These are known as close periods. (If the company produces quarterly results, the non-trading period is just one month before publication, in the case of the three interim quarterly results, but the same rules apply to the final results.)
- A director must not deal at any time that he or she is privy to price-sensitive information. (Information is 'price-sensitive' if its publication could have a significant effect on the share price.)
- A director must seek clearance from the chairman (or another designated director) prior to dealing in the company's shares. Clearance must not be given during a 'prohibited period'. (A prohibited period is a close period and any period during which there is unpublished price-sensitive information which is reasonably likely to result in an announcement being made.) The chairman must seek clearance to deal from the CEO, and the CEO must seek clearance from the chairman.
- In exceptional circumstances, clearance to deal can be given during a prohibited period where the director has a pressing financial commitment or would suffer financial hardship if unable to deal.
- A director must ensure that none of his or her connected persons deals without clearance. Connected persons include spouse and infant children, and companies in which the director controls over 20 per cent of the equity.

9.4 Notification to the stock market of dealings in shares by directors

The Companies Act 2006 has removed a requirement for companies to maintain a register of shareholdings of directors. However, for listed companies and AIM companies, there are requirements for disclosure of dealings by directors in shares in their company.

The regulations for listed companies are imposed by the Disclosure and Transparency Rules of the FSA. 'Persons discharging managerial responsibilities' in listed companies must notify details of dealings by themselves and connected persons in shares of the company, including details of the quantity of shares dealt and price. The company is then required to disseminate this information to the stock market through a Regulated Information Service (RIS).

Similar requirements apply to dealings in shares by directors of AIM companies.

9.5 Disqualification of directors

Directors may be disqualified from holding office as a director. On disqualification the director has to step down from office immediately. The 1985 Table A Articles of Association provide for the disqualification of a director who is bankrupt or suffering from mental disorder, or who is disqualified by the rest of the board for being absent from board meetings for more than a certain period of time without their permission.

A director may also be disqualified from office by the court. Examples of offences for which directors could be disqualified on this basis include insider dealing in the shares of the company, a failure to keep proper accounting records, and breaches of competition law.

9.6 Disqualification by the court with personal liability

UK law makes a distinction between fraudulent trading (criminal law) and the personal liability of individual directors for fraudulent or wrongful trading (civil law). A court has the power to disqualify a director who has been involved in either fraudulent trading or wrongful trading when the company is insolvent. Where the company is insolvent, the disqualified director could also be held personally liable for the debts of the company. Only the liquidator of the company, not the company's shareholders or other directors, can apply to the court for a declaration of civil liability.

Fraudulent trading during the course of winding up a company means carrying on business with the intent of defrauding creditors 'or for any fraudulent purpose' (Insolvency Act 1986). Examples of fraudulent trading are falsifying the company's accounting records, omitting a material fact from a formal statement about the company's affairs, or making a false representation to creditors with the intention of persuading them to come to a financial settlement with the company.

To disqualify the director and hold him or her personally liable for the company's debts, a court must be satisfied that fraud has occurred. This could be difficult. A lower burden of proof is required for wrongful trading. A court will disqualify a director and hold him or her liable for wrongful trading if negligence, rather than criminal conduct (fraud), is proved. Wrongful trading occurs when a director knew, or should have known, before the start of the official winding up procedures, that the company would be insolvent and go into liquidation but did not take every step to minimise the potential losses for the company's creditors.

10 Other types of directors

The duties, responsibilities and potential liabilities of directors extend to two other types of directors recognised by UK company law: de facto directors and shadow directors.

10.1 De facto directors

A de facto director was defined by Mr Justice O'Neill in Re Lynrowan Enterprises Ltd [2002] as someone who:

- is the sole person directing the company's affairs; or
- conducts the company's affairs equally with other individuals who have not been validly appointed as directors; or
- conducts the company's affairs equally with other individuals who have been validly appointed as directors.

In effect, a de facto director fulfils the role of director even though never formally appointed as such.

10.2 Shadow directors

A shadow director is a person who is not on the board of directors, but who is able to give instructions and directions to the directors with which the directors will comply. The Companies Act defines a shadow director as a person in accordance with whose directions or instructions the directors of a company are accustomed to act. A shadow director exists if just a majority of directors follow his or her instructions, rather than all the board directors. (Individuals giving professional advice, such as accountants or solicitors acting in a professional advisory capacity, are excluded from this definition. For the purposes of various company law matters, holding companies are also exempted from being shadow directors of their subsidiary companies.)

Shadow directors are not common, but where they do exist, shareholders ought to be informed about them. For example, an individual who has been disqualified as a director might be the effective controller of the board of a company (probably a private company) without being a director.

Deciding whether an individual is or is not a shadow director will vary according to the circumstances of the case.

Proof that an individual is a shadow director requires specific evidence that instructions have been given by the individual that were acted on by the company. Re Hydrodan (Corby) Ltd illustrates the very restrictive definition applied by the courts to the definition of a shadow director. The judge in this case ruled that for a person to be a shadow director, there has to be clear evidence that he had interfered in the company's affairs to such an extent that the company's appointed directors simply substituted the shadow director's decisions for their own.

When a company does have a shadow director, various statutory and governance issues arise:

- Shadow directors, as well as ordinary directors, are subject to the provisions of the Companies Act with respect to long-term service contracts, loans from the company, interests in contracts made with the company, and so on.
- Shadow directors can be found guilty of wrongful trading. Like other directors, if they have a service contract with a term in excess of two years, this must be approved by the shareholders.

- The issue of transparency also arises. Companies should inform shareholders about the existence of any shadow director, so that the shareholders are aware of how board decisions might be influenced. The existence of a shadow director offends against some basic principles of corporate governance.
- There is a lack of transparency about the workings of the board and how major decisions are reached.
- A shadow director is not held accountable to the shareholders by having to stand for election and re-election.
- A shadow director may be able to act in his or her own personal interests and not in the interests of the company, without declaring any interest or seeking the company's consent.
- An individual may be a shadow director to avoid legal responsibilities. For example, an individual may be a shadow director because he or she has been disqualified from acting as a director.

CASE EXAMPLE 3.7

In 2000, 'shadow directors' of Euro Express, a West Sussex travel agency owing creditors £4.6 million, were disqualified by the court from future involvement in giving instructions to companies, for periods of up to 16 years. This decision by the Court of Appeal was seen as a legal milestone in attempts by the authorities to prevent 'unfit' individuals from controlling companies.

In this case, two individuals controlled Euro Express without being directors. The company sold 'bucket shop' holiday flights between Gatwick and Nice, and in 1991 had diversified into the schools ski holiday market. To operate in the schools market, the company's directors had to assure the Civil Aviation Authority (CAA) and the Association of Travel Operators (ATOL) that it could pay a compulsory bond of £472,000. It was shown that the two 'shadow directors' had been prime movers in deceiving the CAA about this matter. A High Court had ruled that the individuals could not be considered shadow directors, but on appeal the Court of Appeal overturned this ruling and decided that they were. Euro Express went into voluntary liquidation in 1993.

Chapter summary

- Directors, and not shareholders, may exercise all the powers of the company. These powers are subject to some restraints, such as the provisions of company law and the company's constitution (Articles of Association).

- Directors have some statutory duties, but not many. In common law, directors also have a fiduciary duty and a duty of skill and care to the company. This duty is owed to the company, not the shareholders.

- There are three tests for a breach of fiduciary duty, which is difficult to prove in practice. Similarly, it is difficult in practice to bring action for a breach of the duty of skill and care.

- In the UK, the directors are required by law to 'have regard' to the interests of the company's employees. UK law also protects outsiders against 'irregular contracts' entered into with directors acting outside their authority.

- Although the law restraining directors' powers does not provide much protection to shareholders, shareholders have certain rights that they can enforce. These include pre-emption rights and voting rights, such as the right to elect or re-elect directors. In the case of listed companies, large transactions must be approved by the shareholders before they are entered into.

- Other measures to protect shareholders against directors include restrictions on share dealings by directors of listed companies and, in extreme cases, measures for the disqualification of certain directors.

- Some companies have shadow directors or possibly alternate directors. The rules applying to these types of director are the same as those applying to 'ordinary' directors.

Chapter 4

Balance of power of the board

1 The role of the board and corporate governance issues

1.1 The role of the board

A key issue in corporate governance is that a company must have an effective board of directors who are dedicated to ensuring that the company achieves its objectives. This raises questions about what the role of the board should be, what might prevent it from fulfilling this role effectively and what governance measures should be taken to create an effective board.

The Combined Code begins with the role of the board, and the main principle (A1) that 'every company should be headed by an effective board, which is collectively responsible for the success of the company'.

A supporting principle spells this out in more detail, stating that the role of the board is to:

- provide entrepreneurial leadership for the company within a framework of prudent and effective risk management;
- set the company's strategic aims;
- make sure that the necessary resources (financial and human) are in place for the company to meet its objectives;

- review management performance;
- set the company's values and standards;
- make sure that the company's obligations to its shareholders are understood and met.

1.2   Corporate governance issues relating to the board

Chapter 3 considered the powers of directors and the rights of shareholders, suggesting that the powers of directors to act on behalf of the company are largely unrestricted by the shareholders themselves. The ability of the directors to act in their self-interest, regardless of the interests of the shareholders and other stakeholders, is therefore a potential problem in any public company where corporate governance is poor.

The board of directors is a collection of individuals, each with his or her personal views, interests and concerns. Some individuals, notably the CEO and the chairman, carry more influence than others. A central issue in corporate governance is therefore the balance of power and influence among individuals on the board. In a well-governed company, there should be checks and balances to prevent one individual, or group of individuals, from dominating the board and its decisions. In a badly governed company, there will be an opportunity for autocratic leadership, where the board is dominated by one individual. Autocratic leadership may be enlightened and even good for the company, but there is also a risk that under a dominant individual a company will be used to serve the interest of that individual.

CASE EXAMPLE 4.1

The dangers of a dominant personality

There are many examples; the case of the UK company Polly Peck International is just one.

Polly Peck, a FTSE 100 company, was effectively run by a single individual, Mr Asil Nadir, who was both CEO and board chairman. The company collapsed without warning in October 1990. On administration, the system of internal controls at the company's London head office was found to be virtually non-existent. As a result, Mr Nadir had been able to transfer large amounts of money from the company's UK bank accounts to personal accounts with a bank in Northern Cyprus, without any questions being asked. After the company collapsed, Mr Nadir fled to Northern Cyprus, where he lives in exile outside the reach of the UK law enforcers.

1.3   The lessons of Enron

The collapse of Enron in 2002 brought issues of corporate governance into prominence. It is is probably the most notorious example of a company collapsing largely because of failures in corporate governance. It is useful to note some of the circumstances surrounding this collapse because they help to illustrate failures of the board of directors, both collectively and as individuals.

The Financial Times website fairly soon after the collapse gave an interesting view on the lessons to be learned from the Enron affair and the serious failures in corporate governance that occurred:

- Executives encouraged or permitted the misleading treatment of transactions in the company's accounts.
- The audit committee gave its approval to a seriously misleading set of accounts.
- Individuals profited personally from transactions they made with the company that employed them.
- The board was ineffective in supervising the actions of its senior executives.
- The board ignored the complaints of whistleblowers.

In the opinion of the Financial Times, the affair demonstrated the need for government and the investment community to insist on a change in culture of boards of directors. There should be genuinely independent non-executive directors, with a clear leader (senior non-executive). The audit committee should have greater powers in dealing with the external auditors and should be able to decide on the accounting treatment of particular items. The committee should also have the power – and the responsibility – to respond to whistleblowers.

Enron had large numbers of non-executive directors, but they did not have a clear leader and did not provide an effective check on the executive management. There were also questions about just how independent some of them were.

A common board structure in the US is for the board to consist of NEDs, with only the CEO and the chairman representing executive management. The Financial Times suggested that this structure is potentially vulnerable to manipulation by the chairman and CEO, who are able, if they wish, to control the flow of information to their fellow directors. A better structure would therefore be a board with more executive management representation, but with a majority of NEDs led by a senior independent director. This structure should improve the knowledge NEDs have about the company.

The Financial Times also saw the need for improvements in the audit committee, which should have the power to act on its own initiative, and should not have to rely on the chief financial officer (finance director). Members of the committee should have accounting expertise or should be able to hire professional advice. There should be no presumption that the audit committee will automatically approve the company's annual accounts when these are presented by the management and auditors, and the auditors should be encouraged to present alternative accounting treatments for contentious issues, such as off-balance sheet items and revenue recognition. The committee should also have a role in the appointment and performance reviews of the chief financial officer. It should also be the committee to which whistleblowers should be encouraged to take their information. (At Enron, the complaints of the whistleblower Sherron Watkins, a senior employee, were passed to a law firm with a close relationship with the Enron management.)

A Senate sub-committee report in July 2002 on the role of the Enron directors in the firm's collapse gave examples of the financial engineering by the company that was known to the board and tolerated by them. For example, in October 2000, about a year before the collapse, the board's finance committee was told that the group had $60 billion of assets, of which nearly half ($27 billion) was held by 'unconsolidated affiliates' – in other words, by off-balance sheet organisations. The board was also told in 2000 that one of these affiliates, LJM, had produced more than $2 billion for the group in just six months. In spite of the oddity of the financial structure of the group, the board apparently did not ask any questions.

Several issues in corporate governance relate to the qualities of individual directors and the balance of power on the board of directors. These include:

- the suitability of directors;
- the qualities and character of individual directors;
- the effectiveness of the board as a decision-making body;
- the roles of chairman of the board and CEO;
- the role and independence of NEDs;
- the use of board committees;
- board succession;
- controlling family interests.

2 Suitability

Individual directors should be suitable to hold their position on the board of a public company. 'Suitability' refers to character, experience, skills and other individual qualities. For example, it would be reasonable to expect the finance director of a public company to be a qualified accountant with a track record in finance, accountancy or auditing work. Similarly, it would be reasonable to expect a NED to have experience or skills that can be used to contribute towards decision-making by the board. It is quite common, for example, for large public companies that provide goods or services to government departments to appoint a former government minister or senior civil servant with a knowledge of how the government works and makes its purchasing decisions.

Taken as a group, the board should possess a breadth of experience, skills and knowledge, and each individual should be able to contribute to the decision-making capabilities of the board. There would be little value in having two individuals on the board with a similar background. For example, a large public company that carries out major contract work for the government might choose to have a former government minister or senior government official on the board, for their knowledge of how government works. However, it would probably be unnecessary to have two such individuals on the board.

3 Character and qualities

It almost goes without saying that an individual appointed to the board of a public company should possess personal qualities such that investors should trust his or her honesty and integrity. Individual directors should have a sense of what is right and wrong, and act in an ethical way in business. In practice, this is often overlooked.

CASE EXAMPLE 4.2

A well-known illustrative example is provided by the case history of Robert Maxwell. At one time, he owned a company called Pergamon Press, which was the target of a failed takeover bid in 1969. Following the failed bid, the Department of Trade and Industry (DTI) carried out an investigation into Mr Maxwell's businesses. The resulting DTI report (1971) stated: 'We regret having to conclude that, notwithstanding Mr Maxwell's acknowledged abilities and energy, he is not in our opinion a person who can be relied on to exercise proper stewardship of a publicly-quoted company.'

Maxwell eventually revived his business career, buying the British Printing Corporation in 1980, and building up a publishing and media empire in the 1980s that eventually included Mirror Group Newspapers, US publisher Macmillan and the New York Daily News. Mirror Group Newspapers obtained a stock market listing, but other companies in the group remained privately owned. In spite of the 1971 DTI report, he received enthusiastic backing and funding from investment institutions and bankers.

In November 1991, Mr Maxwell died in mysterious circumstances, drowning whilst cruising off the Canary Islands. Investigations after his death found that he had misappropriated about £900 million from the pension funds of his companies, using the funds to finance his corporate expansion and support his ailing private companies. A subsequent DTI report stated that 'there were no proper corporate or financial controls to prevent this'. The Maxwell companies were forced to file for bankruptcy protection in the UK and the US in 1992.

The Maxwell story would appear to be an example of a company dominated by a tyrannical individual, who expected to be obeyed and who was able to do whatever he wanted with no serious questions asked and no systems in place to prevent him from overstepping the mark.

3.1   Collective integrity

The requirement for personal integrity applies not just to individual directors, but to the board of directors as a body. The decisions they make should take account of ethical issues and issues of good governance. Investigations following the collapse of Enron revealed examples of poor governance by the directors. A Senate sub-committee, reporting in 2002, found that:

- In one financial year, the company paid out cash bonuses of almost $750 million to senior executives when the reported total net income of the group was only $975 million.
- Executives were permitted to run off-balance sheet partnerships with the company, which earned hundreds of millions of dollars at Enron's expense.
- NEDs had financial ties with the company, including payments for consultancy services in some cases.

4 Size and balance of the board

4.1 Composition of a board of directors

A board consists of:

- a chairman;
- there may also be a deputy chairman;
- the CEO;
- the senior independent director (who may also be the deputy chairman);
- executive directors;
- NEDs.

The board is supported by the company secretary.

The size of the board will vary from one company to another. The ideal size is one that balances:

- the need to avoid the board being so large as to be unwieldy; and
- the need to have a board that is large enough so that it has individuals with a balance of skills and experience appropriate for a company of its size and business.

This should seem common sense, but it is also included as a supporting principle in the Combined Code.

4.2 Balance: objective decision-making

The Combined Code typifies corporate governance guidelines by stating that, in order to have an effective board, 'all directors must take decisions objectively in the interests of the company'.

It is important that the directors should contribute constructively to board decisions, and in doing so should give their well-considered views. Although the board should aim to reach agreement on all issues, there might be some on which the directors disagree. A director should have the strength of character to back what he or she believes in, and should certainly not agree with the rest of the board simply to avoid argument. Where necessary, individuals should be prepared to disagree with the majority of the board, and let their views be known.

This is supported by the Combined Code, which states that if directors have concerns about a matter that cannot be resolved, they should ensure that those concerns are recorded in the minutes of the board meetings at which the matter is discussed. If a NED resigns as a result of any concern, he or she should provide a written statement to the chairman, for circulation to the board.

To achieve balance and objectivity at board level:

- no one individual should have excessive powers; and
- there should be a significant number of independent directors on the board: independence is provided by NEDs.

Principle A.3 states:

> 'The board should include a balance of executive and non-executive directors (and in particular independent non-executive directors) such that no individual or small group of individuals can dominate the board's decision-making.'

This principle is concerned more generally with achieving a suitable balance on the board. It also introduces the idea that independent board members (independent NEDs) are important to prevent the domination of a board by one individual or clique.

However, the Code also argues that executive directors bring an important element of balance to the board, and a supporting principle is that:

> 'to ensure that power and information are not concentrated in one or two individuals, there should be a strong presence on the board of both executive and non-executive directors.'

5 The board and decision-making

The main decision-making powers in a company are vested in the board of directors. Although the board delegates many of the operational decision-making responsibilities to executive management, it should:

- retain the most significant decisions to itself; and
- monitor the performance of the executive management.

An aspect of corporate governance is therefore the nature of the decisions that the board reserves to itself (rather than delegating) and the way in which it reaches its decisions.

The board should be able to reach decisions that are well-considered and in the interests of the company. It needs:

- a clear set of decision-making responsibilities;
- access to information to enable the directors to arrive at well-judged opinions;
- a suitable balance of power amongst board members, such that the views of a single individual or group of individuals does not dominate decision-making.

The need for a suitable balance of power on the board was emphasised by the UK's Cadbury Code, whose recommendations were an early attempt to apply principles of good corporate practice to public companies. The Code stated that control over the company should be exercised by the board as a whole, and not by an individual executive director or chairman, or by a small group of executive directors. It made a number of recommendations about decision-making by the board:

- The board should meet regularly and retain full and effective control over the company.
- It should monitor the performance of the executive management.

- Some important decisions should be referred to the board for a decision, and should not be taken by executive managers. Decisions by the board should include, for example, decisions on major new investments or divestments, and decisions about large mergers and takeovers.
- A formal schedule should specify matters about which decisions must be taken by the board and not by executive managers. A clear schedule of decision-making responsibilities should make it difficult for a powerful chief executive to usurp decision-making powers and ensure that the ultimate control of the company remains firmly in the hands of the board.

It has to be recognised that individual board members may not have the technical knowledge to make some important decisions unaided. The Cadbury Code, recognising that occasions will arise when a director needs professional advice in order to form an opinion, recommended that there should be an agreed procedure enabling him or her to obtain professional advice at the company's expense.

5.1 Good boardroom practice

Boardroom practice describes the way in which a board conducts its procedures and reaches its decisions. Two elements of good corporate governance are that:

1   All the directors, particularly the NEDs, should be able to contribute effectively to decision-making. To this end, they must be supplied with sufficient, timely information, in advance of board meetings, relating to all the matters the board will be discussing at the next meeting.
2   The board should reserve certain matters for its own decision-making, and should not delegate these matters to the executive management team.

ICSA has argued that it is not sufficient to rely on unwritten boardroom procedures and practices, and it has issued a Code for Directors and Company Secretaries on Good Boardroom Practice (see Appendix 2). This also contains guidance on matters that the board should consider and, where applicable, formally adopt.

The Code includes the following provisions:

- There should be written procedures for the conduct of board business. Compliance should be monitored, preferably by an audit committee.
- Each director on first appointment should be given sufficient information to enable him or her to carry out the duties of a director properly. This should include details of procedures for obtaining information about the company and requisitioning a board meeting.
- Two fundamental concepts in the conduct of board business are that (i) all directors should be given the same information; and (ii) they should be given sufficient time to consider it.
- The board should identify those matters that should require its prior approval. As a basic principle, all material contracts should be referred to the board for approval before the company is legally committed to them.

- Decisions about the agenda for a board meeting should be taken by the company chairman, in consultation with the company secretary.
- The company secretary should be responsible to the chairman for the proper administration of board meetings, the meetings of board committees and general meetings of the company. To carry out these responsibilities, the company secretary should be entitled to be present at and prepare the minutes for all such meetings. The minutes of meetings should record all decisions taken, and procedures should be established for the approval and circulation of minutes.
- The board should give its prior approval for the membership, terms of reference and powers of any committee of the board that is established. Minutes of board committees should be circulated to all directors prior to the next board meeting, to give them an opportunity to raise questions at that meeting.

The Code is supplemented by the ICSA Guidance Note on Matters Reserved for the Board, which details decisions that should be taken by the board as a whole and not delegated.

5.2   Matters reserved for the board

The ICSA Guidance Note on the matters that should be reserved for the board's own decision-making (see Appendix 3) indicates whether a matter is included in the list because it is a statutory requirement of the Companies Act 1985 or 2006, a requirement of the Listing Rules for listed companies or a provision of the Combined Code. Some decisions, such as major decisions relating to acquisitions and disposals, or major capital expenditure, are included in the list simply because they should clearly be board responsibilities. The Guidance Note also indicates which committee (audit, nomination or remuneration) might consider a particular item first, and make recommendations to the full board for a decision.

It is a useful exercise to study the items on this list, to develop an understanding of the range of issues for which the board itself should retain decision-making responsibilities. It should help to clarify the dividing line between what boards should and should not delegate to executive management.

6   The roles of chairman and chief executive officer

6.1   The chief executive officer

The chief executive officer (CEO) of a company is the person responsible for the executive management of the company's operations. As the title suggests, he or she is the senior executive in charge of the management team to whom all other executive managers report. Other executive managers may also be directors, but the CEO is answerable to the board for the way the business is run and its performance.

6.2   The chairman

Whereas the CEO is responsible for the executive management, the chairman's responsibilities relate primarily to managing the board of directors. A supporting principle in the Combined Code is that:

'The chairman is responsible for leadership of the board, ensuring its effectiveness on all aspects of its role and setting its agenda. The chairman is also responsible for ensuring that the directors receive accurate, timely and clear information. The chairman should ensure effective communication with shareholders. The chairman should also facilitate the effective contribution of non-executive directors in particular and ensure constructive relations between executive and non-executive directors.'

In an appendix to the 2003 Combined Code, the Higgs Suggestions for Good Practice give guidance about what the role of the chairman should be, stating that the role of the chairman is 'pivotal' in creating the conditions for the effectiveness of the board as a whole and the individual directors.

The responsibility of the chairman is to:

- run the board and set its agenda, which should be forward-looking and concentrate on strategic matters;
- ensure that members of the board receive accurate, timely and clear information to help them reach well-informed and well-considered decisions;
- ensure effective communication with the shareholders, and ensure that all board members develop an understanding of the views of the major shareholders;
- manage the board, and make sure that enough time is allowed for discussion of complex or contentious issues;
- take the lead, using the company secretary as facilitator, in providing suitable induction for new directors;
- take the lead, using the company secretary as facilitator, in identifying and meeting the development needs of individual directors;
- ensure that the performance of the board as a whole and of individual directors is evaluated at least once a year;
- encourage active engagement by all members of the board.

The effective chairman is therefore a team-builder. He or she should develop a board whose members communicate effectively among themselves and enjoy good relationships with each other. He or she should develop a close relationship of trust with the CEO, giving support and advice whilst still respecting the CEO's responsibilities for executive matters. He or she should also ensure the effective implementation of board decisions, provide coherent leadership for the company and understand the views of the shareholders.

6.3   Separating the roles of the chairman and chief executive officer

As leader of the management team and leader of the board of directors, the CEO and chairman are the most powerful positions on the board of directors.

It is important for the proper functioning of the company that the chairman and CEO should be able to work well together. Acting in alliance, the chairman and CEO can dominate the board and its decision-making, particularly if the chairman also has executive responsibilities in the company's management.

When the same person holds both positions, there is a risk that he or she will become a domineering influence in the company. There is also a risk that the individual will run the company for his or her own personal benefit, rather than in the interests of the shareholders and other stakeholders. The only way to prevent a chairman-cum-CEO from dominating a company is to have an influential group of directors capable of making their opinions heard and listened to.

It is unlikely that the constitution of a company prevents the same individual from holding the office of both chairman and CEO, but in the interests of good corporate governance the roles should be divided between two people. The chairman and the CEO will then each act as a check on the other, providing a better balance of power on the board.

There might be situations where it is appropriate for the same person to be both chairman and CEO. When a company gets into business or financial difficulties, for example, there is an argument in favour of appointing a single, all-powerful individual to run the company until its fortunes have been reversed. In the UK, this appears to have worked successfully at Marks & Spencer, where M. Luc Vandevelde was appointed as chairman and CEO at a time when its business operations were in difficulty and the share price was falling sharply. By 2002, the company's fortunes had changed to the point where he relinquished the position of CEO and announced his intention to become part-time chairman. The combination of the roles of chairman and CEO might have been necessary in the short term to give the company the strong leadership it needed to get it through its difficulties. In the longer term, however, combining the two roles would be harder to justify.

It is now a generally accepted element of good corporate governance that in public companies the roles of chairman and CEO should be held by two people, independent of each other. In the UK Principle A.2 of the Combined Code states that:

> 'There should be a clear division of responsibilities at the head of the company between the running of the board and the executive responsibility for running the company's business. No one individual should have unfettered powers of decision.'

This principle is supported by three Code provisions:

1   The roles of chairman and CEO should not be exercised by the same individual. The division of responsibilities between these two roles should be set out in writing and agreed by the board.
2   On appointment, the chairman should meet the criteria for independence. (The recommended criteria for independence are described in the next chapter in the context of NEDs. These also apply to the chairman. An implication of the requirement that the chairman should be independent on first appointment is that he or she cannot be an executive director of the company, nor have been an executive director in the recent past.)
3   A chief executive should not go on to be the chairman of the same company. If a CEO on leaving office becomes the company chairman, there is a strong risk that he or she will seek to interfere in the matters reserved for the CEO and so try to exert improper influence over the incoming CEO. The Code provision also states that if in exceptional circumstances the board decides that its CEO should move on

to become the chairman, it should consult major shareholders in advance and set out its reasons to the shareholders both at the time of the appointment and in the next annual report.

In practice, pressure is brought to bear on public companies where the same person holds the position of both CEO and chairman, or where a company proposes that its chief executive officer should move on to become the chairman. In the UK, the pressure comes largely from institutions such as the London Stock Exchange, organisations of investment institutions such as the Association of British Insurers (ABI) and the National Association of Pension Funds (NAPF), shareholder activists and investment bank advisers to the companies concerned. Even so, there have been cases where companies have not complied with the Combined Code and have appointed a former CEO as chairman.

7 Non-executive directors

A non-executive director (NED) is a member of the board without executive responsibilities in the company. NEDs should be able to bring judgement and experience to the deliberations of the board that the executive directors on their own would lack. A NED will therefore attend board meetings and contribute to discussions and decision-making.

NEDs are expected not only to bring a wide range of skills and experience to the deliberations of the board, particularly in the area of strategy and business development, but also to ensure that there is a suitable balance of power on the board. A powerful chairman or CEO might be able to dominate fellow executive directors but, in theory at least, NEDs should be able to bring different views and independent thinking to the deliberations of the board. Decisions taken by the board should therefore be improved and more in keeping with the aims of good corporate governance.

NEDs are an important element in corporate governance, and are dealt with more fully in Chapter 5.

8 Board appointments and the nomination committee

8.1 Board appointments

The membership of a board of directors changes regularly as some individuals resign or retire and new appointments are made. There are no regulations on the overall size of the board (unless a provision about the composition of the board is included in the company's constitution), so that:

- there are no restrictions on making new appointments; and
- with the exceptions of the positions of chairman and CEO, there is no requirement to replace individuals stepping down from the board.

It is an accepted principle of good corporate governance that the power over board appointments should rest with the whole board. In addition, recommendations about new appointments should not belong exclusively to the chairman and/or the CEO. Appointments should be made on merit and against objective criteria; however, in practice there has been criticism of the way in which most appointments are made, particularly appointment of NEDs. The criticism centres on the fact that most NED appointments come from a fairly small circle of successful businessmen, many of whom know each other, whereas the net should be cast much wider and individuals from a greater variety of backgrounds should be chosen.

8.2   Nomination committee

The Combined Code states as a principle that: 'there should be a formal, rigorous and transparent procedure for the appointment of new directors to the board'. The recommended framework for making appointments is that:

- the search for new directors should be carried out by a nomination committee of the board, to which the full board delegates the responsibility;
- the nomination committee should make recommendations to the board; and
- the board should consider the recommendations of the committee, and in normal circumstances should be expected to accept the recommendation.

It is important to note that a nomination committee does not have the authority to make new appointments; it simply carries out the search and makes a recommendation. Appointing new directors is a matter for the board, and decisions should therefore be made by the whole board.

The Combined Code makes the following recommendations. A nomination committee should be established by the board with:

- a majority of members who are independent non-executive directors; and
- a committee chairman who is either the board chairman or an independent NED. If the board chairman is the chairman of the nomination committee, he or she should not chair the committee when it is dealing with the succession to the chairmanship.
- The existence of a majority of NEDs should ensure that the appointments process is not dominated by the chairman and/or CEO of the company.
- The committee should consider new appointments to the board and make recommendations to the full board. The full board should then reach a decision about offering a position to the individual concerned, so that final responsibility for board appointments remains with the board as a whole.

8.3   The principal duties of the nomination committee

The principal duties of the nomination committee are summarised in the Higgs Suggestions for Good Practice, which are attached to the Combined Code. These are that the nomination committee should:

- Be responsible for identifying candidates to fill vacancies on the board, as and when they arise, and nominate them for approval by the board.
- Before making an appointment, evaluate the balance of skills, knowledge and experience on the board and, on the basis of this evaluation, prepare a description of the role and capabilities required for the particular appointment.
- Each year, review the time required from a NED. (Performance evaluation should include an assessment of whether the NED is spending enough time on his or her duties.)
- Consider candidates for appointment from a wide range of backgrounds and look beyond the 'usual suspects'.
- Give full consideration to succession planning.
- Review regularly the structure, size and composition of the board, and make recommendations for any changes to the board.
- Keep under review the leadership needs of the company, both executive and non-executive, with a view to ensuring that the company remains competitive.
- Prepare an annual statement of the nomination committee for inclusion in the annual report. This should include a description of its activities, the process used for appointments (giving reasons if external advice or open advertising has not been used for the appointment of a chairman or NED), the membership of the committee, the number of meetings and attendance over the course of the year.
- Make available its terms of reference, explaining clearly its role and the authority delegated to it by the board.
- Ensure that, on appointment to the board, NEDs receive a formal letter of appointment, setting out what is expected of them, including time commitment and membership of board committees.

Recommendations by the nomination committee to the board should include:

- plans for the succession of NEDs and executive directors;
- recommendations about the reappointment of NEDs at the end of their term of office;
- recommendations about the submission of any director for re-election by the shareholders under the retirement by rotation rules in the Articles of Association;
- matters concerning the continuation in office of any director at any time.

8.4   Combined Code provisions on board nominations

The Combined Code includes several provisions about appointments to the board, some of which are duplicated in the Higgs Suggestions:

- The nomination committee should evaluate the skills, knowledge and experience of the board, and in the light of this evaluation prepare a description of the roles and responsibilities required for any new appointment.

- For the appointment of a chairman, the nomination committee should prepare a job specification, including an assessment of the time required and recognising the need for the chairman's availability in times of crisis.
- The departing chairman should not chair the nomination committee when it is meeting to consider the appointment of his or her successor.
- A new chairman's other significant commitments should be disclosed to the board before an appointment is made and included in the annual report. (Subsequent changes should also be disclosed and reported.) No individual should be appointed to a second chairmanship of a FTSE 100 company.
- A separate section of the annual report should describe the work of the nomination committee. This should include a description of the process used for appointments, and giving reasons if external advice or open advertising have not been used.

It should be apparent that an important aspect of suitability for appointment is being able to make enough time available to perform the role of director properly. Another Code provision looks at this issue from a different viewpoint, and states that the board should not allow one of its own executive directors to take on:

- more than one NED post in a FTSE 100 company; or
- the chairmanship of a FTSE 100 company.

8.5 Practical aspects of board appointments

In practice, a nomination committee is likely to carry out its responsibilities by:

- using a firm of head hunters to find individuals outside the firm who might be suitable for appointment (as NED, CEO, finance director, and so on);
- vetting the candidates put forward by the head hunters; and
- making a selection and recommendation to the full board.

Decisions about new appointments of individuals to the board should ideally take into consideration:

- the desirable personal qualities of a director, including experience;
- the need to maintain sufficient representation on the board of the opinions of executive management (although in some public companies, the only executive directors are the CEO and the finance director);
- compliance with any applicable code of best practice in corporate governance, and the desirable minimum numbers of non-executive directors;
- the independence of any individual appointed to a non-executive position on the board.

When an individual is appointed to the board, the appointment may be for a fixed term (which is usually the case with NEDs) or for an indeterminate length of time, subject to a minimum notice period.

9 Induction and training of directors

9.1 Induction of new directors

Induction is the process by which new directors find out about the business, its products or services and how it operates. New directors need induction in order to become effective contributors to the board decision-making process. The issue is much more important for NEDs than for executive directors, who are more likely to be familiar with much of the business before their appointment to the board. In the UK, the Combined Code states that the induction of new directors should be 'full, formal and tailored', and the company secretary should be responsible for ensuring that the induction process is both effective and completed within a reasonably short period.

The company secretary should agree a programme of familiarisation with the company and its products or services. This might include:

- visits to key company sites;
- product presentations;
- meetings with senior management and staff;
- meetings with major shareholders (should any such shareholders want one);
- meetings with external advisers of the company.

There should also be an assessment of any specific training requirements for the new director, and provision of suitable training programmes.

However, reading is an effective way for an individual to absorb new information quickly, and the company secretary might therefore wish to give a new director a selection of documents as an induction pack. The ICSA Guidance Note on Induction of Directors comments: 'The objective of induction is to inform the director such that he or she can become as effective as possible in their new role as soon as possible. The provision of reams of paper in one go is, obviously, not conducive to this process.' The ICSA's recommendation is therefore that information should be provided to new directors in an induction pack in stages:

- essential information to be provided immediately;
- material to be provided over the first few weeks following the appointment, at the most appropriate time.

9.2 Induction of an executive manager as an executive director

The induction process described above is much more relevant to an individual joining as a director from outside the company.

For an individual who is already an executive manager of the company and now appointed as executive director, the induction process needs a different focus. A senior executive of the company should already be familiar with many aspects of the company's operations (although the induction might include visits to parts of the company he or she has not worked with before).

An executive manager appointed to the board is much more likely to lack knowledge and experience about being a director and corporate governance. (Some large companies try to give their senior executives experience as a director by allowing them to take a position as a NED in another company.)

An induction programme for such an individual may therefore need to cover areas such as:

- the role of the board, including matters reserved for the board and oversight of management;
- the powers and duties of directors, and the rights of shareholders (the new director should be given a copy of the Articles of Association);
- the role of board committees;
- the role of the board in monitoring risk and internal control;
- membership of the board and its committees, how the board operates and the role of the company secretary;
- frequency of board meetings;
- what the new director will be expected to contribute;
- the major shareholders and their relationship with the company;
- compliance with corporate governance requirements;
- the laws relating to fair dealing by directors;
- the duties of directors;
- the laws on insider trading and market abuse;
- the Listing Rules and the Model Code on share dealing by directors;
- the potential liabilities of directors: directors' liability insurance;
- company policy on corporate social responsibility;
- arrangements for monitoring the performance of board members.

This list is not exhaustive, although it might be considered too long in some cases. The main point is that an executive manager appointed as a director needs to learn about the differences in the roles of manager and director, and that he or she has not been appointed as a director simply to be a 'high-level' executive of the company.

9.3 Training and professional development

The Combined Code states that all directors should 'regularly update and refresh their skills and knowledge' and that the company secretary should assist with the professional development of directors as required.

- In the case of a non-executive director, the training process will include learning about the company's business, and getting to know its key executives.
- In the case of all directors, training could also involve learning about the statutory and regulatory duties, responsibilities and potential liabilities of directors.

The chairman should be responsible for ensuring that new directors are suitably trained, but the chairman might ask the company secretary to arrange for a training programme to be devised and provided. This proposal was put forward in the Higgs Report.

The Report commented:

'On appointment, non-executive directors will already have relevant skills, knowledge, experience and abilities. Nevertheless, a non-executive director's credibility and effectiveness in the boardroom will depend not just on their existing capability but on their ability to extend and refresh their knowledge and skills ... The word 'training' in this context is not altogether helpful as it carries rather limited connotations of formal instruction in a classroom setting ... By contrast, what I envisage is continued professional development tailored to the individual.'

The need for continuing professional development can probably be readily accepted. The Tyson Report, which looked into the appointment of NEDs, commented that NEDs require continual training and development, with specialist training necessary for individuals appointed to the remuneration committee or audit committee of the board.

It is not clear, however, what forms continuing professional development should take or how easily it can be provided. However, the Tyson Report commented that training courses are becoming more widely available, for example in business schools. This might suggest a different view from that taken by Sir Derek Higgs, that formal classroom training might be suitable.

10 Re-election of directors

The re-election of directors by the shareholders at annual general meetings is primarily a matter for the company's Articles of Association. However, the Combined Code includes the principle that: 'All directors should be submitted for re-election at regular intervals, subject to continued satisfactory performance. The board should ensure planned and progressive refreshing of the board.'

The specific Combined Code provisions are as follows:

- All directors should be subject to election by shareholders at the first annual general meeting after their appointment, and to re-election thereafter at intervals of no more than three years. This Code provision applies to all board members, including the CEO.
- NEDs should be appointed for specified terms subject to re-election (and to Companies Acts provisions relating to the removal of directors). When a NED is proposed for election, the board should inform shareholders why it thinks the individual should be appointed.
- When proposing re-election of a NED, the chairman should confirm to the shareholders that, following a formal performance evaluation, the individual's performance continues to be effective and shows a commitment to the role.
- Any term beyond six years (two three-year terms) for a NED should be subject to particularly rigorous review and take into account the need for progressive refreshing of the board.

- NEDs may serve longer than nine years (i.e. more than three three-year terms), but doing so could be relevant to the determination of whether the individual is independent (see Chapter 5).

These provisions allow the shareholders some powers over board appointments, but in practice they are difficult to apply. In a large public company, it is difficult for activist shareholders to gather a majority of votes against the re-election of particular directors.

Even so, the threat by some major shareholders to vote against the re-election of an individual, and the associated bad publicity this often attracts, could influence board thinking on certain contentious issues where the shareholders disagree with the board. Some activist investors have argued in favour of the annual re-election of all directors, giving the shareholders an opportunity each year to remove any individual from the board.

The requirement for the board to ensure planned and progressive refreshing means that re-election of current directors should not be 'automatic'.

11 Succession planning

The key positions on the board of directors are the chairman and CEO. The individuals holding these positions will retire or resign at some time, for example because the individual has reached retirement age or has come to the end of a fixed-term contract.

The board of directors should try to ensure a smooth succession, with a replacement lined up to take the place of the departing individual. In the case of a departing CEO, the successor may be an existing executive manager who has been groomed for the succession. In the case of a departing non-executive chairman, the successor may be an external appointment. A smooth succession is desirable to avoid disruptions to the company's decision-making processes or unexpected changes in policy or direction. The succession can also be planned well in advance, so that the newly appointed individuals will have an opportunity to learn about their role before the actual succession occurs.

A supporting principle in the Combined Code states that:

'The board should satisfy itself that plans are in place for orderly succession for appointment to the board and to senior management, so as to maintain an appropriate balance of skills and experience within the company and its board.'

Principle A.7 also requires the board to ensure that there is a planned and progressive refreshing of the board membership, which should have implications for succession planning.

Succession planning could be a matter delegated to the nomination committee. If the board intends to breach the Combined Code by appointing the current CEO as the next chairman, it would be advisable for a suitable representative of the board to discuss with major shareholders (and possibly representatives of institutional shareholders) the reasons for this choice. These discussions should take place well in advance of any final decision about the appointment.

12 Performance evaluation

A possibly contentious issue in corporate governance is the extent to which the performance of directors should be monitored and assessed, and what form such assessments should take. A requirement for directors to undergo formal performance appraisals each year was introduced by the 2003 Combined Code, following the recommendations of the Higgs Report.

The Combined Code (Principle A6) states that the board should undertake a 'formal and rigorous' annual evaluation of its own performance and that of its committees and individual directors.

A supporting principle states that individual evaluation should aim to show whether each director:

- continues to contribute effectively; and
- continues to demonstrate commitment to the role (for example, in terms of time spent in carrying out the director's duties, attendance at board and committee meetings, and so on).

The evaluation of performance is particularly important for NEDs. Executive directors commit all or most of their time to the company and should be fully familiar with the business and the company's operations. In contrast, NEDs spend only a part of their time with the company, even though they make up the membership of key board committees (the audit and remuneration committees in particular). The Combined Code states that the performance evaluation of individual directors 'should aim to show whether each director continues to contribute effectively and to demonstrate commitment to the role, including commitment of time for board and committee meetings and any other duties'.

12.1 How is performance evaluation carried out?

The Combined Code does not state how a performance evaluation should be carried out or who should do it. It appears to be common practice, however, that, except for the performance review of the chairman, it is the chairman who organises the performance review process and is closely involved in it.

One approach is for the chairman to carry out the reviews personally, possibly with advice and assistance from the company secretary. Some companies use the services of specialist external consultants.

The Higgs Suggestions for Good Practice included some guidance on performance evaluation (see Appendix 5). The guidance does not go into detail about how the evaluation process should be conducted, nor what target measures of performance might be used in the evaluation. It simply suggests that:

- The board should state in the annual report how the evaluation has been conducted.
- The chairman is responsible for selecting an effective process of evaluation and acting on its outcome. Where appropriate, the chairman should propose that new members should be appointed to the board, or should seek the resignation of current directors.

- Using an external third party (external consultants) to carry out the evaluation will bring objectivity to the process. This might suggest that unless the assistance of an external firm of consultants is used, there is a risk that the process will not be objective.

The Suggestions are limited mainly to providing a list of questions that should be considered, but the list is not exhaustive or definitive, and companies may take a different approach to suit their own particular circumstances. The answers to the questions should make an assessment of performance possible, and indicate in which areas performance might be improved. (The Higgs Guidance is reproduced in Appendix 8.)

One approach to performance evaluation is to mix the approaches used. A company might use external consultants in one year and then the chairman might use the lessons obtained from the consultants to carry out an internal performance evaluation for the next two years. In year 4, external consultants might be used again as a way of learning new lessons or checking the quality of the internal evaluation process.

The NEDs, led by the senior NED, should be responsible for the performance evaluation of the chairman, 'taking into account the views of executive directors'. However, the actual performance review of the chairman may be conducted for the NEDs by external consultants.

A survey by ICSA Corporate Services was reported in 2007, which indicated that less than a quarter of the UK's top 200 companies had used external consultants to assist with the annual performance review of the board in 2005 or 2006. The survey covered 92 companies, of which only 19 had used an externally developed or managed evaluation process. The report commented that the failure to use external consultants raises questions about whether the performance review process in many companies is sufficiently rigorous.

12.2 Using the results of a performance review

The Combined Code makes the following provisions concerning how the performance review should be used:

- The board should state in its annual report how the review of performance (of the board, its committees and individual members) has been conducted.
- The chairman should act on the results of the performance evaluation by recognising the strengths of the board and its weaknesses. This might suggest that the chairman should use the performance review to provide an opportunity for the chairman to review the balance of skills and talents on the board, and consider whether changes to the composition of the board might be appropriate. For example, the chairman might believe that the time has come to change one of the NEDs by not renewing his or her contract when it expires.
- Alternatively, the chairman might discuss with underperforming directors the need for training or professional development to improve skills or knowledge.

12.3 *The effectiveness of a board*

The annual performance review assesses the performance of the board as a whole, as well as its committees. To get practical value from an annual review, the board should be prepared to act on its findings whenever performance is not considered to be as good as it should be.

The possible reasons for an ineffective board may be any of the following:

- Insufficient information provided to the directors to enable them to make properly considered decisions.
- Directors not given sufficient time before a board meeting to read relevant papers, and so arrive at the meeting not properly briefed.
- Directors not bothering to take time before a board meeting to read relevant papers, and so arrive at the meeting not properly briefed.
- Individual directors failing to attend meetings of the board or meetings of board committees.
- Individual directors not being given enough opportunity to contribute to discussions at board meetings. (This is arguably a failing of the chairman rather than an indication of an ineffective board.)
- The board failing to carry out its responsibilities in full.
- The board failing to take its annual performance evaluation seriously.
- The board making ill-considered (bad) strategic decisions.

13 Two-tier boards

Companies in most countries have unitary boards, in other words, just one board of directors accountable to the shareholders. The origins of the unitary board lie in the seventeenth century and early British joint stock companies such as the East India Company. As the company grew, the East India Company organised itself into a court of 24 directors, reporting to a 'court of proprietors' or shareholders.

Another approach to corporate governance is to have two-tier boards. A two-tier structure is used in some countries, notably France, Germany and the Netherlands. With a two-tier structure, there is a supervisory board and a management board.

- The management board is responsible for oversight of management issues, and is led by the CEO.
- The supervisory board is responsible for general oversight of the company and of the management board.

In a two-tier structure, there has to be a functional relationship between the management board and the supervisory board, and here the chairman of the supervisory board plays a key role. The chairman of the supervisory board is responsible for making sure that the two boards work well together, and the most powerful individuals in the company are the chairman of the supervisory board and the CEO who is in charge of the management board. The CEO reports to the supervisory board chairman. If the relationship between these two individuals works well, the chairman will effectively speak for the management at meetings of the supervisory board.

The management board consists entirely of executive directors. The supervisory board consists entirely of NEDs. In Germany, which has been described as the 'apostle of the stakeholder principle', supervisory board members include:

- representatives of trade unions and/or the company's employees;
- representatives of a major shareholder, such as one of the German banks (who have extensive shareholdings in German companies);
- former executives of the company.

The supervisory board NEDs are therefore not necessarily independent, particularly employee representatives. It can therefore be difficult to reconcile the differing views of employee representatives and representatives of major shareholders without antagonising the executives on the management board. On the other hand, where there is a large number of former executives on the supervisory board, there is a risk that the supervisory board will take a lenient and easy-going view of what management are doing. In addition, some independent supervisory board directors might well be senior managers of other companies, where they are management board members. These individuals might therefore sympathise with the views of the management board.

A government-appointed commission set up in Germany to look into corporate governance issues, reporting in 2002, suggested that supervisory boards should give much greater attention to their watchdog role, and made some recommendations about the structure of the board. The committee's recommendations included proposals that:

- The supervisory board should contain no more than two former members of the management board.
- The work of the supervisory board should be delegated to small committees, consisting of directors who are competent in the work concerned.
- A member of the management board of one company should sit on the supervisory board of no more than five other unrelated companies.

Chapter summary

- A central issue in corporate governance is the balance of power and influence between individuals on the board. This is needed to avoid autocratic leadership by an all-powerful individual, which can be damaging to a company and harmful to its shareholders and other stakeholders.

- Individual directors should have a suitable character, with useful skills and experience that can be brought to bear on decision-making by the board. Personal honesty and integrity are essential.

- The board of directors should have a clear set of decision-making responsibilities. It should meet regularly and one of its responsibilities should be to review the performance of executive management.

- The chairman of the board is responsible for the functioning of the board of directors. The chief executive officer is the head of the executive management. In the UK, recommended best practice is that these two positions should not normally be held by the same person.

- Non-executive directors are expected to provide more balance to a board of directors, and prevent dominance by executive management.

- The board of directors might delegate to a nomination committee the task of recommending new appointees to the board. In the UK, the Combined Code recommends that a majority of the nomination committee should be NEDs and that its chairman should be either the chairman of the board or the senior NED.

- The ICSA has issued a guidance note on the terms of reference for the nomination committee.

- The board should plan for succession to the top board positions (especially the chief executive officer and chairman of the board). There should also be suitable training for new directors.

- The company secretary can play a valuable practical role in applying best corporate governance practice.

- In countries such as Germany, there is a two-tier board structure rather than an Anglo-American unitary board of directors. In a two-tier structure, there is a supervisory board of non-executive directors (many of whom are not independent) and a management board of executive directors. The chief executive leads the management board and reports to the chairman of the supervisory board. A corporate governance issue for two-tier boards is the balance of power between the two boards.

Chapter 5

Non-executive directors

1. The role of non-executive directors
2. NEDs on the board and board committees
3. Independence
4. The appointment of a new NED
5. Senior independent director
6. Criticisms of non-executive directors
7. The Tyson Report on the recruitment and training of NEDs
8. The potential liability of a non-executive director: duty of skill and care

1 The role of non-executive directors

A NED is a member of the board of directors without executive responsibilities in the company. NEDs should be able to bring judgement and experience to the deliberations of the board that the executive directors on their own would lack. A NED will therefore attend board meetings and contribute to discussions and decision-making.

One function of NEDs is to improve the quality of decision-making by the board by:

- bringing a range of skills and experience to the deliberations of the board;
- acting as a counterbalance, where necessary, to the influence of the chairman or CEO over board decision-making.

To be effective, a NED has to understand the company's business, but there appears to be a general consensus that the experience and qualities required of a NED can be obtained from working in other industries or in other aspects of commercial and public life. NEDs might therefore include individuals who:

- are an executive director in another public company;
- hold non-executive director positions and chairmanship positions in other public companies;
- have professional qualifications (for example, partners in firms of solicitors);
- have experience in government, as politicians or former senior civil servants.

However, research has been carried out into identifying and recruiting suitable individuals as NEDs from a wider variety of sources and backgrounds (see below).

NEDs are expected not only to bring a wide range of skills and experience to the deliberations of the board, particularly in the area of strategy and business development, but also to ensure that there is a suitable balance of power on the board. A powerful chairman or CEO might be able to dominate fellow executive directors, but – in theory at least – independent NEDs should be able to bring different views and independent thinking to the deliberations of the board. Decisions taken by the board should therefore be better and more in keeping with the aims of good corporate governance.

1.1   *Higgs guidance on the role of the NED*

The Higgs Report, published in January 2003, looked at the role and effectiveness of NEDs, and many of the Higgs recommendations were included in the 2003 Combined Code.

The Higgs Suggestions for Good Practice, which were appended to the Combined Code, include guidance on the role of the NED. This states that this role has several key elements, which NEDs are perhaps in a better position to provide than executives. These are:

- Strategy. NEDs should constructively challenge and help to develop proposals on strategy.
- Performance. NEDs should scrutinise the performance of executive management in achieving agreed goals and objectives, and monitor the reporting of performance.
- Risk. NEDs should satisfy themselves about the integrity of financial information and that the systems of internal controls and risk management are robust.
- People. NEDs are responsible for deciding the level of remuneration for executive directors and should have a prime role in appointing directors (and removing them where necessary) and in succession planning.

These roles explain the requirements for audit, remuneration and nomination committees consisting of independent NEDs.

The Higgs inquiry prompted a large number of responses from organisations with an interest in corporate governance. ICSA's responses are set out in Case Example 5.1, and are indicative of attitudes to NEDs, their role and effectiveness.

CASE EXAMPLE 5.1

The ICSA view of NEDs

ICSA's response to the Higgs inquiry is revealing about the Institute's views on NEDs, which stresses the role of the company secretary in corporate governance, as a provider of support to NEDs.

The other key points in ICSA's response are as follows:

- The unitary board structure is appropriate, and responsibility for actions and decisions by the board should be the same for all directors. However, the role of 'independent' directors should also be recognised and only those individuals who are 'truly independent' should sit on key board committees.

- Many of the perceived problems of the unitary board structure may be due to a failure by executive directors to appreciate their legal responsibilities as directors, as distinct from their other responsibilities as executive managers of the company.
- NEDs must be able to give sufficient time to their work and should be remunerated properly, A suitable balance has to be drawn between paying a fair reward to NEDs and not paying them so much that their independence from the company is compromised.
- The optimum size for a company's board is normally 8–12. An effective board will have a balance of skills, abilities and ages among its directors, and there is also a need for a balance of executive directors, NEDs who are not independent and independent NEDs. There is a role for all three types of director.
- It should be a requirement of the Combined Code that a board of directors should undergo a regular review of its effectiveness It is particularly important that NEDs should have the strength of character to stand up to their fellow directors. However, ICSA does not agree with the view that the NEDs should meet separately with major shareholders.

    The key role of NEDs is to bring an external 'real world' focus to the board's discussions, particularly with regard to strategy and business development. Although the board should aim for unity and agreement, NEDs should also play the role of 'devil's advocate' especially in cases where one of the executive directors is so forceful that the other executive directors tend to concur with his or her views. Other aspects of the role of the NED might be:

- opening up business opportunities through new contacts and experience;
- giving advice to executive directors;
- serving on board committees;
- safeguarding the interests of the shareholders and other stakeholders by making sure that these are considered when the board makes decisions;
- helping to maintain an ethical climate and encouraging probity in the conduct of the company's affairs;
- monitoring and reviewing excesses of executive directors.

2 NEDs on the board and board committees

2.1 Number of NEDs on the board

A key principle of good corporate governance is that there should be a sufficient number of independent NEDs on the board of directors to create a suitable balance of power and prevent the dominance of the board by one individual or by a small number of individuals.

The Combined Code sets out different requirements for large listed companies and for smaller companies. (Smaller companies are defined as companies outside the FTSE 350 for the whole of the year immediately prior to the reporting year.) Except for smaller companies, at least one half of the board, excluding the chairman, should be independent NEDs.

For smaller companies, there should be at least two independent NEDs.

2.2 NED membership of board committees

Independent NEDs are appointed to provide a counterbalance to powerful executive directors and to give the benefit of their experience and know-how to decision-making by the board. A further aspect of corporate governance is the extent to which executive directors should be kept away from some decision-making or monitoring responsibilities, through the delegation of certain responsibilities to committees of the board. A board committee might consist entirely or mostly of NEDs, and might be given:

- the power to make certain decisions on behalf of the board;
- responsibility for investigating particular issues and making recommendations to the full board.

In the UK, there are no statutory requirements to establish board committees, but three committees are recommended by the Combined Code:

1   a nomination committee;
2   an audit committee;
3   a remuneration committee.

The role of the nomination committee was described in the previous chapter. The roles of the remuneration and audit committees are described in later chapters.

Table 5.1 *The Combined Code and board committees*

	MEMBERSHIP
NOMINATION COMMITTEE	A majority of the members should be independent NEDs. The chairman of the committee should be the chairman of the board or an independent NED.
REMUNERATION COMMITTEE	All members should be independent NEDs. Large companies should have at least three members. Smaller companies should have at least two members. The chairman of the board may be a member of the remuneration committee if he or she was considered independent when first appointed as chairman. However, the board chairman should not should not chair the committee.
AUDIT COMMITTEE	All members should be independent NEDs. Large companies should have at least three members. Smaller companies should have at least two members. At least one member of the committee should have recent financial experience.

Some boards might establish other committees, such as a risk management committee, where there are issues of particular importance to the company that warrant close monitoring. For example, a company might have an environment committee, where its business activities are likely to have important consequences for the environment, involving government regulation, the law and public opinion.

Table 5.1 summarises the Combined Code's recommendations about membership of board committees.

3 Independence

Executive directors cannot be independent. They are involved in the running of the company's operations, and report (and are accountable to) to the CEO for this aspect of their work. They also rely on the company for most (if not all) of their remuneration.

NEDs are either independent or non-independent. A NED is not independent if his or her opinions are likely to be influenced by someone else, in particular by the senior executive management of the company or by a major shareholder.

Independent non-executive directors are supposed to bring an independent view to the deliberations of the board. However, they are in a difficult position.

- They are legally liable in the same way as executive directors. For example, they have the same fiduciary duties to the company, and the duty of skill and care.
- As fellow directors, they might also be reluctant to blow the whistle on their executive director colleagues.
- If they have been selected and appointed by the chairman or the chief executive officer, they will be less likely to ask tough questions about the way the company is being run. This is sometimes known as the St Thomas à Becket problem, after the twelfth-century Archbishop of Canterbury. Becket was appointed to his position as archbishop by Henry II, but then took a stand against him on issues concerning the roles of the king and the church in the governance of the country.

If a NED is likely, for one reason or another, to take sides with the CEO, he or she is unlikely to bring the much needed balance of power to the board. The independence of a NED could be challenged, for example, if the individual concerned:

- has a family connection with the CEO (a problem in some family-controlled public companies);
- until recently used to be an executive director in the company;
- until recently used to work for the company in a professional capacity, for example as its auditor or corporate lawyer;
- receives payments from the company in addition to their fees as a non-executive director.

A key principle of good corporate governance is that there should be a sufficient number of independent NEDs on the board of directors to create a suitable balance of power and prevent the dominance of the board by one individual or by a small number of individuals.

The provisions of the Combined Code (and corporate governance regulations and guidelines in other countries) refer specifically to independent NEDs. So what is meant by 'independent'? A NED is not independent if his or her opinions are likely to be influenced by someone else, in particular by the senior executive management of the company or by a major shareholder.

A person cannot be independent of a company if he or she personally stands to gain or otherwise benefit substantially from:

- income from the company, in addition to his or her fee as a NED;
- the company's reported profitability and movements in the company's share price.

A NED cannot be properly independent, for example, if he or she accepts a fee from the company for consultancy work. Consultancy involves the individual in the operational aspects of the company, and by implication puts him or her on the side of the executives. Nor can an individual be independent if he or she has been awarded with a large number of share options by the company. Holding share options gives the individual a direct interest in the share price of the company around the time the options can be exercised. He or she might therefore favour decisions that improve the reported profitability of the company at this time, because good financial results are likely to be good for the share price.

A committee of the board of directors of the New York Stock Exchange, reporting in June 2002 on corporate governance in NYSE-listed companies, commented as follows:

'No director qualifies as "independent" unless the board of directors affirmatively determines that the director has no material relationship with the listed company (either directly, as a partner, shareholder or officer of an organisation that has a relationship with the company). Companies must disclose these determinations.'

The report added, however:

'We do not view ownership ... of a less than controlling amount of stock as a per se bar to an independence finding.'

A former executive director might be appointed as a NED on his or her retirement. When this happens, his attitudes and judgements are likely to remain on the side of the executive management, and he or she is unlikely to make criticisms of the executive management that might indirectly reflect adversely on his own performance as an executive manager prior to retirement.

Occasionally, NEDs are appointed to represent the opinions of a major shareholder. In such cases, the individual can be expected to voice the wishes of the shareholder and so could not be regarded as independent.

To ensure that NEDs should not rely for their tenure in office on one or two individuals, the Cadbury Code recommended that they should be selected through a formal process. This is now a principle of the Combined Code.

3.1 Criteria for judging independence

The Combined Code requires the board to identify in the annual report each NED it considers to be independent. Although this is a matter for the board's judgement, the Code provision sets out circumstances in which independence would usually be questionable where:

- The director has been an employee of the company within the past five years.
- The director has a material business relationship with the company (or has had such a relationship within the past three years). This relationship might be as a partner, shareholder, director or employee in another organisation that has a material business relationship with the company.
- The director receives (or has received) additional remuneration from the company other than a director's fee, or is a member of the company's pension scheme, or participates in the company's share option scheme or a performance-related pay scheme.
- The director has close family ties with the company's advisers, directors or senior employees.
- The director has cross-directorships or has significant links with other directors through involvement in other companies or organisations.
- The director represents a significant shareholder.
- The director has served on the board for more than nine years since the date of his or her first election.

These criteria of independence should be applied to a chairman as well as other NEDs.

CASE EXAMPLE 5.2

The Kazhakstan mining company Kazakhmys attracted attention by becoming a listed UK company in October 2005 and a member of the FTSE 100.

Although the company took steps to strengthen its corporate governance, its practices still fell short of normal UK listed company practice. Its chairman was not independent, and were some doubts about the independence of the non-executives, in view of the requirement of the Combined Code that independence means being free from relationships that affect, or could appear to affect, the judgement of the director.

One NED was a director of a company that has a large secured interest-free loan from Kazakhmys. Another NED received payment for services to the company in relation to its London listing. A third NED was vice chairman of investment banking at J P Morgan Cazenove, financial advisers to Kazakhmys.

A more general debate arose as a result of this case around whether corporate governance standards in the UK will come under threat as more foreign companies join the London market. Index-tracking funds will have to buy shares in these companies, even if their corporate governance regimes are not up to Combined Code standards.

3.2   The nine-year rule on independence

The rule that a NED should not be considered independent after serving on the board for over nine years arises from the general view that the independence of an NED is likely to diminish over time, as the NED becomes more familiar with the company and executive colleagues. The risk is that the NED will take more of the views of executive colleagues on trust and will be less rigorous in his or her questioning.

The Higgs Report commented: 'There will be occasions where value will be added by a non-executive director serving for longer, but I would expect this to be the exception and the reasons explained to shareholders.' On the other hand, the Quoted Companies Alliance (QCA) commented in a submission to the Financial Reporting Council in 2005 that if a NED ceases to be considered independent after nine years, this should not be a reason to end his or her appointment as director, if he or she is still making a valuable contribution to the board. The QCA added that this is particularly important for smaller quoted companies, because effective NEDs are often difficult to find and (unlike a larger quoted company) when a director ceases to be independent, there is no change in the number of independent NEDs required on the board – the requirement remains for just two.

Even larger quoted companies appear reluctant to lose NEDs after nine years of service, due largely to a perceived lack of potential candidates with suitable qualifications to be an effective NED. It is therefore worth remembering that the Combined Code is pragmatic in its approach to the nine-year rule. If the board of directors considers that a director is still independent even after nine years of service, he may still be considered 'independent' for the purposes of the corporate governance provisions.

3.3   Protecting the independence/effectiveness of board committees

As a way of protecting the independence and improving the effectiveness of board committees, the Combined Code includes the following supporting principles:

- When deciding the chairmanship and membership of board committees, consideration should be given to the benefits of ensuring that committee membership is refreshed (i.e. membership rotation) and that undue reliance is not placed on particular individuals.
- The only individuals who are entitled to attend meetings of the nomination, remuneration and audit committees are the chairman and members of the committee, although other individuals may attend at the invitation of the committee.

CASE EXAMPLE 5.3

In July 2002, the National Association of Pension Funds (NAPF) issued a report detailing the failure of property company British Land to comply with certain elements of the UK Combined Code on Corporate Governance. The Code requires independent non-executive directors to play a role in the governance of listed companies. At the time of these reports, the company was approaching its annual general meeting, at which a non-executive, Mr Michael Cassidy, was standing for re-election. Mr Cassidy was a partner in a law firm that had been paid £190,000 in the previous year by British Land for its services. Mr Cassidy was also a non-executive director of UBS Warburg, British Land's investment bankers. NAPF urged its members to abstain from voting on Mr Cassidy's re-election, on the grounds that he could not be considered sufficiently independent.

In its same report, NAPF suggested that the company's deputy chairman, non-executive Mr Derek Higgs, was also not independent. Mr Higgs was an adviser to UBS Warburg and also a non-executive director of property valuers Jones, Lang LaSalle, the valuers of the overseas property portfolio of British Land. Mr Higgs was not standing for re-election, but the NAPF criticism had some significance because Mr Higgs had recently been appointed by the Secretary of State for the Department of Trade and Industry to carry out an investigation into the effectiveness of non-executive directors in UK public companies.

CASE EXAMPLE 5.4

PIRC (Pensions Investment Research Consultants Ltd), a shareholder pressure group, issued a report on Telewest, the UK cable television company in June 2002, describing the company as a 'corporate basket case'. PIRC recommended to its clients that they should oppose the re-election of four of the seven non-executive directors at the forthcoming annual general meeting, including the chairman, on the grounds that they were not independent. In PIRC's view, the chairman could not be independent because he held share options in the company, giving him a financial interest. Other non-executives were not independent because they were appointees of a 25 per cent shareholder in the company. The independence of yet another non-executive was questioned because he had been on the company's board for nine years.

PIRC also criticised aspects of directors' remuneration. It was concerned by a bonus payment of £170,000 to the finance director for securing new credit facilities, because this should be a normal part of the finance director's job, and not something worthy of a bonus. It also criticised the payment of £690,000 in bonuses to directors, despite increasing losses in the company and a collapsing share price, and in its view, the remuneration committee did not consist wholly of independent non-executives.

---

4 The appointment of a new NED

The formal procedures for appointing a new NED are the same as for the appointment of an executive director. However, a NED will be less familiar with the company than a senior executive manager and he should not accept an appointment unless he is satisfied that there are no matters of concern. The Higgs Guidance therefore recomended that before accepting an appointment, a prospective NED should carry out a 'due diligence' check or examination of the company. The ICSA has commented: 'By making the right enquiries, asking the right questions and taking care to understand the replies, a prospective director can reduce the risk of nasty surprises and dramatically increase the likelihood of success.'

Questions that the prospective NED should ask will cover:

- Questions about the business – for example, its nature and size, and the company's market share, financial performance and financial position.
- Questions about governance and investor relation – who are the major shareholders, and what is the structure of the board of directors and its committees?
- Questions about the role that the NED would be expected to perform, including membership of board committees. The prospective NED should be satisfied that he or she has the necessary qualities or experience to make an effective contribution to the work of the company's board.
- Questions about the company's risk management systems and controls.
- Questions about ethical issues, and whether there are any ethical matters that might give cause for concern.

Answers to many of these questions can be obtained from published documents that are available, in paper form or on a website, to the general public. These include the annual report and accounts of the company, the company's articles of association, any sustainability report or social and environmental report that the company publishes and press reports about the company.

4.1   Terms of engagement

If a prospective NED decides to accept the offer of the appointment, terms of engagement should be agreed with the company (either the board as a whole or its nomination committee). The terms that must be agreed are as follows:

- The initial period of tenure in office: this is normally three years.
- Time commitment. The company must indicate how much time the NED is likely to be expected to commit to the company, and the NED should make this commitment: the expected time commitment should be included in the formal letter of appointment. Typically NEDs are expected to commit between 15 and 30 days each year. A main principle in the Combined Code is that: 'Care should be taken to ensure that appointees have enough time available to devote to the job. This is particularly important in the case of chairmanships.'
- Remuneration. The annual remuneration of the NED should be agreed. This may be a fixed annual fee. It is generally considered inappropriate for NEDs, including the chairman, to be remunerated on the basis of incentive schemes linked to company performance, because this could undermine the independence of the individual.

The terms of engagement should be set out in a formal letter of appointment. As well as including details of the role that the NED will be required to perform (including initial membership of board committees), the expected time commitment, the tenure and the remuneration, the letter of engagement should also:

- specify that the NED should treat all information received as a director as confidential to the company;
- indicate the arrangements for induction;
- give details of directors' and officers' liability insurance that will be available;
- indicate the need for an annual performance review process for directors;
- state what company resources will be made available to the NED, such as a desk, computer terminal and telephone.

5 Senior independent director

In the UK, there has been some discussion about the role of the senior independent director (SID). The discussion arose from the view that there could be occasions when institutional shareholders might be in disagreement with the board of directors of a company, but unable to make their opinions heard due to the negative attitudes of the chairman and CEO. It was therefore suggested that the board of directors of large companies should nominate an independent NED as the senior NED, whom shareholders could approach to discuss problems and issues when the 'normal' communication route through the chairman had broken down.

In addition, if the chairman failed to pass on the views of the institutional shareholders to the NEDs, there should be another channel of communication that could be used instead. In the UK, corporate governance guidelines have come down in favour of having a senior NED.

The Combined Code states that the board should appoint one of the independent NEDs to be the senior independent director. Such an individual 'should be available to shareholders if they have concerns which contact through the normal channels of chairman, chief executive or finance director has failed to resolve, or for which such contact is inappropriate'.

The senior independent director is therefore, in effect, a channel of communication between the company and its shareholders when normal channels don't work – for example, when the principles of good corporate governance are not being applied.

Critics of the concept of SID argue that the chairman should resolve difficulties between a company and its shareholders, and the position of a SID should be superfluous. Opening up the possibility of an additional channel of communication for shareholders is perhaps more likely to confuse company–shareholder relationships rather than improve them. The Combined Code includes the following provision with respect to the chairman, SID and other non-executive directors:

- The chairman should hold meetings with the NEDs, without the executive directors present. (It is the chairman's responsibility to make sure that the NEDs contribute effectively to the board.)
- Led by the SID, the non-executive directors should meet at least once a year, without the chairman being present, to discuss the chairman's performance and 'on other occasions as are deemed appropriate'.

5.1 NED meetings with institutional shareholders

The Combined Code states that companies should offer major shareholders the opportunity to meet newly appointed NEDs and that there should be opportunities for subsequent meetings if shareholders want them. Many institutions will perhaps decline the opportunity to meet with new NEDs, but some may be keen on such meetings. Hermes Investment Management (www.hermes.co.uk) went so far as to issue the Hermes Guide for Shareholders and Independent Outside Directors, setting out the nature of the conversations it would expect to have with NEDs.

The Hermes Guide suggested that induction meetings (i.e. meetings with a NED as part of the induction process) are likely to be brief. The number of meetings that a NED should expect will vary between companies, but there ought to be sufficient to give the NED an insight into the views held by its shareholders about the company.

The guide also suggested the key issues that are likely to be discussed at induction meetings:

- The appointment process. Who made first contact with the individual? Did the appointment process work well, or could it have been better? Does the company have a formal list of the roles and responsibilities of its NEDs?
- Skills and attitude. What attracted you to the company? What do you think attracted the company to you? What unique skills and outlook do you bring to the board? How much time do you expect to spend on board duties? Do you expect to take on a specific role?
- Perspectives on the company. Do you see any problems at the company? What does the company do well? What is the company's competitive advantage, and is it being properly exploited? Are there further investment opportunities for the company to pursue? Where do you see the company in ten years' time?
- Investment. How many shares do you hold in the company? Do you expect to add to this shareholding? Explain the nature of the shareholder's investment (passive or active, long- or short-term) and the reasons for investing in the company.

Hermes suggested in its guide that regular meetings between major shareholders and NEDs after the induction meeting should not be necessary, although if a shareholder has a genuine concern, it should expect NEDs to make themselves available to meet and discuss the problem.

Meetings between major shareholders and the company will normally be with the independent chairman, but if the chairman is an executive or has some other potential conflict of interest, the shareholder should meet with either the independent deputy chairman or the senior independent director (SID). (Hermes argues that the positions of deputy chairman and SID should be held by the same individual.) On occasion, a meeting with another NED might be more appropriate, such as a meeting with the chairman of the audit committee to discuss a concern about the audit process or risk management, or a meeting with the chairman of the remuneration committee to discuss concerns about senior executive remuneration.

Hermes also commented that any communication between a major shareholder and the SID should be in addition to existing channels and should not replace them, and should be rare events. 'When it does occur it is almost invariably because of a crisis situation.'

6 Criticisms of non-executive directors

There are differing views about the effectiveness of NEDs. The 'accepted' view is that NEDs bring experience and judgement to the deliberations of the board that the executive directors on their own would lack.

An alternative view is that the effectiveness of NEDs can be undermined by several factors:

- a lack of knowledge about the business operations of the company;
- insufficient time spent with the company;
- the weight of opinion of the executive directors on the board.

6.1 Insufficient knowledge

The quality of decision-making depends largely on the quality of information available to the decision-maker. The Combined Code states that the board as a whole should be 'supplied in a timely manner with information in a form and of a quality appropriate to enable it to discharge its duties'. However, the senior executives in a company control the information systems, and so control the flow of information to the board. It is quite conceivable, for example, that the CEO and other executive directors might have access to management information that is withheld from the board as a whole, or that is presented to the board in a distorted manner. Lacking the 'insider knowledge' of executive managers about the business operations, and having to rely on the integrity of the information supplied to them by management and executive directors restricts the scope for NEDs to make a meaningful contribution to board decisions.

6.2 Insufficient time

NEDs often have executive positions in other companies and organisations, where most of their working time is spent. As a general rule, NEDs do not have an office at the company headquarters and may spend at most one or two days a month on the company's business. A further criticism of non-executive directors is that some individuals hold too many NED positions, so that they cannot possibly give sufficient time to any of the companies concerned. It would be argued, for example, that an individual cannot be an effective NED of a company if he is also the chief executive officer of another public company and holds four or five other NED positions in other companies.

6.3 Overriding influence of executive directors

Yet another criticism of NEDs is that if a difference of opinion arises during a meeting of the board, the opinions of the executive directors are likely to carry greater weight, because they know more about the company. NEDs may be put under pressure to accept the views of their executive director colleagues. This danger has been recognised by the New York Stock Exchange (NYSE). Among its recommendations for corporate governance reform, the NYSE recommended that a framework should be established to allow non-executive directors to meet regularly on their own, as a means of promoting open discussion among themselves without any influence or pressure from executive directors. 'The non-management directors of each company must meet at regularly scheduled executive sessions without management. The independent directors must designate, and publicly disclose the name of, the director who will preside at the executive sessions.' The NYSE therefore lends its support to the concept of a senior non-executive director, whose function is to act as a centre of resistance to pressure from the executive management.

6.4 Myners Report and criticisms of NEDs

Further criticism of the system of NEDs in the UK came in February 2002 from Paul Myners, author of a government-backed report into pension fund investment and former head of Gartmore Investment Management, the institutional investment firm. He accused boards of directors of public companies of being a 'self-perpetuating oligarchy', which failed to stand up for shareholders' rights against over-powerful executives. He condemned NEDs as the 'missing link' in the chain of good corporate governance. In particular, he criticised the way in which NED appointments were made and the number of NED positions that some individuals held.

- Some individuals held too many NED positions in large public companies, more than they could possibly serve effectively.
- Non-executive directorships were frequently given to the executive directors of other listed companies, giving rise to the concerns about a 'You scratch my back and I'll scratch yours' mentality. A NED might tacitly undertake not to ask difficult questions or take a stand against executives on the board, provided that the non-executives of his own company act in the same way.
- NEDs should help to make the board more accountable to the shareholders. However, shareholders only have opportunities to discuss the company's affairs with the NEDs in a formal setting, at general meetings of the company. Any other discussions between shareholders and NEDs must be informal, if they take place at all.
- The law makes no distinction between executive and non-executive directors. In principle, the NEDs could be equally liable with the executive directors for negligence and failure of duty. Arguably, this threat of criminal or civil liability could make non-executives more inclined to support their executive colleagues.

Faith in NEDs to bring sound corporate governance practice to public companies could therefore be misplaced – a view that has been expressed by some individuals. Lord Young, outgoing president of the UK Institute of Directors, argued in a speech to the Institute of Directors (IoD) annual convention (2002) that NEDs cannot hope to govern their company better than the executive directors, because they cannot know as much about the company as full-time executives. He said:

> 'The biggest and most dangerous nonsense is the role we now expect non-executive directors to perform. Even if they spend one day a week in the company, can the non-execs ever know the business as well as the execs? No, they can't. So why bother with non-execs at all?'

7 The Tyson Report on recruiting and training of NEDs

It was suggested in the previous chapter that, in practice, there could be a tendency for NEDs to be recruited from a narrow circle of potential candidates. The Higgs Report on NEDs (January 2003) found that only 7 per cent of NEDs on UK public limited company boards were non-British nationals, only 6 per cent were women and only 1 per cent were from ethnic minorities. The majority of NEDs were white, middle-aged males, many with previous experience as a plc board director.

Following publication of the Higgs Report, a task force under the chairmanship of Laura Tyson, Dean of the London Business School, looked into the recruitment and development of NEDs. The Tyson Report on the Recruitment and Development of Non-Executive Directors was published in June 2003.

The main focus of the report is on the recruitment of NEDs. It:

- argues that a range of different experiences and backgrounds amongst board members can enhance the effectiveness of the board; and
- suggests how a broader range of NEDs can be identified and recruited.

7.1 The need for a range of experiences and backgrounds

The report argues that NEDs have four broad responsibilities:

1 To provide advice and direction to the company's management on the development and evaluation of strategy.
2 To monitor the implementation of strategy by management and monitor performance against the strategic objectives.
3 To monitor the legal and ethical performance of the company.
4 To monitor the truthfulness and adequacy of the financial information provided by the company to investors and other stakeholders.

These responsibilities include appointing and appraising senior management, and where necessary removing them from office, and succession planning.

The Tyson Report suggests that to fulfil these responsibilities, a board with a range of backgrounds and experience is likely to be more effective than a board consisting of individuals with similar backgrounds and experience.

The Report also refers to the identification in the Higgs Report of four personal qualities required of NEDs, and argues that in deciding whether an individual possesses these qualities, background and experience is not relevant. The four personal qualities are:

- integrity and high ethical standards;
- sound judgement;
- the ability and willingness to challenge and probe;
- strong interpersonal skills.

The Report therefore recommends that NEDs should be recruited by a formal process, advertising vacancies and preferably with formal interviews. The aim should be to ensure that the board as a whole possesses the necessary balance and range of skills and experience. 'A company should begin a NED search by articulating its specific board needs taking into account the composition of existing board members. Only by analysing what its board lacks in skills and expertise can a company move forward to identify the best talent.'

7.2   Recruiting NEDs

The Report criticises the predominant current practice of appointing individuals to the position of NED through an informal process and without formal interviews. This 'traditional' method of recruitment has tended to overlook a number of potentially rich sources of NEDs, such as:

- the 'marzipan layer' of corporate management, just below board level. The CEO of a company might be willing to allow managers to act as NEDs of companies that are not competitors, although might be less willing if the demands on the individual's time become significant. Another advantage of this source of NEDs is that the 'marzipan layer' includes a large number of women;
- individuals in private sector companies;
- individuals in the public sector/non-commercial sector;
- individuals working for business consultancies or professional firms (lawyers, accountants) and retired professional accountants.

Some search firms specialise in looking for suitable individuals.

8   The potential liability of a non-executive director: duty of skill and care

In principle, NEDs on a unitary board have the same legal duties and potential liabilities as their executive director colleagues. NEDs owe a duty of care to the company and must perform their role with suitable skill and diligence. However, unlike their executive director colleagues, they do not work full-time for the company, and they will not know the company and its operations in the same detail.

The differences in time commitment and in-depth knowledge of the company might be relevant in the event of a legal claim against the directors of a company. The courts would need to establish the level of care and skill that an NED might reasonably be expected to exercise.

Some guidance on this matter is provided in a Schedule to the Combined Code, which states that it is for each NED to reach his or her own view about what is necessary to comply with the duty of care, skill and diligence. This is a view that the individual should begin to consider before accepting an appointment as NED of the company The position should then be kept continually under review throughout the NED's period in office.

8.1 Issues to consider before taking up an appointment as NED

The Combined Code states that the letter of appointment for a NED should state the commitment of time that the individual will be expected to give to the company. The individual should agree to this commitment, and a failure subsequently to spend this agreed amount of time with the company could result in an accusation of lack of care or diligence.

The Combined Code also states that the board should be supplied with timely and appropriate information to enable it to discharge its duties. It is the responsibility of the chairman to ensure that this information is provided, but there is also a responsibility on all directors to ensure that they are receiving the information that they need, and in good time.

After appointment as NED, an individual has an obligation to provide the level of care, skill and diligence that should be expected from him or her. The Schedule to the Combined Code states that NEDs should make sure themselves that they do the following:

- After appointment they should undertake appropriate induction (which might be arranged with the advice and assistance of the company secretary). They should also regularly refresh their skills, knowledge and familiarity with the company.
- Where necessary, obtain clarification on the information they receive. If necessary, they should obtain suitable professional advice.
- If they have concerns about the running of the board or a proposed action, they should ensure that these concerns are considered by the board. If the problem is not resolved to the satisfaction of the NED, he or she should ensure that the concerns are recorded in the board minutes, as an official record that the NED raised the issue but was out-voted.
- If the NED resigns and has an unresolved concern on resignation, he or she should provide a statement about the matter to the board.

8.2 Personal risk review

NEDs might be well advised to keep their potential liabilities under continual review, possibly by carrying out a personal risk review regularly throughout their term of office. It might be useful to go through a tick list of items for review.

- Has the NED spent enough time on his or her duties? If not, is it likely that the NED has been negligent in some way?
- Has the NED kept his or her skills and knowledge refreshed?
- Have there been any concerns with financial reporting, narrative reporting or any other information issued by the company?
- Is the NED satisfied that the company remains a going concern?
- Does the company appear to have sound systems for monitoring and controlling risks?
- Are there any regulatory issues involving the company that might expose the NED to legal liability?
- Is the NED satisfied that the company has complied with the provisions of the Combined Code, or that reasons for any non-compliance are justified?

Chapter summary

- NEDs should bring a range of skills and experience to a board of directors and its decision-making process. They might also act as a counter-balance to the power and influence of a strong chairman or CEO.

- In the UK, independent NEDs should make up all or a majority of key board committees, the audit committee, nomination committee and remuneration committee.

- The independence of NEDs is a critical issue. There should be enough independent NEDs on the board for their opinions to carry weight. In the UK, the Combined Code recommends that there should be a senior independent director, to act as an additional channel of communication for institutional shareholders.

- NEDs have been widely criticised for their lack of effectiveness and (in countries such as Germany) for their lack of independence from the persons or organisation they represent. Lack of knowledge about the company and insufficient time to do the job properly have been given as reasons for their frequent ineffectiveness. In the UK, the Combined Code recommends that each new director should receive suitable induction and training.

- Another criticism has been the method of appointment of non-executives, and a belief that many appointments are made within a relatively small circle of senior executives who do not want to make trouble for each other by acting as 'devil's advocate' at board meetings or challenging the chief executive officer. In the UK, the Tyson Committee looked into this problem.

- A NED has a legal obligation to provide a duty of skill and care and could be liable for a breach of this duty. An individual should therefore consider the risks before accepting an appointment as NED and take steps that demonstrate that this duty has been performed properly to an appropriate standard.

Chapter 6

Relations with shareholders

1. The relationship between the board and the shareholders
2. The shareholders
3. Shareholder expectations
4. Regulatory requirements for shareholder involvement
5. The company's relations with its shareholders
6. Electronic communications and electronic voting
7. The role of institutional shareholders in corporate governance
8. Institutional shareholder guidelines

1 The relationship between the board and the shareholders

In listed public companies, the management is separate from the ownership. The shareholders need to rely on management to run the company in the interests of the shareholders. Management in return should be able to rely on the support of the shareholders, particularly where new initiatives, such as a proposed takeover, have to be put to a vote at a general meeting. In practice, however, the relationship between shareholders and management can be difficult. Shareholders might suspect management of either putting their own interests first or being incompetent. Management might suspect shareholders of not understanding the business or not showing enough interest.

At the same time, shareholders can be indifferent to their company boards, often failing to attend general meetings or even submit proxy votes and seeming to show little interest in the company's affairs, apart from the immediate share price and dividend prospects, until something goes wrong.

Relations between the company's board and its shareholders are an important aspect of corporate governance. There are two interrelated issues:

1   From the company's perspective, the directors should recognise that although their legal duties are to the company, the shareholders of the company are its owners. The board should therefore keep the shareholders well informed about what the company is doing.

2   From the shareholders' perspective, only institutional shareholders have the time, as well as the understanding, to monitor the performance of companies and the activities of their boards.

Traditionally, institutional investors have taken the view that if they disapprove of a particular company or its management, they can always sell their shares and invest somewhere else. Another view is that many investments by institutional shareholders may be of a long-term nature. 'Activist' shareholders would argue that, over the long term, companies that are better governed will create more value than those that are badly governed. It is therefore in the interest of institutional investors, and the clients or beneficiaries they represent, to encourage companies to adopt best practices in corporate governance.

1.1 The Combined Code and relations with shareholders

The Combined Code takes the view that good relations between a company and its shareholders are desirable. The responsibility for good relations ought to be shared by the boards of companies and institutional shareholders. The Code therefore has sections on:

- The company's relations with all its shareholders. This section includes not just principles, but also provisions. As with the other provisions in the Code, listed companies should comply with them or explain their non-compliance.
- The responsibilities of institutional investors. This section consists of main principles and supporting principles, but there are no Code provisions. However, the Code is consistent with statements and guidelines issued by the main UK institutional shareholder representative groups.

CASE EXAMPLE 6.1

The shareholders of listed UK company SkyePharma, after successfully ousting the chairman of the board of directors, requisitioned an extraordinary general meeting (EGM) at which a proposal would be made for the installation as new chairman of the nominee of a shareholder group. The shareholders requisitioning the EGM also asked for the suspension of any attempts to break up the company before the new chairman was appointed. The shareholder initiative was led by an activist group, North Atlantic Value (NAV), which claimed the support of 37 per cent of the shareholders.

The board of directors defied the shareholders and their demands. In February 2006, it appointed a new chairman of its own choosing and announced the sale of a US-based subsidiary. NAV accused the directors of 'astonishing arrogance' and stated that it was 'surprised that a board that contains a number of seasoned operators should behave in such a cavalier way towards shareholders. We as shareholders are owners of the company, it is not their company.'

---

2 The shareholders

The potential problems in a relationship between a company board and its shareholders arise largely from their different interests and perceptions. The executive directors are mainly full-time professionals, whose main source of income could well be the company itself. Many have a long-term personal involvement in their company. The shareholders in contrast are a mixture of investors, who can be grouped into the following categories:

- institutional shareholders;
- small private shareholders;
- large private shareholders;
- corporate shareholders.

2.1   Institutional shareholders

Institutional shareholders are organisations that have considerable funds to invest and put a large amount of these into company shares. In the UK, the main institutional investors are pension funds, insurance companies and collective investment institutions such as unit trust funds and open-ended investment companies. Between them, institutional investors hold the majority of shares in UK-listed companies.

Institutional investors do not confine themselves to holding shares in domestic companies. US institutions in particular, and to a lesser extent UK institutions, are extensive investors in shares of companies in other countries, such as in continental Europe. All listed companies will have some shareholders who are foreign institutional investors. The international nature of investment can add to the difficulties of establishing a good relationship between a company and its shareholders.

Some institutional shareholders might choose to 'play the stock market' and buy and sell shares regularly. Although they might be long-term investors in some companies, they might treat other shareholdings as short-term investments. If shareholders come and go regularly, a company's board of directors cannot possibly get to know them or develop a relationship with them.

Another development in recent years has been the activism of some institutions, particularly hedge fund investors in company shares. These institutions might pursue an investment policy of identifying under-valued companies with a view to acquiring a shareholding and then applying pressure on the board of directors for measures to improve the performance and value of the company. This type of institutional investor is significantly different from the more 'traditional' type that might be more prepared to support the company's management and invest for the longer term.

Even when shareholders are long-term investors, their interests might be much more in the financial returns from their investment than in anything that the company does. The relationship between a company and its institutional investors cannot be properly understood without recognising that large institutional investors will hold shares in a large proportion of the major stock market companies, but their shareholding will not often be significant. Since large institutions hold shares in many listed companies, it could be argued perhaps that they cannot show a concern for every company in which they invest. For example, suppose that an institution owns 0.5 per cent of the ordinary share capital of an oil exploration company. The board of directors might be concerned about short- and long-term profitability, long-term supplies of oil and environmental issues. An institutional investor might be much more focused on profits, dividends, growth prospects and the share price.

2.2   Small private shareholders

Some individuals own shares directly. In general, private shareholders hold only small quantities of shares and have very little communication with the company, other than through formal communications from the company. The votes of small shareholders are unlikely to affect the outcome of any shareholder vote at a general meeting of the company, where the block votes of institutional shareholders or large private shareholders carry much more weight. It is easy for a company to overlook the interests of small shareholders, and a corporate governance issue is the extent to which the company should try to establish a relationship with them.

2.3   Large private shareholders

Occasionally, a large proportion of the shares in a company are held by private shareholders. For example, in a company floating its shares on the stock market for the first time, a large proportion of the shares might be held by individuals who were shareholders when the company was private and who might still be executive directors. Family shareholders are another example in companies of which, although listed on a stock market, the original family owners continue to hold a position of influence. Ford is a notable example.

2.4   Corporate shareholders

A significant shareholder in a public company could be another company. Shareholdings by one company in another could be either welcome or a source of concern and mistrust. In some cases, two companies might have cross-shareholdings, so that each holds a block of shares in the other. When cross-shareholdings exist, the companies might have some form of strategic alliance or mutual understanding. In other cases, one company might hold a block of shares in another, possibly with a view to using the investment as a potential base for launching a takeover bid in the future.

2.5   Substantial shareholdings and directors' shareholdings

Public companies must be kept informed of who their main shareholders are. Shareholders are required to notify their company when their shareholding reaches 3 per cent of the issued share capital, and then whenever their shareholding changes by 1 per cent or more, up or down. For example, if a shareholder's interest in the share capital of ABC plc reaches 3 per cent, the company must be notified. The company must then be informed each time there is a change, for example, if the shareholding subsequently rises to 4 per cent or more, or drops below 3 per cent. (For institutions that manage share portfolios for other investors, the notification threshold is 10 per cent of the share capital rather than 3 per cent.)

UK quoted companies are also required to notify the stock market of these changes, so that the market as a whole should be kept aware of increases or reductions in large shareholdings.

The notification of substantial shareholdings is required to conform to the requirements of the Transparency Directive, which came into force in 2007. The Directive requires significant shareholders to disclose changes in their interests in shares in a company when the shareholding crosses a 5 per cent, 10 per cent, 15 per cent, 20 per cent, 25 per cent, 30 per cent, 50 per cent and 75 per cent threshold. However, UK public limited companies are still required to disclose changes in their shareholding when this crosses the 3 per cent threshold, and subsequently changes up or down by each full percentage point. There is no fundamental change UK law for UK companies, although responsibility for enforcing the regulations has been transferred to the FSA.

3 Shareholder expectations

As far as institutional investors are concerned, the most important elements of good corporate governance are:

- accountability of the board of directors to the shareholders;
- an openness in communications by the board with the shareholders; and
- minimising conflicts of interest between the directors and the shareholders by structuring the remuneration package for directors so as to link the size of the reward closely with the achievement of the company's objectives.

The Myners Committee was set up to look into the relationship between listed companies and their investors, and to consider how companies and institutional investors could work more closely together. The committee reported in 2001 and made a number of recommendations. It suggested that the board of a company should have:

- clear objectives;
- a well-formulated strategy for achieving these objectives;
- a financing policy to pay for implementation of the strategy; and
- capital expenditure and revenue plans;

– all of which it communicates annually to institutional investors and brokers.

The board should also arrange regular meetings with the shareholders to discuss long-term issues facing the company. In addition, it should have a clearly defined and articulated policy for the remuneration of executive directors that it also discusses openly with shareholders.

A similar theme was discussed by financial journalist Peter Martin in a Financial Times article in 2002. He suggested that the crisis of US corporate responsibility was a reflection of a breakdown in the 'fundamental bargain' or 'agency relationship' between the professional managers on the board of directors and the company's shareholders. This relationship, which had worked well until recently, allowed the professional management to run the company in the interests of the shareholders, within a framework of:

- board oversight of the management;
- accountability through the company's financial statements;
- a reasonable division of the financial spoils.

The scandals at Enron, WorldCom and other companies had, he argued, undermined confidence in this relationship and its ability to work:

- It had failed to prevent improper activities by senior managers in some companies, and had failed to prevent bad strategic decision-making in others (Ford, Marconi and Vivendi Universal, for example).
- There has been a loss of consensus about what the purpose of a company's annual report and accounts should be. At one time, its main purpose was to allow the shareholders and other investors to assess the value of their company in comparison with other similar companies. Increasingly, however, the accounts of a company have been used for public relations purposes, and 'earnings management' has been seen as a legitimate way of propping up the share price through manipulation of the financial results within the permitted accounting rules.
- With the collapse in share prices and company profits in 2001 and 2002, the division of the spoils between shareholders and professional managers also seemed unfair. Senior executives continued to be rewarded with large bonuses and increases in basic salaries, even though the value of the company had been decimated, and profits had plunged.

An analysis of the relationship between a company and its shareholders might therefore be summarised as follows:

- There is a tacit understanding between shareholders and the board about what shareholders expect and what the board should try to deliver.
- A part of this understanding depends on open communications between the board and its shareholders, either through formal or informal channels.
- If this understanding and openness in communications do not exist, standards of corporate governance will be inadequate.

4 Regulatory requirements for shareholder involvement

To a limited extent, the UK listing regime gives shareholders some rights by obliging a company to keep them informed of certain developments and to obtain shareholder approval for certain transactions. Listed companies are required to provide certain information to the stock market, such as profit warnings, changes in major shareholdings, changes in directors' shareholdings, and so on. In addition, listed companies must obtain prior approval from the shareholders, by vote in a general meeting, for:

- transactions above a certain size, relative to the size of the company; and
- transactions with related parties.

Large transactions for which prior shareholder approval is required are known as Class 1 transactions; these include major takeovers or the disposal of a large part of the company's business operations. Transactions with related parties are transactions outside the normal commercial business operations of the company between the company and a major share-holder or a director, or someone closely associated with a major shareholder or director (such as a relative or business partner). One example of a transaction with a related party is the sale of a company property to one of its directors.

When major transactions or transactions with related parties are planned, the board will have to send out a circular to its shareholders, explaining the reason for the transaction and justifying it, in order to win shareholder approval. In some sense, the company is therefore obliged in these situations to communicate with its shareholders and seek their support.

5 The company's relations with its shareholders

Achieving good relations between a company and its shareholders is desirable, however, on a more regular and established basis. This calls for measures by both the board and the shareholders, particularly the institutional shareholders.

The Combined Code identifies two areas of responsibility for companies:

1 maintaining a dialogue with their institutional shareholders; and
2 making constructive use of the AGM.

5.1 Maintaining a dialogue with institutional shareholders

A principle of the Combined Code is that:

> 'There should be a dialogue with shareholders based on the mutual understanding of objectives. The board as a whole has responsibility for ensuring that a satisfactory dialogue with shareholders takes place.'

Dialogue with institutional shareholders calls for not just regular formal announcements by a company to the stock market generally, but also for regular, informal contact with the larger shareholders in the company. The responsibility for maintaining the dialogue might be shared between the chairman of the board, the CEO and possibly the senior NED.

- Large listed companies have a much more onerous task than smaller listed companies. They have a large number of institutional shareholders. Shares in the largest companies in the UK are held by the majority of institutional investors (and certainly by all institutions that operate index-tracking funds for the UK stock market). For these companies, communicating with institutions is a time-consuming and resource-consuming task. Even so, it would be considered as both necessary and desirable for good corporate governance.
- Smaller companies have fewer institutional shareholders to communicate with, and might not in any case be regarded as a significant investment by the institutions that do hold their shares. Even so, occasional meetings should be arranged, possibly organised by the company's stock market advisers or investment bank.

The Combined Code recognises that for shareholders most contact with a company is contact with the CEO or finance director. However, the chairman (and senior independent director and other directors as appropriate) should maintain enough contact with shareholders to understand their issues and concerns.

The board should keep in touch with shareholder opinion in whatever ways are most suitable. The Code states a number of practical requirements for maintaining dialogue:

- The chairman should ensure that the views of the shareholders are communicated to the board as a whole.
- The chairman should discuss strategy and governance with the major shareholders.
- Non-executive directors should be given the opportunity to attend meetings with major shareholders.
- If requested to attend meetings with major shareholders, NEDs should expect to attend them. (The Combined Code states that companies should offer major shareholders the opportunity to meet newly appointed NEDs, although it is uncertain whether major shareholders will wish to take the opportunity.)
- The senior independent director should attend enough meetings with a range of major shareholders to listen to their views, in order to develop a 'balanced understanding' of their concerns and views.

In the annual report, the board should report on the steps that have been taken to ensure that members of the board, especially the NEDs, develop an understanding of the views of the shareholders, for example through face-to-face meetings, analysts' or brokers' briefings or surveys of shareholder opinion.

5.2   Non-financial reporting and voluntary disclosure

A company's annual report and accounts package are key tools for communicating with shareholders. However, financial reporting is often seen as an opaque and uninformative process, which is not a particularly effective way of disseminating good, accessible information. In an attempt to improve shareholder communications, there is an increasing emphasis on the disclosure of non-financial information, much of it on a voluntary basis. Examples include:

- a letter or statement by the company's chairman and/or CEO, summarising company performance;
- within the EU, quoted companies are required to publish an annual business review;
- an annual sustainability report, or social and environmental report, published as a separate document, whose target audience includes shareholders but is wider.

5.3   Constructive use of the AGM

The UK's Combined Code states that: 'The board should use the AGM to communicate with investors and to encourage their participation'. It suggests that relations with shareholders should be maintained through constructive use of the annual general meeting. The provisions of the Code are concerned mainly with:

- encouraging attendance at the AGM;
- giving shareholders an opportunity to ask questions and to hear about the company during the meeting;
- giving shareholders the opportunity to use their vote and greater openness in voting procedures at the annual general meeting.

The Code provisions are as follows:

- Encouraging attendance. The company should arrange for the notice of the AGM and the related papers to be sent to the shareholders at least 20 working days before the meeting. The minimum notice of a public company AGM required by the Companies Act, is just 21 calendar days.
- Giving shareholders an opportunity to ask questions. The board chairman should arrange for the chairmen of the audit, nomination and remuneration committees to be available to answer questions, and for all directors to attend the AGM.
- Voting procedures. At the AGM, there should be a separate resolution for each substantially separate issue. This requirement is intended to prevent the practice of combining two or more issues, one 'popular' and the other more controversial, into a single resolution. Each issue will then be voted on separately.
- The company should count all proxy votes. An amendment to the Combined Code in 2006 introduced a requirement that proxy voting forms should include a 'vote withheld' box. This is in addition to the 'for' and 'against' boxes for each resolution. The 'vote withheld' box allows shareholders to indicate their displeasure about a company's proposals without actually voting against the resolution in question. However a vote withheld is not a vote in law and so does not count towards the proportion of votes cast in favour of or against a resolution (for the purpose of deciding whether a resolution has been passed or rejected).
- Disclosure of information about proxy votes. After a resolution has been dealt with on a show of hands, the company should indicate the level of proxy votes lodged for and against the resolution, and the number of shares in respect of which there was a specific instruction to withhold a vote. This information should be given at the meeting itself and made available as soon as practicable afterwards on the company's website. By announcing the level of proxy votes, companies will give some recognition to the views of shareholders unable to attend the meeting, and will not be able to pass controversial resolutions simply on a show of hands of shareholders present and attending the meeting.

5.4   Changes introduced by the Companies Act 2006

Under the provisions of the Companies Act 2006, s. 324, all registered shareholders have the right to nominate one or more proxies, with each proxy having the right to attend and speak at general meetings, demand a poll, and vote on any resolution (both in a vote by show of hands and in a poll vote).

The right to appoint more than one proxy, with each proxy representing a different part of the shareholder's total shareholdings, might make it easier for proxies to demand a poll vote on a resolution after the chairman has taken a vote by a show of hands. (This would be consistent with the view of many institutional shareholders, including the Shareholder Voting Working Group, that chairmen of companies should use poll votes rather than voting by show of hands for all resolutions at company meetings.)

The Act also requires quoted companies to make available on their website details of polls taken at their general meetings, although the requirement is to show the number of votes cast in favour for and against the resolution.

6 Electronic communications and electronic voting

For some years, it has been argued that communications between companies and shareholders (both ways) could be improved with greater use of electronic methods, particularly websites and email. Changes in corporate governance practice should be expected to follow changes in everyday practice in both business and personal life. Several reasons have been argued in favour of more electronic communication between a company and its shareholders.

- Companies are able to communicate more effectively with their shareholders and provide a greater range and depth of information more quickly than by using written communications by post. For example, there is a greater probability that information posted by a company on its website or sent by email will be seen by senior managers in an institutional investor organisation, as well as by more junior administrators. If so, senior managers might be encouraged to take a greater interest in votes at company meetings, and to use the institution's voting rights more actively.
- Shareholders might be more willing to participate in voting at general meetings if they are able to submit proxy votes conveniently by email or via the company's website, rather than by voting form and post. (A problem in practice has been that proxy voting forms are often dealt with by relatively junior administrators, who either do not submit a form to the company, or submit a form giving the chairman of the company discretion to use the votes in whatever way he or she chooses.)

There are two differing views about the efficacy of electronic communication. One is that electronic communications will improve the quality of communications between the company and its shareholders, especially as a result of electronic voting. An alternative view is that electronic communications should save a company in printing and postage costs, but will do little to improve the quality and effectiveness of corporate governance.

6.1 UK law on electronic communications

The Electronic Communications Act 2000 legalised 'e-signatures', and the Companies Act 1985 (Electronic Communication) Order 2000 gave companies and shareholders the option of communicating electronically in some instances where communication in writing was previously compulsory.

- A company could seek the agreement of its shareholders to the distribution of certain documents (such as the annual accounts and notices of meetings) by email or by website, rather than in writing.
- Shareholders were also permitted to appoint proxies electronically, by email or fax, to vote on their behalf at general meetings. However, the law did not permit shareholders or their proxies to vote electronically.

However, the changes introduced by this Order meant that companies could only communicate with their shareholders by email or by website if the shareholders gave their specific consent, and supplied an email address to the company.

Companies Act 2006

The Companies Act 2006 has introduced more changes in the rules on electronic communications. The Act permits documents to be sent to or from a company in either hard copy or electronic form, and the company's website can also be used for communication with shareholders.

Companies that do not have authority from their shareholders to use their website to communicate with them must pass a shareholders' resolution or amend their Articles to permit the company to use its website as a default method of communication.

Once companies have the authority to use their website to communicate with shareholders, individual shareholders must now opt out of receiving communications from a company through the company website, rather than opt in to electronic communications. If they do not opt out, a company can assume that they have chosen to receive communications through the website. The company must therefore obtain the agreement of each individual shareholder to this method of communication.

However, if a company adopts a system of electronic communications for shareholders, it is required to notify the shareholders whenever a message has been posted on the website. Oddly, perhaps, this notification to shareholders must currently be sent in hard copy form unless the shareholder has agreed to receive their notification of notices by email or fax therefore be persuaded to provide their email address.

6.2 *ICSA guidelines on electronic communications with shareholders*

The ICSA has issued a Guidance Note, Electronic Communications with Shareholders, most recently updated in 2007. The Guide deals with two broad issues.

1. Guidance on issues relating to the introduction of the Companies Act 2006 provisions on electronic communications.
2. Practical guidelines for best practice in communication in electronic form.

It is recommended best practice that a company should seek shareholder approval, by means of a shareholder resolution or a change in the Articles of Association, if the company intends to make use of the deemed agreement provisions in the Act. These are the provisions that will allow the company to deem that a shareholder has agreed to communication in electronic form if the shareholder does not specifically state that he or she wants communications to be sent in hard copy form.

A shareholder resolution may be an ordinary resolution, whereas a resolution to amend the Articles must be a special resolution. An advantage of changing the Articles is that shareholders can see more clearly the company's practice on electronic communications, and this is likely to reduce the amount of complaints from shareholders and investors.

The Guidance also discusses the need for companies to obtain the consent of new shareholders to communication in electronic form, and the problem that companies cannot deem agreement to electronic communications from shareholders more than once every 12 months. Companies using the deemed agreement provisions should therefore arrange to contact shareholders once a year, probably when notice of the AGM is sent out, so that the deemed agreement provisions can be applied for another year.

The points of Recommended Best Practice in relation to communications in electronic form are largely common sense, and include the following:

- The facility to communicate in electronic form should be offered to all shareholders on equal terms.
- Shareholders should be able to retain a copy of any document or information sent to them in electronic form.
- Any electronic communication sent by a company giving notice of a general meeting and proxy voting should not include any electronic address unless the company intends that this address may be used by shareholders to respond to their communication.
- When information or notifications of availability (of information on the website) are sent out to shareholders, the company should use a system for producing a list of recipients or a total number of messages sent, as 'proof of sending'.
- Shareholders opting to communicate electronically should be warned that if they file an electronic proxy voting form containing a virus, the company will not accept it.
- The company should alert shareholders to the fact that the company's obligation to communicate electronically ends with the transmission of the message, and the company cannot be responsible for failed transmissions that are outside their control. However, in the case of failed transmissions, the company should send a written communication to the shareholder within 48 hours of the failure.

6.3 Initiatives on electronic voting and proxy voting

The current state of electronic voting varies between countries, but in the UK, virtually all shares owned by institutional investors are in electronic form. Shares in UK companies are held on the CREST system. The shares of pension funds and insurance companies are often held by fund management organisations on their behalf; and it is the fund managers rather than the beneficial owners of the shares (i.e. the pension funds or insurance companies) who are legally entitled to vote. The pension funds or insurance companies must therefore instruct the fund manager or custodian of the shares on how to cast proxy votes at company meetings.

There is consequently a complex voting chain whereby institutions might have to cast proxy votes, and the widely used paper-based proxy voting system is known to work inefficiently. It was reported in 2003 that Unilever, the foods and household products group, asked ten of its largest shareholders why they had failed to register all their votes at the company's recent AGM. Three of the shareholders replied that they had voted all their shares held, but that they had been lost in the balloting process and so had not been registered. It was generally accepted that the problem of 'lost votes' could be resolved by electronic voting, with a clear audit trail showing when and how proxy votes have been cast electronically.

Report to the Shareholder Voting Working Group 2005

In November 2005, Paul Myners made an updating report to the Shareholder Voting Working Group entitled 'Review of the Impediments to Voting UK Shares'. The report provided an update on progress in shareholder voting practice, and much of the report dealt with the increase in electronic voting.

- Voting levels by institutional shareholders had increased, and fewer votes were 'getting lost' due to administrative weaknesses.
- Electronic voting by shareholders had increased and was expected to increase further.
- Only two FTSE 100 companies did not allow electronic voting, and these would do so during 2006.
- The report also welcomed the provisions in the proposed Companies Act relating to shareholder voting.
- It also repeated a recommendaton of Mr Myners that votes at general meetings should be taken by means of a poll and not by a show of hands. This recommendation, the report suggested, should be implemented by means of an amendment to the Combined Code.

7 The role of institutional shareholders in corporate governance

7.1 *Expecting companies to comply with best corporate governance practice*

Developing good relations between a company and its shareholders is as much a task for the shareholders as for the board. Institutional investors, as 'professional' shareholders with large investments in public companies, should be particularly responsible for improving the dialogue and conveying the concerns of shareholders to the board.

Institutional shareholders now show active concern for good corporate governance from the companies in which they invest. In the UK, this concern is demonstrated in public largely through the various representative bodies of the institutional investor organisations, particularly the ABI and NAPF. The interests of institutional investors in good corporate governance can be explained as follows:

- Investors expect a return on their investment. Most available evidence suggests that well-governed companies deliver reasonable returns over the long term, and shareholders in these companies are less exposed to downside risk than shareholders in companies that are not so well governed.
- Institutional investors also have legal responsibilities (fiduciary duties) to the individuals on whose behalf they invest. For pension funds, these individuals are the beneficiaries of the funds. In fulfilling their responsibilities, institutions should try to ensure that they make a decent return on investment, and promoting good corporate governance is one way of trying to do this.

7.2 The Combined Code on institutional shareholders

The Combined Code sets out a number of principles relating to the responsibilities of institutional shareholders for ensuring good corporate governance. For institutional investors, however, more significant guidance has been provided by their own professional and voluntary organisations, such as the ABI and NAPF. However, the Combined Code is consistent with the views of the main institutional investor organisations.

The Combined Code on institutional investors has three sets of principles, relating to:

1 dialogue with companies;
2 evaluating the corporate governance disclosures by companies;
3 shareholder voting.

The Combined Code on dialogue with companies

Just as companies should maintain a dialogue with shareholders, so too should institutional shareholders enter into a dialogue with companies 'based on the mutual understanding of objectives'.

The Combined Code on evaluation of corporate governance disclosures

The Code encourages institutional investors to take a reasoned and flexible approach to judging the compliance of companies with corporate governance requirements.

- When evaluating company disclosures on corporate governance, particularly those relating to board structure and composition, institutional shareholders 'should give due weight to all relevant factors drawn to their attention'.
- Institutional shareholders should consider carefully the explanations by companies for any departure from the Combined Code provisions 'and make reasoned judgements in each case'.
- If they do not accept the company's position, they should explain their views in writing to the company, and be prepared to enter a dialogue if necessary.

They should avoid a 'box-ticking' approach to checking compliance with the Code and assessing a company's corporate governance.

In making their evaluation of a company's corporate governance arrangements, institutional investors should bear in mind in particular the size and complexity of the company and the size and nature of the risks that it faces.

The Combined Code on shareholder voting

The Combined Code encourages attendance at AGMs by institutional investors and reasoned use of their votes. The Code states that: 'Institutional investors have a responsibility to make considered use of their votes'.

- They should take steps to ensure that their voting intentions are being translated into practice. (Although the Code does not go into further detail, this supporting principle addresses issues such as the way in which discretionary proxy votes are given and used.)
- On request, institutional shareholders should make available to their clients information on the proportion of resolutions on which votes were cast and non-discretionary proxy votes cast. (The accountability of institutional investors to their clients for the way they have voted is an issue that has been recognised by the institutions' shareholder representative bodies.)
- Major shareholders should attend AGMs 'where appropriate and practicable'. Companies and registrars should facilitate this.

7.3 Shareholder engagement (shareholder activism)

In response to a suggestion that shareholders should be given more extensive rights under company law, a frequent counter-argument is that shareholders already have adequate rights, but do not use them constructively enough. Corporate governance would be improved if shareholders were more active in making their views known to their company, and using their votes against the board of directors if the company failed to respond in a satisfactory way to their concerns.

A number of organisations such as PIRC support shareholder activism, also called shareholder engagement, and draw attention to corporate governance issues where shareholders ought to bring their influence to bear by voting at general meetings. In particular, shareholders could cast their votes against:

- directors standing for re-election at the annual general meeting;
- the reappointment of the company's auditors;
- the directors' remuneration report, including its remuneration policy. (In the UK, it is a legal requirement that shareholders of listed companies should be given the right to vote on this report at the AGM, although this is only an advisory vote and the directors are not required to act on the vote of the shareholders);
- a proposed new remuneration scheme for which the directors are required to obtain shareholder approval.

Shareholder activism attracts publicity. Its potential strength is that it brings pressure to bear on companies from the negative publicity that shareholder opposition to the board can create. It is unlikely in most cases, given current corporate governance practice, that activist shareholders will secure a majority of the votes against a resolution in general meeting. This is because organising opposition to the board would be a time-consuming exercise and a very large number of shareholders would have to give their backing.

CASE EXAMPLE 6.2

There are a number of reported instances where the views of shareholders have led to changes in the boards of major UK companies.

In 2003, institutional investor Fidelity International led a shareholder 'revolt' against the arrangements for the board of the newly merged Carlton Communications and Granada Television companies. As a result of the pressure, Mr Michael Green was ousted as chairman-designate of the company.

In 2004 the supermarket group Sainsbury's announced the appointment of Sir Ian Prosser as deputy chairman of the company, and the future chairman to succeed Sir Peter Davis in 2005, without consulting shareholders beforehand. The negative reaction to the appointment from shareholders and institutions led to the appointment being withdrawn. The Financial Times commented (18 February 2004): 'Though details of the new procedure for finding a deputy chairman have not yet been set, one element looks certain: in the next act of the drama, Sainsbury investors will have a chance to speak their piece before the final script is written'.

In 2007 the board of Photo-Me International, a company operating passport photo booths, came under criticism from activist shareholder Principle Capital Holdings. Principle Capital was dissatisfied with the slow progress of a strategic review by the company, and announced its intention to call an extraordinary general meeting to demand the resignation of four of the company's directors. About one week later, the four directors resigned and the company agreed to announce within six weeks its plans regarding the possible sale of its vending division. Principle Capital withdrew its threat to call an EGM.

CASE EXAMPLE 6.3

There have also been cases where activist shareholders with only a fairly small shareholding in a company have attempted, sometimes with apparent success, to influence the decisions of company management.

In March 2007 confectionery and drinks group Cadbury-Schweppes announced its intention to split the drinks division from the confectionery division, with a view to a possible demerger or a sale of the drinks division. This followed an announcement by the company in February that it had no such plans to split the group.

Some City observers believed that the company management had been pushed into a change of mind by the acquisition of 3 per cent of the company's shares by an activist hedge fund that wanted the company to be split up (although the company denied that it had given way to any pressure).

A leading UK fund manager commented in the Financial Times in June 2007 that the suspicion that Cadbury-Schweppes had given way to activist pressure 'could represent a come-on to every corporate raider and activist investor.'

During 2007, Dutch bank ABN Amro was the target of takeover bids from Barclays Bank and a consortium led by the Royal Bank of Scotland. It was reported that ABN Amro had been forced to break itself up or offer itself for sale as a result of pressure led by The Children's Investment Fund, a 1 per cent shareholder. As the takeover battle progressed, it was also reported in June 2007 that Atticus Capital, holder of a 1 per cent stake in Barclays, had called on the bank to drop its bid for ABN Amro.

Developments such as these raised questions about the extent to which activist investment groups holding a fairly small proportion of the equity shares should be able to bring significant pressure to bear on company management.

7.4   Disclosure of voting by institutional shareholders

The Companies Act 2006 gives the government reserve powers to require institutional shareholders to disclose how they have voted on issues at general meetings of the companies in which they invest.

In April 2007, the fund manager Hermes became the twelfth major UK fund manager to announce that in the next few months it would start to publish its entire voting record at shareholder meetings. This voluntary move is consistent with Investment Management Association (IMA) policy.

7.5   The Myners Committee and relations between companies and institutional investors

Although it is tempting to think of activism as confrontational, it is more appropriate to explain it in terms of encouraging shareholders, institutional shareholders in particular, to have a more active involvement with the companies in which they invest. Active involvement will normally mean supporting the board, constructive dialogues with the board and a considered use of votes at general meetings.

The Myners Committee's 2001 report suggested that in an ideal world, the board of a company would have:

- clear objectives for the company;
- a well-formulated strategy for achieving these objectives;
- a financing policy to pay for implementation of the strategy; and
- capital expenditure and revenue plans;

– all of which it communicates annually to institutional investors and brokers.

The board should also arrange regular meetings with the shareholders to discuss long-term issues facing the company. In addition, it should have a clearly defined and articulated policy for the remuneration of executive directors that it also discusses openly with shareholders.

Paul Myners criticised the lack of activism among institutional investors, favouring government regulation to force institutions to take involvement with their companies more seriously. He wrote:

'In the world we now face, an ever-higher premium is likely to be placed on efficiency and flexibility. This review's conclusion is that our present structures fall short on both counts. In short, it finds that savers' money is too often being invested in ways that do not maximise their interests. It is likely to follow too that capital is being inefficiently allocated in the economy. This report therefore sets out a blueprint for change. At the heart of it is a belief that clear incentives and tougher customer pressures need to be driven throughout the savings and investment industry.'

7.6 Practical difficulties with shareholder activism

A problem for effective shareholder activism is that powers over a company are held by the board of directors, not by the shareholders. In the face of a continuing refusal by the board to listen to their concerns, shareholders can only make their opposition felt by voting against the board's proposals at general meetings. To do this successfully, they need a majority of the votes. Since most shareholders in large public companies hold a relatively small percentage of the total number of shares, organising a group of dissident shareholders into a voting majority is extremely difficult, if not impossible. A campaign to organise an 'anti' or 'no' vote might be undertaken by a leading shareholder (or by an organisation such as PIRC) but examples of dissident shareholders winning votes at general meetings are rare.

7.7 The interests of small shareholders

The interests of small shareholders are often overlooked in reporting on company relationships with their shareholders, and attention is usually focused on institutional shareholder interests. The UK Shareholders Association (UKSA) is a non-profit-making group established to represent the views of non-institutional shareholders. It suggests that not only are many companies managed more for the benefit of managers than in the interests of shareholders, but also that institutional investors can act in a way that is contrary to the interests of the small shareholder. When difficulties arise in particular companies the UKSA might establish a small shareholder action group, or give an established action group its support.

CASE EXAMPLE 6.4

Examples of informal pressure by shareholders resulting in changes in a company's governance are often reported in the financial press.

A number of individuals have resigned as chairman or CEO of struggling companies, where shareholder confidence in the individual had eroded. For example, in October 2002, the chief executive of MyTravel, the UK's largest tour operator, resigned following profits warnings that angered investors. Other companies affected during 2001 and 2002 have included British Telecommunications (both chairman and CEO resigned), Royal and Sun Alliance (CEO resigned), Rolls Royce and Cable and Wireless (chairman).

In 2002, for example, it was reported that Prudential Assurance, having devised proposals for a remuneration policy for its directors, was persuaded to re-think its proposals due to shareholder concerns. Vodafone consulted shareholders about a new executive remuneration package after shareholder dissatisfaction in the previous two years.

Following pressure from institutional investors, Six Continents demerged its hotels business from its pubs and restaurants business, and returned £700 million in cash to shareholders. The UK government was persuaded to offer compensation to shareholders in Railtrack after the company had been forced into administration (with suspicions of government influence in the matter).

Case Example 6.5

In January 2007 the share listing of Torex Retail plc was suspended, making it difficult for shareholders to sell their shares in the company. The company was in financial difficulties and was highly geared. Following changes to the board, it became apparent that the company was up for sale and some private equity firms expressed an interest in buying parts of its business. The UKSA established an action group to represent the interests of small shareholders in the company, fearful that these might be ignored in any dealing leading to a break-up of the company.

---

8 Institutional shareholder guidelines

The main guidance on corporate governance and shareholder activism is provided to institutional investors by their various representative bodies, which in the UK include:

- the Association of British Insurers (ABI);
- the National Association of Pension Funds (NAPF);
- the Institutional Shareholders Committee (ISC), a joint body representing the largest institutional investor associations in the UK: the Association of British Insurers, the National Association of Pension Funds, the Association of Investment Trust Companies and the Investment Management Association.

8.1 ISC Statement of Principles

In 2002, the ISC published a statement of principles on the responsibilities of institutional shareholders and their agents, the fund managers, as they should be applied to UK listed companies. This Statement of Principles was reviewed and revised in 2007. It can be seen as a statement on shareholder activism, or 'shareholder engagement'. The introduction to the statement comments:

'The policies of engagement set out below do not constitute an obligation to micro-manage the affairs of investee companies, but rather relate to procedures designed to ensure that shareholders derive value from their investments by dealing effectively with concerns over under-performance. Nor do they preclude a decision to sell a holding, where this is the most effective response to such concerns.'

Setting out policy on the discharge of responsibilities

Institutional investors and their agents should have a clear statement of their policy on engagement and how they will discharge the responsibilities they assume. The responsibilities should address each of the following matters:

- how investee companies will be monitored. For monitoring to be effective, there should be an active dialogue with the company's board and senior management;
- the policy for meeting an investee company's board and senior management;
- how situations where institutional shareholders have a conflict of interest will be minimised or dealt with;
- the strategy on intervention;
- an indication of the circumstances when further action might be taken and what the nature of that action might be;
- the policy on voting.

Institutional shareholders and their agents (fund managers) should agree which of them should discharge these responsibilities and make arrangements for agents to report back.

Monitoring performance

Institutional shareholders and/or their agents will review annual reports and accounts, circulars issued by companies and general meeting resolutions. They may attend general meetings where they may raise questions. Investee companies will also be monitored to decide when and if it is necessary to enter into an active dialogue with its board and senior management. Monitoring may require sharing information with other shareholders or their agents, and agreeing a common course of action. The monitoring process should include measures to obtain satisfaction that the company's board of directors and sub-committees are effective, and that the NEDs have 'adequate oversight'.

Institutional investors must remain aware that if they become too involved in the affairs of a company and too knowledgeable (i.e. in receipt of information that has not been publicly disclosed), they could become insiders. As insiders they would be restricted from dealing in the company's shares under the insider dealing legislation (Criminal Justice Act 1993) or market abuse legislation (Financial Services and Markets Act 2000).

'In summary, institutional shareholders ... will endeavour to identify problems at an early stage to minimise any loss in shareholder value. If they have concerns and do not propose to sell their holdings, they will seek to ensure that the appropriate members of the investee company's board are made aware of them. It may not be sufficient just to inform the Chairman and/or Chief Executive. However, institutional shareholders ... may not wish to be made insiders. Institutional shareholders ... will expect investee companies to ensure that information that could affect their ability to deal in the shares of the company is not conveyed to them without their agreement.'

Intervention

Effective monitoring of investee companies will enable institutional investors to exercise their votes, and if necessary intervene, in an informed way. Institutional investors should set out the circumstances in which they will actively intervene, which might be in connection with concerns about:

- strategy;
- the company's operational performance;
- the company's acquisitions or disposals strategy;
- a failure by the NEDs to hold executive management properly to account;
- a failure of internal controls;
- inadequate remuneration policy/packages;
- inadequate succession planning; or
- the company's approach to corporate social responsibility.

Institutional shareholders should vote all their shares at general meetings. They should not automatically support the board, and if they have been unable to obtain a resolution of their concern, they should either abstain or vote against the appropriate resolution. It is good practice to notify the company about this voting intention in advance, giving the reasons why.

Evaluating and reporting

Institutional shareholders should monitor and evaluate the effects of their engagement (activism). Their agents (fund managers) should report regularly to their clients (institutional investors) giving details on how they have discharged their responsibilities.

This initiative by the ISC was seen in 2002 as an attempt by institutional investors to avoid legislation by the government compelling them to become more active in exercising their shareholder rights. The head of investment affairs at the ABI was reported to have commented, with respect to voting against the board of directors if they did not respond to shareholder concerns: 'We will have a red card in the pocket and we will not be afraid to use it. Clearly, we hope this will focus minds on improving shareholder value.'

8.3 ABI guidelines

The following principles are included in the ABI's guidelines to its members:

- Shareholders should be concerned about the composition and structure of the board of directors and should support the role played by non-executive directors and the creation of remuneration, audit and nomination committees.
- Shareholders should practise responsible voting. Responsible voting is defined as the application of informed decisions about how to vote, within the framework of a

'considered' corporate governance policy. This policy should be based on the principles and provisions in the Combined Code. As a guiding rule, the board of directors should be given positive support by shareholders, unless there are reasons for voting against any particular resolution. In other words, the starting premise is that the board should be given strong support unless there are clear reasons for opposition. The ABI argued that positive support from institutional shareholders over a period of time should alert the board to the importance of retaining and maintaining this support and should make the board concerned whenever this support is not given on any particular issue. The guidelines also recommend that whenever an institutional investor judges it appropriate to vote against a resolution at a general meeting, it is important if possible to let the company know in advance. This will give time for the problem to be considered by the board and for consultations to take place before the vote.

- Although shareholders are recommended to support the board of directors, the ABI guidelines also suggest that they should also be ready to defend their rights and interests. Shareholders should support incentive schemes for executives, but within prudent limits that avoid excessive dilution of the earnings of existing shareholders. Performance-related incentive schemes that align the interests of the executives and the shareholders are favoured. The guidelines also express concern about arrangements that provide for excessive amounts of new shares to be issued by a company to persons other than existing shareholders, for example under share option schemes. Members are recommended to oppose any resolution by a company that would give the directors authority to issue new shares except by way of a rights issue, where the number of new 'non-rights issue' shares would exceed a certain limit. The limit is set at 5 per cent of the issued share capital in any one year and 7.5 per cent of the issued share capital over any rolling three-year period.

8.4   ICGN guidelines for members

In 2003, the International Corporate Governance Network (www.icgn.org), a group of major international institutional investors, published a similar statement on the responsibilities of institutional investors. This statement was reviewed and amended in 2006. A significant feature of ICGN policy pronouncements arises from the fact that the ICGN is an organisation of global investment institutions, and its policy guidelines apply to the activities of its members in all countries in which they invest.

The ICGN statement is compatible with the more detailed corporate governance practices in different countries. It comments:

'High standards of corporate governance will make boards properly accountable to shareholders for the companies they manage on their behalf. They will also help investee companies to make decisions and manage risks to deliver sustainable and growing value over time. Pursuit of high standards of governance is therefore an integral part of institutions' fiduciary obligations to generate value for beneficiaries.'

Corporate governance considerations should therefore be integrated within the investment process by investment institutions. The general benefits from higher standards of corporate governance will only accrue over time if all investment institutions play an appropriate part.

The aim of the involvement in investee companies by investment institutions should be the preservation and growth of the long-term value of the companies in which they invest. Appropriate actions for discharging their responsibilities might be:

- Voting. Responsible shareholders should make use of their voting rights.
- Maintaining constructive dialogue with the board on governance policies and practices in general.
- Supporting the company in respect of good corporate governance.
- Having a clear approach for dealing with situations where dialogue has been a failure, such as:
  - expressing specific concerns to the board, either directly or in shareholders' meetings;
  - making a public statement;
  - submitting proposals for inclusion on the agenda of a general meeting;
  - submitting a nominee for appointment to the board;
  - convening a shareholders' meeting;
  - forming an alliance with other investment organisations, either in general or in specific cases;
  - taking legal action.

The ICGN considers that showing concern about good corporate governance is a key issue and a responsibility to vote is a major aspect of this.

> 'Voting is not an end in itself but an essential means of ensuring that boards are accountable .... Institutions should therefore seek to vote their shares in a considered way ... They should develop and publish a voting policy so that beneficiaries and investee companies can understand what criteria have been used to reach decisions.'

The ICGN statement concludes with the view that institutional investors should follow up on any corporate governance concerns they might have with individual companies, and that such concerns might relate to:

- transparency and the performance of the company;
- board structures and procedures;
- shareholder rights.

8.5 Responsible voting

The meaning of responsible voting is well defined in a joint statement (1999) by the Association of British Insurers and the National Association of Pension Funds.

> 'Responsible voting involves the application of informed decisions reached within the framework of considered corporate governance policy.'

Institutional shareholders should support the board of directors unless they have good reason not to. When a shareholder thinks that it should vote against the board, it should first make representations to the board in time for the problem to be considered, with a view to reaching a satisfactory solution.

The ABI and NAPF guidelines to their members support the principle of responsible voting, and these organisations also liaise closely with members through their respective voting (advisory) services.

Chapter summary

- Relations between a company and its shareholders can be poor, particularly when there is a lack of meaningful communication and dialogue.

- A company might have a majority shareholder, and/or a mix of institutional shareholders and other shareholders. Other shareholders might be corporates or private individuals, and large or small shareholders. The interests and concerns of each type of shareholder, and their relations with the company, will differ.

- Regulations exist for listed companies with regard to the notification of changes in shareholdings of significant shareholders and directors and to the requirement of the company to obtain prior shareholder approval for major transactions. These regulations provide some basis for the need to establish communications and relationships between the company and its shareholders.

- Companies should make efforts to improve communications with shareholders. In the UK, the Combined Code encourages companies to enter into constructive dialogue with their institutional shareholders and to use the AGM to communicate with smaller private shareholders.

- The Combined Code also encourages institutional investors to enter into constructive dialogue with the companies in which they invest. Associations of institutional investors encourage their members to use responsible voting, generally giving support to the board of directors.

- Shareholder activism might be encouraged to bring pressure to bear on companies to pay greater attention to the wishes and concerns of their shareholders. Activism might involve voting against resolutions at general meetings, such as resolutions for the re-election of directors retiring by rotation.

Chapter 7

Financial reporting and auditing

1. Financial reporting and corporate governance
2. Misleading financial statements
3. The role of the external auditors: the audit report
4. Auditor independence
5. Financial reporting: directors' duties and responsibilities
6. Additional reporting by companies
7. The audit committee

1 Financial reporting and corporate governance

The annual report and accounts of a company (and the interim financial statements of a listed company) are the principal way in which the directors make themselves accountable to the shareholders. The financial statements present a report on the financial performance of the company over the previous financial year and the financial position of the company as at the end of that year. The directors' report and other statements that are published in the same document provide supporting information, much of it in narrative form rather than in numbers. Shareholders and other investors use the information in the annual report and accounts to assess the stewardship of the directors and the financial health of the company.

It is an important document for corporate governance because it is a means by which the directors are made accountable to the shareholders, and provides a channel of communication from directors to shareholders. The report and accounts enable the shareholders to assess how well the company has been governed and managed. It should therefore be:

*   clear and understandable to a reader with reasonable financial awareness; and
*   reliable and 'believable'.

The reliability of the annual report and accounts depends on several factors:

*   The honesty of the company in preparing them: if allowed to do so by accounting regulations, companies might indulge in 'window dressing' of their financial performance or financial position through the use of accounting policies (methods) that hide the true position of the company.
*   The care used by directors to satisfy themselves that the financial statements do give a 'true and fair view' and that everything of relevance has been properly reported

- The opinion of the external auditors, which the shareholders should be able to rely on as an objective and professional opinion.

So-called aggressive accounting policies might be permissible within existing accountancy regulations and standards, and accepted by the company's external auditors. Nevertheless, they have the effect of hiding information from shareholders, at least in the short term. The financial performance of a company for the current financial year might be flattered by using certain accounting policies, but in the longer term (say, in one or two years' time) the 'bad news' will eventually emerge.

Trustworthy financial reporting and auditing is probably the most significant issue for corporate governance. Good corporate governance should ensure that financial reporting is reliable and honest, and that the opinion of the external auditors is objective and unbiased.

1.1 Financial reporting and investor confidence

As we saw in Chapter 1, the Cadbury Committee was set up as a direct consequence of concerns about the quality of financial reporting in the UK and the ability of the auditing profession to provide sufficient assurances to the investment community about the reliability of company financial statements. Similar concerns were expressed in the US during the stock market depression of 2002. If investors have doubts about the honesty or transparency of financial reporting, they will hold back from investing, and share values will suffer as a result.

The problem also extends to the corporate bond markets. Many companies have borrowed heavily by issuing bonds to investors. Bond investors rely on bond credit ratings in making their investment decisions. Investors are unlikely to purchase a company's bonds unless they have been rated for creditworthiness by at least one, and more usually two, top ratings agencies. In the US, the top three agencies are Moody's, Standard & Poor's and Fitch, which have the status of nationally recognised statistical ratings organisations (NRSROs).

The US crisis of investor confidence about financial reporting in mid-2002 brought the role of the credit rating agencies into question. The agencies defended themselves publicly against allegations that they failed to identify the financial problems in companies such as Enron, when they should have been much more alert and in a position to forewarn investors about companies that were getting into financial difficulties.

When a company proposes to issue new bonds, a ratings agency carries out an investigation and then gives a rating to the bonds. The interest rate the company has to offer on the bonds will depend on the rating awarded. After the bonds have been issued, the ratings agencies review the rating continually and adjust it if the financial condition of the company either improves or worsens.

Bond investors therefore use the ratings agencies as 'gatekeepers to the financial markets'. Their decisions whether or not to invest in bonds, and the rate of interest they require for doing so, depend on the judgement of the agencies.

However, the ratings agencies themselves rely on honest financial reporting from the companies they monitor. They are not experts in identifying accounting fraud or dubious accounting practices. The chairman of Moody's has commented (Financial Times, 23 July 2002) that in spite of the need to review their ratings methods in the wake of the Enron collapse: 'We still do not believe that we are going to be in a position systematically to detect fraud. Full and fair financial disclosure is critical to us to do our jobs, just as it is critical for many others in the market to do their jobs.' Standard & Poor's similarly defended the credit ratings it gave to Parmalat bonds before the company's collapse in December 2003 on the grounds that it had relied on audited financial statements for much of its information.

The point to note about credit ratings agencies is that the reliability of financial reporting has consequences for bond markets as well as equity markets, i.e. for the capital markets as a whole.

1.2   Responsibilities of the directors for financial reporting

There is often confusion and misunderstanding about responsibilities for financial reporting, because it might be assumed that the external auditors are responsible for the 'true and fair view' in the financial statements. If financial statements are produced that are misleading and incorrect, it might therefore be assumed that the auditors have been negligent and must be to blame. This view is incorrect. The directors are responsible for the financial statements: they prepare the financial statements and have the primary responsibility for the reliability of the information they provide.

- Management and the directors are therefore responsible for identifying and correcting any errors or misrepresentations in the financial satatements.
- The responsibility of the external auditors is to obtain reasonable assurance, in their professional opinion, that the financial statements are free from material error or misstatement.

The Combined Code states that the directors should explain in the annual report and accounts their responsibility for preparing the financial statements, and they should also report that the business is a going concern 'with supporting assumptions or qualifications as necessary'.

It is not the primary responsibility of the external auditors to detect fraud, although the external audit might act as a deterrent to fraud. The auditors might also discover fraud during the course of their audit work.

An area for dispute, however, is whether the auditors ought to be able to identify fraud or a significant error during the course of their audit work, whenever a fraud or error occurs. Although they are not responsible for the financial statements, it can be argued that a failure by the auditors to discover a fraud or material error might be the result of professional negligence. If they are negligent, they should be held liable to the company and its shareholders. Uncertainty about the extent to which auditors might be held liable for professional negligence has led to new rules in the Companies Act 2006 that enable companies to limit auditor liability.

CASE EXAMPLE 7.1

When WorldCom announced its $3.8 billion accounting fraud, its auditors Andersen tried to lay the blame squarely on the company's chief financial officer, who had, Andersen claimed, withheld important information from them, preventing them from carrying out their audit properly. The fraud had been discovered by an internal auditor of the company in a routine audit check, and not one of the external audit team. The Financial Times commented in an editorial (27 June 2002) that the practice of expenses manipulation is well known to accountants, and found it 'astonishing' that Andersen should try to pass all the blame to the chief financial officer. 'What is the purpose of an audit if it is not to ask about hefty transfers in the accounts?'

CASE EXAMPLE 7.2

In 2006 PricewaterhouseCoopers in the UK was fined £495,000 by the Accountants' Joint Disciplinary Scheme (JDS), and ordered to pay £1 million in costs, as a result of audit failures by Coopers & Lybrand in connection with the collapse of the engineering company TransTec in 1999. This was the second highest penalty ever in the UK against an accountancy firm. (The highest penalty ever in the UK was a fine on Coopers & Lybrand in 1999 for its audit work on companies in the business empire of Robert Maxwell.)

Coopers & Lybrand were found to have placed too much reliance on what they were told by the company's management, and their audit procedures had been inadequate. A number of senior executives of TransTec had colluded to conceal from the company's full board of directors and the auditors some critical information about debit notes issued to the company by Ford. The auditors had not spotted the fraud, although they had been misled.

The JDS concluded that the audit form had 'failed to carry out adequate audit procedures in relation to the debit notes, including investigating conflicting explanations as to what the debit notes were ... In the 1998 audit they did not clearly express their own concerns and so did not find fault with the management.'

In 2003, a DTI report into the collapse of TransTec had found that the collapse of the company was due to 'fundamental failings of executive leadership exacerbated by poor corporate governance'.

In view of the JDS report, it is worth remembering perhaps that the original cause of concerns in the UK during the 1980s about poor corporate governance was poor corporate leadership and inadequate auditing, resulting in unreliable corporate financial reporting and, ultimately, the collapse of several major companies.

2 Misleading financial statements

There are three ways in which published financial statements could be misleading:

1   There could be a fraudulent misrepresentation of the affairs of the company, where the company's management deliberately presents a false picture of the financial position and performance.

2   The company might use accounting policies whereby it presents its reported position and profits more favourably than would be the case if more conservative accounting policies were used.

3   The financial statements could be complex and difficult for investors to understand. It is a relatively easy matter for accountants, particularly in companies whose business is itself quite complex, to present financial statements in a way that readers will find difficult to comprehend properly.

It is recognised that some companies on occasion might want to report strong growth in revenues and profits, or even to improve the look of its balance sheet by 'hiding' debts or other liabilities. A company can probably succeed in presenting an excessively favourable picture of its performance for a number of years, particularly when the economy is strong and business is growing. Eventually, however, it will become impossible to 'massage' the figures any further. Unless the business can sustain a strong 'real' growth in its operations, it cannot achieve strong profits growth indefinitely. Eventually, a company that uses 'creative accounting' methods will have to report declining profits.

Improving the reported financial position, at least in the short term, shows the board of directors in a favourable light, and helps to boost the share price. Individual directors could therefore stand to benefit from higher annual bonuses and more valuable share options.

The worldwide falls in stock markets, particularly in 2002, were prompted to a large extent not simply by concerns about the financial collapse of companies such as Enron and WorldCom. A number of other major US corporations reported serious financial problems, and the investment community, not surprisingly, wanted to know why some of the largest companies in the world faced financial collapse without any hint of problems being evident in their published financial statements.

Having lost confidence in the reliability of financial statements, investors lost faith in equities as an investment, and share prices tumbled.

2.1 Ways of improving financial reports

There are several ways in which a company might improve its reported financial position or reported performance. The methods used might sometimes be deliberately incorrect. More often, a company might use accounting policies that are acceptable to the auditors, but succeed in giving a more flattering picture of the company's position.

- A company might claim to earn revenue and profits earlier than it probably should. For example, a company that enters into a three-year contract that will earn £12 million in total might try to claim all the revenue of £12 million in the first year instead of spreading the revenue over the three-year life of the contract.

- A company might try to take debts off its balance sheet. This can sometimes be achieved by means of setting up separate companies, sometimes referred to as 'special purpose vehicles'.
- A company might try to disguise money from loans as operating income, to increase its reported cash flow from operating activities.

It is probably useful to look at a selection of reported examples of investor concerns about financial statements and company announcements. All are from the period of stock market turmoil during mid-2002. In each of these examples, concerns about the accuracy of financial reporting helped to undermine investor confidence in companies, because the financial report and accounts remain the principal method of communication between a public company and the investment community. If the report and accounts can't be trusted, what can?

CASE EXAMPLE 7.3

In June 2002, US telecommunications group Qwest Communications ousted its CEO, partly over concerns about the reliability of the company's financial statements. In July, the company disclosed that it had incorrectly accounted for large amounts of revenue over the past three years. Apparently, the company had recorded millions of dollars of income at the end of each quarter that should properly have been attributed to the next quarter. In this way, the company reported revenue and profits before they properly occurred. It was suspected that the company manipulated the accounts because it was under pressure from the investment community to reach certain revenue and profit targets for each quarter. In addition, the company's new auditors were investigating the company's accounting policies for over $1 billion of 'swap transactions', in which the company bought and re-sold network capacity to the same companies, thereby boosting reported revenues. It was questionable whether these swap transactions were genuine business transactions, or simply a ruse for increasing reported revenues.

CASE EXAMPLE 7.4

In June 2002, US telecommunications company WorldCom announced a huge $3.8 billion accounting fraud. The Justice Department launched a criminal investigation, and the announcement by WorldCom, following the collapse of Enron and reported accounting problems with other US corporations, triggered a loss of confidence by the investment community in the stock markets. The Chairman of the Securities and Exchange Commission, Harvey Pitt, responded to the WorldCom announcement by saying that chief executives and chief financial officers would now be personally liable for the accuracy of the information in their company's accounts and could go to prison if the financial statements were fraudulent. Instead of charging the expenses against profits, the cost had therefore been capitalised and reported as assets in the balance sheet, even though no assets existed. Another consequence of this fraud was that the company's reported cash flows looked much better than they actually were. Investment analysts judged the strength of the cash flows of telecommunications companies according to the cash generated by their business operations, and disregarded cash spent on capital expenditure, which was seen as necessary for growing capital-intensive businesses such as WorldCom. By reporting running costs as capital expenditure, the company therefore improved the look of its cash flows by $3.8 billion. The nature of the fraud was apparently quite simple. WorldCom had incurred running costs of $3.8 billion

3   The role of the external auditors: the audit report

Investors, creditors and other stakeholders in a company rely on the information contained in the annual report and accounts, which are audited each year by a firm of independent auditors. The purpose of an independent audit is to make sure, as far as reasonably possible, that the financial statements are objective and can be relied on.

After completing their annual audit, the auditors are required to prepare a report to the shareholders of the company. (This is included in the published report and accounts of public companies.) The audit report has two main purposes:

1   to give an expert and independent opinion about whether the financial statements give a true and fair view of the financial position of the company as at the end of the financial year covered by the report, and of its financial performance during the year;
2   to give an expert and independent opinion on whether the financial statements comply with the relevant laws.

Auditors of listed companies are also required to review the company's compliance with the Combined Code, and to obtain evidence to support the company's statement (in the annual report and accounts) of its compliance with the Code.

3.1   The purpose of the external audit

The purpose of the audit report is to give users of a company's financial statements some reassurance that the information in the statements is believable. Users of accounts want reassurance that there has not been any fraud or error. 'Fraud' is intentional; 'error' is unintentional and results in:

- incorrect use of accounting policies;
- omissions of fact; or
- misinterpretation of fact.

3.2　Responsibility for detecting fraud and error

As indicated earlier, there is a popular misconception that the auditor is responsible for detecting fraud or error in a company's financial statements. This is not the case.

- The management of the company has the responsibility for preventing and detecting fraud and error. This is achieved by implementing an adequate system of accounting and internal controls.
- The auditor has no responsibility for detecting fraud or error. However, the auditor will assess the risk or possibility that fraud or error might have caused the financial statements to be materially misleading. The auditor should therefore design audit procedures that will provide reasonable reassurance that material fraud or error has not occurred, and that the financial statements give a true and fair view of the company's financial position and performance.

No matter how well an audit is planned and carried out, there will always be some risk that fraud or error has occurred but not been detected. Given the nature of auditing, for which there is only a limited amount of time and resources, and which is carried out through a process of sampling and testing, it would be impossible to ensure that all errors are detected. Accounting systems and internal control procedures are also vulnerable to fraud and error, arising for example from:

- criminal collusion between employees; or
- decisions by management to override the system of controls.

3.3　The liability of auditors for negligence

Auditors are potentially liable to shareholders and others who suffer loss as a result of negligence in carrying out an audit. Negligence would arise from failure to comply properly with professional audit guidelines, and from a failure to carry out the audit with due skill, care, diligence and expedition.

Auditors are not liable to shareholders and lenders to a company if the company suffers a financial collapse and becomes insolvent, unless negligence can be shown. However, audit firms have argued that they are unfairly targeted by shareholders of collapsed companies because they are seen as having pockets that are deep enough to pay large sums of money in compensation. For example, Equitable Life, the life assurance organisation, brought an action against auditors Ernst and Young, claiming compensation for negligent audit work. The action failed in 2005, but Ernst and Young had faced the threat of a potentially huge liability if the case had gone against them.

3.4　Liability limitation agreements

The Companies Act 2006, ss. 534–8 introduced some important new rules on auditors' liability for negligence, breach of duty or breach of trust in connection with the conduct of the audit. Shareholders of both public and private companies can vote by ordinary resolution to limit the potential liability of the external auditors, by means of a liability limitation agreement (LLA).

The main features of the rules in the 2006 Act are as follows:

- Shareholder approval for the LLA may be obtained either before or after the company has entered into the agreement with the auditors. (Private companies may resolve to waive the need for shareholder approval.)
- An LLA with the auditors must be disclosed in the annual report and accounts.
- An LLA is only valid if it applies to acts or omissions by the auditors in the course of one audit for one financial year.
- An LLA cannot limit the liability of the auditors to an amount that is less than what is fair and reasonable in the circumstances, having regard to the circumstances and the professional standards expected from the auditors.
- The limit on the auditors' liability might be expressed as a sum of money, a formula or a proportion of any loss suffered by the company, having regard to the auditors' liability for such loss.

The audit profession expressed its concern that when a legal action is brought against a collapsed company, the court might decide that it is reasonable for the auditors to compensate for the entire loss suffered by the company, on the grounds that only the auditors had enough money to cover the cost of the losses incurred. The Act therefore states that in considering what is fair and reasonable in the circumstances, the court should have no regard to the possibility or otherwise of recovering compensation from other persons who are jointly or partly responsible for the loss that has been incurred.

The scope and format of auditor liability agreements is currently being addressed by a Financial Reporting Council (FRC) working party.

3.5   Criminal liability of auditors for recklessness

Although the 2006 Act provides the possibility of some protection for auditors against liability for negligence or breach of duty with LLAs, it also introduced two new criminal offences for auditors in connection with the auditors' report (s. 507). It is a criminal offence, punishable by a fine, knowingly or recklessly to cause an audit report to:

- 'include any matter that is misleading, false or deceptive in any material particular', or
- omit a statement that is required by certain specified sections of the Act.

It is too early to know at this stage whether the introduction of these criminal offences will make the auditors more cautious about the audit opinion they give in their audit report.

3.6   The audit report

The audit report itself provides only limited information to shareholders, even though shareholders often assume that an unqualified audit report means that the financial statements of the company are accurate and reliable.

Unqualified opinion

An unqualified audit report is given when the auditor believes that the accounts give a true and fair view of the company's financial position and performance. The wording of an unqualified audit report is usually fairly standard, although reports are longer for public companies (where the auditors might also report on some corporate governance statements) and differ between countries.

The framework of an audit report for a company might be as follows:

To the shareholders of ABC Company

We have audited the accompanying balance sheet of ABC Company as of 31 December 20XX and the related statements of income and cash flows for the year then ended.

Respective responsibilities of directors and auditors

The financial statements are the responsibility of the Company's management. Our responsibility is to express an opinion on these financial statements based on our audit.

Basis of opinion

We conducted our audit in accordance with International Standards on Auditing (or the report might refer to the relevant national auditing standards). Those Standards require that we plan and perform the audit to obtain reasonable assurance about whether the financial statements are free of material misstatement. An audit includes examining, on a test basis, evidence supporting the amounts and the disclosures in the financial statements. An audit also includes assessing the accounting principles used and significant estimates made by management, as well as evaluating the overall financial statement presentation. We believe that our audit provides a reasonable basis for our opinion.

Opinion

In our opinion, the financial statements give a true and fair view of (or 'present fairly in all material respects') the financial position of the Company as of 31 December 20XX, and of the results of its operations and its cash flows for the year then ended in accordance with [the international accounting standards or relevant national accounting standards] and comply with [relevant national statutes or regulations].

Auditor signature and name (and address)

Date

An audit report is occasionally not unqualified, but 'modified' by a qualified opinion, a disclaimer or an adverse opinion.

Qualified opinion

A qualified opinion is an opinion in which the auditor believes the financial statements give a true and fair view, except for a particular matter. However, the disagreement of the auditors with the company's management is not so great as to justify a disclaimer or an adverse opinion. For example, the auditors might state that they have been unable to check by a physical count the inventory quantities at a particular location, and have accepted the company's inventory records as being sufficiently accurate. If the amount of inventory involved is unlikely to be large, a qualified audit opinion should be sufficient.

Disclaimer of opinion

A disclaimer of opinion is a refusal by the auditor to give an opinion on a particular item in the financial statements. A disclaimer is appropriate where the auditor has been unable to obtain sufficient audit evidence, and the amount involved could be material. A disclaimer of opinion might state:

> 'Because of the possible effect of the limitation in the evidence available to us, we are unable to form an opinion as to whether the financial statements give a true and fair view ... and whether the statements have been prepared in accordance with [the relevant legislation].'

Adverse opinion

An adverse opinion is the most negative type of modified audit report. This is given when there is a disagreement between the auditors and the company's management, and the auditor believes that the financial statements are misleading or incomplete in a material or pervasive way. An adverse audit opinion will make a statement such as:

> 'In our opinion, because of the effects of the matters discussed in the preceding paragraph, the financial statements do not give a true and fair view of the financial position of the Company as at 31 December 20XX, and of the results of its operations and its cash flows for the year then ended'

Modified audit opinions are quite rare, and adverse opinions are the least common form of modified opinion. In practice, public companies will normally expect to have an unqualified audit report. As a result, investors might assume that the company's financial statements are trustworthy. If the financial statements turn out to be misleading, investors may suppose that either:

- the auditors failed to do their job properly, because they should have spotted the problem and provided a modified audit opinion; or
- the auditors are too close to management and have lost their independence, so that they were unwilling to provide a modified audit opinion.

3.7   Suggested improvements in the audit report

The Audit Quality Forum (AQF) is a working group on audit reporting, set up by the ICAEW to consider whether the wording of audit reports meets shareholder expectations. In 2007, the AQF issued a paper 'Fundamentals – Auditor Reporting'. The paper recognised that audits are becoming a commodity service and do not provide much meaningful information to investors. Investors would probably like to see more information about the issues that were considered by the auditors in making their judgements and reaching their audit opinion.

The paper made recommendations for the short term:

- The opinion paragraph in the audit report should adopt as soon as possible the wording and structure in s. 495(3) of the Companies Act 2006, regardless of when this provision in the Act actually comes into force. This opinion paragraph will be in three parts: the audit report must state clearly whether in the auditor's opinion the accounts:
  - give a true and clear view;
  - have been prepared in accordance with the relevant financial reporting framework; and
  - have been prepared in accordance with the requirements of the Companies Act 2006.
- There should also be a positive statement that proper accounting records have been kept.
- There should be a positive statement that there are no matters the auditors wish to draw to the attention by way of emphasis, without qualifying the audit report.
- The report should be made easier to read by moving the opinion paragraph to the front and moving most of the standard 'boilerplate' text to the back or to an appendix.

The paper also made some proposals for the longer term. It suggested that the requirements in the Combined Code for disclosures by the audit committee could be reviewed and amended, so that audit committees would be expected to include more specific information in their report to shareholders about key issues and significant accounting and reporting matters that were discussed with the auditors as a result of the audit.

3.8   Auditors' liability to third parties

The auditors have a legal duty of care to the company and its shareholders. There is some doubt as to whether they might also have a duty of care to other parties. In the UK, the extent of auditor liability to external parties has been tested in two legal cases.

CASE EXAMPLE 7.5

Caparo and Bannerman

In Caparo Industries plc v Dickman and others [1990], it was held by the House of Lords that auditors did not owe a duty of care in audit reports to third parties that they did not know at the time. The auditors of a company had negligently audited its accounts, and as a result the company reported a profit of £1.2 million instead of a loss of £400,000. Replying on these accounts, the respondents in the case made a successful takeover bid for the company. They subsequently brought an action against the auditors for breach of duty of care and skill. In ruling in the auditors' favour, the House of Lords held that there was no liability, since the auditors did not owe a duty of care to a member of the public. Their duty was simply to the company and its shareholders.

As a result of the *Caparo* case, it was considered that the auditors of a company did not hold a duty of care to any third party, until the subject came up for consideration again in the Royal Bank of Scotland v Bannerman Johnstone Maclay [2002]. This was a case in the Scottish courts, and so was not binding on English courts, but it drew from leading English court cases and so is considered to have significant legal implications for England and Wales as well as Scotland. In this case, Bannerman were the auditors of a company that arranged an overdraft facility with the bank. The overdraft facility letter between the bank and the company contained a requirement for the company to send the bank a copy of its audited annual accounts at the end of each year. In 1998, the company went into receivership owing over £13 million to the bank, which claimed that due to fraud, the accounts for the previous year were materially incorrect and the auditors were negligent. The bank also claimed that it had relied on the auditors' unqualified opinion to continue providing the overdraft facility to the company. In its defence, the audit firm claimed that it had no duty of care to the bank. The judge ruled that although there had been no direct contact between the audit firm and the bank, the auditors would have known about the facility letter. The knowledge they would have gained during the course of their audit work was therefore sufficient, in the absence of any disclaimer, to create a duty of care to the bank. In the judge's view, the absence of a disclaimer was a crucial feature of the case.

In response to the outcome of the Bannerman case, PriceWaterhouseCoopers decided to include a disclaimer of liability to third parties using its audit reports. In January 2003, the Institute of Chartered Accountants in England and Wales recommended the inclusion of a disclaimer in audit reports.

A disclaimer within the audit report might be worded as follows:

'Our report is made solely to the company's members, as a body, in accordance with of the Companies Act 2006. To the fullest extent permitted by law, we will not accept or assume responsibility to anyone, other than the company and the company's members as a body, for our audit work, for the audit report or for the opinions we form.'

4 Auditor independence

The external auditor should be independent of the client company so that the audit opinion will not be influenced by the relationship between the auditor and the company. The auditors are expected to give an unbiased and honest professional opinion to the shareholders about the financial statements. An unqualified audit report is often seen by investors as a 'clean bill of health' for the company. However, doubts have been expressed about the independence of the external auditors. It might be argued that unless suitable corporate governance measures are in place, a firm of auditors might reach opinions and judgements that are heavily influenced by their wish to maintain good relations with the management of a client company.

4.1 Ethics and the accounting profession

Like other professionals, qualified accountants are expected by their professional body to act with integrity and honesty, and to follow a code of ethics in the work they do. However, there can be pressures on accountants to ignore ethical considerations and to allow their judgement to be affected by other considerations. These pressures might apply to both accountants in industry and those in the profession acting as auditors.

In the UK, the Ethical Standards Board (ESB) recognised the conflict faced by some accountants between their responsibilities to their company and their responsibilities as accountants to act in the public interest. In a consultation paper published in 2002, the ESB gave several examples of such conflict:

- 'An accountant employed as a finance director may be under considerable pressure, when preparing accounting statements, to ensure that reported results meet pre-determined expectations or, in the case of public sector entities, to conform with cash limits, by selecting inappropriate accounting policies or unduly stretching judgements as to what is acceptable when forming accounting estimates.'
- 'An accountant employed in a corporate tax department may become involved in a tax planning scheme that crosses the boundary that separates tax avoidance from tax evasion.'

4.2 Threats to auditor independence

Perhaps the most significant threat to auditor independence is that the audit firm relies on the company's management to secure its appointment and reappointment as the company's auditor. Although some public companies have given greater responsibility for appointing the auditors to the audit committee (see section 6), the opinions of senior management are often decisive in the matter of auditor selection. The auditor is therefore reliant for future audit work from the company on the views of the management whose financial statements it is their job to audit. In addition, the audit firm has to rely extensively on management for the information and explanations needed to enable them to carry out their audit work. The UK's Ethical Standards Board has commented about this situation that: 'Any reasonable and informed third party – for example, a shareholder – is likely to regard this as a significant threat to the auditor's objectivity.'

Professional guidelines are given to auditors by national and international accountancy bodies, notably the International Federation of Accountants (IFAC). The IFAC Code of Ethics for Professional Accountants identifies certain ways in which the integrity, objectivity and independence of the auditors might be put at risk.

- An audit firm should not have to rely on a single company for a large proportion of its total fee income, because undue dependence on a single audit client could impair objectivity. IFAC does not specify what amounts to 'undue dependence' on a single client. However, in the UK, the rules of the Association of Chartered Certified Accountants (ACCA) state that the fee income from a single audit client should not exceed 15 per cent of the gross annual income of the audit practice.
- A risk to objectivity and independence arises when the audit firm or anyone closely associated with it (such as an audit partner) has a mutual business interest with the company or any of its officers. Similarly, objectivity could be threatened when there is a close personal relationship between a member of the audit firm and an employee of the company.
- The audit firm should not have a client company in which a partner holds a significant number of shares.
- The IFAC Code does not have any objection in principle to an audit firm providing non-audit services (such as consultancy services) to a client, although the auditor should not perform any management functions in a company nor take any management decisions.

CASE EXAMPLE 7.6

Energy corporation Enron, which had been one of the largest corporations in the world by stock market value, collapsed towards the end of 2001. In January 2002, the company's auditor, Andersen, announced that its employees had shredded documents relating to Enron after it had received a subpoena from the Securities and Exchange Commission in November 2001. This announcement was part of a chain of events that led to Andersen being prosecuted for its role in the Enron affair.

In June 2002, Andersen was found guilty by a US court of obstructing justice during investigations into the collapse of Enron. The Enron scandal and the alleged role of Andersen prompted moves in both the US and the UK to review accounting and auditing standards. The successful prosecution of Andersen also added fuel to speculation that the accountancy profession would face a shake-up, and that self-regulation by the accountancy profession was likely to give way to some form of governmental regulation.

4.3   Auditing and the public interest

In the UK, it has been recognised that the accountancy profession should be required to recognise the public interest when formulating its codes of conduct, and issuing guidelines and regulations to its members. The 'public interest' is seen as a rational balance between public opinion and rational expectations. The UK Ethical Standards Board has written:

'ESB believes that the public interest cannot be determined without reference to public opinion: correctly identifying the public interest involves forming a balanced view of public opinion, taking account of both what the public are reasonably entitled to expect and what accountants can reasonably be asked to deliver.'

The main recent areas of debate about how to ensure auditor independence have been:

- whether auditors should be prevented from carrying out non-audit work for clients, or whether the amount of non-audit work they do should be restricted;
- whether there should be a regular rotation of either the audit firm or the audit partner and other senior members of the audit team.

4.4 Non-audit work for a client by an audit firm

The codes of conduct of national professional accountancy bodies are similar to the IFAC Code, and lack any clear restrictions on the performance of non-audit work for an audit client.

Suggestions for regulatory measures to ensure auditor independence have included proposals to restrict the amount of non-audit work, or the type of non-audit work, that the firm of auditors is permitted to carry out for a client company. Non-audit work might include:

- consultancy on taxation issues, for example helping a group of companies to minimise tax liabilities by setting up subsidiaries in countries with a low-tax regime;
- investigating targets for a potential takeover bid;
- helping a company to construct a bid for a major government contract;
- providing advice and expert assistance on IT systems;
- internal audit services;
- valuation and actuarial services;
- services relating to litigation;
- services relating to recruitment and remuneration.

The main problem with auditors doing non-audit work is that when the firm audits transactions recommended by its consultancy arm, it is unlikely to take an independent view.

The risk to auditor objectivity and independence from carrying out non-audit work became apparent in the wake of the Enron collapse. Arthur Andersen were the auditors of Enron, and in the financial year prior to the company's collapse in 2001, Andersen earned more fee income from non-audit work than from audit work. The audit firm was suspected of failing to carry out a proper audit of the company, with two main reasons being suggested:

1   It was claimed that the audit firm would have been reluctant to question the accounts of Enron because it would risk losing not just the audit work but also the substantial non-audit fee income.
2   In addition, it was suggested that since the information in the company's financial statements reflected the non-audit consultancy advice given by the audit firm, the firm's auditors would be unlikely to challenge the fairness and accuracy of the statements. In other words, Andersen's auditors would not challenge the opinions of Andersen's consultants.

Audit firms have denied that fees from non-audit work will affect their independence, arguing that the individuals who work as consultants for a client company, for example on IT projects, are not the same individuals who work on the company audit. Even so, activist shareholder groups continue to challenge this assertion.

Companies (Disclosure of Auditor Remuneration) Regulations 2005

In the UK, the Companies (Disclosure of Auditor Remuneration) Regulations 2005 came into force on 1 October 2005. The purpose of the regulations is to give shareholders (and others) information that can be used to make a judgement about whether the provision of non-audit services is a threat to a company auditor's objectivity or independence.

Previously, companies have been required to publish only the aggregate amount paid to their auditor for non-audit services. The new regulations require a company to use a standard categorisation (definition of services) of the non-audit services it has purchased from its auditor (and associates of the auditor). Disclosure will be required in the notes to the accounts.

Small and medium-sized enterprises (SMEs) are not covered by the disclosure requirements.

Low-balling

Low-balling is a term used to describe the alleged practice by auditors of pricing the cost of audit work at a loss-making amount in order to win consultancy business at much higher and lucrative fee rates. The problem with this is that the auditor becomes dependent on the consultancy work for its profits, and the audit work is seen as being of lesser importance. When this attitude prevails, the independence of the auditor could be put at risk.

4.5   Approaches to the regulation of non-audit work

There are three broad approaches to the regulation of non-audit work by audit firms:

1   There could be no restrictions at all on non-audit work by the audit firm. Some audit firms have argued that they have already separated their audit partnerships from their consultancy partnerships, and the risk to auditor independence from non-audit work is therefore receding. In 2002, for example, most of the big accountancy firms separated their audit practice from their consultancy practice. A problem with this argument is that there is nothing to prevent the audit side of the business from developing a new consultancy arm. This has actually happened, and all the 'big four' firms now have consultancy practices again.

2   There should be a total prohibition on non-audit work for a corporate client by the audit firm. The large audit firms have argued that this would be an unreasonable and unnecessary restriction.

3   There should be a partial prohibition on non-audit work for a corporate client by the audit firm. This could take either of two forms. There could be a prohibition on audit firms from taking on certain types of consultancy work where their independence as auditors could be put at risk, for example tax planning advice work. However, audit firms would be free to carry out other types of non-audit work. The second approach to restricting non-audit work would be to set a limit on the amount of fees

an audit firm could earn from non-audit work, expressed perhaps as a proportion of the fees it earns from the audit. For example, a limit might be imposed restricting non-audit fees to, say, 50 per cent of the fees from the audit work.

The difficulty with a partial restriction on non-audit work is that rules would have to be devised and agreed as to what permissible and non-permissible non-audit work should be, or what the maximum amount of non-audit fee income should be.

4.6 Rotation of audit firm or audit partner

Whilst recognising the importance of auditor independence, there has been disagreement about the extent to which regulatory measures should be imposed.

Audit firm rotation

One suggestion is that there should be a rotation of auditors, whereby the auditors of a company should be replaced by another firm after a given number of years. Rotation would enhance auditor independence because a firm of auditors would have little to gain by going along with the wishes of the client company, and carrying out a less than rigorous audit, if it knows that it will soon lose the audit work anyway. The work of outgoing auditors would also be subject to review – and criticism – by the firm of auditors taking their place.

Rotation of audit partners

An argument put forward by the major accountancy firms is that the requirement for rotation should apply not to the firm of auditors, but to the individual partner of a firm in charge of the audit. For example, it might be acceptable for ABC Corporation to retain the services of Ernst & Young indefinitely, provided that the partner in charge of the company audit is replaced every, say, five or seven years. Supporters of this argument claim that the independence of the auditor is threatened by the personal relationship an audit partner builds up with the client company.

In the case of large companies, there is also an argument for a regular rotation of other senior audit managers, as well as the lead partner.

A counter-argument is that audit partner rotation would not have prevented the problem that arose between audit firm Andersen and its clients Enron and WorldCom. Although Andersen as a whole was not over-dependent on Enron as a client, the company was a vital client for the firm's Houston office, which carried out the audit. Similarly, the Andersen office in Jackson, Mississippi was heavily dependent on the work that it did for WorldCom. To prevent loss of audit independence, audit partner rotation would almost certainly have been ineffective, whereas audit firm rotation might have been much more effective.

EU 8th Company Law Directive

The 8th Company Law Directive on the statutory audit of annual accounts was approved in 2005. It must be implemented in the national law of EU member states by 29 June 2008 and the UK government intends to implement the requirements of the Directive during April 2008.

In its approved form, the Directive includes a requirement that companies should rotate the key partner of their audit firm at least every seven years in order to ensure independent scrutiny by the auditors.

4.7 Directorships for former auditors

Yet another potential threat to auditor independence is the practice whereby public companies appoint a former auditor to their board, as chief financial officer/finance director. It could be reasoned that if an auditor sees the possibility of a lucrative promotion to the board of a major public company, he or she will do nothing to threaten the relationship he or she has with the management of the company.

A suggestion for countering this risk is that public companies should not be allowed to appoint a former auditor of the company to the board for at least two years after the individual concerned has left the audit firm.

5 Financial reporting: directors' duties and responsibilities

It is important to remember that the company's directors are responsible for the preparation and content of the financial statements. The directors of a company have certain legal duties with regard to financial reporting.

- They have a duty to prepare annual company accounts and, in the case of a parent company, consolidated accounts for the group (Companies Act 2006, ss. 394 and 399). The accounts must be approved by the board and signed on behalf of the board by a director.
- They have a duty to prepare a directors' report, which must also be approved by the board and signed on its behalf by a director or the company secretary (ss. 415 and 419). Unless the company is subject to the small companies' regime, the directors' report must contain a business review (s. 417). The business review is described in more detail in Chapter 8.
- The directors of a quoted company have a duty to prepare a directors' remuneration report, which must be approved by the board and signed on its behalf by a director or the company secretary (ss. 420–2).
- These accounts and reports of a public company must be laid before the shareholders in general meeting (s. 437) and the shareholders of a quoted company must be invited to approve the directors' remuneration report (s. 439).
- In respect of each financial year the directors must file with the Registrar of Companies a copy of the annual accounts, the directors' report, the auditors' report and, in the case of quoted companies, the directors' remuneration report (s. 441).

The Combined Code places additional requirements and responsibilities on the directors with regard to financial reporting, and states that the financial reports should be balanced and understandable.

- 'The board should present a balanced and understandable assessment of the company's position and prospects. 'This requirement applies not only to the statutory financial reports, but also to interim reports, other price-sensitive reports and reports to the regulators.

- The directors should explain in the annual report their responsibility for preparing the accounts.
- The auditors must provide a statement about their reporting responsibilities.
- The directors should also report that the business is a going concern. This requirement is also included in the UK Listing Rules, which require listed companies incorporated in the UK to include in the annual report and accounts a statement by the directors that the business is a going concern, 'with supporting assumptions or qualifications as necessary'. This statement should be reviewed by the auditors before publication.

A typical statement of directors' responsibilities for a UK listed company might be as follows:

'The directors are required by company law to prepare financial statements for each accounting period that give a true and fair view of the company and group as at the end of the period and the profit or loss of the group for that period.

The directors confirm that appropriate accounting policies have been used and applied consistently, and reasonable and prudent judgements and estimates have been made in the preparation of the accounts for the year ended [date]. The directors also confirm that applicable accounting standards have been followed, any material departures being disclosed and explained in the notes to the financial statements, and that the financial statements have been prepared on the going concern basis.

The directors are responsible for ensuring proper accounting records are kept which disclose with reasonable accuracy at any time the financial position of the company and the group and which enable them to comply with the Companies Act. They are also responsible for taking steps to safeguard the assets of the company and the group and to prevent and detect fraud and other irregularities.'

Having made such a statement of responsibilities, the directors must also accept liabilities arising out of a failure to carry them out.

Going concern statement

In the context of corporate governance, an important part of the corporate governance report of UK listed companies is the going concern statement. This is a statement by the directors that the company is a going concern, and will be for the next twelve months. If, for any reason, the company subsequently suffers financial collapse, each director could be liable to anyone suffering a loss (e.g. shareholders, bond-holders, lending banks) having relied on that statement.

A typical going concern statement within a corporate report might be as follows:

'The directors, on the basis of current financial projections and facilities available, have a reasonable expectation that the company and group have adequate resources to continue in operational existence for the foreseeable future. The directors accordingly continue to adopt the going concern basis in the preparation of the group's financial statement.'

6 Additional reporting by companies

This chapter has concentrated on the annual report and financial statements and the annual audit of companies. It should be remembered that listed companies are also required to issue additional reports by the Disclosure and Transparency Rules of the FSA. These rules were amended from 2007 by the introduction of the requirements of the EU Transparency Directive.

Listed companies are required to issue an interim financial statement for the first six months of the financial year. This is not audited.

Companies are also required to announce to the stock market relevant information affecting their business (for example, a profits warning). This information must be issued to the stock market through a Regulated Information Service.

The Transparency Directive has introduced reqirements for listed companies that do not publish quarterly reports. Companies are now required to issue two interim management statements, one during the first half and the other during the second half of the financial year. These should include information on trading performance, financial position and any major transactions or events that have occurred during the relevant period.

For a listed company whose financial year begins on 1 January, the timetable of reporting requirements is as follows. (2008 requirements re-occur in every subsequent year.)

Accounting year report 2007/2008

- 1st interim management statement / Not required / No sooner than 10 weeks after 1 January and no later than 6 weeks before 30 June.
- Half-yearly report / By end of September 2007 (within 90 days of the end of the half year) / By end of August 2007 (within 60 days of the end of the half year).
- 2nd interim management statement / Not required / No sooner than 10 weeks after 1 July and no later than 6 weeks before 31 December.
- Annual report and accounts / By end of June 2008 (within six months of the year end) / By end of April 2009 (within four months of the year end).

Voluntary disclosure

Increasingly, listed companies are providing a range of information with their annual report and accounts above and beyond the statutory and regulatory requirements. The voluntary disclosure of non-financial information, for example sustainability reporting is covered in more detail in Chapter 8.

7 The audit committee

As stated above, the Combined Code requires a board of directors to present a balanced and understandable assessment of the company's position and prospects. The Code also requires the board to maintain a sound system of internal control (see Chapter 10). A further principle (C.3) is that the board should establish formal and transparent arrangements for:

- considering how they should apply the financial reporting and internal control principles; and
- maintaining an appropriate relationship with the company's auditors.

Formal and transparent arrangements can be put in place by setting up an audit committee, which should be a sub-committee of the board of directors. It is now a well-established principle of good corporate governance in the US and UK that companies' extensive responsibilities should be delegated to this committee.

Listed companies will be required by law to have an audit committee when the requirements of the EU 8th Company Law directive are implemented in 2008. However, the detailed responsibilities of an audit committee in the UK have been established by the Combined Code and Smith Guidance.

7.1   Role and responsibilities of the audit committee

According to the Combined Code, the main roles of an audit committee should be:

- to monitor the integrity of the company's financial statements and any formal announcements relating to the company's financial performance. In doing so, it should review 'significant financial judgements' that these statements and announcements contain;
- to review the company's internal financial controls;
- unless the role is assigned to a separate board risk committee, or taken on by the full board, to review the company's internal control and risk management systems;
- to monitor and review the effectiveness of the company's internal audit function;
- to make recommendations to the board in relation to the appointment, reappointment or removal of the company's external auditors, for putting to the shareholders for approval in general meeting of the company;
- to approve the remuneration and terms of engagement of the external auditors;
- to review and monitor the independence and objectivity of the external auditors, and also the effectiveness of the audit process, taking into account relevant UK professional and regulatory requirements;
- to develop and implement the company's policy on using the external auditors to provide non-audit services. This should take into account any relevant external ethical guidance on the subject. The committee should report to the board, identifying actions or improvements that are needed and recommending the steps to be taken.

A separate section of the annual report (an audit committee report) should describe the work of the audit committee. This 'puts the spotlight on the audit committee and gives it an authority that it might otherwise lack' (Smith Guidance).

Other provisions in the Combined Code elaborate on the responsibilities of the audit committee. In addition, guidance on audit committees is provided in the Smith Guidance, which is annexed to the Combined Code and based on the recommendations of the Smith Report. The Smith Report was published in January 2003 (at the same time as the Higgs Report) by a committee set up by the FRC to consider the role of audit committees. The Smith Guidance is reproduced in full in Appendix 6.

The Smith Guidance on the responsibilities of the audit committee

The Smith Guidance (see Appendix 6) makes the following comments about the role and responsibilities of the audit committee:

- The audit committee arrangements within each company need to be proportionate to the task, and will differ according to the size, complexity and risk profile of the company.
- All the board directors have a duty to act in the best interests of the company, but the audit committee has a particular role, 'acting independently from the executive, to ensure that the interests of shareholders are properly protected in relation to financial reporting and internal control'.
- The principle of the unitary board is not affected by the creation of an audit committee. All directors are equally responsible in law for the company's affairs. The audit committee is a committee of the board, and any disagreement within the board, including disagreement between the audit committee members, should be resolved at board level.
- Where there are disagreements between the audit committee and the rest of the board that cannot be resolved, the audit committee should have the right to report the issue to the shareholders as part of the report to shareholders on its activities.
- The company's management is under an obligation to make sure that the audit committee is kept properly informed and should take the initiative in providing the committee with information, instead of waiting to be asked. The executive directors should also have regard to their common law duty to provide all directors, including the audit committee members, with all the information they need to discharge their duties as directors of the company. This guidance is crucial. The audit committee can only do its work properly if it is kept properly informed by the executive management.)
- The core functions of the audit committee are concerned with 'oversight', 'assessment' and 'review' of other functions and systems in the company. It is not the committee's duty to carry out those functions; for example, management remains responsible for preparing the financial statements and the auditors remain responsible for preparing the audit plan and carrying out the audit.
- However, the high-level oversight function can sometimes lead to more detailed work. The Smith Guidance gives as an example a situation where the audit committee are unhappy with the explanations of management and the auditors about a particular financial reporting decision, 'there may be no alternative but to grapple with the detail and perhaps seek independent advice'.
- For groups, the audit committee of the parent company will usually have to review activities relating to subsidiaries within the group. The board of the parent company must ensure that there is adequate cooperation within the group to allow the audit committee of the parent company to do its job properly.
- The board should decide just what the role of the audit committee should be, and the terms of reference should be tailored to the company's particular circumstances. However, the audit committee should review its terms of reference and effectiveness annually, and recommend any necessary changes to the board. The board should also review the effectiveness of the audit committee annually.

7.2 Composition of the audit committee

The Combined Code states that an audit committee should consist of at least three members (or at least two members in the case of smaller companies, outside the FTSE 350). All its members should be independent NEDs. The Smith Guidance adds that:

- the chairman of the company should not be a member of the committee, and appointments to the committee should be made to the board on the recommendation of the nomination committee (if there is one), in consultation with the audit committee chairman;
- appointments should be for a period of up to three years, extendable by no more than two additional three-year periods, and provided that the committee members remain independent during that time.

The Code also states that the board should satisfy itself that at least one member of the committee has recent and relevant financial experience. The Smith Guidance adds that it is desirable that this person should have a professional qualification from one of the professional accountancy bodies. The degree of financial literacy required from the other committee members will vary according to the nature of the company.

The Higgs Guidance adds that, as a matter of good practice, the company secretary should act as secretary to the audit committee.

Remuneration, induction and training of committee members

The Smith Guidance adds that the audit committees have wide-ranging and time-consuming work to do, and companies must make the necessary resources available. This includes making suitable payments to the members of the audit committee, in view of the responsibilities they have and the time they must commit to the work. The amount of remuneration paid to the audit committee members should take account of the remuneration paid to other members of the board. The committee chairman's responsibilities and time commitments will normally be greater than those of the other committee members, and this should be reflected in his or her remuneration.

The committee should have the support of the company secretary and should have access to the services of the company's secretariat.

Audit committee members must also be given suitable induction and training. Ongoing training should include keeping the committee members up to date on developments in financial reporting and related company law. It may, for example, include understanding financial statements, the application of particular accounting standards, the regulatory framework for the company's business, the role of internal and external auditing, and risk management. Both induction and training can take various forms, including attendance at formal courses and conferences, internal company talks and seminars and briefings by external advisers.

Audit committee meetings

The audit committee chairman should decide the timing and frequency of committee meetings, in consultation with the company secretary, and there should be as many meetings as the role and responsibilities of the committee require. The Smith Guidance (notes 2.7–2.10) suggests that:

- There should be no fewer than three committee meetings each year, timed to coin cide with key dates in the financial reporting and audit calendar. For example, meetings might be held when the audit plans are available for review and when interim statements, preliminary announcements and the full annual report are near completion. Most audit committee chairmen will probably want to call meetings more frequently.
- Sufficient time should be allowed between audit committee meetings and meetings of the main board to allow any work arising out of the committee meeting to be carried out and reported to the board as appropriate.
- Only the audit committee chairman and members are entitled to attend meetings of the committee. It is for the committee to decide whether other individuals should be invited to attend for a particular meeting or a particular agenda item. It is expected that the audit lead partner and the company's finance director will be invited regularly to attend meetings.
- At least once a year, the audit committee should meet the external and internal auditors without management being present, to discuss matters relating to its responsibilities and issues arising from the audit.

7.3   Financial reporting and the role of the audit committee

The Combined Code emphasises that it is the responsibility of management, not the audit committee, to prepare complete and accurate financial statements. It is the responsibility of the audit committee to review the significant financial reporting issues and judgements that are made in connection with these statements:

- The audit committee should consider significant accounting policies used to prepare the statements, and any changes to them, and any significant estimates or judgements on which the statements have been based.
- Management should inform the committee about the methods they have used to account for significant or unusual transactions, where the accounting treatment is open to different approaches.
- Taking the external auditors' views into consideration, the committee should consider whether the company has adopted appropriate accounting policies and made appropriate estimates and judgements.
- The committee should also consider the clarity and completeness of the disclosures in the financial statements.

If the committee is not satisfied with any aspect of the proposed financial reporting by the company, it should report its views to the board (Smith Guidance).

The committee should also review related information presented with the financial statements, including the business review and the corporate governance statements relating to audit and risk management.

7.4   Responsibility of the audit committee for internal audit

Another Combined Code requirement is that the audit committee should monitor the effectiveness of the company's internal audit activities. If the company does not have an internal audit function:

- the committee should consider annually whether there is a need for an internal audit function and make a recommendation to the board, and
- the absence of an internal audit function should be explained in the relevant section of the annual report.

7.5 Appointment, reappointment or removal of the external auditors

The audit committee is the body responsible for oversight of the company's relations with its external auditors (Smith Guidance).

The Combined Code states that the audit committee has the primary responsibility for making a recommendation to the board on the appointment, reappointment or removal of the external auditors. If the board does not accept this recommendation, it should:

- include in the annual report, and in any papers recommending the appointment or reappointment of the auditors, a statement from the audit committee explaining its recommendation, and
- giving the reasons why the board has taken a different position (Code provision C 3.6).

If the audit committee recommends to the board that new external auditors should be selected, the committee should 'oversee' the selection process (Smith Guidance, note 4.15). The committee's recommendation should be based on the following assessments:

- the qualification and expertise of the auditors;
- the resources of the auditors;
- the independence of the auditors;
- the effectiveness of the audit process.

The assessment should cover all aspects of the audit service provided by the audit firm, and in carrying out the assessment the committee should obtain from the audit firm a report on its own internal quality control procedures (Smith Guidance).

If the external auditors resign, the audit committee should investigate the issues that gave rise to the resignation, and consider whether any action is needed.

Terms and remuneration of the auditors

The audit committee should approve the terms of engagement of the external auditors and the remuneration to be paid to the auditors for their audit services. (Note: the committee should approve the terms and remuneration, but is not required to negotiate them itself.) It should satisfy itself that the amount of the fee payable for the audit services is appropriate, and that an effective audit can be carried out for such a fee. The fee should not be too large, but neither should it be too low. A low audit fee creates a risk that the audit might be of an inadequate scope or quality.

The committee should review and agree the engagement letter issued by the external auditors at the start of each audit, to make sure that it has been updated to reflect any changes in circumstances since the previous year.

The committee should also review the scope of the audit with the auditor. If it is not satisfied that the proposed scope is adequate, the committee should arrange for additional audit work to be undertaken (Smith Guidance).

7.6   Audit committee responsibilities with regard to the independence of the auditors

The Combined Code also gives the audit committee the responsibility for monitoring and ensuring the independence of the external auditors. If the external auditors provide non-audit services to the company, the annual report should explain how auditor independence and objectivity are safeguarded.

The audit committee should have procedures for ensuring the independence and objectivity of the external auditors annually (Smith Guidance). The Smith Guidance suggests various measures for the committee to take:

- The committee should seek reassurance that the auditors and their staff have no family, financial, employment, investment or business relationship with the company (other than in the normal course of business).
- The committee should seek from the audit firm, annually, information about the firm's policies and processes for maintaining independence and monitoring compliance with relevant requirements, such as those regarding the rotation of audit partners and staff.
- The committee should agree with the board the company's policy on employing former employees of the external auditor. Particular attention should be given to the company's policy on former employees of the auditor who were members of the audit team and then moved directly to the company. This policy should be drafted, and the audit committee should monitor its application. The committee should monitor the number of former employees of the external auditor who now hold senior positions within the company, and consider in the light of their findings whether there may be some impairment (or appearance of impairment) in the auditors' judgement and independence with regard to the audit.
- The committee should monitor the audit firm's compliance with ethical guidance in the UK about the rotation of audit partners, and the level of fees the company pays as a proportion of the overall fee income of (i) the firm, (ii) the office of the firm responsible for the audit and (iii) the audit partner.
- The audit committee should develop and recommend to the board the company's policy in relation to the provision of non-audit services by the external auditors. The committee's objective should be to ensure that the provision of such services does not impair the independence or objectivity of the auditors.

7.7   Provision of non-audit services: factors for the committee to consider

A claim made after the Enron collapse in the US was that its external auditors, particularly the Houston office of the partnership, relied too heavily on the company for income from non-audit work, and as a consequence compromised their independence. An issue in corporate governance is therefore the extent to which the external auditors should be permitted to take on non-audit work from a company for which they are the external auditors. The

Combined Code gives the responsibility for monitoring this situation and developing the company's policy on the provision of non-audit services by the external auditor. The audit committee should consider:

- whether the skills and experience of the audit firm make it a suitable supplier of the non-audit services;
- whether there are safeguards in place for ensuring that there would be no threat to the objectivity and independence of the auditors arising from the provision of these services;
- the nature of the non-audit services and the fees for these services;
- the level of fees for individual non-audit services and the fees in aggregate for these services, relative to the size of the audit fee;
- the criteria governing the compensation of the individuals who perform the audit.

The audit committee should set and apply a formal policy specifying the types of non-audit work:

- from which the external auditors are excluded;
- for which the external auditors can be engaged without referral to the audit committee;
- for which a case-by-case decision is necessary. In these cases, it may be appropriate to give a general pre-approval for certain classes of work, subject to a fee limit decided by the audit committee and ratified by the board. If the external auditor subsequently provides any of these services, the engagement of the auditors should then be ratified at the next audit committee meeting.

The policy may also set fee limits generally or for particular classes of non-audit work.

In deciding its policy on the provision of non-audit work by the external auditors, the committee should take into account relevant ethical guidance, but a guiding set of principles should be that the external auditor should not be engaged for non-audit work if the result is that:

- the external auditor audits work done by itself;
- the external auditor makes management decisions for the company;
- a mutuality of interest is created; or
- the external auditor is put in the role of advocate for the company (Smith Guidance, note 4.28).

If the external auditors do provide non-financial services, the annual report should explain to shareholders how auditor independence and objectivity is safeguarded.

7.8 The audit committee and the annual audit cycle

The Smith Guidance goes into some detail on the annual audit cycle, and the relationship between the audit committee and the external auditors during this process.

- At the start of each annual audit, the audit committee should make sure that appropriate plans are in place for the audit.

- The committee should consider whether the auditors' overall work plan (including the planned levels of materiality and the proposed resources to carry out the audit) seems consistent with the scope of the audit engagement. This assessment should have regard to the seniority, expertise and experience of the audit team.
- The audit committee should review, with the external auditors, the findings of their work. As a part of this review, the committee should (i) discuss with the auditors any major issues that arose during the audit (and whether these have been resolved) (ii) review key accounting or audit judgements and (iii) review levels of errors identified during the audit and obtain explanations as to why certain errors might remain unadjusted.

The Smith Guidance states that the audit committee should review:

- the audit representation letters from management, before they are signed, and consider whether the information provided is complete and appropriate, based on the knowledge the committee has;
- the management letter from the auditors, and the responsiveness of the company's management to the auditors' findings and recommendations.

Management representations

Representation letters from the company's management are a part of the audit evidence collected and considered by the auditors. These deal with matters for which other audit evidence does not exist; therefore the auditors are relying on what the management tells them. Representations are required:

- from the directors, acknowledging their collective responsibility for the financial statements and confirming that they have approved them; and
- with regard to matters where knowledge of the facts is confined to management (e.g. management's intention to sell off a division of the business) or where there is a matter of judgement and opinion (for example, with regard to the trading position of a major customer and debtor, or the likely outcome of litigation in progress).

Management letter

As a by-product of the audit process, the auditors will normally make recommendations to management about improvements in internal controls. These recommendations are known as management letters.

Audit review by the committee

At the end of the audit cycle, the audit committee should assess the effectiveness of the audit process. As a part of this assessment, the committee should:

- review whether the auditors have met the agreed audit plan and consider the reasons for any changes;
- consider the 'robustness and perceptiveness' of the auditors, in their handling of key accounting and audit judgements, and in their commentary on the appropriateness of the company's internal controls;

- obtain feedback about the conduct of the auditors from key people within the company, such as the finance director and the head of internal audit;
- review the auditor's management letter, to assess whether it is based on a good understanding of the business and to establish whether the auditors' recommendations have been acted on (and if not, why not).

7.9   The audit committee and whistleblowing by employees

The audit committee should review the arrangements by which employees of the company may, in confidence, raise concerns about possible improprieties in financial reporting or other matters. The objective of the audit committee should be to make sure that arrangements are in place for:

- the 'proportionate and independent' investigation of such matters; and
- appropriate follow-up action.

The committee is not required to be part of the whistleblowing procedures itself; it is simply required to review the system and procedures that are in place. Whistleblowing is covered in more detail in Chapter 11.

7.10   The audit committee and communication with shareholders

The Smith Guidance includes some matters relating to the communication by the audit committee to the company's shareholders. The terms of reference of the audit committee should be made available.

The separate section in the annual report about the work of the audit committee should include:

- a summary of the role of the audit committee;
- the names and qualifications of the audit committee members during the period;
- the number of audit committee meetings;
- a report on the way the audit committee has discharged its responsibilities;
- if the external auditors provide non-audit services, an explanation of how auditor objectivity and independence are safeguarded.

The chairman of the audit committee should be present at the AGM to answer questions on the audit committee report and matters within the scope of the audit committee's responsibilities.

7.11   ICSA Guidance Note: Terms of Reference – Audit Committee

An ICSA Guidance Note, Terms of Reference – Audit Committee, presents model terms of reference for an audit committee, which are applicable to organisations in the public and not-for-profit sectors as well as to companies. These are consistent with the Combined Code and Smith Report recommendations.

The Guidance Note stresses the need for formal written terms of reference as follows:

'Not only should companies go through a formal process of considering their internal audit and control procedures and evaluating their relationship with their external auditor, but they must be seen to be doing so in a fair and thorough manner. It is, therefore, essential that the Audit Committee is properly constituted with a clear remit and identified authority.'

In addition to providing model terms of reference, the Guidance Note makes the following points:

- The Higgs Review stated that as good practice the company secretary (or an individual designated by the company secretary) should act as secretary to the audit committee, with responsibility for ensuring that both the board and the committee are properly advised. He or she should be able to play the role of intermediary between them.
- The Smith Report recommended that the company secretary should attend meetings of the audit committee.
- The company secretary is responsible for ensuring that the board of directors and its committees, including the audit committee, are properly constituted and advised.

The Guidance Note also comments that: 'Although the responsibility for internal controls clearly remains with the board as a whole, the company secretary would normally have the day-to-day task of reviewing the internal control procedures of the company and responsibility for drafting the governance report.'

The frequency of audit committee meetings should be specified in the terms of reference. As a general rule, the committee should meet quarterly, although the Combined Code provides that the committee should meet at least three times a year.

The Guidance Note also suggests that the annual report of the audit committee to shareholders will need to disclose:

- the role and main responsibilities of the committee;
- the membership of the committee and the relevant qualifications of the members;
- the appointment process and fees paid in respect of membership;
- the number of meetings and attendance levels;
- a description of the main activities during the year to:
  - monitor the integrity of the financial statements;
  - review the integrity of the internal financial control and risk management systems;
  - review the independence of the external auditors and the provision of non-audit services;
  - oversee the external audit process and how its effectiveness was assessed;
  - provide an explanation of the recommendation of the board to the shareholders on the appointment of the auditors.

Chapter summary

- Concerns of investors about misleading financial statements have been a major factor in the development of corporate governance in recent years. Financial statements can be misleading, due to the selection of inappropriate accounting policies.

- Many companies choose not to let their accounts present an open and transparent report on the company's performance and financial situation.

- Directors are responsible for the accuracy of the financial statements, not the external auditors.

- The external auditors provide an opinion on whether the financial accounts appear to provide a true and fair view of the company's performance and financial position.

- Doubts have been expressed about the independence of auditors from the companies to which they provide an audit service.

- Control over the audit profession is therefore a corporate governance issue.

- An audit committee, properly constituted, could provide a valuable role in improving the relationship between a company and its auditors. ICSA has issued a Guidance Note dealing with this issue.

- The directors of UK listed companies are required by the Combined Code to issue a statement that the company will be a going concern over the next twelve months.

Chapter 8

Narrative reporting

1. The nature of narrative reporting by companies
2. The business review
3. Social and environmental reporting (or CSR reporting)
4. Sustainability reporting: triple bottom line reporting

1   The nature of narrative reporting by companies

Published financial statements are historical in outlook and contain very little non-financial information. Although they can help users to understand the prospects for the company, it has been argued that more information should be provided to give users better understanding.

In addition, it has been argued that international financial reporting standards have possibly made financial statements more difficult for many investors to read and understand. In a search to make financial statements more informative and relevant to investors, the accounting standards bodies may have gone the other way and made them more obscure. (This is a matter of argument and debate.)

The result of this debate, however, has been a general agreement that companies should present information about their company's performance, and possibly also about its future prospects, in a way that is:

- easy to understand; and
- covers non-financial as well as financial aspects of performance and the company's position.

There is a need for transparency in all reporting by companies to shareholders and other stakeholders, and the requirement for transparency in reporting should be seen as a key element of good corporate governance.

Requirements have been introduced for additional reporting by companies to improve the quality of communications with their shareholders. To some extent legal and regulatory requirements have lagged behind best practice and voluntary reporting by some companies.

A statutory requirement for a business review has been introduced into UK law as the result of an EU Directive, but it reflects the demand from investors for more information about companies. The corporate governance movement in the UK originated largely from investor concerns about misleading financial statements. It appears that a situation has been reached where investors believe that even if financial statements are reliable, they are not on their own a sufficient source of information about a company.

1.1 An Operating and Financial Review

It has been best practice for some years in the UK for listed companies to publish an Operating and Financial Review (OFR) with their annual report and accounts, and a statement of best practice was issued by the Accounting Standards Board on this subject (revised 2003). An OFR is largely in narrative form but with supporting figures presented in a way that should be easy to comprehend, and its purpose is to present a review of the company's operating and financial performance, position and prospects for the future.

In the UK, the Companies Act was amended in 2005 by a statutory instrument requiring all quoted companies to include an OFR in their annual report and accounts, for reporting years starting on or after 1 April 2005. The government then changed its mind, and the requirement for a statutory OFR was withdrawn on the grounds that the contents requirements for an OFR represented unnecessary 'gold plating' and imposed requirements on companies that were more extensive than those applying to quoted companies in other EU countries.

The requirements for an OFR were replaced in 2006 by a requirement for an annual business review, which was introduced to the Companies Act 1985. The business review is explained later. It is useful first, however, to look in more detail at the intended contents of an OFR.

The scrapped OFR regulations were based on a White Paper for Modernising Company Law (2002), which proposed a statutory requirement for companies (with the exception of small companies) to publish an OFR each year, containing certain information to meet a 'high level objective of greater transparency'. In addition, the White Paper proposed that the OFR should reflect those matters which, in the opinion of the board of directors, were relevant to an understanding of the company.

The key issue from a corporate governance perspective was that an OFR would improve the communications between a company and its shareholders, and make the affairs and the prospects of the company more transparent and understandable to shareholders – without disclosing confidential information that would benefit rival companies.

1.2 Contents of an OFR

It was intended that the OFR would provide a balanced and comprehensive analysis, for the company and its subsidiaries, of:

- the development and performance of the business during the financial year;
- the position as at the end of the year;
- the main trends and factors underlying the development, performance and position of the business during the financial year;
- the main trends and factors likely to affect the development, performance and position of the business in the future.

It was also proposed that an OFR should include, for the company and its subsidiaries:

- a statement of the business, its objectives and strategy;
- a description of the resources available to them;
- a description of the main risks and uncertainties facing them;

- a description of the capital structure, treasury policies and liquidity of the company and its subsidiaries.

The information should be sufficient to enable shareholders to assess the strategies of the company and their potential to succeed.

Other information might have to be included in an OFR relating to:

- employees;
- environmental matters;
- social and community issues;
- business relationships;
- receipts from and returns to shareholders;
- key performance indicators (both financial and non-financial in nature, for example relating to employee and environmental matters).

It was expected that the information appearing in the OFR would be a mix of quantitative and qualitative information and financial and non-financial information.

The DTI published a report by the OFR Working Group, The Operating and Financial Review: Practical Guidance for Directors (2004) which stated:

'A balance between historic(sic) review and a focus on the future is key to the OFR. To meet its objective, the OFR has to enable members to understand what has driven past performance but also what are the main trends and factors in its operating environment likely to affect future performance.'

2   The business review

The requirement for a statutory OFR was replaced with a requirement to publish an annual business review. This was introduced into the Companies Act 1985 from 2006, although companies that continue to publish an OFR voluntarily should meet all the requirements of the business review.

2.1   Requirements introduced by the Companies Act 1985 amendment (2006)

The requirements introduced into the 1985 Companies Act were as follows:

- A business review should be included in the directors' report.
- The review should provide a 'balanced and comprehensive analysis' of the development and performance of the business of the company during the financial year and the position of the company as at the end of the year. The review should be consistent with the size and complexity of the business.
- The directors' report must contain:
  - a fair review of the business of the company, and
  - a description of the principal risks and uncertainties that the business faces.

- Trends and factors affecting the development, performance and position of the business should be included where necessary to provide a comprehensive analysis of the performance and position of the business or to describe the principal risks that it faces.
- Information on environmental, employee, social and community matters and policies should be included where necessary to provide a fair review of the business, a description of the principal risks and uncertainties and a balanced and comprehensive analysis of the development, performance and position of the business.

The business review would be largely narrative in form, but should include key performance indicators. These should be financial key performance indicators and also, where appropriate, other key performance indicators relating to environmental matters and employee matters.

The auditors must state in their audit report whether in their opinion the information given in the directors' report is consistent with the company's accounts for the financial year.

2.2   The business review and the Companies Act 2006 requirement

The Companies Act 2006, s. 417 has retained the requirement for a business review as part of the directors' report. Small companies continue to be exempted. The Act states that the purpose of the business review is to inform shareholders and help them to assess how the directors have performed their statutory duty to promote the success of the company.

The statutory requirements for the business review have been expanded, particularly for quoted companies.

For quoted companies, the business review must contain, to the extent necessary for an understanding of the development, performance or position of the business, information about the following matters:

- The main trends and factors likely to affect the future development, performance and position of the business.
- Information about:
  - environmental matters, including the impact of the company's business on the environment,
  - the company's employees,
  - social and community issues.

  This should include information about any policies of the company in relation to these matters and the effectiveness of those matters.
- Information about 'persons with whom the company has contractual or other arrangements which are essential to the business of the company.'

The business review must also, to the extent necessary for an understanding of the development, performance or position of the business, include:

- analysis using financial key performance indicators; and
- where appropriate, other key performance indicators relating to environmental matters and employee matters.

(Medium-sized companies need not comply with this requirement for the business review to include key performance indicators.)

There was considerable concern amongst companies about the requirements for information in the business review about the future development of the business and for information about persons who are essential to the company's business, and several further provisions were included in the Act to remove these concerns.

- Companies are not required to disclose information about future developments ('impending developments or matters in the course of negotiation') that would in the opinion of the directors be seriously prejudicial to the company's interests.
- Companies are not required to disclose information about any person if this disclosure would in the opinion of the directors be seriously prejudicial to that person and 'contrary to the public interest'.

2.3   Directors' 'safe harbour' provisions

Concerns were expressed about the potential liability of directors for statements they make in a business review, especially those that are forward-looking in nature. To meet general concerns about the potential liability of directors for the contents of reports, the 2006 Act includes so-called 'safe harbour' provisions (s. 463).

Section 463 applies to the directors' report (including the business review) and the directors' remuneration report and deals with untrue or misleading statements in a report, or the omission from a report of information that should be included in it.

A director will only be liable for untrue or misleading statements if he or she knew them to be untrue or misleading, or was 'reckless' as to whether they were untrue or misleading. A director will only be responsible for an omission if he or she knew the omission to be a 'dishonest' concealment of a material fact.

When a director is found liable for an untrue or misleading statement or an omission, he or she will be liable to compensate the company for any loss it has suffered as a result. 'No person shall be subject to any liability to a person other than the company' (s. 463(4)).

2.4   ASB review of narrative reporting

In January 2007, the Accounting Standards Board (ASB) published 'A Review of Narrative Reporting by UK Listed Companies in 2006'. The purpose of the review was to highlight strengths and weaknesses in narrative reporting and to encourage the adoption of best practice by companies. It was based on an analysis of the report and accounts of 23 companies, of which 15 were FTSE 100 companies, four were in the FTSE 250 and the other four were companies in the FTSE Small Capitalisation index.

The paper commented that the ASB's Reporting Statement on the Operating and Financial Review is still 'the most authoritative source of best practice guidance', even though it goes beyond the legal requirements for disclosure in narrative reports (the business review).

The ASB's review found that there were some areas of reporting where disclosures by companies were of a high standard. These were:

1   descriptions of the company's business and markets;
2   strategies and objectives (although there was scope for improvement in the description of the company's external environment);
3   the current development and the performance of its business.

Most companies reported environmental, social and employee issues, but few companies discussed contractual arrangements in any depth.

The paper suggested that there was a need for improvement in narrative reporting on forward-looking provisions:

1   Companies need to think about describing the resources that are available to them, in particular intangible assets not on the balance sheet.
2   Companies need to make a careful assessment of the principal risks and uncertainties that they face, and provide disclosures on how these are being managed. The number of principal risks is unlikely to be large. However, too many companies in 2006 simply provided a long list of risks. One company included 33 risks in its principal risks, which the ASB considered implausible.
3   Improvements could be made in providing disclosures about key performance indicators, both financial and non-financial.

The paper concluded that there were problems with the overall structure and presentation of narrative reporting and cross-referencing, and improvements could be made so that the narrative flows better. In the absence of guidance on the statutory business review, quoted companies (especially FTSE 100 companies) appeared to be adopting the principles in the ASB's Reporting Statement on the OFR.

2.5   ABI position paper on developments in narrative reporting

In November 2006, the ABI published a position paper on developments in narrative reporting. The paper examined the state of narrative reporting, and was based on the view that the introduction of the statutory requirement for a business review marked a transition from reliance by investors on voluntary social and environment reports by companies. The position paper regarded the business review as a significant narrative report for the future, commenting that investors 'see narrative reporting as a useful communications opportunity rather than a compliance burden.'

The ABI's views on this transition are evident in the following statements in the position paper:

- 'Social, environmental and ethical (SEE) issues are an important dimension of [the risks and opportunites facing companies], but not the only one. Strategic, financial and market risks and opportunities are also key components of narrative reporting.'
- 'The essential principle will remain that Boards should confirm they have reviewed and are managing risks and opportunities. However the emphasis will no longer be exclusively on social, environmental and ethical issues.'

The ABI's view is that the priority areas for investors in narrative reporting will be forward-looking information and non-financial key performance indicators. It indicated that the guidelines in the OFR Standard published by the Accounting Standards Board/Financial Reporting Council will provide a useful benchmark for good practice.

The position paper also identified six key criteria that, in its opinion, distinguish the best narrative reporting. These are:

1   forward-looking information on the company's strategy and market environment;
2   the quality of reporting on the company's individual business units;
3   the reporting of risks to the company's future value. (In the past, some companies have reported on risks such as the impact of safety and environmental issues on the company's operations, the importance of having a suitably motivated and incentivised workforce, the financial and reputational consequences of non-compliance with legislation, and the impact on demand of changes in customer requirements or preferences);
4   the presentation of key performance indicators (KPIs) and key performance targets;
5   information on whether and how Boards have used the data in KPIs to monitor and review the effectiveness of their risk management strategies;
6   information on the role of the board and its committees.

It recognised that companies had been reluctant in the past to provide much forward-looking information.

- Directors were concerned about their potential liability for providing false or misleading information in forward-looking statements. The ABI considered that this problem should be removed by the safe harbour provisions for directors in the Companies Act 2006.
- There was also concern about providing commercially sensitive information to rival companies by publishing forward-looking information. The ABI paper suggested that this problem will eventually disappear as a 'critical mass' of companies start to publish forward-looking information in the light of the Companies Act legislation.

At the time of revising this text, the ABI planned to revise and rename its Socially Responsible Investment Guidelines as a result of the reporting changes introduced by the business review.

3   Social and environmental reporting (or CSR reporting)

The business review has introduced requirements for companies to report on environmental and social aspects of their business. The business review is a part of the directors' report and as such it is written primarily for shareholders of the company.

3.1 *The reason for social and environmental reports*

Many large companies have recognised a responsibility to other corporate stakeholders as well as to their shareholders and are aware of the concerns of the public in general for the impact that companies are having on society and the environment, as well as on the economy.

The social and ethical responsibilities of companies as an issue in corporate governance are considered more fully in Chapter 11. This chapter is concerned more specifically with narrative reporting as a means of communication by a company with its shareholders and other stakeholders.

There is no legal requirement for companies to report on social, ethical and environmental issues (SEE issues), other than the requirements in the business review. However, many listed companies voluntarily publish a report on these issues each year. They do so as a means of communicating with a wider group of stakeholders, including not only shareholders but also employees, investors and the community in general.

There are various reasons why companies might want to report voluntarily on SEE issues.

- They might have a genuine concern for social and environmental issues, and consider that they are fulfilling their responsibilities to stakeholders by reporting on these matters.
- The company might recognise that its reputation with the public might be at risk because of the nature of their business activities. Mining companies and oil and gas extraction companies are obvious examples, since the public is aware that these companies deplete the world's natural resources and pollute the environment. Reporting on social and environmental issues allows the company to demonstrate that it understands the concerns of society and explain how it is addressing these concerns with its social and envionmental policies.
- A company might see an opportunity to gain a competitive advantage over rival companies by reporting on its social and environmental policies. A company whose policies are greener and more environmentally-friendly than its competitors might hope to build their reputation and attract more customers.
- There might be pressure on companies to report more extensively on SEE issues from major shareholders or bodies representing investment institutions (the ABI or NAPF for example).
- Companies might recognise that there has been a loss of trust by the general public in the ethics of companies, and reporting on SEE issues is a way of trying to rebuild public trust.

The mining group Xstrata has explained its reasons for publishing annual Sustainability Reports as follows:

'Our commitment to the principles of sustainable development is based on our belief that operating responsibly and to the highest international standards ... mitigates risk, creates opportunities and enhances our reputation and competitive position. In particular, a strong reputation for operational and environmental excellence and industry-leading community engagement enables us to gain access to new resources, maintain a social licence to operate from the communities associated with our operations, attract and retain the best people and access diverse and low-cost sources of capital.'

3.2   Reasons against voluntary social and environmental reporting

Although many listed companies do publish social and environmental reports, they can control the content of their reports. There might be a natural inclination to include good news only and exclude aspects of the company's social and environmental performance that would attract stakeholder disapproval. For example, a chemical manufacturing company might include a section on health and safety measures at its processing plants without reporting the actual number of accidents and injuries sustained by employees during the year.

There are various reasons why companies might not report social and environmental issues voluntarily:

- The company's directors and senior management might be insufficiently aware of social and environmental issues.
- Companies might be deterred by the cost of obtaining relevant information for reporting, or the difficulty in collecting reliable and useful social and environmental information.
- The company might be reluctant to disclose any information that it is under no legal requirement to provide, possibly to avoid giving sensitive data to competitors or regulators.
- The company might want to avoid the risk of damage to its reputation if it were to present unfavourable information about itself.

3.3   Risk society theory of social and environmental reporting

In spite of reasons against social and environmental reporting, it seems probable that voluntary reporting by companies will increase, because stakeholders in companies want to be given the information that these reports contain.

In Corporate Governance and Accountability, Jill Solomon makes an interesting reference to risk society theory as a possible explanation of the big changes in society's attitudes to SEE issues. Risk society theory was developed in the early 1990s by Ulrich Beck, a German sociologist. He has argued that in today's society there has been an increase in 'high consequence risks' such as global warming and the risk of a major nuclear accident or incident. The whole of society is affected by these risks, at a global level, and although human and corporate behaviour has contributed to these problems, they are largely unmanageable and the blame cannot be placed entirely on specific causes and specific companies. A clear connection between cause and effect does not exist.

As a consequence, people have lost their trust in leaders and in institutions. They do not believe that companies have genuine ethical, social or environmental concerns, and they believe that companies act unethically and damage society and the environment through their self-centred activities.

Risk society theory can be used to suggest that companies see voluntary social and environmental reporting as an attempt to rebuild public trust. Communicating with stakeholders on these issues is a necessary step towards re-establishing trust.

3.4 The content of social and environmental reports

Social and environmental reports, also called corporate social responsibility reports, might be produced as a separate document (usually at the same time that the annual report and accounts document is published) or it might be included in the (non-statutory) report of the chairman or chief executive officer within the annual report and accounts.

Because they are voluntary publications, the content of social and environmental reports does not follow a set pattern:

- The information that they contain varies according to the nature of the company's business. For environmental reporting, it is generally accepted that a company's impact on the environment can be measured in terms of its impact on the air, water or land, or noise pollution. However, companies can either measure their consumption of resources (total energy use for lighting and heating, total fuel use for transport, total water usage) or they can provide measurements of pollution they have created such as the volume of waste produced and discharged into the air, rivers, sea or land.
- The method of presenting the information also varies. Some companies produce a separate social and environmental report. Others give information about SEE issues in the chairman's report or report of the CEO in the published annual report and accounts.

CASE EXAMPLE 8.1

Tesco plc has a corporate responsibility committee which publishes a corporate responsibility review each year. Its 2007 Review comments that 'the retail sector is undergoing rapid change, with increasing expectations of business on sustainability and community'. The Committee sees the annual review as the main method of reporting to stakeholders generally on SEE issues.

Its 2007 Review presents a narrative report with separate sections on:

- Being a good employer
- Climate change (and the 'carbon footprint' of the Tesco Group)
- Sustainable consumption
- Waste, packaging and recycling
- Farmers and local sourcing
- Retail and the high street (including the provision of convenience local stores)
- Health, nutrition and well-being
- Ethical trade and developing countries
- Charities and community.

The Review ends with a series of key performance indicators in each of these social, ethical and environmental areas. The targets for the year just ended are specified, with a comment on whether the target was missed, achieved or exceeded, and targets for the next year are also given.

CASE EXAMPLE 8.2

Each company's social and environmental report deals with issues specific to that company and its business. The SEE report of Vodafone, the mobile phone operating company, includes a section on handset recycling.

The company's 2006 report comments that the average consumer upgrades his or her mobile phone every 18 months. If thrown away, old telephones generate waste and can release harmful substances into the atmosphere if not disposed of properly.

The report explains how the company collects used handsets from customers at retail stores and through a Freepost address, and how the handsets are either refurbished for resale and re-use in lower income countries, or are recycled. Money received for refurbished handsets is donated to a charity, the National Autistic Society.

This is another example of how a major company recognises the reputational and commercial advantages of SEE policies.

4 Sustainability reporting: triple bottom line reporting

The term 'sustainable development' has emerged as a social and environmental objective for major companies. However, there is no generally accepted definition of what sustainable development actually means. The Brundtland Report (for the World Commission on Environment and Development, 1987) defines it as 'development that meets the needs of the present without compromising the ability of future generations to meet their own needs'.

However, although this definition might seem broadly acceptable, there are difficulties with what it means exactly in practice:

- There can be disagreement about the meaning of 'needs of the present'. Presumably these are more than the bare minimum needs for survival, because in much of the world consumption is well above survival level and affluent societies do not accept the need to reduce consumption to levels in other countries of the world.
- Similarly, it is not clear what the needs of future generations are. If they are just survival needs, there must be an inherent assumption that at some time in the future economic wealth must decline in the more affluent societies.
- It is not clear over what period of time the needs of future generations should be considered and measured. In theory, society's long-term needs should be recognised. However, governments and companies are likely to plan over much shorter time-scales. Since companies plan for the future and report their performance within fairly short time-frames, reporting for sustainable development by companies is likely to focus on relatively short-term measures of sustainability.
- Should sustainability be measured collectively for all people in all societies of the world, or should it be measured in terms of individual countries or regions?

4.1 Environmental footprints

A company might report its environmental footprint as a series of measurements. The measurements for each individual company might vary according to the nature of its business, but should relate to the following environmental issues:

- the company's use of key resources such as land, and also its consumption of materials subject to depletion (such as quantities of livestock, wild fish or forest timber) and non-renewable resources (such as coal, oil and natural gas);
- pollution caused by the company's activities, measured in terms of carbon dioxide emissions, chemical waste or spillages of oil;
- an assessment in either qualitative or quantitative terms of the broader effect of the company's resource consumption and pollution on the environment.

4.2 Triple bottom line reporting

The term 'triple bottom line' was coined in 1994 by J. Elkington. Its aim is to encourage companies to recognise social and environmental issues in their business reporting systems. This method of reporting is encouraged by the Global Reporting Initiative (GRI), an internationally recognised body that promotes sustainability reporting.

The term 'triple bottom line' comes from the fact that sustainability reports should provide key measurements for three aspects of performance:

1 economic indicators;
2 social indicators; and
3 environmental indicators.

Triple bottom line reporting therefore provides a quantitative summary of a company's economic, environmental and social performance over the previous year.

Economic indicators are measures typically associated with financial reporting, such as measurements relating to:

- sales revenue;
- profits, earnings and earnings per share;
- dividends per share;
- global market share (the percentage share of the global market captured by the company's products or services);
- in industries manufacturing standard products, such as car production, units of sale worldwide.

Social indicators might include measures relating to employment and employees, and measurements relating to society and the community, such as:

- employee diversity: for example, the percentage of its employees who were female and the percentage who came from minority groups;
- the recordable injury rate per 1,000 employees;
- donations to communities and sponsorships.

Environmental indicators might include measurements relating to targets for:

- reducing the consumption of materials in products and services;
- reducing energy use;
- minimising the release of toxic materials/pollutants;
- improving the recycling of materials;
- maximising the use of renewable resources;
- extending the life of a product.

CASE EXAMPLE 8.3

Xstrata, the Swiss mining group that has listings in both Switzerland and London, produced a Sustainability Report in 2006 based on the GRI guidelines for triple bottom line reporting. A significant feature of triple bottom line reporting is that performance should be quantified by measurements. Actual performance might be compared against a target.

The report includes, for example, the following comparison of environmental targets and actual performance for 2006.

Environment: Target 2006	Actual performance
No fines or penalties	4 fines paid (US$8,100 in total)
Zero Category 3, 4 or 5 incidents	24 Category 3 incidents. No Category 4 or 5 incidents
Extend biodiversity plans to cover every managed site	Achieved at every operation except 3 sites. Plans scheduled for implementation in 2007
Every Australian operation to implement Greenhouse Challenge Plus agreements with the Australian government.	Agreements in place. Formal reporting begins 2007

The company's performance targets are specific and measurable. The following are examples of its 2007 targets.

Health, Group	No new occupational illnesses
	Implement VCT programmes for HIV and AIDS at all higher risk operations
Climate change	
Xstrata Alloys	Achieve 5% energy reduction per tonne of materials produced
Xstrata Coal	Contribute $75 million to clean coal technologies over the next five years
	Reduce greenhouse gas emissions per ROM tonne by 5% by 2010

Water management	
Group	Implement water conservation [plans for all operations in water-scarce regions
Xstrata Alloys	Achieve 5% water usage reduction per tonne of materials produced
Xstrata Coal	Achieve 10% reduction in fresh water consumption per ROM tonne by 2011
Xstrata Zinc	Spain smelter to reduce water consumption by over 4% and water discharge by 9%

4.3   *Limitations of triple bottom line reporting*

There are several limitations to triple bottom line reporting:

- There are no widely established standards for triple bottom line reporting, and no standard methods for measuring social and environmental impacts. It is therefore not possible to compare the sustainability of one company with the sustainability of another.
- The Global Reporting Initiative (GRI) is attempting to standardise measurements for the triple bottom line and has been publishing Sustainability Reporting Guidelines since 1999.
- If the social and environmental measures are not subject to independent audit, there might be doubts about the reliability of the data presented in a company's report. Companies have a vested interest in presenting 'good news' but withholding 'bad news' in any form of voluntary reporting.

Chapter summary

- Financial statements published by companies contain historical financial information, often in a form that is complex and difficult to understand. The lack of transarency in much financial reporting has led to a demand from investors for more comprehensible reporting, largely in a narrative form, with content that is both forward-looking as well as historical and covering non-financial as well as financial issues.

- It is argued that this form of reporting by companies will improve transparency, and enhance corporate governance through improved communications.

- In response to demands from investors for improved corporate reporting, the UK government planned briefly to require quoted companies to publish an Operating and Financial Review (OFR) in their annual report and accounts, and the Accounting Standards Board published a reporting standard on OFRs.

- The proposal for a statutory OFR was abandoned in favour of a statutory requirement for companies (excluding small companies) to include a business review in their directors' report. This is now a requirement of the Companies Act (Companies Act 2006, s. 417).

- The requirements for the content of the business review are more extensive for quoted companies than for other companies. A business review should provide a balanced and comprehensive analysis of the development, performance and position of the company and the main risks and uncertainties that it faces. Where appropriate, quoted companies should provide information about trends and other significant factors and information on environmental, employee, social and community issues.

- The potential liability of directors for false or misleading statements in a business review have been restricted by 'safe harbour' provisions in the Act.

- The busines review is a report for shareholders of the company. Many large companies are also aware of reputational risk and recognise a need to engage with the general public or broader community on environmental and social issues.

- In recognition of this need, many companies voluntarily produce a social and environmental report each year (or corporate social responsibility report). This may be published as a separate document or possibly included within the (non-staututory) report of the chairman or CEO in the annual report and accounts document.

- Social and environmental reports are largely narrative reports covering a range of issues relevant to the company, although many reports also include performance measurements on social and environmental issues. Sustainability reports might provide 'triple bottom line' reporting, with quantified performance measurements on economic (financial), social and environmental factors.

- However, there is an awareness that social and environmental reports contain whatever information the company chooses to provide, and reports might therefore be published as 'PR' documents, emphasising a company's positive achievements on CSR issues but ignoring the negative factors.

- A general potential problem with narrative reporting is the lack of standardisation in format and content.

Chapter 9

Directors' remuneration

1 Directors' remuneration as a corporate governance issue

Until the 1990s in the UK and 2002 in the US, directors' remuneration was not seen as a major problem of corporate governance. A sense that something might be wrong arose when:

- the general public, informed by the media, criticised some top executives for being paid much more money than they were worth; and
- investment institutions criticised directors for receiving ever-increasing rewards even when their company performed badly.

Directors' remuneration has tended to rise rapidly regardless of company performance, whereas a principle of good corporate governance is that remuneration should be linked to some extent to company performance, so that a director will earn more if the company does well, but less if it does badly.

In the UK, the problem was further aggravated by the fact that in many listed companies, the CEO and chairman were involved in deciding their own remuneration package.

1.1 Public attitudes

A general belief that directors pay themselves far too much can have a damaging effect on the stock market. Private investors may be reluctant to invest in companies that reward their leaders far more than they deserve. It can be particularly damaging to the capital markets when public anger is stirred against directors who continue to pay themselves more when their companies are performing badly.

The problem emerged in the UK during the 1990s, largely as a result of the privatisation of state-owned industries, such as water and electricity supply companies. The same individuals who had run the former state-owned enterprises were appointed as directors of newly established listed companies, with a much improved remuneration package. For doing exactly the same jobs as before, they were paid much more money. The popular press led a campaign against 'fat cat' directors, such as the leaders of British Gas and United Utilities.

Similar concerns have arisen in the US. Alan Greenspan, chairman of the US Federal Reserve, commenting in July 2002 on the collapse in the stock markets, accused senior executives of 'infectious greed' during the period of the stock market boom in the late 1990s, when the size of reported corporate profits and rapidly increasing value of shares provided an 'outsized increase in opportunities for avarice'.

CASE EXAMPLE 9.1

In 2006 US corporation Home Depot was heavily criticised by its shareholders, and attracted considerable press attention, for the remuneration of its CEO Bob Nardelli. The company was expected to come in for intense shareholder questioning at its general meeting. However, no directors turned up to the meeting, except for Mr Nardelli himself, who then restricted the length of the meeting and discouraged shareholder questioning. Proposals seeking to allow shareholders more say in the CEO's remuneration and to restrict retirement pay for senior executives were both defeated. Even so, the level of criticism directed at the company provided evidence of the growing concern in the US about excessive executive pay.

In the UK during 2002–3, there was institutional investor concern, supported by widespread media coverage, about large remuneration packages for senior directors where the size of the reward did not seem sufficiently linked to performance, and large severance payments to outgoing senior executives who had been ousted from their job following poor company performance. High severance payments to unsuccessful directors were seen as 'rewards for failure'.

However, a distinction should be made between:

- the unethical 'corporate greed' of some senior executives; and
- a reasonable desire by senior executives to be well-remunerated for what they do.

Similarly, it important to make the distinction between:

- high rewards that are justified by performance; and
- high rewards that are earned in spite of poor performance.

1.2   Directors' remuneration and corporate governance

In a system of good corporate governance, the remuneration of directors and key senior executives should be sufficient to attract and retain individuals of a suitable calibre. At the same time, the structure of an individual's remuneration package should motivate the individual towards the achievement of performance that is in the best interests of the company and its shareholders, as well as those of the individual.

The Combined Code states as a principle that:

'Levels of remuneration should be sufficient to attract, retain and motivate directors of the quality required to run the company successfully, but a company should avoid paying more than is necessary for this purpose. A significant proportion of executive directors' remuneration should be structured so as to link rewards to corporate and individual performance.'

Despite popular resentment of high salaries for top directors, the central issue for corporate governance is concerned with the link between pay and performance.

- The remuneration package of a director should include a performance-related element. If the director successfully achieves predetermined levels of performance, he or she should be rewarded accordingly. There could be some debate as to how much remuneration should be performance-related, but there is a view that a substantial part of a director's total potential remuneration should be linked to performance.
- The purpose of performance-related remuneration is to give a director an incentive to achieve the performance targets. This is why potential performance-related pay should be substantial.
- It is clearly in the interest of good corporate governance that directors should be motivated to perform, but it is equally important that the performance targets set for each individual director are (a) sufficiently challenging, and (b) related to objectives that are in the interests of the company and its shareholders.
- The best remuneration packages align the interests of the individual directors with those of the company and its shareholders.
- When directors are unsuccessful, they might be dismissed. If they are dismissed, they will have a contractual right to some compensation for loss of office. However, the compensation should not be excessive, because large payments to an outgoing director could be seen as 'rewards for failure' which are inconsistent with good corporate governance.

Another concern has been the problem of who decides a director's remuneration. An individual who decides the remuneration of another will inevitably have an influence (conscious or not) over that person. If the chairman or CEO has the power to decide the remuneration of the other executive directors, or the fees and other rewards for NED directors, there could be a serious threat to the independence of the board members. It is therefore a well-established principle of corporate governance that there should be a formal procedure for deciding on remuneration for directors and senior executives and that no individual should be involved in setting his or her own remuneration.

2 Elements of remuneration for executive directors

It is widely accepted that senior executives should be able to earn a high level of remuneration in return for the work they do and the responsibilities they carry. If a company does not offer an attractive package, it will not attract individuals of the required calibre. It is also generally accepted that the level of remuneration should be linked in some way to satisfactory performance. If an executive performs well, he or she should receive more rewards than if he or she performs only reasonably well.

Linking remuneration, wholly or in part, to performance is not an easy task, however:

- Unsuitable measures of performance may be selected, so that although the individual executive succeeds in achieving targets that earn high rewards, the company itself and its shareholders do not obtain a comparable benefit.
- Many performance measures are based on the short term, possibly linked to annual results. This may not be in the interests of the company's longer-term development and performance.
- Remuneration systems are normally designed to provide the reward after the performance has been made. This time delay means that if the company has poor results in the current year after having done well in the previous year, an executive may be paid high remuneration (for the previous year) at a time the company is doing badly.
- Severance payments have been high for executives who are seen to have failed, having led their company to setbacks in business strategy or even financial catastrophe (e.g. Marconi).

The problem of seeming to pay rewards for failure was evident in the stock market crash in the US in 2001–2. This was highlighted by an investigation by the Financial Times (31 July 2002) into the pay-outs to the directors of the 25 largest US corporations that had gone bankrupt since January 2001. The investigation found that the top executives of these companies had obtained about $3.3 billion in pay-outs and share sale proceeds, almost irrespective of company performance. The executives concerned were reaping the benefit of remuneration packages that had been agreed when the economy was booming and there was no foreseeable end in sight to the good times. When their company's profits fell and the share price tumbled, the executives were still receiving rewards under their contractual agreements. To the investment community, it appeared that the executives were being rewarded for failure.

2.1 The component elements of executive directors' remuneration

The remuneration package for a senior executive is likely to consist of a combination of:

- a basic salary;
- a payment by the company into a personal pension scheme arrangement for the individual;
- an annual bonus, tied perhaps to the annual financial performance of the company;
- long-term incentives, usually in the form of share option awards or the granting of fully-paid company shares (sometimes called 'restricted stock awards');

- In addition, executives might enjoy a number of other 'perks' such as free private medical insurance, a company car and the use of a company airplane or apartment.

Remuneration can be divided into two elements – a fixed pay element and a variable element:

- The fixed elements are the remuneration received by the director regardless of performance, such as fixed salary and salary-related pension, and other perks.
- The variable elements are the performance-related elements (cash bonuses, awards of share options or shares depending on performance, etc.) The size of the remuneration depends on the performance achieved.

A problem in negotiating a remuneration package with an executive is to decide on the balance between the fixed and the variable elements, and to agree on measures of performance as the basis for deciding on how much the performance-related payments should be.

An executive might also have a severance payment arrangement, whereby the company is committed to giving the individual a minimum severance payment if he or she is forced to leave the company.

2.2 The overall size of the remuneration package

The remuneration package offered to a senior executive has to be sufficient to attract him or her to accept the position. There is a perception that there are not enough individuals available to meet the demand with sufficient skills and talent to fill a senior executive post successfully. If this perception is correct, it is a sellers' market and talented executives can command ever-increasing remuneration packages, which companies are forced to pay to get the person they want.

Companies often use remuneration consultants, who give advice on remuneration packages, including basic salary levels for senior executives. Consultants might use competitive pay data to recommend a basic package for senior executives. Competitive pay data are simply information about the rewards that are being paid to senior executives in other top companies. At first sight, it would seem that this is a sensible way of setting a total value for a remuneration package.

Unfortunately, over-reliance on competitive pay data is likely to result in a sharp upward spiral in executive remuneration.

A supporting principle in the Combined Code is that the remuneration committee should judge where to position the company relative to other companies, but they should use caution in making this judgement 'in view of the risk of an upward ratchet of remuneration levels with no corresponding improvement in performance'. The committee should also consider pay and employment conditions elsewhere within the group, especially when deciding the annual salary increases for the executive directors.

One of the arguments in favour of high remuneration for top executives of international companies has been that high pay is necessary to stop executives being poached by other global companies. In the UK, for example, this argument has been used to justify comparisons of UK executives' salaries with those of top US businessmen. However, a report in 2002 by the International Corporate Governance Network (ICGN) argued that there is no international market for top executives, and so there is no point in structuring remuneration packages to prevent top executives from being lured to companies in other countries, the US in particular.

The ICGN report admitted that some multinational companies face global competition for top executives, and so have to offer packages that match those paid to top US executives. However, ICGN argued that the number of multinationals in this position was much smaller than the number of companies using the international competition argument to boost top executives' pay. Measures should, therefore, be taken to prevent a senior executive remuneration spiral from getting even further out of hand.

2.3 The structure of the remuneration package

The remuneration package for an executive director should be a mixture of fixed payments and a performance-related element. The Combined Code states that: 'A significant proportion of executive directors' remuneration should be structured so as to link rewards to corporate and individual performance.' The Code goes on to state that the performance-related elements should be designed to align the interests of the executive director with those of the company's shareholders, and should give the director 'keen incentives to perform at the highest levels'.

2.4 Performance-based cash bonus incentives

Performance-based incentives reward executives, usually with one or more cash bonus payments, if actual performance during a review period reaches or exceeds certain predetermined targets.

A performance target might be for an annual period, with the executive rewarded according to the financial performance of the company. However, there are different ways of measuring financial performance. Here are just a few possible measures:

- annual profit after taxation;
- annual profit before interest and taxation (PBIT);
- annual earnings before interest, taxation, depreciation and amortisation (EBITDA);
- the annual increase in profit, PBIT or EBITDA, compared with the previous year.

There are several problems with using profit measures as a basis for a reward system:

- Annual profitability can often be manipulated within the accounting rules, so that executives seeking a high current annual bonus might be able to make the profit more than the profit that would be reported if more conservative accounting policies and judgements were applied.
- Achieving profit targets does not necessarily mean that the shareholders benefit. Higher annual profits do not guarantee higher dividends and higher share prices. However, an ideal bonus system is one that links rewards to executives with the benefits accruing to shareholders, so that the interests of directors and shareholders are in alignment.

Other types of remuneration scheme are to reward executives on the basis of achieving:

- a number of different performance targets, some of them non-financial; or
- longer-term strategic objectives.

A CEO might have two or more bonus schemes, with one bonus payment linked to short-term financial results and another linked to longer-term strategic achievements. A problem with rewarding executives for long-term performance, however, is that an incoming CEO inherits the long-term results of the efforts of his or her predecessor. The CEO might also move on to another position before the full impact of his or her own efforts is fully appreciated.

It is important to recognise that there are different ways of arranging a bonus payments scheme for executives, but none of them is perfect because it is difficult to devise a scheme for individuals that ties bonus payments in a satisfactory way to performance that benefits shareholders in the long term.

2.5   Long-term incentives: share plans

Long-term incentive plans usually take the form of an award of either share options or fully-paid shares in the company. The award of share options or shares should be conditional on the director or senior executive meeting certain performance targets.

For example, a scheme might award shares to a director provided that the company achieves targets for total shareholder return (TSR) over a three-year period relative to comparator companies. The individual might receive 30 per cent of the available shares, say, if the company matches the TSR of comparator companies and 100 per cent of the available shares if the company's TSR is comparable with the top quartile (25 per cent) of comparator companies.

A company might also offer a deferred annual bonus scheme whereby participating executive directors and other senior managers are entitled to use some or all of their annual cash bonus to buy shares in the company. These shares might then be held in trust for three years, after which the individual is entitled to the award of additional free matching shares from the company, subject to a requirement that the company should have met a target growth objective for the three-year period.

The purpose of each element of a remuneration package for an executive director can be summarised as follows:

ELEMENT OF REMUNERATION

Basic salary

Annual cash bonus

Deferred annual bonus scheme

Share options or share awards

Element of remuneration continued

Example of a performance measure

Earnings per share and other specified annual corporate objectives

Growth in TSR or earnings per share, or the achievement of other specified corporate objectives

TSR over a three-year period

Purpose

To attract and retain talented people

To motivate the individual to achieve year-on-year growth in profitability and other priority corporate targets

To motivate the individual to achieve medium-term targets

To motivate the individual to achieve longer-term corporate targets and objectives. Also encouages greater shareholding by directors (and alignment of the director's interests with those of the other shareholders in the company)

3 Problems with linking rewards to performance

The purpose of incentive schemes is to provide an incentive to an executive director or senior manager to improve the company's performance, by linking rewards to performance. However, experience has shown that there are a number of severe practical problems in devising a satisfactory scheme.

- There may be disagreement about what the performance targets should be and at what level they should be set. For example, should short-term incentives be based exclusively on one or more financial targets, or should there be rewards for the achievement of non-financial targets?
- Executives are usually rewarded with a cash bonus for achieving a short-term (annual) financial target, such as a target for growth in earnings per share. Short-term profit-based incentives are often set without any consideration being given to the potential long-term consequences for the company.
- Executives might develop an expectation that they should receive annual rewards regardless of the actual performance of the company.
- Newly appointed executives might benefit from a 'legacy effect' from their predecessor in the job. The bonuses paid to a new director, for example, might arise because of the effort and work of his or her predecessor in the job.
- Occasionally, rewards are paid to incentivise directors for doing something that should be a part of their normal responsibilities, such as rewarding a CEO for helping the nomination committee to find a successor to replace him when he retires.

3.1 Drawbacks to rewarding executives with options

There are several drawbacks to using share options and restricted stock awards. Rewarding executives with share options or shares is intended to align the interests of shareholders and directors (and other senior executives rewarded with options). However, an excessive use of options can result in a serious misalignment of interests:

- They reward the option holder for increases in the share price. Although shareholders also benefit from a rising share price, many might prefer higher dividends. For example, given the choice between a 10 per cent increase in dividends and no increase in dividends but a 1 per cent increase in the share price, many shareholders might prefer the higher dividends. Option holders do not benefit from dividend pay-outs, and executive directors holding share options may have a personal interest in a low dividend pay-out policy, in order to reinvest the company's profits to achieve further growth.

- Share price movements are unpredictable over the short to medium term. When the stock markets have a bull run, share prices tend to rise regardless of the underlying long-term strength of the company's business. In these circumstances, option holders can make profits on their options without really having to do much to earn them. On the other hand, when the stock markets go into decline (a 'bear phase') options lose value and might even become worthless. In 2001 and 2002, when the major stock markets went from a bull phase to a bear phase, many senior executives were able to cash in their profits on share options whilst share prices were still high, and then see the value of the company's shares tumble. Investors were angered by the ability of senior executives to make profits when their shareholders were suffering heavy losses.

- Share options lose all their value when their exercise price falls below the current market price of the shares. Options that are 'out-of-the-money' or 'under water' lose their ability to act as incentives to executives. When this happens, the remuneration committee of a company's board might decide to re-price the options or to reissue new options at a lower exercise price. The problem with re-pricing options, or issuing new options at a lower exercise price, is that executives are protected from the risk of a falling share price, whereas their shareholders have no such protection. The option scheme therefore fails to align the interests of executives and shareholders.

International Financial Reporting Standard 2 (IFRS2) requires companies to recognise the award of share options as an expense, chargeable against the company's profits, from the time that the share options are granted. The potential effect of share option awards on reported profits might discourage some companies from using options as an incentive.

4 Combined Code provisions on the design of performance-related remuneration

The Combined Code contains provisions for the design of performance-related remuneration schemes that remuneration committees are expected to apply. Some of these provide a useful insight into how incentive schemes might be structured and approved. The Code suggests the following:

4.1 Short-term incentives

The remuneration committee should consider whether the directors should be eligible for annual bonuses. If so, performance criteria should be 'relevant, stretching and designed to enhance shareholder value'. There should be upper limits to annual bonuses, and these limits should be disclosed. There may be a case for an annual bonus to be part-paid in shares which the director is required to hold for a 'significant period'.

4.2 Long-term incentives

The committee should consider whether the directors should be eligible for benefits under long-term incentive schemes. Traditional share option schemes should be weighed against other types of long-term incentive scheme. In normal circumstances the benefits under such schemes should not be receivable in less than three years (for example share options should not be exercisable within three years, and the granting of fully-paid shares should not be within three years). Directors should be encouraged to hold their shares for a further period after they have been granted or share options have been exercised (subject to the need to finance any costs of purchase or any associated tax liabilities). Awards of share options and shares should normally be phased over time rather than granted in a single large block.

4.3 Any proposed new long-term incentive scheme should be approved by the shareholders

A new scheme should preferably replace an existing scheme, or should at least form part of a well-considered overall plan that incorporates the new scheme with existing schemes. The total rewards that are potentially available under such schemes should not be excessive.

4.4 Performance criteria

Pay-outs or grants under all incentive schemes (including new grants under share option schemes) should be subject to challenging performance criteria that reflect the company's objectives. Consideration should be given to criteria that reflect the company's performance relative to a group of other companies in some key measure, such as Total Shareholder Return.

5 Compensation for loss of office: severance payments

A company might come under pressure from its institutional shareholders to limit severance payments to senior executives who are unsuccessful and so are forced to leave the company, having lost the support of both shareholders and fellow directors. When an executive director or other senior executive is dismissed from office, there is usually a compensation payment for loss of office. There are various reasons why an individual might leave the company:

- He or she might be regarded as having failed to do a good job, and someone else should do the job instead. A high severance payment would be seen as 'rewarding failure'.
- There could be a disagreement or falling out between directors, resulting in one or more directors being asked to leave.

The service contract of a director might provide for the payment of compensation for loss of office. Alternatively, a company might be required to give the individual a minimum period of notice, typically one year or six months in the UK. If an individual is asked to leave, he or she might be paid for the notice period without having to work out the notice.

Shareholder concerns with compensation for loss of office arise in cases where an individual is dismissed for having performed badly. A large compensation payment can seem annoying because it seems that the individual is being rewarded for failure. The actual amount of compensation that is paid for loss of office could be a matter of long and difficult negotiations, involving solicitors on both sides. From a good corporate governance perspective, it is generally undesirable that a confidentiality agreement should apply to the details of any compensation agreement.

The Combined Code contains two provisions about service contracts and compensation for termination of office:

1 When negotiating the terms of appointment of a new director, the remuneration committee should consider what compensation commitments the company would have in the event of early termination of office. More specifically, the aim should be to avoid rewarding poor performance. The committee should 'take a robust line' on reducing the amount of compensation to reflect a departing director's obligation to mitigate losses.
2 Notice periods in a contract should be set at one year or less. If it is necessary to offer a longer notice period to a director coming into the company from outside, the notice period should subsequently be reduced to one year or less 'after the initial period'.

The reference to taking a robust line on a director's duty to mitigate losses is a suggestion that a director's contract should provide for a payment of compensation in stages, which would be halted in the event of the director finding employment elsewhere.

6   The remuneration of NEDs

It is usual for a NED to receive a fixed annual fee for his or her services. This might be in the region of £20,000–£60,000 each year, for attending board meetings, some committee meetings and general meetings of the company. A conscientious NED might also spend some time visiting parts of the company, to meet its executives and see how it operates. A provision in the Combined Code is that the board (or, if required by the Articles of Association, the shareholders) should decide the remuneration of NEDs and that the level of remuneration for NEDs should reflect the time commitment and responsibilities of the role.

Concerns for better corporate governance have resulted in a growing role for the NEDs, particularly through membership of board committees. Membership of the audit committee in particular could be very time-consuming if it is done properly.

It seems likely that as the demands on the time of NEDs grow, and as they take on more responsibilities – and potential personal liabilities – they will expect higher rewards. If so, it is probable that these will take the form of a higher fixed annual fee.

6.1   Additional fees

Non-executive directors may receive other forms of remuneration or reward from the company, in addition to a basic fee. This is not so much a problem in the UK as it is in the US. When Enron collapsed, it was revealed that a number of NEDs obtained benefits from the company in addition to a basic fee as a NED. For example, a NED might be paid additionally as a consultant to the company. No matter how genuine and useful these consultancy services are, they put the independence of the NED at risk. This is because the size of a consultancy fee is decided by executive management. Management also has the decision about extending or renewing a consultancy agreement.

If a NED creates trouble for executive management in board meetings or at board committee meetings, there is always the chance that the consultancy agreement will be axed. If the NED is supportive, the fees may be raised.

A consultancy agreement could also bring a NED and the executive management into a close working relationship, such that the independence of the NED is compromised, possibly through friendship and possibly through learning to look at problems from a management perspective.

CASE EXAMPLE 9.2

In 2006, Coca Cola in the US attracted considerable attention for a remuneration initiative for its non-executive directors. In April, Coca Cola announced major changes in the remuneration structure for its (non-executive) directors. Previously, directors had been paid a fixed annual fee of $125,000 ($50,000 in cash, and the rest in Coca Cola stock) and with extra fees for chairing board committees and attending board meetings and committee meetings. Under the new 'all-or-nothing' arrangement, directors would receive no remuneration unless earnings per share grew by at least 8% compound over three years. The aim of this new policy was to achieve greater alignment of the directors' interests with those of the shareholders.

Critics of the new scheme argued that linking NED pay to company performance could threaten the independence of the directors from executive management, rather than align the interests of NEDs and shareholders. In addition, it was argued that by delaying payment of non-executive remuneration for three years, it would be more difficult for the company to recruit directors from less affluent socio-economic backgrounds (on the assumption that this is a desirable objective).

7 The remuneration committee

A fundamental issue with the remuneration of directors and senior executives is who should be responsible for remuneration policy – i.e. who should make the judgements and decisions about what the component elements of a remuneration package should be, and how large the total package might reasonably be. In the past, it has been quite common for the top executives in a company, notably the CEO and chairman, to be involved in setting their own remuneration. Such a system, however, is open to abuse. Without controls and restraints, there is a risk that executives will pay themselves excessively.

Concerns about directors' remuneration found expression in the UK in the mid-1990s, with the Greenbury Committee Report, whose recommendations were subsequently incorporated in the original 1998 combined code (see Chapter 12). Significantly, the Greenbury Committee reached the following conclusions:

- The formulation of remuneration packages for senior executive directors was a fundamental issue for good corporate governance.
- However, the system was open to abuse if executives could decide their own remuneration levels.
- Shareholders are not in a position to decide directors' remuneration, although they had a right to extensive information about it.
- Remuneration for executive directors should therefore be decided by a remuneration committee of the board, consisting entirely of independent NED directors.

7.1 Combined Code requirements for a remuneration committee

The Combined Code states that:

> 'There should be a formal and transparent procedure for developing policy on executive remuneration and for fixing the remuneration packages of individual directors. No director should be involved in deciding his or her own remuneration.'

It goes on to make a provision that 'the board should establish a remuneration committee ... [which] should make available its terms of reference, explaining its role and the authority delegated to it by the board'. The remuneration committee is responsible for both developing remuneration policy and for negotiating the remuneration of individual directors. Although these two matters are related, they are different.

- The remuneration committee should consist entirely of independent NED directors. In larger companies, the committee should consist of at least three members, and in smaller companies (i.e. companies below the FTSE 350) at least two members. The company chairman may be a member of the committee, but not its chairman, provided that he or she was considered to be independent on appointment as company chairman.
- The remuneration committee should have delegated responsibility for setting the remuneration for all executive directors and the chairman (including pension rights and any compensation/severance payments). The remuneration committee should also recommend and monitor the level and structure of remuneration for senior management.
- The board itself (or the shareholders, where required by the Articles of Association) should determine the remuneration of the NED directors. However, if permitted by the Articles, the board may delegate this responsibility to a committee, which might include the CEO.

The Code recognises that it is common in practice for a remuneration committee to use the services of external remuneration consultants. Where remuneration consultants are appointed by the committee, the company should also make publicly available a statement of whether they have any other connection with the company.

The principal duties of the remuneration committee

The principles and provisions of the Combined Code with regard to the remuneration committee include the following points:

- The remuneration committee should consult the chairman and/or CEO about their proposals for the remuneration of executive directors.
- The committee should judge where to position their company relative to other companies (for the purpose of benchmarking). The committee should be sensitive to pay and employment conditions elsewhere in the group, especially when deciding the level of salary increases.
- The remuneration committee should have responsibility for setting the remuneration packages of 'senior management' in addition to executive directors. 'Senior management' is not defined but should include the first layer of management below board level.
- Shareholders should be invited to approve specifically all new long-term incentive schemes and all significant changes to existing schemes.
- Deciding the remuneration of the NEDs should be the responsibility of the board (or the shareholders if required by the articles of association). Where permitted by the articles the board may delegate this responsibility to a committee which might include the CEO. (As a basic principle, no one should be involved in any decisions as to their own remuneration.)
- The chairman of the company should ensure that the company maintains contact as required with its principal shareholders about remuneration issues.

The Higgs Suggestions for Good Practice, which was annexed to the 2003 Combined Code, provided a list of duties of the remuneration committee. Higgs suggested the following main duties:

- The committee should determine and agree with the main board the remuneration policy for the CEO, the board chairman, and any other designated executive managers. This policy should provide for executive managers to be given appropriate incentives for enhanced performance.
- To maintain and assure his or her independence, the committee should also decide the remuneration of the company secretary.
- The committee should decide the targets for performance for any performance-related pay schemes operated by the company.
- It should decide the policy for and scope of pension arrangements for each executive director.
- It should ensure that the contractual terms for severance payments on termination of office are fair to both the individual and the company, that failure is not rewarded and that the director's duty to mitigate losses is fully recognised.
- Within the framework of the agreed remuneration policy, it should determine the remuneration package of each individual executive director, including bonuses, incentive payments and share options.
- It should be aware of and advise on any major changes in employee benefit structures throughout the company and group.
- It should agree the policy for authorising expense claims from the chairman and chief executive.
- It should ensure compliance by the company with the requirements for disclosure of directors' remuneration as required by the Directors' Remuneration Report Regulations 2002 (written into the Companies Act).
- It should be responsible for appointing any remuneration consultants to advise the committee.
- In the company's annual report, it should report the frequency of committee meetings and the attendance by members.
- It should make available to the public its terms of reference, setting out the committee's delegated responsibilities. Where necessary these should be reviewed and updated each year.

ICSA Guidance Note on the terms of reference of the remuneration committee

An ICSA Guidance Note on the terms of reference of the remuneration committee has been issued as a 'guiding document for the effective operation of the remuneration committee'. This contains a list of duties for the committee that was compiled for the Higgs Review and appended to the revised Combined Code. Its content is therefore entirely consistent with the Higgs Report and the Combined Code. Its purpose is to provide a documentary framework that companies can use to draw up their own formal terms of reference for the committee.

It recommends (in agreement with the Higgs Review) that the company secretary (or a designee) should act as secretary to the remuneration committee, because it is his/her responsibility to ensure that the board and its committees are properly constituted and advised. The company secretary can also play a role as intermediary and coordinator between the committee and the main board.

It also addresses how frequently the committee should meet to carry out its duties effectively. Its recommendation is that there should be at least two meetings each year. For UK listed companies, one meeting should be held close to the year end, to review the Remuneration Report that must now by law be included in the annual report and accounts and submitted to the shareholders for approval at the AGM.

8 Disclosure and approval of remuneration details

The main arguments about directors' remuneration can be summarised as follows. Top executives have to be paid high remuneration in order to attract and retain them. A remuneration package for a senior executive should offer incentives for achieving performance targets, and incentive-based payments should be a substantial element in the total package. However, it is very difficult to devise an incentive-based system that properly aligns the interests of top executives with those of the shareholders. Top executives should not be allowed to decide their own remuneration packages. The responsibility for executive remuneration decisions can be given to a remuneration committee of NEDs. This committee should try to find the elusive balance between rewarding their top executives sufficiently, but at the same time structuring the reward package so as to bring the interests of shareholders and executives into alignment.

It is noticeable that within these arguments, the interests of shareholders are mentioned, but there is no suggestion that shareholders should get involved in making remuneration decisions themselves. Shareholder involvement, however, is desirable, and there are two ways in which this might happen:

1 disclosure;
2 shareholder voting on remuneration.

8.1 Directors' remuneration report

The Directors' Remuneration Report Regulations 2002 apply to quoted companies, which are UK companies whose shares are listed on the Official List of the London Stock Exchange or on an official exchange of any other EEA state, the New York Stock Exchange or NASDAQ. They do not apply to AIM companies.

Directors' remuneration report

Quoted companies are required to prepare a directors' remuneration report, which must be approved by the board and signed on its behalf. A copy must be circulated to shareholders in the same way as the annual report and accounts, and it is normal for the report to be included in the same document.

Shareholders must vote at the annual general meeting on a resolution (ordinary resolution) to approve the report. This is an advisory vote only.

The report must contain extensive disclosures about directors' remuneration. A distinction is made between items that are not subject to audit and items that are. The auditors in their audit report must state whether in their opinion the part of the report to be audited has been prepared properly in accordance with the Act. A signed copy of the report must also be filed with the Registrar of Companies, in the same way as the annual accounts, directors' report and auditors' report.

Information not subject to audit

Items to be included in the directors' remuneration report that are not subject to audit are as follows:

- The names of the directors who were members of the remuneration committee, and details about any remuneration consultants that were used (name, nature of services provided).
- A statement of the company's policy on directors' remuneration for the next financial year and the years after that (i.e. a forward-looking policy statement).
- A line graph showing the total shareholder return (TSR) on the company's shares over a five-year period, and the TSR on a holding of a portfolio of shares over the same period representing a named broad equity market index. The graph can therefore be used to compare shareholder returns on the company's shares with those of a market index. The Act specifies how TSR should be calculated.
- Information about the service contract for each director: the date of the contract, its unexpired term and details of any notice periods; any compensation payable for early termination of the contract and any other provisions in the contract affecting the liability of the company in the event of early termination (i.e. severance terms).
- The forward-looking statement on the company's policy on directors' remuneration must include the following details, for each director:
  - details of the performance conditions that apply to decide the director's entitlement to share options or an award under a long-term incentive scheme, and an explanation of why these performance conditions were chosen;
  - a summary of the methods used to decide whether these performance conditions have been met, and an explanation of why these methods were chosen;
  - a description of any proposed significant amendment to the terms and conditions affecting the director's entitlement to share options or awards under a long-term incentive scheme (and an explanation of the reasons for the proposed change);
  - where the director's entitlement to share options or award under a long-term incentive scheme are not subject to meeting certain performance conditions, an explanation of why this is the case;
  - the relative importance of those elements of the director's remuneration that are related to performance and those which are not.

The policy statement should also summarise and explain the company's policy on the duration of contracts with directors and the notice periods and termination payments under these contracts.

Information subject to audit

The remuneration report must contain the following items which are subject to audit:

- A table showing, for each director, the total remuneration for the year, broken down into salary and fees, bonuses, expenses received, compensation for loss of office and other severance payments, and non-cash benefits.
- A table showing, for each director, details of interests in share options, both beneficial and non-beneficial. (Beneficial options are options held in the name of the director or a connected person, such as the director's spouse or child under 18.) The information disclosed should include details of options awarded or exercised during the year, options that expired unexercised during the year, and any variations to the terms and conditions relating to the award or exercise of options. For options exercised during the year, the disclosures should show the market price of the shares when the options were exercised. For options not yet expired, the disclosures should give details of the price paid for their award (if any), the exercise price, the date from which the options may be exercised and the date they expire. Also the market price of the shares at the end of the year, and the highest and lowest market prices reached during the year.
- For each director, details of any long-term incentive schemes (other than share options). These should show the director's interest in each scheme at the start of the year and the end of the year, any changes during the year, and details of when the awards/entitlements can be taken.
- For each director, details of pension contributions or entitlements. The nature of the disclosures will vary according to whether the pension scheme is a defined benefit scheme or a defined contribution scheme.
- For each director, details of any excess pension benefits received or receivable in the year (i.e. benefits in excess of the director's contractual entitlement).
- Significant payments made during the year to former directors of the company.
- The total amount of any payments made to third parties for the services of any director.
- An explanation and justification of any element of directors' remuneration, other than basic salary, which is pensionable.

Additional requirements recommended by the Combined Code

The statutory regulations for quoted companies on directors' remuneration are now quite extensive. The significant elements are:

- the shareholders' right to vote on the directors' remuneration report, which includes a statement on remuneration policy, and the extensive disclosures of remuneration details.
- The Combined Code, however, makes further recommendations:
  - Shareholders should be asked to approve all new long-term incentive schemes.
  - If grants under a share option scheme or long-term incentive scheme are made in one block, rather than phased over time, this should be explained and justified.

8.2   Shareholder approval of directors' remuneration

Giving shareholders the right to vote on directors' remuneration is more contentious that providing shareholders with more information. A distinction should be made, however, between two different types of shareholder vote on executive remuneration:

1   Shareholders might be invited to vote on the company's remuneration policy for the directors. This vote could be binding on the company, so that if the shareholders voted against a remuneration policy, the remuneration committee (or whoever is responsible for remuneration policy in the company) would have to devise a new policy. Alternatively, a shareholder vote might not have the power to bind the company, but simply be treated as a form of advice.

2   Shareholders might be invited to vote on the remuneration package of individual directors. If the package has been negotiated subject to shareholder approval, a shareholder 'no' vote would force the company to renegotiate with the individual (who might choose to leave the company, having failed to win the support of the shareholders). Once a remuneration package has been agreed between a company and a director, there is a binding contract, and shareholders could not be allowed the right to alter the contract details, since this would put the company in breach of contract.

The Directors' Remuneration Report Regulations to invite shareholders to vote on the remuneration policy, although the vote is not binding on the company. For example, in 2005 shareholders of United Business Media voted against the company's remuneration report, in protest against a decision by the company to award an ex gratia payment to its departing CEO. Although the vote was not binding, it had sufficient effect to persuade the CEO, Lord Hollick, to ask the company not to make the payment.

CASE EXAMPLE 9.3

The problems of setting suitable remuneration packages for senior executives was well illustrated by the case of Vodafone and its chief executive, Sir Christopher Gent. The company consulted widely with institutional investors about a new remuneration package for the CEO, and obtained their approval for the principles of the package. However, when the company eventually applied the principles to devise a detailed package, many shareholders were dissatisfied. Three particular controversies were reported in the run-up to the company's 2002 annual general meeting.

1   Sir Christopher was awarded a special payment of £10 million for his role in the acquisition of German company Mannesmann. The problem with payments based on successful takeovers is that there is often no way of knowing for some time whether a takeover has been a success or not. In the case of Vodafone and Mannesmann, the takeover occurred at a time when the telecommunications industry appeared to be growing rapidly and share prices in telecommunications companies were rocketing. Two years or so later, after the worldwide share price collapse in 2001, the wisdom of the Mannesmann deal was called into question.

2 A second problem was that Sir Christopher received large bonus payments for the year to 31 March 2002, when the company reported a loss of £13.5 billion, the largest in UK corporate history. Here, the problem is one of trying to ensure, as far as possible, that bonus payments are linked to the achievement of satisfactory performance targets, although these could include longer-term targets and non-financial targets.

3 A third problem was the announcement of a new remuneration policy, in response to investor criticisms of the old policy. The company consulted with City institutions when formulating the new policy, with the intention of winning their approval. However, investment institutions might be willing to support the principle of a remuneration policy, yet still be angered by the details. Regardless of the general aims of a remuneration policy, the problem is in getting the detail right. In particular, there could be general approval of which performance measures should be used, but disagreement about how challenging should the performance targets be, and what limits, if any, should be placed on the size of bonus payments. When the shareholders voted on the remuneration package at the company's annual general meeting in July 2002, the package was approved, but there was a fairly large vote against.

9 Directors' service contracts

The service contract of a director with his or her company should ideally be in written form, but might not be. A service contract sets out the terms and conditions of the director's appointment, including the duration of the appointment (with a fixed-term contract) or the required minimum period of notice of termination (with a 'rolling' contract).

Companies are required under Companies Act 2006, s. 228 to keep a copy of all written service agreements with directors. Each written service contract should be available for inspection by shareholders free of charge, and a copy should be kept at the company's registered office, or its principal place of business, or in the same place as its register of shareholders.

Individuals who are not shareholders may also inspect a director's service contract on payment of a prescribed fee.

In addition, UK Listing Rules require, for listed companies, that:

- Directors' service contracts should be available for inspection by shareholders during normal business hours.
- Copies of directors' service contracts must be available for inspection at the AGM for at least 15 minutes before the meeting starts and until it ends.
- The notice convening the AGM must specify that copies of written service contracts will be available for inspection, or that no such written contracts exist.

In the directors' report in the annual report and accounts, there should be a statement of the unexpired term of the service contract of any director who is being proposed for re-election at the AGM.

The issues that raise the most concerns about directors' service contracts are:

- remuneration, including pension rights;
- the term of the contract or period of notice;
- payments to which the director would be entitled on termination of the contract.

The Combined Code states that notice periods or contract periods should be for one year or less. Should it be necessary to offer a director joining from outside the company a notice period or contract period in excess of one year, the period should be reduced to one year or less after the initial period.

The views of the ABI/NAPF on two-year contracts are that, as a general rule, they should not be offered to incoming senior executives as an inducement to join. The notice period for contracts should be one year or less. If all companies take this line, executives will stop asking for contracts with a notice period in excess of one year. Two-year deals should only be acceptable for struggling companies.

10   Institutional shareholder views on directors' remuneration

UK Institutional investors have developed strong views on directors' remuneration. The ABI and NAPF have issued guidelines on executive remuneration, and regularly issue 'red top' notices to their members recommending that they vote against the boards of companies on resolutions relating to pay.

The Association of British Insurers reviews regularly its guidelines for members on executive remuneration. Revised guidelines were published in December 2007 containing:

- basic principles on executive remuneration;
- a section on remuneration committees and their responsibilities;
- guidance for base pay, bonuses, pensions and contracts and severance;
- guidance on share-based incentive schemes.

10.1 ABI principles for executive remuneration

The ABI's general principles on remuneration policies and practice for executives are as follows:

- Boards are responsible for adopting remuneration policies and practices that promote the success of the company by creating value in the longer term. Remuneration policies and practices should be clearly aligned with corporate objectives and business strategy and they should be reviewed regularly.
- Remuneration committees should maintain a 'constructive and timely dialogue' with the company's major institutional shareholders and with the ABI on matters relating to senior executive remuneration such as changes in remuneration policy and share incentive schemes.

- Executive remuneration should be set at levels that retain and motivate. However, benchmarks used for setting targets and rewards should be used with caution, because of the risk that remuneration levels might 'ratchet' upwards without any corresponding improvement in company performance.
- Executive remuneration should be linked to individual and corporate performance through graduated targets that align the interests of the executives with those of shareholders.
- Shareholders will not support arrangements that entitle executives to rewards that are not justified by performance. Remuneration committees should ensure that service contracts contain provisions that are consistent with this principle.

10.2 Remuneration committees and their responsibilities

The main aspects of ABI guidance on remuneration committees are as follows:

- The remuneration committee is responsible for 'ensuring that the mix of incentives reflects the company's needs, establishes an appropriate balance between fixed and variable remuneration, and is based on targets that are stretching, verifiable and relevant'.
- The remuneration committee should ensure that remuneration levels for executives properly reflect the contributions of executives, and they should be rigorous in selecting a comparator group of companies.
- When designing share-based incentives, the remuneration committee should guard against the possibility of 'unjustified windfall gains'.
- The committee should consider legal redress where performance achievements are subsequently found to have been overstated significantly, so that bonuses and other incentives that were paid should not in fact have been paid.
- The committee should also ensure that variable and share-based rewards are not payable unless the performance measurement governing this is 'robust'.
- The committee should pay particular attention to the remuneration of key executives who are not directors.

10.3 ABI guidance for base pay, bonuses, pensions and contracts and severance

The ABI's guidelines for remuneration structure go into some detail on specific aspects of remuneration packages. They include the following.

Base pay and bonuses

On base pay, the ABI guidelines state simply that base pay should reflect the contribution of the executive concerned and policy on base pay should be fully communicated to the shareholders. If a company seeks to pay base salaries above this median level, this policy should be justified.

The remuneration committee should scrutinise all other benefits, including benefits in kind, to ensure that they are justified, appropriately valued and disclosed.

The remuneration committee should be 'robust' in setting and monitoring targets for bonuses, and bonus payments should reflect actual achievements against these targets.

The other main provisions relating to bonuses are as follows:

- Any material ex gratia payments to an executive must be fully explained and justi- fied, and should be subject to shareholder approval before being paid.
- Shareholders are not supportive of 'transaction bonuses' that reward directors or other executives for effecting transactions irrespective of the future financial conse- quences of those transactions.

Additional guidance on bonuses is provided, including the following:

- Following the payment of a bonus, shareholders expect to see a full analysis in the Remuneration Report of the extent to which targets were actually met.
- Maximum participation levels in bonus schemes for each individual should be dis- closed, and any increase in the maximum participation level from one year to the next should be disclosed.
- Annual bonuses should not be treated as pensionable pay.
- The remuneration committee should retain the right to reduce or reclaim a bonus if it is subsequently discovered that performance achievements were 'significantly misstated'.

Pensions

The remuneration committee should recognise the impact that pension arrangements can have on the mix between fixed pay (base salary) and variable pay (bonuses). The commit- tee should recognise that pension costs can be very expensive and pension payments to a former executive are not directly linked to performance.

Contracts and severance

The remuneration committee should ensure that service contracts protect the company from exposure to the risk of payments to an executive in the event of failure. 'Contracts should commit companies not to pay for failure.'

There should be a clear link in the service contract between payments of variable pay and performance, and in the event of an early termination of employment for an executive there should be no automatic entitlement to bonuses or share-based payments.

'Phased payments are generally appropriate for fulfilling compensation on early termi- nation.' Shareholders are less supportive of a 'liquidated damages' approach, whereby the company and the executive agree at the outset on the amount that will be paid in the event of severance.

The remuneration committee should also ensure that the full benefit of mitigation is obtained. This includes a legal obligation on the part of a departing executive to mitigate his or her loss incurred on severance of the service contract by seeking other employment and so reducing the need for compensation.

CASE EXAMPLE 9.8

In August 2006, the Association of British Insurers (ABI) sent a letter to the FTSE 350 companies, asking them to review their pension arrangements for senior executives, warning that some major shareholders would be concerned about the pensions aspect of excessive severance packages. The specific matter of concern was that executives might have employment contracts that entitle them to a large increase in their pension fund, as part of any severance package. The letter asked the remuneration committees to look at the pension arrangements in executives contracts, to make sure that they were in line with best practice.

The reason for the letter was a payout to four former directors of Scottish Power, who had all retired with large increases in their pension funds. The former chief executive had benefited from a doubling of his pension fund arrangements. The company admitted that the cost of the retirement of the four directors had been £11 million, but justified its action by stating that it was contractually obliged to make the pension increases, but was now reviewing its pension arrangements for senior executives.

The ABI expressed its concern that other companies might have similar arrangements that the shareholders were unaware of. Although the ABI has expressed its strong disapproval of any such arrangements that might exist, it would not necessarily be easy for companies (even if they wanted to do so) to persuade executives to agree to changes in the pension arrangements in their contracts.

10.4 ABI guidance for share-based incentive schemes

The main provisions of the ABI guidelines on share-based incentives are as follows. (The guidelines also include extensive additional guidance on share-based awards.)

- The ABI supports share incentive schemes that link remuneration to performance and align the interests of senior executives with those of the company's shareholders. The vesting of share awards or share options should therefore be based on performance conditions measured over a period of time that is appropriate to the strategic objective of the company. This will not be less than three years.
- All new share-based incentive schemes and any substantial changes to existing schemes should be subject to prior approval by the shareholders. Their operation, rationale and cost should be fully explained so that the shareholders can make an informed judgement.
- The operation of share incentive schemes should not lead to a dilution in the equity holding of the other shareholders in excess of acceptable limits.
- Share options should not be granted at an exercise price below the prevailing market price for the shares.
- It is desirable to align the interests of the chairman and independent NEDs with those of the shareholders, for example through payment in company shares bought at market prices. However, shareholders consider it inappropriate for the chairman

or independent NEDs to receive incentive awards geared to the share price or corporate performance, since this would impair their ability to provide impartial oversight and advice.

- Shareholders encourage companies to require their executive directors and senior executives to build up 'meaningful' shareholdings in the company.

10.5 Joint ABI/NAPF statement on severance pay

The ABI and NAPF have also produced a joint statement (December 2003; reviewed December 2004) on severance pay. The main issues concerning severance pay are now included in the ABI guidelines, but it is interesting to look at the response of the institutional investors to 'rewards for failure' when the issue first became an issue of concern.

The statement was issued as a result of the concern about severance payments to senior executives ousted from their companies as a result of poor corporate performance. High levels of compensation on leaving office were seen as unjustifiable 'rewards for failure'. The joint statement commented:

> 'It is unacceptable that failure, which detracts from the value of an enterprise and which can threaten the livelihood of employees, can result in large payments to its departing leaders. Executives, whose remuneration is already at a level which allows for the risk inherent in their role, should show leadership in aligning their financial interests with those of their shareholders.'

On the other hand, the ABI/NAPF acknowledge that incoming executives should be offered some protection against downside risk in their contracts, and that having agreed a contract with the company, the individual is protected by contract rights.

Nevertheless, the joint statement argues that boards should have remuneration policies that avoid making payments that are not properly merited. From the outset, when agreeing a remuneration package with an individual senior executive, boards should both calculate the potential cost of a sudden termination of employment and also consider the potential reputational risk to the company of being obliged to make a high severance payment to an unsuccessful departing executive. Although shareholders should hold the board of directors accountable for excessive severance payment terms, the main responsibility for arranging suitable severance terms in an individual's contract lies with the remuneration committee.

Principles for negotiating severance terms

- The terms of an individual's contract should not commit companies to making payments for failure. Boards should resist pressure from incoming individuals for generous severance terms in their contract.
- 'It should be clearly understood that investors do not expect executives to be automatically entitled to contract payments other than basic pay. Bonuses should be cut or eliminated when individual performance is poor.'
- Although the maximum notice period should be one year, a shorter notice period might be appropriate where severance pay would otherwise be too high.

When a dismissed director takes a dispute to litigation, the courts take some account of variable pay (performance-related pay or bonuses) when deciding on the appropriate award. However, the size of this payment can be limited by attaching clear performance conditions to variable pay in the individual's contract (rather than wording the performance conditions in unclear or ambiguous terms).

Contract details

- The ABI/NAPF would approve of a contract that provided for phased payments to an individual after termination of employment, with the payments ceasing if the individual finds fresh employment.
- The employment contract should include a provision that it is the duty of the individual, in the event of severance of employment, to mitigate his or her losses.

The ABI/NAPF statement goes on to discuss the problem that in UK law, it is not normally possible for underperformance to be established as grounds for summary dismissal of an individual without compensation. It then refers to the Employment Act 2002, under which a statutory disciplinary procedure is implied into every employment contract, including those of executive directors, and suggests that boards should be prepared to make use of these statutory procedures against underperforming executives where appropriate.

An executive's contract might therefore include a provision that following dismissal as a result of disciplinary procedures against the individual, a shorter notice period will apply than the normal notice period in the contract (typically twelve months). The ABI/NAPF statement suggests one week's notice for every year of service up to a maximum of 12 weeks. However, without a specific provision in the contract for shorter notice periods, the individual will be entitled to the full contractual notice period, even if dismissed following disciplinary procedures.

The statement also makes certain comments about pension settlements for an outgoing executive. Boards should make a clear distinction between the individual's contractual entitlement to pension arrangements and discretionary enhancements agreed as part of the severance settlement. Contracts for executives should state that the individual's pension will not be enhanced in the event of early termination unless the board is satisfied that the enhancement is merited. Ominously perhaps, the statement adds that shareholders are likely to question enhancement decisions that do not seem merited, and might vote against the remuneration policy if they are not satisfied.

Chapter summary

- Public hostility to excessive remuneration for directors can affect investor confidence in companies and the stock markets. Senior executives should be well rewarded, but not excessively so.

- An attractive basic salary should be offered to directors to attract and keep capable and talented individuals. A large part of an executive's remuneration package, however, should be in the form of incentives.

- Incentives could be bonus payments linked to short-term performance (e.g. growth in earnings per share) or possibly long-term performance. Unless appropriate incentives are selected, executives could earn a high bonus even when the company performance is disappointing. The UK Combined Code requires companies to seek shareholder approval for new long-term incentive schemes.

- A major concern with corporate governance is that incentive schemes do not achieve their intended purpose, which is to attract and retain talented executives, and then to motivate them to achieve performance targets that are in the best interests of the company's shareholders.

- A problem is to find a suitable balance between fixed base pay (and pension entitlements) and variable rewards, and also to find a suitable balance between short-term cash bonuses and longer-term share-based incentives.

- NEDs should be paid a flat fee and should not be given incentive-linked rewards.

- To avoid a situation where executives are involved in setting their own remuneration, the Greenbury Committee recommended that remuneration policy for directors and the remuneration packages of individual directors should be decided by a remuneration committee consisting entirely of independent NEDs. The requirement for a remuneration committee is included in the Combined Code.

- The Companies Act requires listed companies to provide extensive information about directors' remuneration in the annual report and accounts. This report, which should also contain a statement of remuneration policy, should be submitted to the shareholders for approval at the AGM.

- Institutional shareholders have indicated their concerns about the details of directors' remuneration packages, and the ABI and NAPF have issued guidelines on the subject.

Chapter 10

Risk management and corporate governance

1. The nature of risk
2. Internal control system
3. The UK corporate governance framework
4. The Turnbull Committee Report on internal control
5. The role of internal audit
6. Risk management
7. The role of the board (or audit committee) in risk management
8. The board's statement on internal control
9. Sarbanes–Oxley Act, s. 404

1 The nature of risk

Risk refers to the possibility that something unexpected or unplanned will happen. In many cases, risk is seen as the possibility that something bad might happen. This type of risk can be described as downside risk, because it is a risk that something will happen that would not normally be expected.

There is upside risk too. This is the possibility that actual events might turn out better than expected. In a business context, an example of upside risk is the possibility that sales volumes will be higher than planned or that workdays lost through industrial action will be lower than anticipated.

- Businesses also need to manage their risks and risk management involves making decisions about upside risks as well as downside risks.
- Just as individuals make decisions about accepting risks, avoiding risks or mitigating risks through insurance and other measures, businesses do the same. Risk insurance is an important aspect of risk management, and a large organisation might employ specialist risk managers. In some companies, the responsibility for risk management is given to the company secretary.
- Businesses are exposed to the risk of losses through errors and omissions by their employees or by fraud and dishonesty. Many of the errors and omissions relate to the activities of the accounts department, such as failing to send out invoices to customers, or failing to carry out sufficient credit checks on a new customer asking

for credit. Fraud is often related to the accounts department too, because it deals with payments and receipts of money for the business.

- Businesses also make investment decisions. Every investment is risky. Actual returns could be either lower or higher than expected. In deciding whether or not to undertake an investment, the risks as well as the potential returns should be taken into consideration. Shareholders would like to see their company earning high returns, but might be unwilling to see the management taking excessive investment risks in trying to achieve those returns.

1.1   The connection between risk management and corporate governance

Risk management is relevant to corporate governance in two ways:

1   It is the responsibility of the board of directors to look after the assets of their company and to protect the value of their shareholders' investment. This includes a duty to take measures to prevent losses through error, omission, fraud and dishonesty. Control measures are provided through a system of internal control. A principle of the Combined Code is that 'The board should maintain a sound system of internal control to safeguard shareholders' investment and the company's assets'.

2   It is also argued that the board of directors should be responsible for making sure that all risks are managed properly. A company should protect itself against serious downside risks, such as losses through fire damage, flood damage, theft, accident claims by employees, and so on, and the board should be satisfied that a management system is in place for monitoring and controlling these risks. Executive managers take many business decisions where returns are difficult to predict, and there is upside risk as well as downside risk. The board should be satisfied that, in their decision-making, managers take risk into account as well as expected returns. Similarly, when the board takes major investment decisions itself or decides on corporate strategy, risks as well as expected returns should be properly assessed.

The Cadbury Committee described risk management as 'the process by which executive management, under board supervision, identifies the risk arising from business ... and establishes the priorities for control and particular objectives'. The Committee, reporting on corporate governance in 1992, took the view that risk management should be systematic and embedded in the company's procedures and that there should be a culture of risk awareness. The importance of risk management for a company is that a failure to monitor, control and contain risks could lead to financial collapse.

The Cadbury Committee argued the need not just for an effective system of internal control but also for broader risk management. This view was not generally accepted at the time, but the significance of risk management and of the board's responsibility to shareholders for proper risk management, was eventually accepted 'officially' as an element of corporate governance with the publication of the Combined Code in 1998. The provisions of the current Combined Code relating to risk management are outlined in more detail below.

Although ultimate responsibility for internal control and risk management lies with the board of directors, the task of detailed oversight might be delegated to the audit committee, or even a separate board committee with specific responsibility for managing risk.

2 Internal control system

An internal control system consists of a 'control environment' and control procedures. A useful definition of internal control was given by the Committee of Sponsoring Organizations of the Treadway Commission (COSO) in the US. The COSO Framework defied internal control as 'a process, effected by an entity's board of directors, management and other personnel, designed to provide reasonable assurance regarding the achievement of objectives' in the areas of:

- effectiveness and efficiency of operations (through operational controls);
- the reliability of financial reporting (through financial controls); and
- compliance with relevant laws and regulations (through compliance controls).

The COSO Framework identified five elements to a system of internal control.

1   A control environment describes the awareness of (and attitude to) internal controls in the organisation, shown by the directors, management and employees generally. It therefore encompasses corporate culture, management style and employee attitudes to control procedures.
2   Risk identification and assessment. There should be a system or procedures for identifying the risks facing the company (and how these are changing) and assessing their significance. Controls or management initiatives should be devised to deal with significant risks.
3   Internal controls. Controls should be devised and implemented to eliminate, reduce or control risks. Internal controls are described in more detail later.
4   Information and communication. All employees who are responsible for the management of risks should receive information that enables them to fulfil this task.
5   Monitoring. The effectiveness of risk controls and the internal control system generally should be monitored regularly. Internal audit is one method of monitoring the internal control system.

Internal controls

There are several types of internal control, and each organisation will use some or all types to a greater or lesser extent. Some organisations have more extensive and more effective controls than others. A useful method of categorising internal controls was used in an old guideline of the UK Auditing Practices Board, and remembered by the mnemonic SPAMSOAP. Internal controls can be categorised as:

> **S – Segregation of duties.** Where possible, duties should be split between two or more people, so that the work done by one person acts as a check on the work done by another. With segregation of duties, it is more difficult for fraud to take place, because several individuals would have to collude in the fraud. It is also more difficult for accidental errors to occur, because when several people are involved in a task, they act as a check on each other.

P – Physical controls. Physical controls are measures to ensure the physical safety of assets, such as putting cash in a safe, banking cash receipts immediately, and preventing unauthorised access to computer systems through the use of passwords and internet firewalls.

A – Authorisation and approval. All financial transactions should require the authorisation or approval of an appropriate responsible person, and there should be an authorisation limit to how much spending each responsible person can approve.

M – Management controls. Management should exercise control over financial systems, for example by preparing a budget and then monitoring actual performance by comparing it with the budget. Management controls can also be exercised by reviewing other financial statements, such as a balance sheet, profit and loss account and cash flow statement.

S – Supervision. The day-to-day work of employees should be properly supervised. Good supervision will reduce the likelihood of errors or fraud.

O – Organisation. Everyone should be fully aware of his or her responsibilities, and lines of authority, lines of reporting and levels of responsibility should be clear. Errors and fraud are much more likely where it is uncertain who is responsible for what and who should be reporting to whom.

A – Arithmetical and accounting controls. These are procedures in an accounts office to check the accuracy of the records and the numbers. They include the use of control totals and reconciliations.

P – Personnel. The quality of internal controls is dependent on the quality of the individuals working in the organisation, and personnel selected to do a job should have the right personal qualities and be properly trained and/or qualified.

The nature and extent of the internal controls in an organisation will depend to a large extent on the size of the organisation, what controls it can afford and whether the benefits obtained from any particular control measure are sufficient to justify its cost. The internal control system should, however, be sufficiently robust and effective to minimise the risk of serious losses through error or fraud.

3 The UK corporate governance framework

The connection between good corporate governance and risk management has been recognised for some years, with the inclusion of provisions in the original Combined Code. The key issues to note are that the board has a responsibility to monitor the risk management and internal control systems, and if the company does not have an internal audit team, to review the need for one each year.

3.1 Combined Code requirements: internal control and risk management systems, and internal audit

A principle of the Combined Code is that: 'The board should maintain a sound system of internal control to safeguard shareholders' investment and the company's assets.' The Code goes on to state that the board should establish formal and transparent arrangements for considering how they should apply the financial reporting and internal control principles.

The board is required, at least annually, to conduct a review of the group's systems of internal controls, and should report to the shareholders that they have done so. 'The review should cover all controls, including financial, operational and compliance controls and risk management.' In other words, the board's responsibility for reviewing internal controls and risk management extends beyond financial matters to the business operations and regulatory compliance.

The Code also states that the audit committee should have delegated responsibilities for some or all of these matters, and it includes in the main responsibilities of the audit committee:

- to review the company's internal financial controls;
- unless reviewed by a separate board risk committee consisting of independent directors or by the board as a whole, to review the company's internal control and risk management systems (i.e. extending beyond just internal financial controls);
- to monitor and review the effectiveness of the internal audit function.

Where there is no internal audit function, the audit committee should consider annually whether there is a need for one, and make a recommendation to the board. The reasons for the absence of an internal audit function should be explained in the relevant section of the annual report.

4 The Turnbull Committee Report on internal control

Following the inclusion of provisions relating to risk management and internal controls in the 1998 Combined Code a working party, known as the Turnbull Committee, published guidelines to listed companies on how to apply the principles of the Combined Code with respect to internal controls and risk management. The Report, originally called 'Internal Control: Guidance for Directors on the Combined Code' is now known as The Turnbull Guidance.

The Financial Reporting Council, which now has responsibility for The Turnbull Guidance, initiated a review in 2005 and a revised version came into effect for financial years beginning on or after 1 January 2006 (see Appendix 9).

4.1 Maintaining a sound system of internal control

The board of directors is responsible for maintaining a sound system of internal control. The Turnbull Guidance states that the board should:

- set appropriate policies on internal control;
- seek regular assurance to satisfy itself that the system is operating effectively;
- ensure that the system of internal control is effective in managing risks in the way that it has approved.

In deciding its policies for internal control and assessing what constitutes an effective system of internal control, the board should consider the following factors:

- the nature and extent of the risks facing the company;
- the extent and categories of risk that it regards as acceptable for the company to bear;
- the likelihood that the risks will materialise;
- the company's ability to reduce the incidence and impact on the business of the risks that do materialise;
- the costs of operating particular controls relative to the benefits to be obtained from managing the risks they control.

The Turnbull Guidance, in keeping with the Combined Code, identifies three categories of internal controls that should be managed, reviewed and monitored:

1 operational controls, to ensure the efficiency and effectiveness of operational performance;
2 financial controls, to protect assets, prevent or detect fraud and ensure the accuracy of financial record-keeping and financial reporting;
3 compliance controls, to ensure compliance with regulations.

The internal control system should:

- 'be embedded in the operations of the company and form part of its culture';
- be capable of responding quickly to risks to the business as they emerge and develop;
- include procedures for reporting immediately to the management responsible and for controlling failings that have been identified and any corrective action that has been undertaken.

The report emphasises that a sound system of internal control cannot provide certain protection against a company suffering losses or breaches of laws or regulations or failing to meet its business objectives. The possibility will always exist of 'poor judgement in decision-making, human error, control processes being deliberately circumvented by employees and others, management overriding controls and the occurrence of unforeseen circumstances'.

4.2   Reviewing the effectiveness of internal control

The Turnbull Guidance states that 'reviewing the effectiveness of internal control is an essential part of the board's responsibilities'. The board needs to form its own view on the effectiveness, based on the information and assurances it receives. Management is accountable to the board for monitoring the system of internal control and for providing assurance to the board that it has done so.

This authority to conduct the review might be delegated to the audit committee, but the board as a whole is responsible for the statements on internal control in the company's annual report and accounts.

- An essential feature of a sound system of internal control is a continuous monitoring of the system.
- The board should not rely solely on the monitoring processes that are built into the system as internal controls. It should also receive regular reports on internal control. 'Internal controls considered by the board should include all types of controls including those of an operational and compliance nature, as well as internal financial controls' (Turnbull Report).

Management is accountable to the board for monitoring the internal control system, and should provide an assurance to the board that it has done so. 'The reports from management to the board should ... provide a balanced assessment of the significant risks and the effectiveness of the system of internal control in managing those risks.' Any significant control failings or weaknesses that have been identified should be discussed in the management reports, including the impact they have had or could have, and the measures that have been taken to rectify them.

When reviewing management reports, the board should:

- consider what are the significant risks and assess how they have been identified, evaluated and managed;
- assess the effectiveness of the related system of internal control in managing those significant risks (having particular regard to any significant failings or weaknesses in internal control that have been reported);
- consider whether the necessary actions are being taken to deal with identified failings or weaknesses;
- consider whether the findings of the review indicate a need for more extensive monitoring of the internal control system (Turnbull Guidance).

The board should undertake an annual assessment for the purpose of making its public statement on internal control. This should consider, in particular:

- the changes, since the previous annual assessment, in the nature and extent of significant risks and the company's ability to respond to changes in its business and external environment;
- the scope and quality of management's risk monitoring, the system of internal control and the work of the internal audit function (and other providers of assurance);
- the extent and frequency of reports to the board on risk monitoring and internal control;
- the incidence of significant failings or weaknesses in control that have been identified in the period, and their actual or potential impact on the company's financial performance or condition;
- the effectiveness of the company's public reporting processes.

Whenever the board becomes aware at any time of a significant failing or weakness in internal control, it should:

- find out how the failing or weakness arose;
- reassess the effectiveness of management's processes for designing, operating and monitoring the system of internal control.

4.3   The board's statement on internal control

'The annual report and accounts should include such meaningful, high-level information as the board considers necessary to assist shareholders' understanding of the main features of the company's risk management processes and system of internal control, and should not give a misleading impression.'

In its statement the board should summarise the process it has applied for reviewing the effectiveness of the system of internal control, and confirm that action has been taken to deal with any significant weaknesses or failings identified from the review.

5   The role of internal audit

Internal audit is defined as 'an independent appraisal activity established within an organisation as a service to it. It is a control which functions by examining and evaluating the adequacy and effectiveness of other controls' (CIMA Official Terminology). 'The objective of internal auditing is to assist members of the organisation in the effective discharge of their responsibilities. To this end internal auditing furnishes them with analyses, appraisals, recommendations, counsel and information concerning the activities reviewed' (Institute of Internal Auditors).

An organisation might have an internal audit unit or section, which carries out investigative work. An internal audit function should act independently of executive managers, and would report either to the board itself, the audit committee, the chief executive officer or the finance director.

The work done by any internal audit unit is not prescribed by regulation, but is decided by management or by the board (or audit committee). The possible tasks of internal audit include the following:

- Reviewing the internal control system. Traditionally, an internal audit department has carried out checks on the financial controls in an organisation, possibly in collaboration with the external auditors. The checks would be to establish whether suitable financial controls exist and, if so, whether they are applied properly and are effective. It is not the function of internal auditors to manage risks, only to monitor and report them, and to check that risk controls are efficient and cost-effective.
- Special investigations. Internal auditors might conduct special investigations into particular aspects of the organisation's operations.
- Examination of financial and operating information. Internal auditors might be asked to investigate the timeliness of reporting and the accuracy of the information in reports.

- A VFM (value for money) audit is an investigation into an operation or activity, to establish whether it is economical, efficient and effective.
- Reviewing compliance by the organisation with particular laws or regulations.
- Risk assessment. Internal auditors might be asked to investigate aspects of risk management, and in particular the adequacy of the mechanisms for identifying, assessing and controlling significant risks to the organisation, from both internal and external sources.

Internal auditors might be involved in providing continuous support to the risk management process. If a company has established a risk oversight committee, with responsibility for the oversight and reporting of risks, a senior internal auditor might be one of the committee members. The internal audit department might even have responsibility for coordinating risk management within the company, and reporting to the board or audit committee about risks on a company-wide basis.

5.1   Investigation of internal controls

Internal auditors are commonly required to check the soundness of internal financial controls. In assessing the effectiveness of individual controls, and of an internal control system generally, the following factors should be considered:

- Whether the controls are manual or automated. Automated controls are by no means error- or fraud-proof, but might be more reliable than similar manual controls.
- Whether controls are discretionary or non-discretionary. Non-discretionary controls are checks and procedures that must be carried out. Discretionary controls are those that do not have to be applied, either because they are voluntary or because an individual can choose to disapply the controls. Risks can creep into a system, for example, when senior management choose to disapply controls and allow unauthorised or unchecked procedures to happen.
- Whether the control can be circumvented easily, because an activity can be carried out in a different way where similar controls do not apply.
- Whether the controls are effective in achieving their purpose. Are they extensive enough or frequent enough? Are the controls applied rigorously enough? For example, is a supervisor doing his job properly?

Reports by internal auditors can provide reassurance that internal controls are sound and effective, or might recommend changes and improvements where weaknesses are uncovered.

5.2   The objectivity and independence of internal auditors

The line manager of an operation or department should monitor the internal controls within the operation, and should try to identify and correct weaknesses. However, a line manager cannot be properly objective, because he or she could face 'blame' for control failures.

In contrast, internal auditors ought to be objective, because they investigate the control systems of other departments and operations.

The independence of internal auditors is more questionable, because they are employees within the organisation and report to someone on the organisation structure. If the internal auditors report to the finance director, they will find it difficult to be critical of the finance director himself. Similarly, if the internal auditors report to the chief executive, they will be reluctant to criticise the chief executive. In this respect, the independence of the internal auditors could be compromised.

5.3   The need for an internal audit function

The Combined Code requires the audit committee to monitor and review the effectiveness of the internal audit function. Where there is no internal audit function, the audit committee should consider annually whether there is a need for one, and make a recommendation to the board.

The Turnbull Guidance suggests that the need for an internal audit function will depend on the nature of the company and its activities, and on factors such as company size, diversity and complexity of activities, number of employees, and so on. Some particular aspects of risk and internal control might be monitored by specialist units, such as health and safety experts, lawyers and environmental experts. The Turnbull Guidance adds:

'In the absence of an internal audit function, management needs to apply other monitoring processes in order to assure itself and the board that the system of internal control is functioning as intended. In these circumstances, the board will need to assess whether such processes provide sufficient and objective assurance.'

6   Risk management

Many risks face an organisation. The nature and severity of risks varies from one organisation to another. Risks also change over time. Some become less significant, whilst new risks emerge. It is useful to categorise risks, in order to develop a better understanding of risk management.

6.1   Categories of risk

For companies, risks can be broadly divided into business risks (or strategic risks) and financial risks.

Business risks are risks to a company's business such that actual performance could be much worse (or better) than expected. When a company develops a new product or service, it will have an expectation of the likely sales demand. Actual demand could be higher or lower than expected. With some new products, the risk that demand will differ from expectation could be much more severe than with other new products.

Another example of business risk is obsolescence. A company might operate in a market where there is a high risk of technological change. For manufacturers of typewriters, the risk of obsolescence was realised with the arrival of the personal computer and word processing software. For manufacturers of analogue television sets, there has been the risk of replacement by digital television. For producers of pocket diaries and paper-based personal organisers, there was a risk of obsolescence with the arrival of electronic personal organisers.

Business risk arises from new competition, or from the possibility of a merger of two existing competitors. A company operating in a competitive market needs to be aware of the initiatives a rival firm might take, and what responses might be needed to deal with them.

Financial risks arise from the possibility that the financial situation will turn out to be different from what was expected. Financial risks can be grouped into sub-categories, such as credit risk, foreign exchange risk and interest rate risk:

- Credit risk faces companies that lend money or give credit, and is the risk that losses from bad debts will be much higher (although they could also be lower) than anticipated. In an economic downturn, many borrowers default on debt repayments, and losses for lenders can be severe. Banks in particular suffer bad debt losses.
- Foreign exchange risk arises from the possibility that a volatile currency exchange rate might change, and become much worse (or better) than expected. For example, a non-US company that buys crude oil in large quantities is exposed to a risk of a rise in the value of the US dollar, since oil is priced in US dollars in the world markets.
- Interest rate risk arises from the possibility that interest rates will rise or fall and result in unexpected losses (or gains). Banks in particular have exposures to interest rate risks, because they both borrow and lend huge amounts of money, and their profits or losses depend on the respective rates at which they can borrow funds and lend funds.

The management of financial risks has reached a high level of sophistication in the banking industry. Internationally accepted rules (known as the Basel Accord) require banks to maintain a minimum amount of capital relative to the size of their business to cover their credit risk. These rules are intended to ensure that if a bank suffers from severe bad debt losses due to defaults by borrowing governments or multinational companies, it will have sufficient capital resources to cover the losses, without putting the funds of depositors at risk. In a similar way, banks are required to maintain a minimum amount of capital to cover market risk. This is the risk of losses on their financial market trading activities, in equities, bonds, the foreign exchange markets and money markets, and so on.

The banking industry has developed a new set of capital adequacy rules to replace the existing rules (known as Basel 2). These will require banks to maintain a minimum amount of capital to cover their operational risks. These are risks of losses that would occur as a result of a failure in their operational systems.

Each industry and each company within an industry faces different risks. The questions that management should ask are:

- What are the risks facing this company?
- For each of these risks, how would the company be affected if the worst outcome happened, or if a fairly bad outcome happened?
- What is the likelihood of a bad outcome for that risk item?

- What should the company be doing to manage the risk, either by avoiding it altogether or planning to deal with the problems that will arise in the event of a bad outcome?

Controversially, perhaps, these issues of risk management have been introduced as a matter of good corporate governance by the Combined Code. The board's responsibility for risk management extends beyond financial controls, and to all aspects of risk, including operational risk and compliance risk.

Regulatory risk and compliance risk refer to the risks to a company from breaking the law or failure to comply with regulations. The business environment is now highly regulatory, with laws or regulations applying in areas such as health and safety, the environment, product safety, competition law, financial services regulations, data protection, bribery and corruption, taxation and company law in general. Regulatory and 'watchdog' organisations exist for each of these areas, such as the Office of Fair Trading and Competition Commission, the Health and Safety Commission and the Financial Services Authority.

Breaches of regulations might be punished with fines, but there are also the hidden risks of damage to reputation and effect on employee morale.

Reputational risk, which has links to corporate social responsibility and regulatory risk, refers to the risk to a company's reputation, particularly with customers and the general public, from adverse reaction to its products or activities. Environmental groups, for example, might target companies who are considered to be carrying out non-sustainable business that is causing irreversible damage to the environment. Public warnings about the risk to health or safety from particular products can damage the reputation of the companies making and selling them.

6.2 Principles for effective risk management

There are four basic elements to risk management:

1 risk identification;
2 risk evaluation;
3 risk management measures; and
4 risk control and review.

These are four of the elements in a system of internal control, referred to earlier.

Risk identification

An organisation should have a procedure for reviewing the risks it faces, to identify what they are. Risks change over time, and risk reviews should therefore be regular.

The board (and management) should look at all the significant risks facing the company, not just financial risks. For example, companies seeking to expand in global markets and develop a worldwide brand name could find reputation risk a matter of some importance, and should consider how to respond to international and local pressure groups. In this context, environmental risk is also important. Causing environmental damage will lead not just to large direct costs (remedial expenditure, fines), but will also damage the company's international reputation.

Risk evaluation

The evaluation of risks calls for procedures to assess the potential size of the risk. The expected losses that could occur from adverse events or developments depend on:

- the probability that an adverse outcome will occur; and
- the size of the loss in the event of an adverse outcome.

Where a risk is unlikely to result in an adverse outcome and the loss would in any case be small, no management action might be necessary. Where a risk is not very likely to materialise, but the losses could be high, measures should be taken to protect the organisation. Some of these risks are insurable.

When a risk is quite likely to materialise and the liabilities or losses could be high, some risk management measures should be taken.

Risk management measures

The measures taken to deal with each risk are decided by management and management is accountable to the board for the measures they take. In broad terms, risks can be dealt with using internal controls, in the ways suggested earlier in this chapter:

- Some risks can be insured, so that if losses are incurred, they will be met by a third party (the insurance company).
- Some risks might be avoided. For example, a car manufacturer might be concerned about the risk of losses at a subsidiary specialising in car repairs, due to the strength of competition in the car repair industry. It could decide to avoid the risk by selling off the subsidiary.
- Many risks have to be accepted, as an inevitable feature of business. For significant risks, a company should decide what measures might be necessary to reduce the risk to acceptable proportions. Financial risks can be reduced through a variety of hedging measures, using forward contracts and financial derivative instruments. Business risks might be reduced through measures such as a diversification of product range (to avoid over-reliance on a single product), joint ventures (to share new venture risks) and cost reduction measures (to reduce the risks from competition).

From a corporate governance perspective, it should be a responsibility of the board to make sure that risks are reviewed regularly, and that management take suitable measures to deal with them.

Risk control and review

Control systems should be established to monitor risks. There should be a system for identifying situations that are getting out of control or where significant events have developed or are developing. This control system should include a system of internal controls. However, as indicated earlier, the Turnbull Report suggests that embedded control systems should be overlaid by a system of regular risk reviews by the board of directors, to check that the control system is working properly.

7 The role of the board (or audit committee) in risk management

The Combined Code states that unless either there is a separate board risk committee consisting of independent directors or the full board considers the matter itself, the audit committee should be responsible for reviewing the company's internal control and risk management systems, not just financial controls.

The Turnbull Guidance provides guidelines to directors on the review of risk and internal controls. An important issue to remember is that although the report refers to internal controls and the internal control system, it does not restrict the meaning of controls to financial controls. All risks should be monitored and controlled: business risks and operational risks as well as financial risks, and strategic risks as well as procedural risks.

With this point in mind, it is useful to study the Turnbull recommendations on risk reviews by the board of directors.

'When reviewing reports during the year, the board should:

- consider what are the significant risks and assess how they have been identified, evaluated and managed;
- assess the effectiveness of the related system of internal control in managing the significant risks, having regard, in particular, to any significant failings or weaknesses in internal control that have been reported;
- consider whether necessary actions are being taken promptly to remedy any significant failings or weaknesses; and
- consider whether the findings indicate a need for more extensive monitoring of the system of internal control.'

In addition to its regular reviews, the board should also carry out an annual review for the purpose of making a statement on internal control in the annual report and accounts.

The Guidance also states that should the board become aware at any time of a significant failing in internal control, it should find out how it arose and 'reassess the effectiveness of management's ongoing processes for designing, operating and monitoring the system of internal control'.

8 The board's statement on internal control

The Combined Code requires listed companies to include in their annual report and accounts a statement from the board on internal control. This should be a narrative statement, and should include, as a minimum, a statement that:

- there is an ongoing process for identifying, evaluating and managing significant risks;
- this process has been in place for the year under review;
- it is reviewed regularly by the board;
- it is in accordance with the Turnbull Guidance.

The statement should also include an acknowledgement that the board is responsible for the system of internal control and for reviewing its effectiveness. There should also be an explanation that the system of internal control is designed to manage risk but cannot eliminate the risk of failure to achieve business objectives. It can also only provide reasonable reassurance against material misstatements and loss, and cannot provide an absolute assurance.

The Turnbull Guidance appears to recognise that the requirements for disclosure are by no means rigorous, when it suggests that 'the board may wish to provide additional information in the annual report and accounts to assist understanding of the company's risk management processes and system of internal control'. In recognition perhaps that the statement by the board on internal control might simply contain high-flown but empty language, the guidelines also add: 'The board should ensure that its disclosures provide meaningful, high-level information and do not give a misleading impression.'

8.1 Carrying out an assessment of risks

Some guidance is given by the Turnbull Report to the board of directors on how to carry out an assessment of risks. An appendix to the report provides a list of questions to which there ought to be satisfactory answers.

On risk assessment

- Does the company have clear objectives? Have these been communicated in a way that provides effective direction to employees on risk management and control issues?
- Are significant risks assessed on an ongoing basis? Significant risks could relate to market risk (adverse movements in market prices, including the company's own share price), and credit risk, liquidity risk, technological risk, legal risk, health and safety risk, environmental and reputational risk, and business probity issues.
- Do management and others have a clear understanding of what risks are acceptable to the board? In other words, is the board satisfied that management know the extent of the risks they can expose the company to without taking appropriate risk reduction or risk hedging measures?

On the control environment and control activities

- What is expected of them, and the scope of their freedom to act? The guidelines indicate the scope of this question by stating that it applies to areas such as customer relations, service levels, health and safety and environment protection, security of assets and business continuity issues.
- Does the board have a clear strategy for dealing with significant risks, and is there a policy on how to manage them?
- Do the company's culture and performance reward systems support the business objectives and risk management and internal control systems? In other words, does the incentive system for senior management recognise the need for risk management as well as profit growth?
- Does senior management demonstrate through their actions as well as their policies a commitment to both competence and integrity?

- Are authority, responsibility and accountability clearly defined, so that decisions are made and actions are taken by the appropriate people?
- Does the company communicate to its employees expenditure, accounting and financial reporting?
- How are processes and controls adjusted to adapt to new risks or operational deficiencies?

On information and communication

- Do management and the board receive regular and relevant reports on actual performance compared with business objectives and the related risks, suitable for decision-making and management review purposes?
- Are periodic reporting procedures effective in communicating a proper account of the company's performance and prospects?

On monitoring

- Are processes embedded within the company's operations for monitoring the effective application of internal control and risk management?
- Is there appropriate communication to the board (or board committees) on the monitoring of risk and control matters?
- Are there specific arrangements for management monitoring and reporting to the board on risk and control matters of particular importance? These matters would include fraud and other illegal acts that could adversely affect the company's reputation or financial position.

8.2   The scope of risk reporting

The Combined Code has gone much further in the UK than corporate governance codes in other countries in recognising the responsibility of the board of directors for risk. Risk management is not widely understood, but the bottom line is quite clear. The board of directors is responsible for anything that goes wrong in the company's business. Experience has shown that many companies have collapsed or suffered a severe setback because they ignored risk and were not prepared for dealing with adverse events.

The Combined Code states that the board of directors are as responsible for risk as they are for the company's returns, and that good corporate governance practice must provide for the review of risk management and internal control.

9   Sarbanes–Oxley Act, s. 404

Although the UK has taken a lead in developing the risk management aspects of corporate governance, there have been important developments internationally.

The terrorist attacks on the United States on 11 September 2001 forced many companies, particularly large international or multinational companies, to reassess their disaster recovery plans. The attack on New York caused severe disruption to the banking system, and in some banks both the normal operational systems and the back-up operational arrangements were disrupted by the attack. As a result of this experience, companies have turned their attention to the arrangements they should have in place in the event of a major disruption to their front-line operations from a devastating terrorist attack.

The banking industry continues to provide a lead in the development of risk management systems and controls, with plans for a new system of capital adequacy controls. International banks will be expected to have sufficient capital to cover the risk of losses from bad debts, market trading and operational mishaps (credit risk, market risk and operational risk).

A significant development in internal control and corporate governance was introduced by the Sarbanes–Oxley Act 2002 (SOX) following the collapse of Enron and the other US corporate scandals in 2002.

Section 404(a) directs the Securities and Exchange Commission (SEC) to set rules requiring companies ('SEC registrants') to include an internal control report in their annual report:

'The Commission shall prescribe rules requiring each annual report ... to contain an internal control report, which shall –

- state the responsibility of management for establishing and maintaining an adequate internal control structure and procedures for financial reporting; and
- contain an assessment, as of the end of the most recent fiscal year of the issuer, of the effectiveness of the internal control structure and procedures of the issuer for financial reporting.'

The SEC applied the requirements of s. 404(a) in its own Rule 33–8238. This Rule includes the requirements that:

'The management of each ... issuer ... must evaluate, with the participation of the issuer's principal executive and principal finance officers ... the effectiveness, as of the end of each fiscal year, of the issuer's internal control over financial reporting. The framework on which management's evaluation of the issuer's internal control over financial reporting is based must be a suitable, recognized control framework ...

The management of each issuer ... must evaluate, with the participation of the issuer's principal executive and principal finance officers ... any change in the issuer's internal control over financial reporting that has occurred during each of the issuer's fiscal quarters, or fiscal year in the case of a foreign private issuer, that has materially affected, or is likely to materially affect, the issuer's internal control over financial reporting.'

Companies should also maintain evidence, including documentation, to provide reasonable support for management's assessment of the effectiveness of internal control over financial reporting.

Management are required to disclose any material weaknesses in the company's internal control system for financial reporting, and are not permitted to conclude that the internal control is effective if one or more material weaknesses exist.

Section 404 of SOX requires companies to include in their annual report a report on 'internal control over financial reporting'. This report should set out:

- a statement of management's responsibility for establishing and maintaining adequate internal controls over the company's financial reporting;
- a statement identifying the framework used by management for evaluating the efficiency and effectiveness of the internal control over financial reporting;
- an assessment by management of the effectiveness of the internal control over financial reporting, as at the end of the most recent fiscal year (and any 'material weakness' in internal control);
- disclosure of any material weakness in the company's internal control over financial reporting that management has identified;
- a statement that the external auditors have issued an 'attestation report' on management's assessment of the company's internal control over financial reporting. This attestation report by the auditors should be filed as part of the company's annual report.

In order to prepare this report on internal control, management must:

- undertake a review of the effectiveness of internal controls over financial reporting (the 'review' requirements'); and
- maintain evidence to provide reasonable support for management's assessment of the effectiveness of internal controls (the 'documentation requirements').

Section 404 has raised strong criticisms in the US on the grounds that its requirements are taking up much valuable time and resource of management, and that it has added substantially to the cost of audit fees to the external auditors, who must produce their attestation report. The heavy administrative burdens (and the potential liability that exists for the CEO and chief financial officer) were blamed for discouraging foreign companies from listing their shares in the US, and choosing alternative financial centres such as London instead, where the regulatory burden was much lower.

Comparing s. 404 of Sarbanes–Oxley with the Combined Code and Turnbull Guidance

There are significant differences between the requirements of SOX and the Combined Code/ Turnbull Guidance. For UK companies without a US listing:

- there is no requirement for management to report on the effectiveness of internal control, only to state each year that they have reviewed the system of control;
- there is no requirement for the auditors to report to shareholders on the directors' statement on internal control.

Commenting on its review of the Turnbull Guidance, a press release of the Turnbull Review Group commented that 'it would not be appropriate to require boards to make a statement in the annual report about the effectiveness of the company's internal control system'. With its emphasis on a principles-based approach to assessment and review, and the restricted disclosure requirements, the UK regime imposed a much less heavy administrative burden on companies than s. 404.

However, s. 404 applies to internal control over financial reporting only, whereas the review of internal control in the UK covers all types of internal control – operational controls, compliance controls and risk management generally, in addition to financial controls.

Review by the SEC of s. 404 requirements

In December 2006 in response to the continuing criticsms of s. 404 the SEC proposed new interpretative guidance for management, with the intention of improving the implementation of the s. 404 provisions. The SEC also proposed a change to the rules whereby a company performing an evaluation of internal controls in accordance with this new interpretive guidance would satisfy the requirements of s. 404 for an annual evaluation.

The new guidelines are intended to allow the management of companies more discretion in how the annual review of internal controls is carried out. They are also intended to free companies from a highly cautious 'box-ticking' approach to compliance with s. 404, to reduce reliance on advice from external auditors and to reduce the quantities of documentary evidence required.

By easing the regulatory and compliance burden of s. 404, it was hoped that these changes might help to restore the attractiveness of New York as a stock market.

The new guidance is principles-based:

- Management should evaluate the design of the company's internal controls over financial reporting. The purpose of this evaluation should be to determine whether there is a reasonable possibility that a material misstatement in the financial statements would not be prevented or detected by those controls. This evaluation will allow management to focus on the controls that are needed to prevent or detect a material misstatement.
- Management should then gather and analyse evidence about the operation of these internal controls over financial reporting, and assess the risk associated with them. This should allow management to focus their evaluation procedures on those areas of financial reporting where they believe that the greatest risks to reliable financial reporting exist.
- The proposed guidance will address four specific areas:
  - Identification of risks to reliable financial reporting and the related controls for dealing with those risks. The guidance suggests a risk-based approach requiring the use of judgement by management to decide those areas that are material for financial reporting and where the risks are greatest. Management should then identify the controls that address those risks, including the risk of material misstatement due to fraud. The guidance will not require that every control in a process be identified and evaluated. (This will reduce the administrative burden considerably, compared with the original rules.)
  - Evaluation of the effectiveness of the controls. Once management has decided which controls should come within the scope of their evaluation, they should then gather and analyse evidence about the operation of those controls. The proposed guidance provides for a risk-based approach.
  - Reporting the overall results of management's evaluation. Once management has completed its evaluation, they must decide if any identified control deficiencies are material weaknesses. The guidance will provide management with a

framework for making these judgments. If a deficiency is found in a control and the deficiency is a material weakness, management must conclude that internal control over financial reporting is not effective and management (as with the current requirements) must report those material weakness.

- Documentation. The amount of documentation required (to provide documentary evidence) would be much less than under the original rules.

Chapter summary

- A fundamental element of a system of risk management is a system of internal control. This is a combination of culture and attitude to risk control, and a large number of internal controls. Internal controls can be categorised into different types.

- In the UK, following publication of the 1998 Combined Code, the Turnbull Committee issued guidelines on how to establish and maintain a sound system of internal controls. Responsibility ultimately rests with the board of directors.

- Risks can be analysed into different types or categories. For any business, some will be more significant than others.

- There are four basic elements to risk management: risk identification, risk evaluation, risk management measures and risk control and review.

- The UK Combined Code requires listed companies to include in their annual report and accounts a statement from the board on internal control. The board's responsibility for risk management extends to all types of risk, not just financial risks.

- In the US, there is a statutory requirement on companies to include a report on internal control in their annual reports to shareholders.

Chapter 11

Ethics and corporate social responsibility

1. Ethics and corporate governance
2. A corporate code of ethics
3. Corporate social responsibility
4. Institutional investors, CSR and SRI
5. Whistleblowers

1 Ethics and corporate governance

Personal and business ethics underlie all the regulations and codification in corporate governance. Laws and regulations alone can never guarantee fair practice. Individuals in positions of influence and authority have to want to apply fair practice and abide by the rules. Some individuals, however, will think far more about themselves than about the collective aims of their organisation. In extreme cases, an individual will think about him- or herself to the exclusion of any other interests, and have only personal interests in mind, regardless of his or her position within the organisation. To some individuals, laws, stock market regulations and corporate governance codes are therefore obstacles to overcome rather than guidelines for conduct.

Laws, regulations, accounting standards and codes are framed on the presumption that they will be followed. For would-be transgressors, there is some threat of punishment in the law. When there is evidence of misdeeds in corporate governance, new laws may be introduced with stiffer penalties, in the expectation that potential wrongdoers will hesitate before doing anything selfish and wrong.

Even so, laws and regulations, with criminal and civil punishments, can never be enough on their own. Good practice in corporate governance practice calls for ethical conduct and a firm sense of what is right and wrong.

- Individuals must follow an ethical code in their personal decision-making. Each individual should abide by a personal moral code in business as well as in private life.
- There might be a code of ethics sustaining the corporate culture of each company. Employees within a company should understand that the company acts morally and by well-established ethical rules. Although it is not necessary, some companies produce their own code of ethics, explaining the rules and guidelines by which they operate and by which they expect all their employees to work. However, a code of ethics is difficult to apply in practice when it differs significantly from the accepted culture of employees in the organisation.

- There should be a generally accepted understanding and acceptance of the purpose of companies, and the need to balance different interests of different groups. The belief that the prime objective of a company is to maximise shareholder wealth should give way to a more stakeholder-based concept or an ethical shareholder concept of corporate objectives.

Conflicts of interest inevitably occur within organisations, particularly in large organisations, but these should be resolved or managed through negotiations and bargaining arrangements that rely on trust between the parties and an implicit assumption of fair dealing.

Without ethical conduct, regulations and codes of practice will not work. Individuals in positions of power will be able to circumvent rules and break the law, and unless they act ethically, might be tempted to do something illegal or improper in order to obtain personal gain.

CASE EXAMPLE 11.1

In 2003 the reputation of banking group Citigroup had been damaged by its associations with companies such as Enron, WorldCom, Adelphia and Parmalat, as a provider of both on-balance sheet and off-balance sheet finance.

The newly-appointed CEO Chuck Prince wanted to improve the image and reputation of the bank. He believed that this meant improving its cultural and ethical outlook. He therefore introduced a code of conduct which stated that the bank should aspire to be a company with the highest standards of ethical conduct and an organisation that people could trust. The bank's executives world-wide were asked to adhere to this code and promote the ethical status of the group.

In 2004, a problem occurred in London on the bank's trading desk for European government bonds. The desk was under pressure to increase its profits, and the management spotted an opportunity to exploit a weakness in an Italian-based electronic trading system for government bonds called MTS. They planned and executed a trade that came to be known as the 'Doctor Evil trade'. They sold a large quantity of bonds early one morning, sufficient to send bond prices falling sharply, and then bought the bonds back at much lower prices later the same morning. The trade earned a profit of over €18 million for Citigroup at the expense of other participant banks in the bond market.

The aftermath of this event was that some banks refused to honour their commitment to make a market in government bonds on MTS, and in the next three months daily trading volumes on MTS fell by 30 per cent. Some European governments expressed worries about whether they would be able to continue issuing bonds (to raise new finance) at a reasonable rate of interest. Some governments withdrew business from Citigroup as an expression of their anger. In the UK, the Financial Services Authority fined the bank £14 million for failing to exercise due skill, care and diligence.

The traders responsible for the Doctor Evil trade were suspended. There had been a serious breach of the bank's new code of conduct that customers, suppliers and competitors would be treated fairly. However, the incident demonstrated that the change in culture that the code of conduct was intended to introduce had not reached the heart of cultural attitudes within the bank. After a brief suspension, the traders returned to work. The bank admitted to bad ethical behaviour and poor professionalism, but no one within the bank was held responsible.

2 A corporate code of ethics

A corporate code of ethics is a code of ethical behaviour, issued by the board of directors of a company. It is a formal written statement and should be distributed or made easily available to all employees. The decisions and actions of all the company's employees must be guided by it.

The effectiveness of a code of ethics depends on the leadership of the company – its directors and senior managers. These individuals must be seen to comply with the ethical code, otherwise employees will see no purpose in complying with the code themselves. The culture of a company drives its ethical behaviour, and a code of ethics provides useful guidance.

It has been suggested that there are three reasons why companies might develop a code of ethics. These reasons are progressive, which means that companies might begin by having a code of ethics for the first reason, but then progress to the second and third reasons as they gain experience with implementing the code and appreciating its potential benefits.

- Compliance and customer service. The company wants to ensure that all its employees comply with relevant laws and regulations and conduct themselves in a way that the public expects. Compliance with a code of ethics is necessary for both legal and commercial reasons. For example, companies providing a service to the general public need to ensure that their employees are polite and well-behaved in their dealings with customers, otherwise it will lose customers.
- Managing stakeholder relations. A code of ethics can help to improve and develop the relations between the company and its shareholders by improving the trust that shareholders have in the company. The code might therefore include the ethical stance of the company on the disclosure of information to shareholders and the investing public (openness and transparency) and respect for the rights of shareholders.
- Creating a value-based organisation. It might be argued that an ethical company, like a well-governed company, is more likely to be successful in the long term. A company might therefore recognise the long-term benefits of creating an ethical culture, and encouraging employees to act and think in a way that is consistent with the values in its code of ethics.

The purpose of a formal code of corporate ethics is for a company to make its employees aware of the ethical issues relating to corporate social responsibility (CSR) that the company's leaders consider important. It provides a statement for employees on both ethics and CSR issues. A typical code of ethics for a company might contain:

- general statements about ethical conduct by employees;
- specific reference to the company's dealings with each specific stakeholder group, such as employees, customers, shareholders and local communities.

2.1 General statements about ethical conduct

A code of conduct might state specifically that compliance by its employees and managers with local laws is essential and that employees should also comply with the policies and procedures of the company. The code might also include a statement about the conduct of business affairs and the need to protect the company's reputation and 'good name'.

There are likely to be statements about the ethical values of the company, such as:

- acting at all times with integrity;
- protecting the environment;
- the 'pursuit of excellence';
- respect for the individual.

2.2 IBE guidelines on a code of business ethics

The Institute of Business Ethics (IBE) has provided the following broad guidelines for the content of a code of corporate ethics.

Preface or introduction

The code should explain its purpose and should describe the values that are important to senior management for the conduct of the business, such as integrity, responsibility and reputation. The code should state the commitment of the directors to maintaining high standards both within the company and in its dealings with others.

The introduction should also refer to the role of the company in the community and state the expectation that the standards set out in the code will be maintained by all the company's employees.

The code should contain the following key elements:

- The purpose and values of the business.
- Employees. There should be a statement on how the business values its employees and its policies on working conditions, recruitment, development and training, rewards, health, safety and security, equal opportunities, retirement, redundancy, discrimination and harassment.
- Customer relations. The code should make a statement about the importance to the company of customer satisfaction and good faith in all agreements, quality, fair pricing and after-sales service.
- Shareholders and other providers of finance. An ethical objective should be the protection of investment made in the company and proper 'return' on money lent, and a commitment to accurate and timely disclosures on the company's business performance and prospects.
- Suppliers. The code might include statements about prompt settlement of invoices, cooperation with major suppliers, cooperation to achieve quality and efficiency, and a policy that no bribery or excess hospitality will be either accepted or given.

- Society/the wider community. A code of ethics should also include a statement about the company and its relationship with the communities in which it operates. The company might state its compliance with the spirit of laws as well as the letter of the law, its obligations to protect and preserve the environment, the involvement of the company and its staff in local affairs, and corporate policy on giving to education and charities.
- Implementation. It is recommended that a code of ethics should include an explanation of the process by which the code is issued and used, and how employees can obtain advice on dealing with ethical problems.

3 Corporate social responsibility

Organisations and individuals dealing with a company expect certain standards of ethical behaviour from the company representatives they deal with, but they also expect similar standards from the company as a whole. There is a view that the best-managed companies are those that are aware of their responsibilities towards all stakeholders and society as a whole. In other words, the best-managed companies show a large degree of corporate social responsibility (CSR).

The website for the pressure group Business for Social Responsibility (see Directory) defines CSR as follows:

> 'While there is no single, commonly-accepted definition of corporate social responsibility, or CSR, it generally refers to business decision-making linked to ethical values, compliance with legal requirements, and respect for people, communities and the environment.'

In 'leadership companies', CSR is viewed as 'a comprehensive set of policies, practices and programmes that are integrated throughout business operations, and decision-making processes that are supported and rewarded by top management'.

Whereas a code of corporate ethics is addressed primarily to a company's employees, CSR is about how a company implements its policies on social, ethical and environmental issues, and how it presents those policies to stakeholders and the general public.

Major issues of CSR vary from one company to another according to its particular circumstances, but include:

- minimising damage to the environment and promoting 'sustainable' business development, i.e. business growth that does not have adverse long-term consequences for the environment and the earth's resources;
- having liberal employment policies;
- investing money in local communities;
- helping in the fight against crime.

Business in the Community, a voluntary group of UK companies working for the application of responsible business practices, has set out five principles that companies should apply:

1   to treat employees fairly and with respect;
2   to operate in an ethical way and with integrity;
3   to respect basic human rights;
4   to sustain the environment for future generations;
5   to be a responsible neighbour in their communities.

Examples of corporate activities that might be prompted by an awareness of social responsibility and the need to sustain the company's reputation include: giving scholarship awards for environmental studies, or giving money or resources to aid the victims of a hurricane or major flood. A multinational mining company operating in less-developed economies might give money to local tribal communities for the purpose of preserving them. A holiday company with centres on 'paradise islands' has developed environmentally and culturally sustainable practices at its resorts to prevent them from being overrun by damaging aspects of commercialism. At least one US company sets aside one day each year for its employees to do voluntary work in their local community.

3.1 The purpose of CSR policies

CSR policies are linked to ethical behaviour and the view that companies should act as 'corporate citizens'. However, there are differing views about the significance of CSR for companies. The National Association of Pension Funds, in a document on the NAPF and CSR/Social Responsible Investment (SRI) (2005), suggested that corporate social responsibility relates to the idea that companies, in addition to their responsibilities to shareholders, have responsibilities to other stakeholder groups and to society at large. The document then comments, interestingly, that these responsibilities can be divided into two distinct elements:

1   generally accepted responsibilities that a board of directors must fulfil in order to succeed in business or comply with legislation or regulations; and
2   functions considered by some parties, including some investors, to be responsibilities that go beyond compliance with the law and regulations, and beyond the measures necessary for achieving commercial success.

Whereas it would be widely accepted by company directors that companies should comply with the law and should give serious attention to the company's reputation risk, there are differences of opinion about the extent to which companies need to go beyond legal, regulatory and commercial requirements in pursuing CSR policies.

3.2 The potential benefits of CSR for companies

There are differing views about the extent to which companies benefit commercially from CSR policies. In 2004, the ABI published a research report on CSR and its impact on company performance and investor relations. The key findings of the report were as follows:

- Some studies have found that companies with active CSR policies benefited financially. The evidence is not conclusive but it points to benefits in areas such as corporate reputation, consumer acceptance, employee loyalty and environmental management.

- The benefits of CSR for companies are not uniform across all companies or sectors.
- Strategic risk aspects of CSR are as important as the effect on short-term profitability. Companies should recognise CSR risks in their strategic planning and management, because they can have important implications for brand value and market acceptability. There was a greater awareness of the importance of risk as well as returns, including risk to reputation. Social, cultural, demographic and technological changes mean that social and environmental risks are now more significant than in the past.

There appears to be a link between public attitudes towards a company and the way in which the company presents itself as an organisation concerned with social, ethical and environmental issues. There is a risk to a company's reputation, depending on the CSR policies it adopts. A company's reputation can be damaged by adverse publicity and public comment from incidents such as a serious environmental spillage or a serious accident. Reputational risk exists for many large companies, not just the obvious examples of companies in mining and extracting, pharmaceuticals and food. As just one example, it has been suggested that rail system operator Railtrack failed to recover from the damage to its reputation from the Hatfield rail crash in 2001, and collapsed in the following year.

The potential significance of CSR from a financial rather than an ethical perspective is therefore:

- brand reputation (reputational risk); and
- stakeholder preferences. Employees might prefer working for ethical organisations, customers might prefer buying from them and suppliers might prefer dealing with them. Perhaps even more significantly, investors might prefer holding the securities of ethical companies (and companies with good governance practices).

However, there is no clear link between CSR and short-term shareholder value.

The significance of CSR is also likely to vary among companies in different industries and companies finding themselves subject to the closest scrutiny will include:

- those with a dominant market position, such as former state-owned utility companies;
- those dealing directly with consumers, such as retailers and commercial banks;
- those producing essentials, such as food and drugs;
- those exploiting natural resources;
- those depending on supply chains in developing counties, such as clothing manufacturers.

Institutional investors have brought some pressure to bear on public companies to report on corporate social responsibility.

- The Association of British Insurers (ABI) issued guidelines in 2001 (subsequently reviewed and amended in 2007) calling on companies to disclose in their annual report that they have assessed the significant reputational risks that could affect their business. The aim of the guidelines is to encourage companies to improve the security and quality of the earnings from their business operations, by removing or reducing risks arising from inadequate regard to social interests and reputation. These ABI guidelines on Responsible Investment Disclosure are described in more detail in section 4.1 below.

- PIRC launched a Socially Responsible Investment (SRI) Service in 2000, providing a web-delivered information service about the practices and policies of major UK companies on social, environmental and ethical issues. PIRC argues that the overall quality of a company's earnings can be judged by its relationships with stakeholders.
- The National Association of Pension Funds has commented that although 'being the best' at corporate social responsibility does not ensure business success, it does reduce risk levels significantly and improves the quality of a company's returns. It therefore argues that 'quality assurance' can be obtained through CSR.

CASE EXAMPLE 11.2

A business case could be put forward that it is in the best long-term interests of a company to pursue a strategy of sustainable economic development and 'corporate social responsibility'.

In 2005, HSBC became the first 'carbon-neutral' bank, offsetting its carbon emissions through tree planting and carbon trading.

The telecommunications company BT has expressed the opinion that: 'We view sustainable development as a vision of a new kind of world – a world in which economic growth delivers a more just and inclusive society, whilst protecting our natural heritage for future generations.' Arguably, corporate social responsibility can enhance both employee and customer satisfaction and provide a company with a competitive advantage. Concerns for society and the environment are likely to have an increasingly important influence on corporate objectives, particularly in the developing world. In 2004, BT became the world's biggest company to take all its energy from 'environmentally sound' sources.

The chemical group ICI comments on its website that: 'ICI's safety, health and environment policy is at the heart of ICI. It is a series of core values that flow through every aspect of our business. Managing ICI's SHE performance is focused around a rolling programme of five-year targets. ... Since 1987 an ICI board director has had responsibility for SHE.'

3.3   Formulating a CSR policy

A company formulating a CSR policy should:

- Decide on its CSR values (and possibly publish a code of ethics).
- Establish the company's current position on these CSR values, and identify the gap between 'where we are' and 'where we want to be'.

- Obtain board support for the policy and identify responsibilities: nominate board leaders and local 'champions'.
- Develop realistic strategies and targets.
- Implement these on a local and global (company-wide) basis.
- Identify key stakeholders whose views the company wishes to influence (employees, pressure groups, customers).
- Communicate the company's activities to the target audiences (see below and Chapter 6);
- Monitor achievements. The company might subscribe to a CSR index or award scheme, such as the schemes operated by Business in the Community in the UK.

3.4   Benchmarking and corporate social responsibility

Developments in corporate social responsibility have been assisted by cooperation between companies that are willing to have their policies and practices assessed and compared with those of other companies, in all industrial sectors. Comparisons provide benchmarks for comparison and standards for attainment. Given suitable data, they can also be used to establish an index for CSR performance measurement.

An interesting development in the UK has been the Corporate Social Responsibility Index published by Business in the Community (BiTC), a UK-based consortium of about 700 companies. Its index is derived from a number of UK companies in different industries that volunteer to be assessed. The assessments are then developed into index scores out of 100 relating to:

- each company's CSR strategies;
- its success in integrating the strategies into its business operations; and
- the company's management practices that have an impact on four key areas: the community, the environment, the marketplace and the workplace.

The published index does not give the actual index scores for individual companies, but the participating companies are divided into five groups, ranging from a top group whose index scores are above a certain level to those in the bottom group whose scores are below a certain level.

It should be expected that each time BITC produces a new index, more companies will participate, aware of the potential for favourable PR from the exercise, as well as the benefits of benchmarking and comparing themselves with other companies.

3.5   Ethical behaviour and corporate self-interest

A more cynical view about the ethical conduct of companies is that whenever there is a conflict between ethical values and corporate self-interest, companies will normally act in their self-interest.

An example is the use of bribery to win major contracts. In some countries, it would appear that government officials and other key decision-makers expect to be paid for their support in winning a contract. When bribery is an established part of a local culture, foreign companies trying to win business have to pay bribes themselves, or lose the business.

Companies might condemn bribery, but in practice they are likely to look after their own self-interest and pay whatever they think is necessary to win major business contracts.

Another example of a conflict of interest would be a European company operating in a highly competitive market that has the opportunity to purchase low-cost supplies from a supplier in a developing country, knowing that the supplier uses slave or child labour. Faced with a choice between condemning slave and child labour and buying supplies at a low price, what will the company do?

4 Institutional investors, CSR and SRI

For institutional investors, there is a close connection between Socially Responsible Investment (SRI) and CSR. SRI, also known as Ethical Investment and Sustainable Investment, is defined as an approach to investment management that takes into account a proper analysis of the CSR responsibilities of companies to society as a whole and particular stakeholder groups. It is a process whereby the principles of the investor affect their choice of which companies to invest in and how they should use their rights as shareholders. It involves the screening and selection process for investment decision-making and also the process of engagement between shareholders and companies.

SRI is therefore a method of managing an investment portfolio whereas CSR relates to the behaviour of companies. Investment institutions each have their own policy towards SRI. Pension funds are specifically required to state their policy towards social, ethical and environmental issues in their Statement of Investment Principles.

In the UK, institutional investors have been involved in the development of company attitudes to CSR, for two reasons:

1   There is a recognition by investors that CSR risks and corporate policies on CSR could affect the long-term prosperity of a company, and boards of directors should be aware of CSR risks for the company. Investors should therefore expect to receive regular disclosures from boards about the CSR risks faced by their company, and the policies they have developed and implemented for dealing with them.
2   Some institutional investors consider that CSR issues should affect their investment decisions, and the choice of shares for their investment portfolios.

4.1   ABI guidelines to companies on CSR/ESG disclosures

The Association of British Insurers has issued guidelines to companies on the sort of disclosures on CSR issues that they expect companies to provide to their shareholders. An updated set of these guidelines on Responsible Investment Disclosure was published in 2007. These are broad guidelines to all companies about the types of disclosure that institutional investors will expect companies to make about social, ethical and environmental issues.

The guidelines, which are consistent with the company law requirements for coverage of environmental, social and governance (ESG) issues in the annual business review, state that shareholders place great value on 'narrative reporting which (a) sets ESG risks in the context of the whole range of risks and opportunities facing a company (b) contains a forward-looking perspective, and (c) describes the actions of boards in mitigating these risks.'

There are three areas of ESG reporting where companies should make disclosures.

1   ESG risk assessment by the Board. The annual report should state whether, as a part of its regular assessment of risk, the board takes accounts of significant ESG risks, whether the board has identified any such risks to the company's short-term and long-term value (and opportunities to enhance value that may arise by making an appropriate response) and that the company has effective systems in place for mitigating the significant risks.

2   ESG risk: policies and procedures. The annual report should also include information about significant ESG risks that could affect value and how they might affect the company, together with a description of the policies and procedures for managing these risks (or a statement that there are no such policies or procedures). The report should also include information about the extent to which the company has complied with its policies and procedures for managing material risks (with Key Performance Indicators where appropriate) and the role of the Board in providing oversight.

3   Remuneration and ESG issues. In the directors' remuneration report, the company should state whether the remuneration committee is able to consider ESG issues when setting the remuneration of executive directors, and whether the committee has ensured that the incentive structure for senior management does not raise ESG risks by 'inadvertently motivating irresponsible behaviour'.

The ABI has commented that if companies provide these disclosures, this should help them to develop appropriate CSR policies and provide a constructive basis for 'engagement' between shareholders and their companies.

4.2   NAPF policy on CSR and SRI

In its 2005 paper on CSR/SRI (referred to in section 3.1), the NAPF explained that it had given some consideration to whether it should be active in promoting good CSR practices in companies, in the same way that, it had been active in promoting good corporate governance. Its conclusion was that unlike corporate governance, CSR should be seen as 'a fundamental part of the normal running of the business'.

- CSR is a management responsibility, and management should be allowed to get on with their task without interference from institutional investors.
- Boards should be accountable to shareholders for the way they run the business, including their CSR policies.
- Boards should develop CSR policies as part of their normal business agenda, which they should disclose to shareholders and other stakeholders in the normal process of disclosure by companies.

The NAPF therefore recognises the potential importance of CSR issues, but does not intend to issue specific guidelines to its members. One of its statements of underlying principles summarises its position:

'At all times the board and Management should be mindful of the wider role of the Company in society, bearing in mind that maximisation of short-term gain in a manner which is deemed unacceptable by society as a whole, can seriously damage the longer term prospects of a Company and lead to real financial losses for shareholders. Such losses may come about as a result of either changing consumer preferences or legislation putting additional cost on the Company, or both.'

Advice to institutional investors on companies and CSR issues

Some organisations provide detailed advice to institutional investor clients about the CSR policies of companies. PIRC Limited, for example, provides institutional investor clients with 'tools to enable them to achieve accountability, transparency and responsibility in their portfolio investments'. PIRC researches corporate governance and CSR issues at companies and provides reports to client.

'In this way we believe that our services ... enable our clients to add value to their understanding of how companies function, to more effectively monitor risks that arise from corporate governance and CSR failure, and to increase their (and their investee companies') wealth-creating potential.'

Similarly EIRIS (The Ethical Investment Research Service), an organisation founded by churches and charities in 1983, provides research information to clients about the social, ethical and environmental policies and performance of companies.

5 Whistleblowers

A whistleblower is an employee who provides information about his or her company which he or she reasonably believes provides evidence of:

- a violation of a law or regulation by the company;
- a miscarriage of justice;
- financial malpractice; or
- a danger to public health or safety.

In the government sector, a whistleblower might also provide evidence of a gross waste of public funds or gross mismanagement.

A feature of whistleblowing is that the individual concerned has been unable to get a response from the company's management through normal lines of reporting, which has forced the individual to go to someone else with the information. The whistleblower presumably hopes that the recipient of the information will take action to deal with the misdemeanour.

Whistleblowing can arise in different situations and for different reasons:

- There have been instances in the past where an employee of a company manufacturing defence equipment has passed information to the press about an illegal arms sale. Presumably, the whistleblower in each case disapproved of the transaction and believed that the company was aware that it was in breach of the law, but intended to go through with the sale.

- An employee may have evidence that his or her superiors are in breach of company regulations and so reports the facts to someone else in a position of seniority within the company, such as a managing director. In these cases, the individual believes the company's senior management to be unaware of the problem, but that it will take action if alerted. This situation arose, for example, with the whistle-blowing at Enron in 2001.

There is a strong connection between corporate governance and whistleblowing. An employee may honestly believe that there is, has been or could soon be serious malpractice by someone within the company, but feel unable to report his or her concerns in the normal way. This could be because the individual to whom he or she normally reports is involved in the suspected malpractice. Serious malpractice or a misdemeanour could be damaging to the company:

- It might suffer financial loss if some employees are indulging in fraud.
- It might be exposed to severe penalties as a consequence of employees breaking the law or regulations.
- There could be damage to the company's reputation if the misdemeanour is uncovered and made public.

The board of directors and senior management have a responsibility for monitoring potential risks within their company. This responsibility includes a need to recognise that whistleblowing by an employee would help to uncover significant risks, and procedures should therefore exist to encourage 'honest' whistleblowing, whilst at the same time discouraging malicious and unjustifiable accusations and allegations from employees against their bosses.

Concerns about whistleblowing have grown in recent years, for three main reasons:

1   A huge amount of information about a company is held on computer files, which are accessible to many employees. Individual employees prepared to spend the time to look closely into a matter are likely to discover a large amount of information that they might not 'officially' be supposed to know, or information that no one else has yet become aware of. Companies are now aware, for example, that they could become liable for information held as email messages in the files of employees.

2   In many companies, there is a strong culture of loyalty to the company. Employees who question or criticise the actions of management might be considered to be traitors. Despite laws designed to protect them, whistleblowers run the risk of retaliatory action from their company. When they report their suspicions, they may be sacked on the grounds of making false and malicious allegations. It would certainly appear to be the case that whistleblowers are more likely to be dismissed than rewarded. This is particularly the case when the whistleblower passes the information to someone outside the company, such as a newspaper.

3   Individual whistleblowers played an important role in uncovering information about financial and accounting mismanagement at Enron (2001) and WorldCom (2002), and in criticising the handling of security information by the FBI before the September 11 terrorist attacks in New York. The public became aware not only that organisations were being mismanaged, but that honest attempts to reveal the problems were being disregarded by senior management.

Case Example 11.7

In the cases of Enron and WorldCom, the whistleblowers were women working in what appears to have been male-dominated corporate cultures. At Enron, senior manager Ms Sherron Watkins, having been disregarded by her superiors, reported directly to the Enron chairman Kenneth Lay that she believed the company to be on the edge of financial collapse. Her complaints were passed to a law firm that had very close relationships with Enron and whose independence of judgement might therefore have been questionable.

At WorldCom, internal auditor Ms Cynthia Cooper found accounting malpractice, whereby the company had reported about $3.8 billion in revenue expenditure as capital spending, thereby falsely increasing the company's profits. She reported her concerns, without any effect, to the company's chief financial officer, then to the head of internal audit and finally to the company's external auditors.

Whistleblowers may put their jobs at risk. An employer taking retaliatory action may claim that sacking the employee had nothing to do with the revelations the employee had made, or claim that the employee was sacked because his or her statements were vindictive and untrue.

5.1   Whistleblowing: best practice

If an employee has a genuine, honest concern about something happening within the company, which he or she believes to be dishonest or improper, there should be a way for the employee's concerns to be brought to the attention of management and dealt with in a constructive way. Having a system for listening to employees' concerns should be a part of an effective risk management system within the organisation, because diligent employees can act as an early warning system of problems.

However, there are several problems with whistleblowing procedures and policies.

Experience in many organisations appears to show that an individual who reports concerns about illegal or unethical conduct is often victimised subsequently by colleagues and management. If the allegations by the whistleblower are rejected, he or she might find themselves failing to receive the same salary increases as colleagues, or being overlooked for promotion. The attitude of colleagues and managers might also be hostile, making it difficult for the individual to continue in the job.

On the other hand, some whistleblowing is malicious and unfounded, the result perhaps of personal dislikes or arguments. A problem facing companies is therefore to establish a whistleblowing system that:

- encourages employees to report illegal or unethical behaviour, but
- discourages malicious and unfounded allegations.

A company might state its policy on whistleblowing in the following terms:

- An employee is acting correctly if, in good faith, he or she seeks advice about improper behaviour or reports improper behaviour, where it is not possible to resolve the individual's concerns through discussions with colleagues or line management. (Whistleblowing is appropriate if the employee does it in good faith and is not being malicious, and there is no other way to resolve the problem.)
- The company will not tolerate any discrimination by employees or management in the company against an individual who has reported in good faith their concerns about illegal or unethical behaviour. (This is a policy statement that whistleblowers will be protected if they have made their report in good faith.)
- Disciplinary action will be taken against any employee who knowingly makes a false report of illegal or improper behaviour by someone else. (Malicious reporting will not be tolerated.)

Unfortunately, there appears to be a high risk in many cases that a whistleblower will not be given adequate protection by the employer.

In practice, employees may feel obliged to take their concerns (possibly anonymously) to someone outside the organisation, risking the anger of the employer for breach of proper procedures if his or her action is discovered. An employee can be disciplined for making groundless complaints and allegations in bad faith about his or her employer. On the other hand, there are some 'official' whistleblowing channels, such as the Whistleblowing Line operated by the Financial Services Authority for the financial services industry (described in some further detail in section 5.4).

5.2 Internal procedures for dealing with whistleblowers' allegations

A company should have a fair system for dealing internally with accusations from whistleblowers, so that an honest individual does not feel under threat when making an allegation. Employees ought to know what those procedures are. Since whistleblowing is not a regular event, a company may simply try to deal with each case on its merits when it arises, without any formal procedures or channels of complaint being established. The employee will therefore not know whom to complain to, and will probably go to the most senior manager available – possibly the chief executive.

A problem with dealing with whistleblowing incidents on an ad hoc basis is that the accusations may relate to the senior executive directors themselves. An employee who believes the CEO or finance director to be guilty of wrong-doing will have no option other than to resign or take the complaint to an external authority, such as the press or the police.

It may therefore be more appropriate to establish a formal internal channel for dealing with whistleblowers:

- If the company has a culture of ethical conduct, it should be prepared to encourage whistleblowing, and should provide a channel for reporting complaints and allegations by employees about their bosses. At the same time, it should make clear its policy about disciplining employees found to have been malicious in making allegations.
- Although it will often be necessary to involve senior executives in the investigation of allegations, the channel for complaints should not be to senior executive management or the board. One possible arrangement would be for allegations to be made to the company secretary, who would then arrange for the senior NED to be notified. This NED, or a committee of NEDs, could then decide how the allegation should be investigated.
- An allegation might be investigated on behalf of a company by a firm of solicitors, because of the possibility of criminal activity or a misdemeanour that could expose the company to a large civil liability. If so, the solicitors asked to do the work should not have a close relationship with the company, so that the investigation can be independent. For example, the company should not be a large client of the solicitors for other legal work.

However, until every company has adopted an enlightened approach to dealing with employee allegations, and every employee can feel that he or she is not risking job security by making an accusation, many individuals will not trust internal procedures and will prefer to go to an external authority. Anyone making allegations about their company and its management to an external authority could be putting their job at risk. In recognition of the risks taken by honest whistleblowers, the law should offer some protection.

5.3   Laws to protect whistleblowers

The Public Interest Disclosure Act 1998 came into force in 1999. Under the terms of this Act, workers are given protection when they disclose information they reasonably believe will expose financial malpractice, dangers to health and safety, or miscarriages of justice in their employer's organisation. Employees making a 'qualifying disclosure' have the right not to suffer any detriment at the hands of the employer, under the pretence of redundancy, demotion or failure to receive promotion. If a whistleblower is penalised by the employer, he or she can take a claim for retaliatory action to an industrial tribunal. (Industrial tribunals also hear cases of unfair dismissal.) There is no limit to the size of award a tribunal can make against an employer and in favour of a dismissed employee.

The Act also states that any 'gagging' clause in an employee's service contract is void. A gagging clause forbids the employee from voicing concerns about illegal activity, etc. in the organisation to the authorities, and gives the employer the right to sack the individual for whistleblowing.

A 'qualifying disclosure' protected by the Act must normally satisfy three criteria:

1   It should be made in good faith.
2   It should be made in the reasonable belief that the information tends to reveal (although might not provide conclusive proof of) a criminal offence, a failure to comply with a legal obligation, a danger to the health or safety of one or more individuals, or damage (or the threat of damage) to the environment.
3   It is made to the employer under an internal whistleblowing procedure (or, in certain circumstances, to another person).

The Act also recognises that it is not always sufficient to have internal whistleblowing procedures and, in exceptional circumstances, individuals making an external disclosure are also protected. These circumstances might arise if four criteria are met:

1   The disclosure must be made in good faith.
2   It should not be made for personal gain.
3   It is reasonable for the disclosure to be made outside the employer organisation.
4   The employee reasonably believes that he or she will be victimised by making the disclosure to the employer, or the employee has already made the disclosure (with no effect), or the employee believes that by making the disclosure to the employer, evidence of the malpractice will be concealed or destroyed.

5.4   Combining internal and external procedures

The Financial Services Authority, responsible for the supervision of firms in the financial services industry, has recognised the potential importance of whistleblowers in revealing corruption and malpractice in an industry where non-professional investors are known to be vulnerable. It would like to see a combination of internal procedures for dealing with whistleblowers, backed by an external system for cases where internal procedures do not exist or are inadequate.

The FSA has suggested that firms should have internal procedures for dealing constructively with information provided by whistleblowers, in their own 'enlightened self-interest'. These procedures could include the following arrangements:

*   The employer should make a formal statement to all employees that it takes seriously any genuine whistleblowing (and the allegations of whistleblowers).
*   The employer should also indicate to employees what it would regard as a 'failure' in the system, sufficient to justify whistleblowing.
*   There should be respect for individuals who 'blow the whistle'.
*   The firm should give an assurance to its employees that it will take every measure to ensure that there is no victimisation of a whistleblower.
*   The system should provide employees with an opportunity to voice their concerns outside the line management structure, but still within the organisation.
*   The FSA suggests that whistleblowers should be able to take their concerns to the internal auditor or the company secretary, who should then investigate the problem. Another suggestion is that the focal point for receiving allegations from whistleblowers should be the audit committee.

- However, employees making false claims or allegations should be subject to disciplinary measures by the employer.

The firm should also indicate how the employee may, if necessary, take the complaint to an outside body for investigation. In the UK financial services industry, the FSA has set up a Whistleblowing Line so that employees of financial services firms can voice their concerns if they do not feel they will be dealt with properly by the firm. Despite the wish of the FSA to rely on internal procedures for handling whistleblowers' accusations, there will almost certainly be a close involvement of external agencies in the investigation of malpractice in the financial services industry.

5.5   ICSA Best Practice Guide: Establishing a Whistleblowing Procedure

The ICSA issued a Best Practice Guide on establishing a whistleblowing procedure in 1999, in response to the Public Interest Disclosure Act. This was revised in 2007.

The Guide states that an internal whistleblowing procedure will be effective only if it has the confidence of the employees, who are its intended users. Confidence in the system will be obtained only if the employer is genuinely committed to the procedure. The Guide recommends that employees' representatives should be involved in establishing the procedure and monitoring its implementation.

The company secretary will often be given an important role in establishing an internal whistleblowing policy and procedures. He or she needs to ensure that there are trained people in the organisation to operate the procedure so that any matters raised by whistleblowers under the internal procedure are dealt with effectively. The Guide adds that if someone does report a genuine concern in good faith, these individuals must be supported. Providing support might be a role for the company secretary to perform.

The Guide suggests that features of an internal whistleblowing policy and procedure should include the following provisions:

- The internal whistleblowing procedures should be documented and a copy should be given to every employee.
- It should set out the key aspects of the procedure, such as the person to whom employees should report their suspicions or concerns. This might be the company secretary or internal audit.
- It should contain a statement that the employer takes malpractice or misconduct seriously, and is committed to a culture of openness in which employees can report legitimate concerns without fear of penalty or punishment.
- It should give examples of the type of misconduct for which employees should use the procedure and set out the level of proof that there should be in an allegation. (Although positive proof might not be required, a whistleblower should be able to provide good reasons for his or her concern.)
- The document should set out the procedures by which an allegation will be investigated.

- It should make clear that false or malicious allegations will result in disciplinary action against the individual making them.
- It should also make clear that no employee will be victimised for raising a genuine concern. Victinisation of an employee for raising a qualified disclosure should be a disciplinary offence.
- An external whistleblowing route should be offered, as well as an internal reporting procedure.
- There should be an undertaking that, as far as possible, whistleblowers will be informed about the outcome of their allegations and the action that has been taken.
- Whistleblowers should be promised confidentiality, as far as this is possible.

5.6 Whistleblowing and the Combined Code

Following a recommendation in the Smith Report on audit committees, the 2003 Combined Code includes a provision making it a responsibility of the audit committee to 'review arrangements' whereby staff may, in confidence, raise concerns about possible improprieties within the company. The aim of this review should be to ensure that arrangements are in place for an independent investigation of allegations, and appropriate follow-up action.

Chapter summary

- Ethical behaviour by individuals is essential if the concepts supporting good corporate governance are to be applied. In addition, the organisation itself should have a culture of ethical behaviour, supported perhaps by a formal code of ethics.

- Investors, and in particular institutional investors, might believe that there is a correlation between well-managed companies and companies that show an awareness of their social responsibility. Investment decisions by shareholders might be taken on the basis of the social policies of different companies.

- Issues in corporate social responsibility include minimising damage to the environment and creating a sustainable business that does not deplete the earth's natural resources, concern for safety and health, and concern for employees and for the local communities within which the organisation operates.

- There is a link between corporate social responsibility by companies and socially responsible investment by investment institutions.

- The ABI has issued guidelines on disclosures it expects from companies on social, ethical and environmental issues.

- The NAPF in the UK takes the view that although CSR and socially responsible investments are important issues for institutional investors, CSR issues are primarily matters for the management of companies to deal with. It has therefore chosen not to issue guidelines to members on CSR/SRI – unlike its approach to other aspects of corporate governance.

- Whistleblowers can be an important source of information about malpractice and misdemeanours by employees within an organisation, but might be at risk of punishment or victimisation for reporting what they know or suspect. Protection for whistleblowers is provided by the Public Interest Disclosure Act of 1998. It is also considered a matter of best practice in corporate governance to establish a system, fully supported by top management, for internal and external whistleblowing procedures.

Chapter 12

A history of corporate governance in the United Kingdom

1 The Cadbury Code (1992)

A number of financial scandals involving UK listed companies during the 1980s undermined confidence in both the quality of financial reporting and also the ability of external auditors to provide sufficient assurances about the financial condition of the companies they reported on. At the instigation of the London Stock Exchange, a committee was established under the chairmanship of Sir Adrian Cadbury, representing the major financial markets institutions.

The committee was asked to look into financial aspects of corporate governance, amid concerns that financial reporting by companies was often misleading and suffered from 'window dressing'. The attention of the committee broadened, however, to include other aspects of corporate governance, particularly the functions and the effectiveness of the board of directors. The stated aim of the Cadbury Committee was to help raise standards of corporate governance and confidence in financial reporting and auditing, by setting out what it saw as the respective responsibilities of those involved and what it believed was expected of them.

The Cadbury Committee issued a range of recommendations for good corporate governance in a Code of Best Practice. Many of these were regarded as best practice already, but were by no means universally applied by UK companies. The Code therefore marked an attempt to force companies, particularly public limited companies, to improve their conduct.

One of the recommendations was that all quoted companies should comply with the best practice as set out in the Code. The Code should be voluntary, but companies should be required to explain in their annual report and accounts the extent to which they had complied with the Code and the reasons for any non-compliance. It was also suggested that the external auditors should be asked to review this statement of compliance as part of their annual report to shareholders.

It was intended that compliance with the Code would help to create a board of independent-minded directors acting in the best interests of the company.

Taking up the Cadbury recommendations, the London Stock Exchange introduced a requirement into its listing rules that listed companies should include such a statement of compliance (or non-compliance) in their annual report and accounts. Institutional investors and investment banks sponsoring and advising listed companies brought pressure to bear on companies to adopt the Cadbury Code provisions, and many companies changed their rules and conduct in compliance.

1.1 Major provisions of the Cadbury Code

The major provisions of the Cadbury Code were the following.

Board of directors

On the question of whether shareholders should have more rights and a stronger voice in decision-making by their company, the committee accepted that it was appropriate for the directors to retain their 'essential powers', and there should be no question of giving more powers to shareholders. On the other hand, although directors should have the essential powers, they should be properly accountable to the shareholders for the way in which they used them.

The Code stated that control over the company should be exercised collectively by the board of directors as a whole. There should be no domination of the board by a single individual, the CEO or chairman, or by a small group of executive directors.

To exercise its authority collectively, it would be necessary for the board to meet regularly. At its regular meetings it should monitor the performance of the executive management. As a matter of course, some decisions should be taken by the board and not delegated to executive management. These decisions should be taken at board meetings. The Code recommended that there should also be a formal schedule of matters that are specifically reserved for board decisions, to make sure that the board retains firm control over the company and does not allow power to transfer to an all-powerful chief executive or chairman. It was suggested that unless the board takes decisions formally and collectively on major matters, such as mergers or acquisitions, power would drift away from the board to the senior executive management.

The Cadbury Committee recognised the risk that some directors might be accused of having insufficient experience or knowledge of some matters, and that their views might be disregarded. The Code therefore stated that on the occasions where a director needs professional advice in order to form an opinion, he or she should be able to obtain professional advice at the company's expense.

Given a history in the UK of public companies being dominated by an all-powerful CEO-cum-chairman, the Code stated that there should be a clear division of responsibilities at the top of the company. The two major roles were those of the CEO, who is in charge of the executive management and the company's business operations, and the chairman, who was responsible for the management of the board of directors. The responsibilities of each role should be clearly defined. The Code argued that it would usually be desirable to separate these roles, so that the same person did not carry out both. It did not state that the same person should never be both chairman and CEO, but recommended that when this did happen, there should be a strong independent element on the board to act as a counter-force, with a recognised senior member to lead them.

In spite of the Cadbury Code, and a similar requirement in the Combined Code that eventually replaced it, a number of listed UK companies still combine the roles of chairman and CEO in one person.

Non-executive directors

At the time of the Cadbury Report, NEDs were heavily outnumbered by executive directors on the boards of UK companies, and many NEDs were appointees of major shareholders or former (retired) senior executives. Some companies did not have any non-executive directors at all.

There was also some concern that where a company had NEDs, these were often supporters of the CEO or chairman and, far from being independent, they provided voting support to the CEO or chairman at board meetings.

The Cadbury Code addressed the issue of NEDs, taking the view that there should be a sufficient number of them for their views to carry sufficient weight. The Code made a specific recommendation as to how many NEDs there should be. Although not all NEDs need be independent, most of them should be, so that they could contribute effectively to decision-making by the board. The view of the Cadbury Committee was that independent NEDs should be able to bring judgement and experience to the deliberations of the board that the executive directors on their own would lack.

It was recognised that the independence of a NED might be put in jeopardy if the individual had to rely on the CEO or chairman for his or her appointment to office or level of remuneration. The Code therefore recommended that NEDs should be selected through a formal process. Initial interviews might be conducted by a nomination committee, which would put forward nominees to the board. Appointment of a new NED should also be a matter for the board as a whole. NEDs should also be appointed for a fixed term, and re-appointment at the end of that term should not be automatic.

The Code appears to have accepted the view that once appointed to the board of a company, a NED might become less independent-minded over time. Even so, the Code did not make any recommendations about the maximum length in office for NEDs.

Executive directors: service contracts and remuneration

The Cadbury Code contained some provisions about the length of service contracts for executive directors and for the disclosure of more information about directors' remuneration in the annual report and accounts. However, there were no major concerns at the time about directors' remuneration, and the provisions in the Code were fairly mild in nature. (They were made more rigorous subsequently by the Greenbury and Hampel Committee recommendations.)

The Code recommended that the service contract of an executive director should not exceed three years without shareholder approval. (This three-year maximum has since been reduced to twelve months.) The purpose of this requirement was to set a limit to the size of the pay-off for a director who is forced to leave the company, for example as a result of poor performance and shareholder pressure. A director forced out of office would normally be entitled to a leaving payment equivalent to the total of his or her pay for the full contract notice period. This would mean, for example, that a director on a four-year rolling contract with an annual salary of £200,000 might be entitled to a 'golden handshake' of about £800,000 for agreeing to leave the company. The three-year limit set by the Cadbury Code still left scope for large leaving payments.

The Code also recommended that the remuneration of executive directors should be decided (subject to board approval) by a remuneration committee, consisting wholly or mainly of NEDs.

Recommendations in the Code for greater disclosure of details of directors' remuneration were not particularly extensive, and were subsequently superseded by the Greenbury Report recommendations.

The accounts of the company

At the time of the Cadbury Report, by no means all listed companies had an audit committee. However, the Cadbury Committee viewed the audit committee as a key board committee, with the task of communicating with both the internal and external auditors, and for providing a forum for the discussion of audit issues. The audit committee should also review the interim and annual financial statements before their submission to the full board for approval.

The audit committee should include at least three non-executive directors, and should have written terms of reference. It was envisaged that the main relationship between the board and the external auditors should be through the audit committee, rather than through the working relationship between the auditors and the executive management.

The board has a duty to present a balanced and understandable assessment of the company's financial position to the shareholders. As a part of this responsibility, the Code stated that the directors should include in the annual report a statement about the company's ability to continue as a going concern. An implication of this recommendation (which is also contained in the UK Combined Code) is that before approving the report and accounts, each director is under a personal responsibility to reassure him- or herself that the company is a going concern.

The Cadbury Committee also made the radical recommendation that the directors should report to the shareholders on the entire system of internal control in the company. The board would therefore be accountable to the shareholders for risk management generally, not just the quality of financial reporting and financial controls. The reaction to this proposal was quite hostile, and the Code was therefore watered down to stating that the directors should report on internal financial controls only. The board's responsibility for the company's entire system of risk management was subsequently revived by the Hampel Report and eventually written into the Combined Code in 1998.

2 The Greenbury Report (1995)

During the early 1990s, directors' remuneration emerged as a problem for corporate governance. The popular press regularly attacked 'fat cat' directors who paid themselves enormous salaries even when their companies were performing badly. A particular target of criticism was the pay of directors in former nationalised industries. A popular perception was that nothing had changed with privatisation, and if anything the quality and level of service to the public had fallen, but the directors had rewarded themselves with large pay rises for doing the same jobs as before.

A much greater concern for institutional investors was the failure of remuneration packages to provide a suitable incentive for directors to perform better. The rewards of executive directors did not appear to be linked to company performance in such a way that directors would be rewarded more if the company's results benefited shareholders, and would not be rewarded as well if results were disappointing. The perception was that directors appeared to be paid well regardless of the company's performance.

A committee under the chairmanship of Sir Richard Greenbury was set up to look into the issue, and it reported in 1995. Like the Cadbury Committee, the Greenbury Committee issued a code of best practice on directors' remuneration, with the recommendation that in the UK all listed companies should comply. In a similar vein to the Cadbury Report, the Greenbury Report recommended that listed companies should include in their annual report and accounts a statement on directors' remuneration. This should explain the extent of the compliance by the company with the Greenbury recommendations on remuneration committees, and should justify any non-compliance.

The London Stock Exchange adopted the recommendations of Greenbury, and incorporated its recommendations into the UK Listing Rules. However, unlike the Cadbury Code, which had been widely welcomed, the Greenbury Report had mixed reviews. There was a widespread opinion that the recommendations did not do enough to deal with the problem of trying to link directors' rewards to company performance in the interests of the shareholders.

Directors' remuneration and service contracts

The Greenbury Committee recommended that a remuneration committee of the board should decide the remuneration of the executive directors. This committee should consist entirely of NEDs, so that no executive director should have the responsibility for setting his or her own remuneration or the remuneration of executive colleagues.

The maximum notice period in an executive director's service contract should normally be twelve months, compared to the three years maximum recommended by the Cadbury Code. (As a result, when the Greenbury recommendations were adopted by the London Stock Exchange, many executive directors with existing three-year rolling contracts were persuaded to agree to a reduction to a twelve-month notice period in their service contract.)

The Report added, however, that notice periods of up to two years might be reasonable in some circumstances. In exceptional circumstances, for example as an enticement to a key individual to join the board, a notice period in excess of two years might occasionally be justified.

The Report included general recommendations about remuneration policy, but most of these were loosely phrased and so open to broad interpretation.

- Executive pay should not be excessive. However, the remuneration committee should offer remuneration packages that are sufficient to attract, retain and motivate individuals of the required quality. This would mean looking at the wider pay scene when setting remuneration levels. In effect, this gives remuneration committees a free hand to set pay levels, because any package can be justified on the grounds of what was needed in order to attract a person of the necessary calibre.
- The performance-related elements of remuneration should create a link between the interests of the director and those of the shareholders. The performance criteria should be 'relevant, stretching and designed to enhance the business'. Matters for the remuneration committee to consider should include the phasing of any reward schemes, the nature of any share option package and the implications of each element of the remuneration package for payments into the director's pension scheme. Setting an upper limit to the award of bonuses should 'always be considered'.
- Share options granted as part of a director's remuneration scheme should not be issued at a discount. Before Greenbury, it was quite usual in the UK to grant share options to directors with an exercise price at a discount to the current market price.
- Share options should be granted to directors in phased amounts over time rather than in single large awards. Frequent smaller awards are much better than occasional awards of a large block of options, since a single large award encourages the director to focus on the share price in the short term rather than the longer term.
- The Report also considered compensation payments to directors for loss of office. Remuneration committees were urged to take a firm line on the payment of compensation to directors dismissed for unsatisfactory performance. In the public perception, a high pay-off to an outgoing chief executive can look very much like a reward for failure. The reduction of notice periods in service contracts to twelve months would help to limit compensation payments, but the Greenbury Committee wanted remuneration committees to go further. When a director has a very high salary and bonus arrangements, together with share options and pension benefits, the compensation for loss of office can still be very high. The committee also recommended that the remuneration committee should think about paying compensation for loss of office over a period of time, instead of in a single lump sum, and to halt the payments if the individual concerned finds another job. However, these recommendations about taking a tough line on compensation are not easily applied in practice, because the outgoing director can insist that the company should honour its contractual obligations to honour the terms of the service contract.

Disclosures about remuneration

The Greenbury Report included extensive recommendations on the disclosure of information about the company's remuneration policy and the remuneration of individual directors.

The Report recommended greater disclosures about the remuneration of individual directors. The annual report and accounts should disclose for each named director the elements of remuneration, such as salaries and fees, annual bonuses, deferred bonuses, and compensation for loss of office. For each director, information should also be given about share options and any other long-term incentive scheme other than share options. An explanation and justification should be provided whenever any element of remuneration other than basic salary is pensionable.

A disclosure should be made of any director with a notice period in excess of twelve months in his or her service contract, together with an explanation of the reasons.

The detailed disclosures on directors' remuneration should be checked by the external auditors.

To provide some accountability to the shareholders, it was recommended that the chairman of the remuneration committee should attend the annual general meeting, where the shareholders should have an opportunity for a question-and-answer session.

The remuneration committee report

The Greenbury Report called for a report in the annual report and accounts on directors' remuneration policy. This should provide details of how the remuneration of directors compares with other, similar companies.

All bonus schemes should depend on satisfactory performance criteria. Long-term incentive schemes should be submitted to the shareholders for approval in advance of introducing them. The Greenbury Report did not give guidelines for deciding what constitutes 'satisfactory performance', and as a result this element of the recommendations has been interpreted widely. For example, there were no guidelines about incentives for short-term performance and incentives for longer-term performance.

The report should also include a statement on the company's policy for granting share options and other long-term incentive schemes, together with a justification for any departure from that policy in the period under review.

The Greenbury recommendations did not include a requirement for shareholder approval of the general remuneration policy for directors, or for shareholder approval of short-term incentive schemes. In practice, companies can decide themselves on whether to submit most elements of remuneration policy to the shareholders for approval.

3 The Hampel Report (1998)

The Hampel Committee was set up in 1996 to continue the review of corporate governance practices in the UK, following the Cadbury and Greenbury Reports. The Hampel Committee suggested that the recommendations of all three committees should be integrated into a single code of corporate governance, which was published in 1998 as the Combined Code.

In its report, the Committee explained that its aim was to restrict the regulatory burden on companies, and to this end it sought whenever possible to recommend principles rather than detailed regulations. Principles are preferable to rules because the most suitable form of corporate governance will depend to a large extent on the particular situation of each individual company. Detailed regulations are a form of governance by box ticking. 'Box ticking takes no account of the diversity of circumstances and experiences among companies and within the same company over time.' For example, commenting on the assumptions that the roles of chairman and CEO should always be kept separate, the committee report stated: 'We do not think there are universally valid answers on such points.' This emphasis on principles rather than detailed rules survived into the Combined Code, which soon followed the Hampel Report. The Combined Code is a combination of a set of guiding principles and a more detailed code of practice.

The introduction to the Report also stated that whilst the Cadbury and Greenbury Reports concentrated on the prevention of abuses, Hampel was equally concerned with the positive contribution that good corporate governance can make.

The introduction to the Hampel Report expressed firm support for the shareholder view of corporate governance. In the view of the Committee, the primary responsibility of the board of directors was towards the shareholders, and the objective of the company and the task of the directors is to enhance the value of the shareholders' investment over time. The directors had no direct responsibility towards the other stakeholders in the company. Relationships with other stakeholders were important, but making the directors responsible to other stakeholders would mean there was no clear yardstick for judging directors' performance.

The corporate governance principles of the Hampel Committee, which were presented under a number of headings, are summarised below. Many of these principles reflect the earlier recommendations of the Cadbury and Greenbury Committees, although are generally less specific.

3.1   The directors

A company should be headed by an effective board, which should lead and control the company. There are two key tasks at the top of each company. One is to run the board of directors and the other is the executive responsibility for running the company's business. These tasks are typically assigned to a chairman and CEO respectively, and should generally be kept separate, but this is not essential. A company should explain publicly how these tasks are carried out and if they are combined in one person, a senior non-executive director of the board should be identified.

There should be a balance on the board between executive and non-executive directors, and some NEDs should be independent. No individual or small group of individuals should be able to dominate the board.

New appointments to the board of directors should be made through a transparent and formal procedure. A nomination committee might be involved. The report stressed the importance of monitoring director performance and recommended that all directors should submit themselves for re-election at regular intervals, and not less than once every three years.

The board should be supplied with timely information, sufficient to enable it to discharge its duties properly.

3.2   Directors' remuneration

Hampel went no further than the Greenbury Committee on directors' remuneration, and put forward the following principles. The remuneration committee should have the responsibility for setting the pay of executive directors. No director should be involved in deciding his or her own remuneration.

This committee should develop a policy on remuneration and devise reasonable remuneration packages for individual executive directors. Remuneration for directors should be sufficient to attract and retain good people. The element in the remuneration package of an individual director should be structured so that rewards are linked to individual and company performance. Companies should try to reduce the period of notice in a director's contract periods to one year or less.

A statement on remuneration policy should be included in the company's annual report to shareholders, with details of the remuneration of each individual director. However, the Hampel Committee saw no need for remuneration policy to be a matter for shareholder approval at the annual general meeting.

3.3   Shareholders

The Hampel recommendations favoured greater shareholder involvement in company matters, but did not recommend any extension of shareholder rights.

Shareholders should be able to vote separately on each substantially separate issue and the practice of 'bundling' unrelated proposals into a single resolution should cease. Notice of the AGM and related papers should be sent to shareholders at least 20 working days before the meeting.

The Hampel Report also encouraged the idea of more dialogue and communication between a company and its shareholders. In this respect, it introduced an emphasis that had been missing in the Cadbury Report. In return, shareholders should be expected to make a greater contribution, partly by being more active in the exercise of their rights. Some of the recommendations in the report were directed against the common practice amongst institutional investors of always giving their proxy votes in favour of resolutions put forward by the board of directors, and avoiding active involvement with companies in which they invested.

- The report recommended that institutional investors should adopt a 'considered policy' on voting their shares.
- There should be a dialogue between a company and its institutional investors, based on a mutual understanding of objectives.
- Institutional investors should evaluate corporate governance disclosures by a company and give 'due weight' to all the relevant factors drawn to their attention in the information provided.
- Companies should use their annual general meeting to communicate with private shareholders, and encourage their participation at those meetings.

These principles of shareholder involvement and dialogue between a company and its institutional shareholders were subsequently repeated in the Combined Code.

3.4   Accountability and audit

The Hampel Report repeated some of the recommendations of Cadbury:

- In its financial reports to shareholders, the board should present a balanced and understandable assessment of the company's position and prospects.
- The board should put in place formal and transparent arrangements for maintaining a suitable relationship with the external auditors.

- The external auditors should report independently to the shareholders. (As a consequence of Hampel Committee and the subsequent Combined Code, the auditors' report in the annual report and accounts of UK listed companies must now include much more than the basic statutory information required by the Companies Act.)

A significant feature of the Hampel Report was the recommendation originally made by the Cadbury Committee, but rejected at the time, that the board should maintain a sound system of internal control, to safeguard the shareholders' investment and the company's assets. This responsibility should apply to all internal controls relating to the achievement of the company's objectives, not just to financial controls. The responsibility of the board for all aspects of risk management was therefore established as 'best practice'. (The Cadbury recommendations were watered down, and until Hampel the board was held responsible for financial controls only.)

However, whilst recommending that directors should report to shareholders on internal control, the Hampel Committee stated that the directors should not be required to report on the effectiveness of those controls. Instead, the opinions of the auditors about internal controls should be reported privately to the directors.

4 The 1998 Combined Code

The Hampel Report was the third report on corporate governance in the UK in the space of about six years, and it was therefore decided that the accepted principles and best practice guidelines of Cadbury, Greenbury and Hampel should be brought together into a single Code. This was the Combined Code, which brought together a set of principles of good corporate governance (as favoured by the Hampel Committee) and provisions for best practice, giving more detailed guidelines to follow. The Code was in two sections, the first setting out principles and a code of best practice for companies, the second proposing principles and a code of practice for institutional investors.

The Code was produced by a Committee on Corporate Governance in 1998 and adopted by the London Stock Exchange. It was included in the UK Listing Rules as an appendix, although it did not form part of the Listing Rules themselves.

4.1   Principles-based guidance: 'comply or explain'

The Combined Code provides principles to guide best practice in corporate governance, and includes some more detailed provisions. Essentially, however, it is a principles-based document that does not contain prescriptive rules that companies must follow. Companies are free to disregard aspects of the Combined Code. However, they must disclose any non-compliance and explain the reasons for it.

The Listing Rules require a statement in two parts from all listed companies in their annual report and accounts, as follows:

1   A narrative statement of how the company has applied the corporate governance principles in Section 1 of the Combined Code. This should be sufficient to allow

the shareholders to make their own evaluation of how the principles have been applied. The Code does not set out a standard form or content for this statement. Instead, it states that: 'companies should have a free hand to explain their governance policies in the light of the principles, including any special circumstances applying to them which have led to a particular approach. It must be for shareholders and others to evaluate this part of the company's statement.'

2   A statement about whether or not the company has complied with the provisions of Section 1 of the Code. If it has not complied with any of the provisions, or has only complied for a part of the financial year, it must specify the provisions it has not complied with or time period in which it has not complied. It should also give reasons for non-compliance.

This approach to compliance with the Combined Code provisions has become known as 'comply or explain'. Listed companies are not compelled to comply with all the provisions of the Code. It is recognised that in certain circumstances, departures from the Code might be appropriate. However, if they do not comply, companies must give their reasons.

Institutional investors have stated that they expect any such explanations to be convincing if they are to win shareholder support. Indeed, pressure on companies from investment institutions and their financial market advisers, together with the requirement for the statement on disclosure, has persuaded most listed companies to comply fully, or almost fully, with all the provisions of the Combined Code.

Although the 1998 Code has now been superseded by the 2003 Combined Code, itself reviewed and revised in 2006 (see below), the principles and reporting requirements it established, its 'comply or explain' approach and its overall structure endure.

5   The Turnbull Report (1999)

The Turnbull Report was produced by a working party of the Institute of Chartered Accountants in England and Wales to give additional guidance to listed companies on how to implement the provisions of the Combined Code with regard to internal control.

By making directors responsible for risk management and internal controls generally, the Combined Code recognises that the objectives of the company are not simply to maximise returns to shareholders in the short term, because shareholders expect their investment to be protected against unnecessary risks. It does not seek to eliminate risk, because taking some risks is necessary to earn returns on investment. There is risk in undertaking new business opportunities, but the prospective returns should justify the foreseeable risks. Companies need to be aware of how much risk they can handle. Risk management is therefore concerned with developing the business as well as with preventing 'disasters'.

The Turnbull guidelines are notable because:

- They require the board of directors to look forward, and not just consider past performance.
- They encourage companies to keep their shareholders informed about risks.

- They require directors to think strategically, and to be aware that the company must continually adapt to its changing environment.
- Risks should be reviewed regularly.
- The risk control procedures should evolve as the business and its environment change.

The Report is now known as The Turnbull Guidance which is described in more detail in Chapter 10 and reproduced in its entirety in Appendix 9.

6 Directors' Remuneration Report Regulations (2002)

One of the provisions in the 1998 Combined Code was that there should be a statement in the company's annual report on remuneration policy and disclosure of certain details of the remuneration of each director. A schedule to the Code indicated what items of remuneration should be included in the disclosures. For listed companies, however, more stringent disclosure requirements were written into the UK Listing Rules specifying the details of what should be disclosed about directors' remuneration.

In 2002, the UK Listing Rules requirements were replaced by legislative change, when the Directors' Remuneration Report Regulations amended the Companies Act 1985. Listed companies must now prepare an annual remuneration report, describing remuneration policy and giving detailed disclosures about the remuneration of each director. The report must be submitted to the shareholders for approval at the annual general meeting. The Regulations are outlined in detail in Chapter 9.

7 The Higgs Report (2003)

The Higgs Report, the Review of the Role and Effectiveness of Non-executive Directors, aimed to develop guidelines for making NEDs more effective. A part of the problem was to ensure that the role of NEDs is properly understood. Other aspects of the problem are to ensure that NEDs are suitably knowledgeable or experienced, understand the company and its affairs sufficiently well, have enough time for their duties, and are given the opportunity to contribute to board decision-making. These issues were addressed in the Report.

Recommendations in the Report included the following.

The board

- The board should be collectively responsible for promoting the success of the company by leading and directing the company's affairs. The Report included recommendations for what the role of the board should be. (By implication, since the board includes NEDs, the NEDs share the collective responsibility and should be involved in the leading and directing of the company's affairs.)
- The annual report should provide information about how frequently the board and committees of the board have met, and about the attendance at meetings of each individual director.

- At least half of the board, excluding the chairman, should be independent NEDs. (The Higgs proposal went further than the 1998 Code, and was incorporated into the 2003 revised Code.)

The chairman

- The Report stated that the role of the chairman of the board is pivotal in creating conditions suitable for an effective board and getting an effective contribution from each individual director. (This pivotal role of the chairman was also written into the 2003 revised Code.)
- The roles of the chairman and CEO should be separate, and the division of responsibilities between the two roles should be set out in writing and agreed by the whole board.
- The CEO should not become the chairman of the same company.
- At the time of his or her appointment, the chairman should be independent.

NEDs

The Report suggested what the role of NEDs should be, for inclusion on the revised Code.

- Prior to their appointment, NEDs should carry out due diligence on the board and the company, to satisfy themselves that they have the knowledge, skills, experience and time to do their job properly.
- There should be a senior independent director, who should be available to shareholders if they have concerns that cannot be sorted out through normal channels of contact with the company (i.e. through the chairman). (At the time, this recommendation by Higgs was controversial and opposed by a number of companies, who saw it as a threat to good relationships between a company and its major shareholders.)
- The Report suggested a definition of 'independence' for inclusion in the revised Code.
- The task of searching for new directors and recommending new appointments to the board should be delegated to a nomination committee. The Report also proposed that the pool from which NEDs are selected should be broadened. (This recommendation led to the Tyson Report later in 2003.)
- NEDs should be given induction on appointment. The chairman should be responsible for the induction of NEDs and for the development of all members of the board, to develop and update their knowledge and skills.
- The company secretary should be accountable to the board as a whole, through the chairman, on all corporate governance matters.
- On appointment, NEDs should give an undertaking that they will have sufficient time to carry out their duties.
- NEDs should be allowed to take a part of their fee as director in the form of shares in the company. However, NEDs should not participate in a company share option scheme.

The Higgs Report was very influential, and most of the Report's recommendations were either written into the revised Combined Code, or included in best practice guidelines that are appended to the Code.

8 The Smith Report (2003)

A committee established by the Financial Reporting Council published the Smith Report in January 2003: 'Audit Committees: Combined Code Guidance'. The purpose of the report was to give guidance to company boards on how to make suitable arrangements for their audit committees, and individual audit committee members on how to fulfil their role and responsibilities.

The recommendations of the Report – The Smith Guidance – are reproduced in their entirety in Appendix 6. The Guidance is also described in more detail in Chapters 7 and 10.

9 The 2003 Combined Code

Following the Higgs and Smith Reports, responsibility for the Combined Code was given to the FRC, which published a revised version in July 2003. Many of the Higgs Report and Smith Report recommendations were written into the revised Code. Like the 1998 Code, the 2003 Code is divided into two sections, one for companies and the other for institutional shareholders. The section for companies is subdivided into four areas of corporate governance:

- directors (covering issues such as the board and its responsibilities, the chairman and CEO, board balance, appointments to the board, etc.);
- directors' remuneration;
- accountability and audit;
- relations with shareholders.

Three Schedules provide:

- provisions on the design of performance related-remuneration;
- guidance on the liability of NEDs;
- a summary of corporate governance disclosure requirements.

Whereas the 1998 Code consisted of principles and provisions (best practice), the 2003 Code consists of main principles, supporting principles and provisions (practical requirements). The 2003 Code is longer than the 1998 Code, but the total number of provisions is not much larger. This was deliberate:

- The accepted view is that corporate governance in the UK should be principles-based, rather than rules-based. Some rules (provisions) are necessary, but should not be excessive provided that companies apply the principles.
- Listed companies are required by the UK Listing Rules to comply or explain their non-compliance with the Code's provisions. It was considered that, given the fact that corporate governance should be mainly principles-based, increasing the number of provisions might create unnecessary reporting requirements.

The Code also explicitly relaxes certain rules, such as the required number of independent NEDs on boards, for smaller listed companies, defined as those which are below the FTSE 350 throughout the year immediately prior to the reporting year.

The Financial Reporting Council (FRC) is now responsible for the Combined Code, and will review the Code regularly. The most recent review, which resulted in minor changes, was in 2006.

The Accounting Standards Board, which is a body within the FRC structure responsible for UK accounting standards, has responsibility for issuing Standards relating to the Operating and Financial Review, although the OFR is not (as originally intended) a statutory document, only a voluntary one.

The FRC is also responsible for reviewing the Turnbull Guidelines.

Most of the principles and provisions of the Combined Code have been described in detail in earlier chapters. The full text of the Code itself is set out in Appendix 1.

10 The Combined Code and institutional investors

Section 2 of the 2003 Combined Code contains main principles and supporting principles for institutional investors. This section is short, with just three main principles. (Section 2 of the 1998 Code contained three principles and three provisions.) Their aim is to encourage institutional investors to take a more active role in the governance of companies in which they invest.

It is argued that institutional investors, such as pension funds, unit trusts and life assurance companies, hold funds on behalf of many individuals, and so in an indirect way are investing on behalf of those individuals. It is therefore incumbent on institutional investors, on behalf of the individuals they represent, to make sure that the boards of directors of companies are made properly accountable and govern the company responsibly.

They should do this by making their views known to the company, forcibly if necessary.

The principles are general and do not provide many practical guidelines, because it has been left to the membership associations of institutional investors, such as the Association of British Insurers (ABI) and the National Association of Pension Funds (NAPF) to issue more detailed guidelines to their members.

Main principle

- Institutional shareholders should enter into a dialogue with companies based on a mutual understanding of objectives.
- When evaluating corporate governance arrangements in companies institutional shareholders should give weight to all the factors drawn to their attention.
- Institutional shareholders have a responsibility to make considered use of their votes.

Supporting principle

- Institutions should apply the principles set out in the corporate governance principles issued by the Institutional Shareholders' Committee.
- Institutions should give careful consideration to any departure by a company from the Combined Code and make a reasoned judgement in each case. They should avoid a box-ticking approach.

- Institutions should ensure that their voting intentions are turned into practice.
- They should attend AGMs where practicable.
- They should make their voting record available, on request, to clients.

11 Corporate governance guidelines for non-listed companies

As best practice in corporate governance has been increasingly recognised or accepted by large listed companies, attention has turned to smaller quoted companies, mainly listed companies outside the FTSE 350 and companies whose shares are traded on the Alternative Investment Market (AIM).

11.1 QCA Guidelines

There is no regulatory requirement for companies other than listed companies to comply with the principles and provisions of the Combined Code. However, The Quoted Companies Alliance (QCA), a body representing smaller quoted companies, has issued two guides:

- Corporate Governance: Guidelines for Smaller Quoted Companies (2004);
- Corporate Governance: Guidelines for AIM Companies (2005).

These were developed in consultation with some institutional investors. The QCA website has included the comment from its chief executive that: 'It is a huge mistake for companies to believe that they are too small to worry about corporate governance. Good practice increases investor confidence and commitment, and improves a company's ability to raise finance through the markets at a lower cost.'

The Guidelines for Smaller Quoted Companies offer guidance on how small companies should adapt the Combined Code to their particular circumstances. The Guidelines for AIM companies are consistent with the Combined Code for listed companies, but not as detailed or rigorous.

Although the Combined Code does not apply to AIM companies, the QCA has commented that: 'Compliance with the Combined Code should continue to be an aspiration for AIM companies as they grow.' Larger AIM companies should be expected to comply with most of the requirements of the full Combined Code, whereas smaller AIM companies should comply with certain minimum guidelines.

The QCA guidelines for AIM companies include the following minimum standards:

- There should be a formal schedule of matters reserved for the board, where decisions must be taken by the board and should not be delegated to executive management.
- The board members should be provided in a timely manner with the information they need to do their job properly.

- The roles of chairman and chief executive officer should not be held by the same individual. If they are held by the same individual, the company should provide a clear explanation of the procedures that are applied to prevent the risk of dominance of the company and its board by that individual.
- Internal controls should be reviewed at least annually. The review should cover financial controls, operational controls, compliance controls and risk management systems.
- The company should have at least two independent NEDs. One of these may be the company chairman.
- There should be an audit committee, remuneration committee and nomination committee of the board. The audit and remuneration committees should have at least two members and the members should all be independent NEDs.
- All directors should submit themselves for re-election by the shareholders at regular intervals.
- There should be a dialogue with shareholders to establish a mutual understanding of the company's objectives.

AIM companies should publish an annual corporate governance statement, stating that the company has complied with the QCA guidelines, or explaining any non-compliance. This statement should be put on the company's website, or included in its annual report and accounts. The QCA therefore hopes to extend the concept of 'comply or explain' to AIM companies.

In practice, many AIM companies do not comply with the AIM guidelines. In particular, not all AIM companies have two or more independent NEDs and many do not have a nomination committee.

11.2 NAPF corporate governance policy for AIM companies

In March 2007, the National Association of Pension Funds issued a policy document, 'AIM Corporate Governance Policy and Voting Guidelines', with regard to corporate governance in AIM companies.

The introduction to the document explains the reasons for its publication. There is now a greater interest in AIM companies, and investors are looking to representative bodies such as the NAPF to provide voting guidelines. The NAPF also believes that by applying certain standards of corporate governance, AIM companies will be better able to manage their growth and attract an institutional investor following. 'We believe that, by encouraging higher standards of corporate governance, AIM companies will be better able to manage their growth and attract a greater institutional investor following, thereby enabling them to raise fresh capital more easily and on potentially more advantageous terms.'

The NAPF policy guidelines are consistent with the QCA's corporate governance guidelines for AIM companies, although there are some differences in the details. One of the points made in the NAPF policy document is a recognition that AIM companies vary substantially in size, and appropriate corporate governance arrangements will vary according to the company's characteristics and circumstances.

Some of the policy guidelines are as follows:

1   The boards of AIM companies should be familiar with the main principles of the Combined Code and should seek to apply them to the extent that they are appropriate to the company's circumstances. NAPF would expect AIM companies with a large market capitalisation to comply with the Combined Code in full or explain any non-compliance. At the other end of the scale, small AIM companies should concentrate on growing their business, but should provide 'good levels of disclosure' in their annual report and accounts.

2   NAPF expects all AIM companies to explain their corporate governance policies and to include in their annual report biographical details of the board directors and details of the board committees.

3   As a general rule, companies should separate the roles of company chairman and CEO, and appoint different individuals to these roles. The NAPF recognises that there are circumstances in which an AIM company might appoint the same person to the role of both company chairman and CEO. When this happens, the company should also appoint a senior independent director. This director should provide a communication channel between the shareholders and the board, should this be needed. The CEO should not subsequently go on to become the company chairman.

4   The NAPF guidelines on the composition of the board differ from those of the QCA. The NAPF recommends that the board of a larger AIM company should have at least two independent NEDs, excluding the chairman. For companies with a smaller board, say four to six members, there should be at least two independent NEDs, one of whom may be the chairman, and these should comprise at least one-third of the total board membership.

5   Like the QCA the NAPF recommends that there should be remuneration, audit and nomination committees. There should be a majority of independent NEDs on all the committees.

6   The NAPF recognises that the definition of 'independence' needs to differ in some ways for AIM companies, compared with listed companies. In listed companies, the independence of a director would be questioned if he or she held more than 1 per cent of the company's shares. For AIM companies this threshold is raised to 3 per cent. The NAPF is also more willing to accept that a NED might be independent even if he or she has served more than nine years (but less than twelve years) in the role.

7   Remuneration guidelines for AIM companies should be similar to those for listed companies. A significant proportion of the remuneration of senior executives should be linked to performance. There should be disclosure by the company of the performance conditions attached to bonuses and long-term incentive plans.

11.3 *London Stock Exchange rules for AIM companies*

In 2007 The London Stock Exchange issued an amended rule book for companies (and also a new publication, 'The AIM Rules for Nominated Advisers', which is additional to the AIM rules for companies). The amended rules include a requirement for all AIM companies to display (free of charge) on a separate section of their website a minimum amount of core management and financial information. This includes:

- a description of the company's business;
- the names and biographical details of its directors;
- the responsibilities of the board of directors and the board committees;
- the company's country of incorporation;
- its constitutional documents (such as Articles of Association);
- the number of AIM securities in issue;
- the percentage of the company's shares that are in the hands of significant shareholders;
- its most recent annual report and any subsequent half-yearly report, quarterly report or similar report;
- all notifications made by the company to the stock market in the past twelve months;
- its most recent admission document;
- details of its nominated adviser and other key advisers.

Chapter summary

- In the UK, the development of a code of corporate governance principles and best practice began with the Cadbury Code in 1992. This identified many of the key issues, including the balance of power on the board and the need for independent NEDs, the transparency of financial reporting and role of the external auditor and the need for risk management.

- The Greenbury Committee subsequently addressed concerns abut 'fat cat' directors, and made recommendations about directors' remuneration and disclosure of information about their remuneration.

- Recognition of the need to keep corporate governance guidelines under review led to the Hampel Report and then the Combined Code.

- The lack of detail in the Combined Code about the responsibilities of the board of directors for risk management prompted the Turnbull Committee guidelines.

- Although there is considerable pressure on listed companies to comply with the Combined Code, it remains a voluntary code rather than a statutory requirement. However, the UK Listing Rules include a requirement for listed companies to disclose details of their compliance or non-compliance with the Code.

- A recognition of the need to provide shareholders with extensive information on directors' remuneration, and to give shareholders a voice in the consideration of remuneration policy led to the Directors' Remuneration Report Regulations and a change in UK company law in 2002.

- Concerns about the effectiveness of NEDs prompted an investigation leading to the Higgs Report in 2003.

- A recognition of the need to give guidance to companies and committee members on the constitution, role and conduct of the audit committee prompted the Smith Report in 2003.

- In the wake of the Higgs and Smith Reports, a revised Combined Code was issued in July 2003. The Combined Code is now the responsibility of the FRC, which will review it regularly and amend it as necessary.

- There have been some initiatives for the encouragement of good corporate governance practice in AIM companies, and guidelines have been issued by both the QCA and the NAPF.

- Some changes have been introduced into UK law affecting corporate governance.

Chapter 13

An international history of corporate governance

1. The OECD Principles of corporate governance
2. Corporate governance and the European Union
3. Corporate governance and the Commonwealth countries
4. The King Reports (South Africa)
5. Corporate governance in the United States
6. Corporate governance in other countries

1 The OECD Principles of corporate governance

1.1 International aspects of corporate governance

The Organisation for Economic Cooperation and Development (OECD) is an international body established to help countries, particularly those with developing economies, by providing advice and assistance on economic matters and on ways of helping them to adapt to the demands of the international economy. In 1998, the OECD set up a task force to produce a set of principles of good corporate governance. A purpose of the OECD Principles, which were published in 1999 and subsequently revised in 2004, was to help governments in their efforts to improve the legal, institutional and regulatory framework for corporate governance in their countries. The Principles were also intended to provide a source of suggestions and guidance for stock exchanges, institutions, companies and other organisations with a role to play in formulating detailed corporate governance practices.

They provide a reference point, and are non-binding on member countries. They are a set of principles and do not provide detailed regulations as to how companies should be governed. However, in 2002 the Emerging Markets Committee of IOSCO (the International Organisation of Securities Commissions) recommended the OECD Principles as a 'benchmark'.

The OECD states in its preamble to the Principles that there is a close connection between economics and institutional structures, and one way of improving a country's economic efficiency is through the development of good corporate governance. If countries are to succeed in attracting inward capital investment through the international capital markets, their corporate governance practices must be understood by and acceptable to the international investment community.

The Principles do not address the issue of how multinational companies should run their foreign subsidiaries. OECD guidelines for this are provided in its Guidelines for

Multinational Enterprises. Nor do the Principles address the problem of bribery as a feature of corporate practice in some countries. This issue is covered by the OECD Convention on Combating Bribery of Foreign Public Officials in International Transactions. The focus of the Principles is on corporate governance problems arising from the separation of the owner-ship of a company (the shareholders) from its control (by the board of directors).

The OECD Principles were also written with a clear understanding of the divergence of corporate governance practices in different countries. They should be studied in particular with an awareness that in some countries controlling shareholders or management might govern companies with disregard for the interest of minority shareholders. The preamble to the Principles states:

> 'Controlling shareholders, which may be individuals, family holdings, bloc alliances, or other corporations acting through a holding company or cross share-holdings, can significantly influence corporate behaviour. As owners of equity, institutional investors are increasingly demanding a voice in corporate governance in some mar-kets. Individual shareholders usually do not seek to exercise governance rights but may be highly concerned about obtaining fair treatment from controlling share-holders and management.'

1.2 The structure of the OECD Principles

The OECD Principles are divided into six sections or areas. These are:

1. ensuring the basis for an effective corporate governance framework;
2. the rights of shareholders;
3. the equitable treatment of shareholders;
4. the role of stakeholders;
5. disclosure and transparency;
6. the responsibilities of the board.

Ensuring the basis for an effective corporate governance framework

The corporate governance framework should promote transparent and efficient markets, be consistent with the rule of law and should clearly specify the division of responsibilities between the supervisory, regulatory and enforcement authorities.

The rights of shareholders

'The corporate governance framework should protect and facilitate the exercise of share-holder rights.'

Shareholders have certain property rights, which ought to be protected. However, a company cannot be managed by shareholder referendum, and shareholders cannot take over the task of management. They should not interfere in the functions that are properly delegated to company managers.

The property rights of shareholders are therefore the right to:

- secure methods of registering their ownership of the shares;
- transfer their shares;

- receive relevant information about the company on a 'timely and regular' basis;
- participate and vote in general meetings of the company;
- elect members of the board of directors;
- share in the profits of the company.

The shareholders should have the right to make the decisions on certain fundamental issues affecting the company, through voting at general meetings. Shareholders should therefore be kept sufficiently informed on and participate in decision-making on matters such as:

- amendments to the company's constitution (e.g. Articles of Association);
- authorising the issue of new shares;
- extraordinary transactions that in effect result in the sale of the company.

Shareholders should have the opportunity to participate effectively and vote in general meetings of the company, and should be informed about the rules and voting procedures for those meetings. They should therefore be given adequate notice about the timing, location and agenda for a general meeting, and about the matters to be decided at the meeting. Shareholders should also have the opportunity to ask questions at general meetings, and the right, within reasonable limitations, to put things on the agenda. In these respects, the OECD Principles differ very little from the Combined Code in the UK. The Principles go further, however, by recommending that shareholders should be able to vote at general meetings, either in person or by means of proxy (in absentia).

The Principles recommend that shareholder participation should be broadened, and that companies should consider ways of encouraging more shareholders to vote.

Shareholders should be given sufficient and timely information about general meetings and the issues that will be decided at each meeting. They should be able to ask questions of the board, including questions about the external audit. They should also be able to vote at meetings either in person or in absentia (for example, by proxy).

Shareholders should also be able to participate in the nomination and election of board directors and to give a view on the remuneration policy for directors and key executives. Equity components of remuneration schemes should be subject to shareholder approval.

There should be a disclosure of any capital structures and other arrangements that allow certain shareholders to obtain a degree of control disproportionate to the size of their shareholding. Cross-shareholdings, shareholder agreements and voting caps are examples. A shareholder agreement occurs when a group of shareholders who individually might hold only a small proportion of the company's shares agree to act and vote in concert, so that they create an effective voting majority, or at least the largest block of shareholder votes. A voting cap is a rule that sets a limit on the percentage of the vote that any one shareholder can have, regardless of the size of the shareholding. For example, if there is a voting cap of 10 per cent, a shareholder with 20 per cent of the shares could only exercise a vote up to 10 per cent. A note to the Principles comments: 'Pyramid structures and cross-shareholdings can be used to diminish the capability of non-controlling shareholders to influence corporate policy.'

The Principles do not suggest that such shareholder arrangements or capital structures should be banned. Such prohibitions would be a matter for national regulation. The Principles simply state that given the ability of such arrangements to affect the balance of influence in a company, it is reasonable to expect that shareholders should be informed about them.

The Principles also address the issue of mergers and takeovers, where problems include giving more favourable treatment to some shareholders in a target company than to others, and devices to make it more difficult for a hostile bidder to succeed with a takeover bid (poison pills).

- The Principles state that 'markets for corporate control should be allowed to function in an efficient and transparent manner'. The price at which transactions in shares are made should be transparent and transactions should be made under fair conditions that protect the rights of all shareholders.
- Anti-takeover devices (poison pills) should not be used to shield management from accountability. The Principles recognise that companies use anti-takeover devices in some countries, and note that stock markets and investors have expressed concern about them. Once again, however, the Principles do not go so far as to recommend that anti-takeover devices should be banned.

The section of the Principles on the rights of shareholders ends with the recommendation that shareholders, including institutional investors, 'should consider the costs and benefits of exercising their voting rights'. Some investors have already recognised that they will benefit financially by exercising their rights more actively, but the Principles do not suggest what would be the optimum level of shareholder activism.

The equitable treatment of shareholders

'The corporate governance framework should ensure the equitable treatment of all shareholders, including minority and foreign shareholders. All shareholders should have the opportunity to obtain effective redress for violation of their rights.'

This section of the Principles is concerned with the protection of shareholders against unfair actions by management, the board of directors or controlling shareholders. As well as recognising the need to protect minority shareholders, the Principles also specifically mention foreign shareholders as well.

To some extent, shareholder rights may be protected by the law, and the effectiveness of the legal system, or any system of regulation, is of particular importance in this respect. In particular, the law might give minority shareholders the right to bring lawsuits where they consider that their rights have been violated. On the other hand, companies and management should be protected against excessive litigation, and a balance needs to be struck between protecting minority shareholders' rights and allowing minority shareholders too much scope to bring cases against their companies or their directors.

The Principles require that all shareholders of the same class should be treated equally. For example, foreign shareholders should receive the same treatment as domestic shareholders.

Within any class of shares, shareholders should have the same voting rights. Any proposed changes in voting rights should be subject to vote by shareholders in the class of shares affected.

The Principles do not support the idea of 'one shareholder, one vote', recognising that when shares are issued with different voting rights or dividend rights, such as preference shares, the differences will be reflected in the market prices of those shares.

Votes cast by nominee shareholders and custodians should have been agreed with the beneficial owner of the shares. (This principle does not apply to trustees.) In many countries, the shares of foreign investors are held and managed on behalf of the beneficial shareowner by nominees or custodians (such as banks). In some countries, it has been customary for nominees or custodians to cast the votes for those shares in favour of the company's management, unless specifically instructed otherwise by the beneficial shareowner. The Principles recommend that the beneficial shareowners should have more input into the way the votes belonging to their shares are cast.

The processes and procedures at a general meeting of shareholders should allow for the equitable treatment of all shareholders. Procedures should not make it unduly difficult or expensive to cast votes. Notes to the Principles comment that:

> 'Management and controlling investors have at times sought to discourage non-controlling or foreign investors from trying to influence the direction of the company. Some companies charged fees for voting. Other impediments included prohibitions on proxy voting and the requirement of personal attendance at general shareholder meetings to vote.'

The Principles encourage the removal of any such barriers to shareholder participation.

Insider trading and 'abusive self-dealing' should be prohibited. 'Abusive self-dealing' occurs when persons with a close relationship to the company exploit the relationship to the disadvantage of the company and its investors. The OECD commented that the enforcement of laws against insider dealing were more rigorous in some countries than in others. (It is worth noting that the lack of success in the UK in obtaining successful prosecutions for insider dealing was one of the factors leading to the introduction of the new offence of 'market abuse' in the Financial Services and Markets Act 2000.)

The Principles also require members of the board and managers of the company to disclose any material personal interests they have in transactions or matters affecting the company. (In the UK, listed companies are required to obtain prior shareholder approval for transactions with related parties for transactions outside the normal run of business operations.)

The role of stakeholders in corporate governance

'The corporate governance framework should recognise the rights of stakeholders as established by law and encourage active cooperation between corporations and stakeholders in creating wealth, jobs and the sustainability of financially sound enterprises.'

The notes to the Principles argue that a key aspect of corporate governance is ensuring the flow of external capital to firms that need to obtain it. The role of creditors is therefore significant. Corporate governance is also concerned with finding ways to encourage the various stakeholders in the firm to undertake socially efficient levels of investment in human and physical capital within their companies. The competitiveness and success of a company depend ultimately on the teamwork of the various stakeholders, including investors, employees, creditors and suppliers. However, in spite of these elevated remarks, the Principles restrict themselves largely to recommending that the legal rights of stakeholders should be upheld by the corporate governance framework, and that stakeholders should have an effective means of seeking redress for the violation of their rights. The Principles do not suggest what stakeholder rights should be provided or protected by law.

The Principles add that the corporate governance framework should permit 'performance-enhancing mechanisms for stakeholder participation'. Examples included are employee representation on the board of directors, employee share ownership, profit-sharing arrangements and the right of creditors to be involved in any insolvency proceedings. The corporate governance framework should be complemented by an effective and efficient insolvency framework and by effective enforcement of creditor rights.

Disclosure and transparency

'The corporate governance framework should ensure that timely and accurate disclosure is made on all material matters regarding the corporation, including the financial situation, performance, ownership and governance of the company.'

The Principles suggest that a strong disclosure regime is a 'pivotal feature' of market-based monitoring of companies, and is essential for allowing shareholders to exercise their voting rights properly. A strong disclosure regime also helps to attract fresh capital and maintain confidence in the capital markets, whereas insufficient or poor disclosure may prevent the markets from functioning properly, add to the cost of capital and result in an inefficient allocation of resources.

The Principles provide a list of matters about which disclosures should be made. Timely disclosures should include, but not be restricted to, material information on:

- Financial and operating results. When the reporting company is part of a group, it is important that the financial statements should relate to the entire group.
- The company's objectives. In addition to commercial objectives, companies are encouraged to disclose policies on business ethics, the environment and other public policy commitments.
- Major shareholdings and voting rights.
- Members of the board and key executives, and their remuneration.
- Related party transactions.
- Material foreseeable risk factors. Notes to the Principles include the comment that: 'Users of financial information and market participants need information on reasonably foreseeable material risks that include: risks that are specific to the industry and geographical areas, dependence on commodities, financial market risk including interest rate or currency risk, risk related to derivatives and off-balance sheet transactions, and risks related to environmental liabilities.' Disclosure of whether or not companies have put in place a system for monitoring risk would also be 'useful'.
- Material issues regarding employees and other stakeholders. Some countries require extensive disclosures about human resources, such as HR policies and programmes for staff development.
- Governance structures and policies. Companies are encouraged to report on how they apply relevant corporate governance principles and practices.

Information disclosed by a company should be prepared, audited and disclosed in accordance with high-quality standards of accounting, financial and non-financial disclosure, and audit. The OECD supports the use of international accounting standards.

The Principles address the issue of the role of the external auditors, and their independence. The Principle is that the annual audit should be carried out by an independent auditor, to provide an objective assurance on the way the financial statements have been prepared. The notes on the Principles recognise the difficulties in obtaining reassurance about auditor independence. The notes recommend:

- the application of high-quality audit standards and codes of ethics;
- strengthening the audit committee of the board;
- increasing the responsibility of the board for the auditor selection process.

Channels for disseminating information can be as important as the content of the information itself. The channels used should therefore provide for 'fair, timely and cost-efficient access to relevant information by users'. The notes to the Principles mention the electronic filing of company accounts and the use of the Internet to put out information.

Responsibilities of the board

'The corporate governance framework should ensure the strategic guidance of the company, the effective monitoring of management by the board and the board's accountability to the company and the shareholders.'

The Principles recognise that board structures and procedures differ widely among OECD countries, and are phrased in such a way as to be applicable to both two-tier boards and unitary boards. In broad terms, the responsibilities of the board are seen as:

- guiding corporate strategy;
- monitoring management performance;
- achieving an adequate return for shareholders;
- implementing systems designed to ensure compliance with laws and regulations whilst at the same time preventing conflicts of interest and balancing the competing demands on the company, and having regard for (and dealing fairly with) stakeholder interests and observing environmental and social standards.

To do their job properly, the board of directors must have 'some degree of independence from management'.

The Principles relating to the responsibilities of the board are similar to those in the Combined Code.

Board members should be fully informed for decisions they take, and should act in good faith and with due diligence and care, and in the best interests of the shareholders.

Where board decisions affect shareholder groups differently, the board should treat all shareholders fairly.

The board should also fulfil certain key functions. Although these can vary from country to country, and according to the constitution of the company, there are some functions that the board should always fulfil. These are listed in the Principles as follows:

- Reviewing and guiding corporate strategy, major plans of action, risk policy, annual budgets and business plans, setting performance objectives, monitoring implementation and corporate performance and overseeing major capital expenditures, acquisitions and disposals.

- Selecting, monitoring and (where necessary) replacing key executives, and ensuring succession planning for top management.
- Reviewing the remuneration of key executives and board members. Ensuring a formal and transparent process for nominating new members to the board.
- Monitoring and managing potential conflicts of interest between management, board members and shareholders. Preventing the misuse of corporate assets and abuse in related party transactions.
- Ensuring the integrity of the company's accounting and financial reporting systems, including the independent audit. Ensuring that appropriate systems of control are in place, in particular for monitoring risk, financial control and compliance with the law.
- Monitoring the effectiveness of corporate governance practices under which it operates, and making changes as needed.
- Overseeing the process of disclosure and communication.

The board should be able to exercise objective judgement on corporate affairs, independent in particular from management. Boards should therefore consider assigning a sufficient number of capable non-executive directors to tasks where there is potential for a conflict of interests, for example, responsibilities for financial reporting, remuneration of executives and board members and nominations to the board.

Board members should devote 'sufficient time' to their activities. In order to fulfil their responsibilities properly, board members should have access to accurate, relevant and timely information.

1.3 The OECD Principles and state-owned enterprises

The OECD Principles state that they are intended mainly for companies whose shares are traded, but that they could also be applied to 'non-traded companies' (private companies and state-owned enterprises).

A particular concern about state-owned enterprises, however, is political interference in the way these organisations are governed. For example, there might be concerns about the way in which boards of state-owned enterprises are appointed and given responsibilities, and how transparency can be ensured. The OECD has therefore issued a draft of non-binding guidelines for the corporate governance of state-owned assets, with a view to issuing these as complementary guidelines to the OECD Principles of corporate governance during 2005.

The OECD is also preparing guidelines on corporate governance for state-owned enterprises. A major concern is increasing political interference in the way these organisations are managed.

2 Corporate governance and the European Union

In May 2003, the EU Commission presented a Communication entitled 'Action Plan on Modernising Company Law and Enhancing Corporate Governance in the European Union'. The aim of this report was to put forward recommendations designed to lead to greater harmonisation of the corporate governance framework for EU listed companies in all countries of the EU. Its approach is similar to the Sarbanes–Oxley Act, in the sense that the report recommended certain changes to company law to enforce some aspects of corporate governance.

The report stated that the biggest problem was not so much differences in corporate governance codes in different EU countries as differences in company law. Even so the Commission argued that on some key issues the EU should introduce certain key requirements. The recommendations in the report for the short term included:

- An EU Directive requiring listed companies to publish an annual statement on corporate governance, including a 'comply-or-explain' regulation whereby the company had to comply with a specific national corporate governance code or explain its non-compliance. The Directive should also include disclosure requirements relating to the composition of the board, the identity of the major shareholders and certain shareholders' rights.
- Another Directive on collective board responsibilities for the disclosure of certain key financial and non-financial information.
- Setting up a European Corporate Governance Forum with the task of persuading member states to work towards the harmonisation of their corporate governance codes.
- Issuing a recommendation on the role of NEDs and supervisory board directors and board committees, which companies should adopt or explain their non-compliance.
- Issuing a recommendation on a regime for the approval of the remuneration programmes for executive directors.
- A Directive aimed at overcoming obstacles to cross-border shareholding and cross-border voting rights.

For the medium term, the report recommended a new Directive for investment institutions on the disclosure of their investment and voting policies, and a Directive allowing companies to choose between unitary and two-tier boards.

New EU Directives or amendments to existing Directives will have to be incorporated into the national laws of all member states of the EU. Any changes that are introduced could therefore be significant. Already, the EU Modernisation Directive has introduced a requirement for an annual review by companies of their development, performance and position (with an enhanced review by quoted companies, providing more disclosures). This is now a requirement of the Companies Act.

The Action Plan proposed that listed companies in the EU should prepare an annual corporate governance statement, based on an EU Code of Corporate Governance, on a 'comply or explain' basis. However, it seems more likely that countries will be able to apply their own national codes of governance, rather than a standard EU-wide code.

2.1 EU draft Directive on shareholders' rights

In 2007, the EU Commission published a draft Directive on shareholders' rights. The aim of the draft Directive is to set minimum standards for EU companies whose shares are traded on a regulated market. It seeks to make it easier in some EU countries for shareholders to obtain information about meetings, to participate at general meetings and to exercise their rights as shareholders (especially if they cannot attend meetings).

For example, there is a proposal that shareholders should be permitted to vote by post, that member states should remove constraints on electronic voting by shareholders and that companies should be required to publish on their website the results of votes on resolutions at general meetings.

There is also a proposal that shareholders should be allowed to appoint anyone as a proxy, and that proxies should have the same rights as shareholders to speak at general meetings and ask questions (unless the shareholder instructs otherwise).

Most of the proposals in the draft Directive are unlikely to affect UK quoted companies following the introduction of the Companies Act 2006. However, there are some aspects of the draft Directive that might affect UK companies.

- It includes a proposal giving shareholders the right to add items to the agenda for a general meeting and to draft resolutions. However, there must be a sufficient notice period to allow other shareholders to be informed.
- It proposes that all votes cast on a resolution must be taken into account. It is not yet clear whether this means that all resolutions will have to be decided by a poll, or whether decisions by a show of hands will be permitted.

3 Corporate governance and the Commonwealth countries

Concern for the need to establish good corporate governance practice has led to an initiative from the Commonwealth countries, which began with the first King Report in 1994. Many commonwealth countries have emerging economies and some such as South Africa have developing stock markets. Good corporate governance is seen as essential to the further development of national economies and the growth of the capital markets in those countries.

For many Commonwealth countries, matters considered of some importance for corporate governance are:

- The significance of state-owned industries, which include political appointees to the board of directors or governors. In view of the importance of state-owned enterprises, it can be argued that these should give a lead to smaller private companies in establishing best corporate governance practices.
- The role of foreign multinationals in the economy of the country.

3.1 Commonwealth Association for Corporate Governance

The work of the first King Committee led to the setting up in 1998 of the Commonwealth Association for Corporate Governance (CACG), with the purpose of promoting good standards in business practice and corporate governance throughout the Commonwealth. It produced a set of corporate governance guidelines in 1999.

The CACG takes an integrated approach to corporate governance, emphasising ethical values and the need to have regard to all the stakeholders in the company. The introduction to the Guidelines states that corporate governance:

'Involves a set of relationships between the management of a corporation, its board, its shareholders and other relevant stakeholders. Accordingly, the board must agree on the corporation's purpose (what it is for), its values (what it stands for) and the strategy to achieve its purpose. It must account to shareholders and be responsible for relations with its stakeholders.'

This point is further emphasised. The Guidelines suggest that the licence a company has to operate is not just regulatory. It:

'Embraces the corporation's interaction with its shareholders and other stake-holders such as the communities in which it operates, bankers and other suppliers of finance and credit, customers, the media, public opinion makers and pressure groups. While the board is accountable to the owners of the corporation (share-holders) for achieving the corporate objectives, its conduct with regard to factors such as business ethics and the environment, for example, may have an impact on legitimate societal interests (stakeholders) and thereby influence the reputation and long-term interests of the business enterprise.'

3.2   CACG's fifteen principles

The CACG Guidelines put forward a list of 15 principles of corporate governance. These might seem fairly similar to the corporate governance guidelines of other organisations. It is useful to look at them, however, in the context of the nature of the Commonwealth. Although the Commonwealth includes some countries with an advanced economy, such as Britain, Australia and Canada, it is more instructive to look at them from the viewpoint of 'emerging market' countries whose economies are in a relatively early stage of development.

The 15 principles can be summarised as follows:

1   The board of directors should exercise leadership and judgement, with enterprise and integrity, so as to achieve continuing prosperity for the corporation. It should also act in the best interests of the business enterprise in a manner based on trans-parency, accountability to shareholders and responsibility to stakeholders. (The specific emphasis on integrity, an ethical issue, is worth noting.)

2   There should be a process of appointing individuals to positions on the board that provides a mix of proficient directors, each able to add value and bring inde-pendent judgement to bear. New directors should be taken through a process of familiarisation with the company, its operations and its senior management. They should be given training if they do not have any previous experience as a director. Appointments to the board should avoid cronyism.

3   The board should decide the purpose and values of the corporation, and its strat-egy for achieving its purpose and implementing its values. The board should also protect the assets and reputation of the corporation. (Again, there is a notable emphasis on ethical issues.)

4   In formulating its strategy, the board should support enterprise and innovation. In motivating management to achieve performance targets, the board should try to ensure that both long-term and short-term performance targets are fair and achievable.

5   The board should monitor and evaluate the implementation by management of strategies, policies, business plans and performance criteria. The board should also retain decision-making responsibility over material matters affecting the business.

6   The board should ensure that the corporation complies with all relevant laws and codes of practice. (Again, there is a concern about illegal or improper conduct by companies.)

7   The corporation should communicate effectively with shareholders and stakeholders. Shareholders need timely accurate information to make informed investment decisions. Unclear or inadequate information undermines investor confidence. Directors should not disclose confidential price-sensitive information unless authorised by the board to do so, and unless the information is made public. Directors should also avoid recklessly giving out false information.

8   The board of directors should serve the legitimate interests of the corporation's shareholders and account to them fully. The directors of a public company should work on the assumption that their shareholders will constantly change, as investors buy and sell shares in the stock market. They should therefore consider the interests of future shareholders as well as current shareholders.

9   The board of directors should identify the internal and external stakeholders and agree a policy on how the corporation should relate to them. Society now demands transparency from corporations, and with the modern inclusive approach to corporate governance, the board has a responsibility to develop relationships with its relevant stakeholders.

10 No single person or group should have unfettered power over the board of directors. There should be a suitable balance of power on the board, with the roles of chairman and CEO held by different individuals. There should also be a suitable balance between executive and non-executive directors.

11 The board should review regularly the processes and procedures used by the corporation to ensure the effectiveness of internal controls. Effective internal controls are needed to maintain at the highest level the decision-making capability of the corporation's leaders and the accuracy of its reported financial results. In its comments on this principle, CACG states that the board should establish and maintain relevant board committees, such as a remuneration committee, audit committee and possibly an environmental committee.

12 The board should regularly assess the performance and effectiveness of the corporation as a whole, and the performance of individual directors, including the CEO.

13 The board should appoint the CEO and at least participate in the appointment of other senior executive managers. It should also ensure a succession plan for senior managers.

14 The board should ensure that all the technology and systems used by the corporation are adequate to run the business properly and remain competitive.

15 The board should identify the key risk areas and key performance indicators of the business, and monitor these.

Each year, the board should also check and confirm that the corporation will remain a going concern for the next fiscal year.

4 The King Reports (South Africa)

The development of a code of best practice in corporate governance is already well established, and dates back to a report of the King Committee in November 1994. The first King Report has now been superseded by the second King Report ('King II') which was published by the Southern African Institute of Directors and came into force in March 2002.

The Report contains a Code of Corporate Practice and Conduct in South Africa, which applies to 'affected companies'. These are companies whose shares are listed on the Johannesburg Stock Exchange, banks and many government departments and agencies. However, as in the UK, the Code does not have the force of law.

The Code promotes the seven characteristics of good corporate governance: discipline, transparency, independence, accountability, responsibility, fairness and social responsibility. Its contents are in many ways similar to those of the UK Combined Code, but they are more detailed and include matters not referred to in the Combined Code. For example, the King Report includes requirements on sustainability and ethical standards, whose significance should be considered in the context of the developing economy in South Africa and the culture of business ethics in Africa.

The features of the Code are summarised briefly below.

The board and directors

The King Report states its belief that a unitary board structure is appropriate for companies in South Africa, with a mix of executive and non-executive directors on the board.

Board responsibilities

The board should be responsible for the exercise of power and authority, and is accountable for the performance and affairs of the company. The Code sets out a detailed list of the responsibilities of the board, and in this respect it is more specific than many other national and international codes and guidelines on corporate governance. The board's responsibilities should include the following matters:

- The board should provide strategic direction and retain full and effective control, at the same time complying with laws and regulations.
- The board should delegate certain powers to management but retain powers over 'material' issues to itself. A charter should be prepared, itemising the responsibilities of the board, and this should be published in the annual report of the company. The minimum responsibilities of the board should include matters such as strategic planning, monitoring operational performance and the performance of management, risk management and the selection and induction of new directors.
- The board should have access to company information and should agree a procedure for enabling directors to obtain independent professional advice.
- The board is responsible for risk management, and should identify and monitor key risk and key performance areas, including non-financial aspects.
- The board should encourage shareholders to attend general meetings, and as many directors as possible should attend, including the chairmen of the audit and remuneration committees.

- The board should 'determine a balance between governance constraints and entrepreneurial performance'. The King Report gives recognition to the problem that 'best practice regulations' in corporate governance can act as a restraint on the company's business activities, and emphasises that some risks have to be taken in business for a company to be successful.

Balance of power

There should be a suitable balance of executive and non-executive directors on the board, but with NEDs making up a majority. 'Sufficient' NEDs should be independent. There should be a nomination committee whose responsibility is to select new directors in a 'transparent manner'. This committee should be chaired by the chairman of the board of directors and consist entirely of NEDs, the majority of whom should be independent. Rotation of directors is considered important, to 'ensure continuity'.

The Report defines an independent director as a non-executive who:

- does not represent a major shareholder;
- has not been employed by the company in the past three years and is not an immediate family member of such a person;
- is not a professional adviser;
- is not a significant supplier to the company, does not have a significant contractual relationship with it, or does not have any business or other relationship with the company that could affect his or her independence.

The positions of chairman and CEO should normally be held by different individuals. When this is not the case there should be a deputy chairman who is an independent NED and also a strong independent element on the board. The performance of the chairman should be evaluated 'annually or on any other basis agreed by the board' and the performance of the CEO should be evaluated at least once a year, by either the chairman or a committee of the board. This performance appraisal should be taken into account when deciding the CEO's remuneration.

No single bloc of individuals should dominate the board, and a division of power is necessary to prevent a risk of this happening. NEDs should have the skill and experience to contribute to issues relating to strategy, performance, standards of conduct and resources.

- Executive directors should be encouraged to hold NED positions in other companies, to develop their own skills and experience.
- NEDs should 'consider' the number of non-executorship positions they hold in companies, to ensure that they are able to perform their role effectively in each.

There should be an orientation programme for new directors, and all directors should be briefed from time to time on new laws and regulations. Normally, the company secretary will be responsible for this induction and training of directors.

Board meetings and committees

The board should meet at least once every three months, and information about the number of meetings held and the attendance of each director should be included in the annual report.

Non-executive directors should have access to management without any executive directors being present.

Committees of the board should have written terms of reference, and there should be transparency and full disclosure of committee matters. All companies should have an audit committee and a remuneration committee, and NEDs should play an important part in all committees of the board. The performance of each board committee should be reviewed regularly.

A board committee, possibly the nomination committee, should carry out a review at least once a year of the effectiveness of the board itself, and also assess its mix of skills, experience and 'demographics'.

The company should have rules prohibiting directors from trading in its shares between the end of its financial year and the publication of its annual results. These rules should be enforced by the company secretary.

Remuneration of directors

The remuneration of directors should be sufficient to attract and retain 'quality' directors. There should be a remuneration committee of the board, consisting mainly (and preferably entirely) of independent NEDs and chaired by an independent NED. This committee should be responsible for making recommendations to the board on executive remuneration. The CEO may attend meetings of this committee by invitation, but should not be allowed to sit in on discussions of his or her own remuneration.

Details of the remuneration of directors should be included in the annual report. Performance-related elements should make up a large element of each executive director's remuneration package.

The grant of share options to NEDs is permissible, but should be subject to approval by the shareholders, normally at the AGM. The report also suggests that it is preferable to issue shares rather than share options to directors as part of their remuneration, 'because of the loss of independence by following the option route'. The re-pricing of the exercise price of out-of-the-money share options of directors to a lower level, or the issue of share options with an exercise price at a discount to the current market price of the company's shares, should also be subject to prior shareholder approval.

Risk management

The King Report recommendations on the board's responsibility for risk management include required practices for establishing internal audit as an 'independent objective assurance activity'. The board should authorise an internal audit charter and an internal audit work plan should be approved by the audit committee. If the board decides not to implement internal audit, it should explain its decision in the annual report and describe what measures are implemented instead to test the effectiveness of processes and systems.

Sustainability reporting

A company should report on its social, ethical, health and safety and environmental policies and procedures. Matters requiring specific attention include:

- issues relating to safety and occupational health objectives, including those for HIV/AIDS;
- environmental reporting and following the business options with the least-damaging effect on the environment;
- social investment policies, including black economic empowerment;
- human capital development, including training and also opportunities for women and the 'previously disadvantaged'.

A company needs to establish a code of ethics for all stakeholders, and give its commitment to upholding the code. A company should also re-evaluate its continuing relationships with any individuals and organisations with lower ethical standards.

Accounting and external auditing

The external auditors should be independent of the company and its management. The audit committee should establish a principle for the use of external auditors for non-audit services, and there should be a disclosure to shareholders of the non-audit services that the auditors have provided.

There should be an audit committee, the majority of whose members should be independent NEDs. The chairman of the board of directors should not be appointed as chairman of the audit committee.

Relations with shareholders and communication

Constructive dialogue with individual directors is encouraged. The notice of a general meeting should explain the effects of any items of special business to be discussed at the meeting, and a reasonable amount of time should be allowed at the meeting for a discussion of each item. The use of a poll for voting at general meetings should be considered for 'contentious issues'.

The board has a responsibility to report to shareholders on significant and relevant matters. Reports should be transparent, objective and comprehensive, and should reflect accountability.

The annual report of the directors should contain a statement:

- that accounting records are kept and that accounting standards are complied with (with any departures from the standards explained);
- on risk management and internal controls;
- that the company will be a going concern in the year ahead;
- on compliance with the Code of Corporate Practice and Conduct.

4.1   King Report and the company secretary

The Code of Corporate Practices and Conduct includes particular mention of the role of the company secretary, who has a 'pivotal role' in corporate governance, through the board. The chairman should be entitled to the strong and positive support of the company secretary in making sure that the board functions effectively. In addition, 'all directors on the board should have access to the advice and services of the company secretary'. Some particular functions of the company secretary were suggested:

- providing directors individually and collectively with detailed guidance on carrying out their responsibilities;
- having a role in the induction of new and relatively inexperienced directors;
- assisting the chairman or CEO in deciding matters of an administrative nature, such as how the board's annual plan should be determined;
- giving advice to the board on matters of good governance and business ethics.

The King Committee saw the company secretary as an individual with knowledge of corporate governance matters, whose advice and assistance should be valued by the directors. The company secretary should also be prepared to remind the board about best practice in corporate governance and about business ethics, should members of the board overlook them.

5 Corporate governance in the United States

The US has taken a different approach to corporate governance from Europe. In Europe, the emphasis is mainly on voluntary compliance with a Code and the application of principles. In the US, the emphasis has been on statutory regulation (the Sarbanes–Oxley Act 2002) and the enforcement of rules. The Securities and Exchange Commission (SEC) plays a key role in the enforcement of corporate governance regulations by companies with a listing in the US and in the application of the Sarbanes–Oxley Act requirements.

5.1 The Sarbanes–Oxley Act 2002

The Sarbanes–Oxley Act came into force in the US at the end of August 2002. Whereas corporate governance issues in other countries have been introduced largely as voluntary measures for listed companies, the Act introduces 'corporate accountability legislation'.

The Act itself contains various specific requirements, and it also directs the Securities and Exchange Commission to issue rules implementing its measures relating to corporate governance. The SEC in turn is required to ensure that the US stock exchanges apply suitable rules for corporations whose shares are traded on the exchange.

The requirements of the Sarbanes–Oxley Act, and some of the subsequent SEC regulations, are set out briefly in the following paragraphs.

CEO/CFO certifications (section 302)

The Act requires that all companies with a listing in the US must provide in annual or quarterly reports of the company a signed certificate to the SEC vouching for the accuracy of the company's financial statements. The certificates, signed by the principal executive officer and principal financial officer, must accompany each periodic report filed with the SEC containing financial information. The principal executive officer and principal financial officer are therefore required to take direct responsibility for the accuracy of their company's financial statements.

This requirement applies to foreign companies with a US listing, as well as to US companies. The authorities have rights of investigation, which means that US regulators have given themselves the powers to investigate the accounts of foreign companies, if they are required to file accounts in the US.

The SEC also requires the principal executive officer and principal financial officer to certify in each quarterly and annual report:

- the accuracy of the information in the report;
- the fairness of the financial information.

The report should contain information about the effectiveness of the company's 'disclosure controls and procedures' and its internal controls over financial reporting. This should be covered by the certifications.

The assessment of internal controls (section 404)

Section 404(a) requirements relating to the annual assessment of internal controls by registered companies are described in chapter 10.

Loans to executives

It is unlawful for any public company to loan money to directors and executive officers, or to modify or renew existing loans (s. 402).

Forfeiture of bonuses

The CEO and CFO must give up bonuses received in the past twelve months, including equity or incentive compensation awards, if their company's accounts are restated due to material non-compliance with accounting rules and standards (s. 304).

Dealing in shares

Dealings in a company's shares by 'insiders', including directors, must be reported within two business days (s. 403). The actual rule is that a Form 4 report must be filed by the end of the second business day after the transaction.

All notifications of beneficial ownership must be filed electronically, and either posted on or linked to the company's website.

Insiders are not allowed to trade in the shares of the company during 'blackout periods' imposed on any retirement or pension fund (s. 306). A regulation has been issued requiring companies to notify its directors and executive officers and the SEC, using Form 8-K, of the imposition of a blackout period. If any director or executive officer breaches this rule, any trading profits they make are recoverable by the company.

Increased disclosures

The Act includes a number of provisions for greater or more rapid disclosure of financial information:

- The company must disclose in its financial reports filed with the SEC the material facts and circumstances of its off-balance sheet transactions, and their material effects (s. 401(a)). A table of future long-term debt and lease obligations is also required.

- The Act also imposes rules relating to the accuracy and completeness of pro-forma financial information appearing in financial reports. This information must not be misleading and should be reconciled to GAAP figures.
- Material changes should be disclosed on a 'rapid and current basis' (s. 409). The Act delegates the creation of detailed regulations to the SEC, but with no formal timetable for their introduction. Material changes would relate to matters such as the creation of new off-balance sheet transactions, credit rating changes, a decision to make a one-off writing down or restructuring charge, the termination of a relationship with a major customer, and so on. The proposal (at the time of writing) was that changes should be disclosed to the SEC within two business days.

Audit committee

National securities exchanges are prohibited from listing the securities of any company not complying with the following audit committee requirements (s. 301):

- Every member of the audit committee should be independent of the company.
- The audit committee must have responsibility for the appointment and compensation of the external auditors and for oversight of their work.
- The committee must establish procedures for whistleblowers who raise concerns about questionable accounting or auditing matters.

The auditors must report to the audit committee on critical accounting policies, material alternative accounting treatments and other written communications with management (s. 203).

SEC rules have been introduced to safeguard the independence of audit committee members by prohibiting any committee member from:

- accepting any consulting fee, advisory fee or any other fee, other than in their capacity as a committee member or director of the company;
- being an 'affiliated person' of the company or any of its subsidiaries.

The Act requires companies to disclose whether or not (and if not, why not) at least one member of the audit committee is an 'audit committee financial expert' and also independent (s. 407). The SEC has introduced rules defining what requirements must be met to be a suitable 'financial expert' for audit committee purposes.

Auditors and the audit

Restrictions have been placed on the types of non-audit work that can be carried out by the audit firm for a client company (s. 201 and 202). Prohibited services include:

- book-keeping services and other services related to the accounting records or financial statements of the company;
- the design and implementation of financial information systems;
- actuarial services;
- valuation services;
- internal auditing (outsourced);

- legal services;
- management functions;
- broker/dealer or investment advice services.

Tax services are specifically permitted by the Act, unless they come within a prohibited category of non-audit services.

All audit and non-audit services carried out by the auditors should be approved in advance by the audit committee.

There is a compulsory five-year rotation of the lead audit partner and concurring partner working on the audit of a corporate client (s. 203). Other audit partners who perform more than ten hours of audit or review services should be changed at least every seven years.

There is a one-year ban on an audit firm providing audit services to a company if a person in a 'financial reporting oversight role' within the company was either the lead partner, concurring partner or any other member of the audit engagement team providing more than ten hours of audit, review or attest services (s. 206).

The auditors must retain records for at least seven years (s. 802).

It is illegal for the directors and officers of a company to coerce, manipulate, mislead or fraudulently influence an auditor, if he or she knew or should have known that such action, if successful, could make the financial statements materially misleading (s. 303).

Protection for whistleblowers

The Act prohibits the termination of employment of any individual reporting a securities fraud of the company (s. 806) and prohibits other forms of retaliation against whistleblowers who are not employees (s. 1007).

The Public Company Oversight Board

An independent five-man board, known as the Public Company Oversight Board, was established (under the supervision of the Securities and Exchange Commission) to oversee the auditing of public companies, with responsibility for enforcing professional standards, ethics and competence for the accounting profession. It is required to enforce auditing, quality control and independence standards and rules in company accounting. It has powers to investigate and punish audit firms that certify inaccurate financial statements. The majority of this board are not professional accountants.

Standard of professional conduct of attorneys

The Act requires the SEC to establish rules for the minimum professional standard of attorneys who represent a company on matters relating to securities law. Attorneys must report evidence of material violations of securities, laws or serious breaches of fiduciary duty by a company or its officers. The attorney should report initially to the chief legal counsel or the CEO of the company. If this individual does not respond appropriately, the attorney should report the evidence to the audit committee or other committee made up entirely of independent directors (s. 307).

Fraud and document shredding

Severe criminal penalties have been introduced for executives involved in financial fraud and document shredding, which can lead to a prison term of up to 25 years.

5.2   Would measures in the Sarbanes–Oxley Act have prevented the corporate scandals?

Legislative measures for corporate governance are considered by some commentators to be unnecessary, on the grounds that rules are often broken, and the forcible imposition of rules is unlikely to be effective unless directors and managers work to a voluntary code of business ethics.

It could be argued, for example, that the requirement for the CEO and CFO of all listed companies to certify the financial statements of their company puts a greater burden on top management to review the financial statements more thoroughly. On the other hand, it can be argued that the rule simply duplicates existing responsibilities and will not stop fraudsters.

It could also be argued that the measures against audit firms will make it difficult for an audit firm to build an inappropriate relationship with audit clients. A counter-argument is that, in the case of large companies, the size of audit fee itself could be big enough to influence the relationship and threaten the independence of the auditor.

The requirement for disclosure of material off-balance sheet transactions should in theory prevent undisclosed corporate loans to directors and officers, which had been a cause of concern in cases such as Mr Bernie Ebbers at WorldCom and the Rigas family at Adelphia Communications. The counter-argument here is that rules can be circumvented and some other way of channelling money to individuals could well be found that is not in breach of the law but would not require disclosure.

It might also be supposed that there is a strong deterrent effect in the requirement for the CEO and CFO to give up bonuses received in the past twelve months if the company's accounts are materially re-stated. Even here, the case is by no means proved, since the rules in place before the Sarbanes–Oxley Act allowed the SEC to demand repayment. It remains to be seen whether this element of the Act will have any practical value

Even so, the Sarbanes–Oxley Act has raised the possibility that corporate governance measures might, to an increasing extent, be enforced through legislative measures rather than voluntary practice.

6   Corporate governance in other countries

The measures for promoting good corporate governance vary between countries. Some countries, such as the UK and USA, are more advanced than others. However, the OECD Principles and ICGN Principles establish guidelines for countries wishing to establish efficient capital markets.

In addition, institutional investors, especially US investors, expect standards of governance similar to those they are familiar with in the UK.

Singapore has introduced a code of corporate governance for its stock market companies based on the UK Combined Code. In contrast, concepts of best practice in corporate governance have not been widely accepted in Japan, a major economic and financial centre.

6.1   *Principles for responsible investment: UN initiative*

Social and environmental issues might also be gaining a wider global recognition. In 2006, the UN Global Compact issued six principles for responsible investment (PRI). The PRI are linked to the Finance Initiative of the UN's Environmental Programme. At the time of its launch in New York, 32 major institutional investors from around the world had signed up to the Principles. This may well give a boost to the inclusion of environmental and social issues in institutional investment policies and relationships with investee companies.

The Principles are 'voluntary and aspirational'. The brochure introducing them comments that: 'There is a growing view among investment professions that environmental, social and corporate governance (ESG) issues can affect the performance of investment portfolios. Investors fulfilling their fiduciary (or equivalent) duty therefore need to give appropriate consideration to these issues, but to date have lacked a framework for doing so. The Principles for Responsible Investment provide this framework.' Signing up to the Principles represents a 'very real commitment' by an institutional investment organisation.

There are six Principles, and each is supported by a list of possible actions that might be taken to put the Principle into effect. These are:

1   We will incorporate ESG issues into investment analysis and decision-making processes.
2   We will be active owners and incorporate ESG issues into our ownership policies and practices.
3   We will seek appropriate disclosure on ESG issues by the entities in which we invest.
4   We will promote acceptance and implementation of the Principles within the investment industry.
5   We will work together to enhance our effectiveness in implementing the Principles.
6   We will each report on our activities and progress towards implementing the Principles.

Chapter summary

- Principles of good corporate governance have been issued by some international bodies, notably the OECD and the Commonwealth Association. These are intended to provide guidelines for individual countries in formulating their own national codes and guidelines.

- The European Commission issued an Action Plan on Modernising Company Law and Enhancing Corporate Governance in the European Union in May 2003.

- The Commonwealth Association guidelines are directed primarily at countries with developing economies.

- As in the UK, South Africa has non-statutory corporate governance guidelines for JSE-listed companies. These are much more detailed than the UK Combined Code, and give greater prominence to ethical and corporate social responsibility issues, including sustainability.

- In the USA, a stricter statutory regime has been introduced by the Sarbanes–Oxley Act 2002, in response to the succession of corporate governance scandals, beginning with Enron in 2001.

- Taking a broad view, the issues addressed in international and national principles and in national codes of best practice are broadly similar, although with some differences of emphasis. These are ethics and corporate social responsibility; the role and responsibilities of the board of directors; the use of the board's powers to act in the best interests of shareholders and possibly other stakeholders; the balance of power on the board and the role of NEDs and board committees; relations and communications between the board and the shareholders; financial reporting, transparency and the independence of the external auditors; directors' remuneration; and risk management and internal audit.

Appendix I

The Combined Code on Corporate Governance

Section I Companies

A Directors

A.I The Board

Main Principle

Every company should be headed by an effective board, which is collectively responsible for the success of the company.

Supporting Principles

The board's role is to provide entrepreneurial leadership of the company within a framework of prudent and effective controls which enables risk to be assessed and managed. The board should set the company's strategic aims, ensure that the necessary financial and human resources are in place for the company to meet its objectives and review management performance. The board should set the company's values and standards and ensure that its obligations to its shareholders and others are understood and met.

All directors must take decisions objectively in the interests of the company.

As part of their role as members of a unitary board, non-executive directors should constructively challenge and help develop proposals on strategy. Non-executive directors should scrutinise the performance of management in meeting agreed goals and objectives and monitor the reporting of performance. They should satisfy themselves on the integrity of financial information and that financial controls and systems of risk management are robust and defensible. They are responsible for determining appropriate levels of remuneration of executive directors and have a prime role in appointing, and where necessary removing, executive directors, and in succession planning.

Code Provisions

A.1.1 The board should meet sufficiently regularly to discharge its duties effectively. There should be a formal schedule of matters specifically reserved for its decision. The annual report should include a statement of how the board operates, including a high level statement of which types of decisions are to be taken by the board and which are to be delegated to management.

A.1.2   The annual report should identify the chairman, the deputy chairman (where there is one), the chief executive, the senior independent director and the chairmen and members of the nomination, audit and remuneration committees. It should also set out the number of meetings of the board and those committees and individual attendance by directors.

A.1.3   The chairman should hold meetings with the non-executive directors without the executives present. Led by the senior independent director, the non-executive directors should meet without the chairman present at least annually to appraise the chairman's performance (as described in A.6.1) and on such other occasions as are deemed appropriate.

A.1.4   Where directors have concerns which cannot be resolved about the running of the company or a proposed action, they should ensure that their concerns are recorded in the board minutes. On resignation, a non-executive director should provide a written statement to the chairman, for circulation to the board, if they have any such concerns.

A.1.5   The company should arrange appropriate insurance cover in respect of legal action against its directors.

A.2   Chairman and chief executive

Main Principle

There should be a clear division of responsibilities at the head of the company between the running of the board and the executive responsibility for the running of the company's business. No one individual should have unfettered powers of decision.

Supporting Principle

The chairman is responsible for leadership of the board, ensuring its effectiveness on all aspects of its role and setting its agenda. The chairman is also responsible for ensuring that the directors receive accurate, timely and clear information. The chairman should ensure effective communication with shareholders. The chairman should also facilitate the effective contribution of non-executive directors in particular and ensure constructive relations between executive and non-executive directors.

Code Provisions

A.2.1   The roles of chairman and chief executive should not be exercised by the same individual. The division of responsibilities between the chairman and chief executive should be clearly established, set out in writing and agreed by the board.

A.2.2   The chairman should on appointment meet the independence criteria set out in A.3.1 below. A chief executive should not go on to be chairman of the same company. If exceptionally a board decides that a chief executive should become chairman, the board should consult major shareholders in advance and should set out its reasons to shareholders at the time of the appointment and in the next annual report.

A.3 Board balance and independence

Main Principle

The board should include a balance of executive and non-executive directors (and in particular independent non-executive directors) such that no individual or small group of individuals can dominate the board's decision taking.

Supporting Principles

The board should not be so large as to be unwieldy. The board should be of sufficient size that the balance of skills and experience is appropriate for the requirements of the business and that changes to the board's composition can be managed without undue disruption.

To ensure that power and information are not concentrated in one or two individuals, there should be a strong presence on the board of both executive and non-executive directors.

The value of ensuring that committee membership is refreshed and that undue reliance is not placed on particular individuals should be taken into account in deciding chairmanship and membership of committees.

No one other than the committee chairman and members is entitled to be present at a meeting of the nomination, audit or remuneration committee, but others may attend at the invitation of the committee.

Code provisions

A.3.1 The board should identify in the annual report each non-executive director it considers to be independent. The board should determine whether the director is independent in character and judgement and whether there are relationships or circumstances which are likely to affect, or could appear to affect, the director's judgement. The board should state its reasons if it determines that a director is independent notwithstanding the existence of relationships or circumstances which may appear relevant to its determination, including if the director:

- has been an employee of the company or group within the last five years;
- has, or has had within the last three years, a material business relationship with the company either directly, or as a partner, shareholder, director or senior employee of a body that has such a relationship with the company;
- has received or receives additional remuneration from the company apart from a director's fee, participates in the company's share option or a performance-related pay scheme, or is a member of the company's pension scheme;
- has close family ties with any of the company's advisers, directors or senior employees;
- holds cross-directorships or has significant links with other directors through involvement in other companies or bodies;
- represents a significant shareholder; or
- has served on the board for more than nine years from the date of their first election.

A.3.2 Except for smaller companies, at least half the board, excluding the chairman, should comprise non-executive directors determined by the board to be independent. A smaller company should have at least two independent non-executive directors.

A.3.3 The board should appoint one of the independent non-executive directors to be the senior independent director. The senior independent director should be available to shareholders if they have concerns which contact through the normal channels of chairman, chief executive or finance director has failed to resolve or for which such contact is inappropriate.

A.4 Appointments to the Board

Main Principle

There should be a formal, rigorous and transparent procedure for the appointment of new directors to the board.

Supporting Principles

Appointments to the board should be made on merit and against objective criteria. Care should be taken to ensure that appointees have enough time available to devote to the job. This is particularly important in the case of chairmanships.

The board should satisfy itself that plans are in place for orderly succession for appointments to the board and to senior management, so as to maintain an appropriate balance of skills and experience within the company and on the board.

Code Provisions

A.4.1 There should be a nomination committee which should lead the process for board appointments and make recommendations to the board. A majority of members of the nomination committee should be independent non-executive directors. The chairman or an independent non-executive director should chair the committee, but the chairman should not chair the nomination committee when it is dealing with the appointment of a successor to the chairmanship. The nomination committee should make available its terms of reference, explaining its role and the authority delegated to it by the board.

A.4.2 The nomination committee should evaluate the balance of skills, knowledge and experience on the board and, in the light of this evaluation, prepare a description of the role and capabilities required for a particular appointment.

A.4.3 For the appointment of a chairman, the nomination committee should prepare a job specification, including an assessment of the time commitment expected, recognising the need for availability in the event of crises. A chairman's other significant commitments should be disclosed to the board before appointment and included in the annual report. Changes to such commitments should be reported to the board as they arise, and included in the next annual report. No individual should be appointed to a second chairmanship of a FTSE 100 company.

A.4.4 The terms and conditions of appointment of non-executive directors should be made available for inspection. The letter of appointment should set out the expected time commitment. Non-executive directors should undertake that they will have sufficient time to meet what is expected of them. Their other significant commitments should be disclosed to the board before appointment, with a broad indication of the time involved and the board should be informed of subsequent changes.

A.4.5   The board should not agree to a full time executive director taking on more than one non-executive directorship in a FTSE 100 company nor the chairmanship of such a company.

A.4.6   A separate section of the annual report should describe the work of the nomination committee, including the process it has used in relation to board appointments. An explanation should be given if neither an external search consultancy nor open advertising has been used in the appointment of a chairman or a non-executive director.

A.5   Information and professional development

Main Principle

The board should be supplied in a timely manner with information in a form and of a quality appropriate to enable it to discharge its duties. All directors should receive induction on joining the board and should regularly update and refresh their skills and knowledge.

Supporting Principles

The chairman is responsible for ensuring that the directors receive accurate, timely and clear information. Management has an obligation to provide such information but directors should seek clarification or amplification where necessary.

The chairman should ensure that the directors continually update their skills and the knowledge and familiarity with the company required to fulfil their role both on the board and on board committees. The company should provide the necessary resources for developing and updating its directors' knowledge and capabilities.

Under the direction of the chairman, the company secretary's responsibilities include ensuring good information flows within the board and its committees and between senior management and non-executive directors, as well as facilitating induction and assisting with professional development as required.

The company secretary should be responsible for advising the board through the chairman on all governance matters.

Code Provisions

A.5.1   The chairman should ensure that new directors receive a full, formal and tailored induction on joining the board. As part of this, the company should offer to major shareholders the opportunity to meet a new non-executive director.

A.5.2   The board should ensure that directors, especially non-executive directors, have access to independent professional advice at the company's expense where they judge it necessary to discharge their responsibilities as directors. Committees should be provided with sufficient resources to undertake their duties.

A.5.3   All directors should have access to the advice and services of the company secretary, who is responsible to the board for ensuring that board procedures are complied with. Both the appointment and removal of the company secretary should be a matter for the board as a whole.

A.6 *Performance evaluation*

Main Principle

The board should undertake a formal and rigorous annual evaluation of its own performance and that of its committees and individual directors.

Supporting Principle

Individual evaluation should aim to show whether each director continues to contribute effectively and to demonstrate commitment to the role (including commitment of time for board and committee meetings and any other duties). The chairman should act on the results of the performance evaluation by recognising the strengths and addressing the weaknesses of the board and, where appropriate, proposing new members be appointed to the board or seeking the resignation of directors.

Code Provision

A.6.1   The board should state in the annual report how performance evaluation of the board, its committees and its individual directors has been conducted. The non-executive directors, led by the senior independent director, should be responsible for performance evaluation of the chairman, taking into account the views of executive directors.

A.7 *Re-election*

Main Principle

All directors should be submitted for re-election at regular intervals, subject to continued satisfactory performance. The board should ensure planned and progressive refreshing of the board.

Code Provisions

A.7.1   All directors should be subject to election by shareholders at the first annual general meeting after their appointment, and to re-election thereafter at intervals of no more than three years. The names of directors submitted for election or re-election should be accompanied by sufficient biographical details and any other relevant information to enable shareholders to take an informed decision on their election.

A.7.2   Non-executive directors should be appointed for specified terms subject to re-election and to Companies Acts provisions relating to the removal of a director. The board should set out to shareholders in the papers accompanying a resolution to elect a non-executive director why they believe an individual should be elected. The chairman should confirm to shareholders when proposing re-election that, following formal performance evaluation, the individual's performance continues to be effective and to demonstrate commitment to the role. Any term beyond six years (e.g. two three-year terms) for a non-executive director should be subject to particularly rigorous review, and should take into account the need for progressive refreshing of the board. Non-executive directors may serve longer than nine years (e.g. three three-year terms), subject to annual re-election. Serving more than nine years could be relevant to the determination of a non-executive director's independence (as set out in provision A.3.1).

B Remuneration

B.I The Level and Make-up of Remuneration

Main Principles

Levels of remuneration should be sufficient to attract, retain and motivate directors of the quality required to run the company successfully, but a company should avoid paying more than is necessary for this purpose. A significant proportion of executive directors' remuneration should be structured so as to link rewards to corporate and individual performance.

Supporting Principle

The remuneration committee should judge where to position their company relative to other companies. But they should use such comparisons with caution, in view of the risk of an upward ratchet of remuneration levels with no corresponding improvement in performance. They should also be sensitive to pay and employment conditions elsewhere in the group, especially when determining annual salary increases.

Code Provisions

Remuneration policy

B.1.1 The performance-related elements of remuneration should form a significant proportion of the total remuneration package of executive directors and should be designed to align their interests with those of shareholders and to give these directors keen incentives to perform at the highest levels. In designing schemes of performance-related remuneration, the remuneration committee should follow the provisions in Schedule A to this Code.

B.1.2 Executive share options should not be offered at a discount save as permitted by the relevant provisions of the Listing Rules.

B.1.3 Levels of remuneration for non-executive directors should reflect the time commitment and responsibilities of the role. Remuneration for non-executive directors should not include share options. If, exceptionally, options are granted, shareholder approval should be sought in advance and any shares acquired by exercise of the options should be held until at least one year after the non-executive director leaves the board. Holding of share options could be relevant to the determination of a non-executive director's independence (as set out in provision A.3.1).

B.1.4 Where a company releases an executive director to serve as a non-executive director elsewhere, the remuneration report should include a statement as to whether or not the director will retain such earnings and, if so, what the remuneration is.

Service Contracts and Compensation

B.1.5 The remuneration committee should carefully consider what compensation commitments (including pension contributions and all other elements) their directors' terms of appointment would entail in the event of early termination. The aim should be to avoid rewarding poor performance. They should take a robust line on reducing compensation to reflect departing directors' obligations to mitigate loss.

B.1.6   Notice or contract periods should be set at one year or less. If it is necessary to offer longer notice or contract periods to new directors recruited from outside, such periods should reduce to one year or less after the initial period.

B.2 Procedure

Main Principle

There should be a formal and transparent procedure for developing policy on executive remuneration and for fixing the remuneration packages of individual directors. No director should be involved in deciding his or her own remuneration.

Supporting Principles

The remuneration committee should consult the chairman and/or chief executive about their proposals relating to the remuneration of other executive directors. The remuneration committee should also be responsible for appointing any consultants in respect of executive director remuneration. Where executive directors or senior management are involved in advising or supporting the remuneration committee, care should be taken to recognise and avoid conflicts of interest.

The chairman of the board should ensure that the company maintains contact as required with its principal shareholders about remuneration in the same way as for other matters.

Code Provisions

B.2.1   The board should establish a remuneration committee of at least three, or in the case of smaller companies two, independent non-executive directors. In addition the company chairman may also be a member of, but not chair, the committee if he or she was considered independent on appointment as chairman. The remuneration committee should make available its terms of reference, explaining its role and the authority delegated to it by the board. Where remuneration consultants are appointed, a statement should be made available of whether they have any other connection with the company.

B.2.2   The remuneration committee should have delegated responsibility for setting remuneration for all executive directors and the chairman, including pension rights and any compensation payments. The committee should also recommend and monitor the level and structure of remuneration for senior management. The definition of 'senior management' for this purpose should be determined by the board but should normally include the first layer of management below board level.

B.2.3   The board itself or, where required by the Articles of Association, the shareholders should determine the remuneration of the non-executive directors within the limits set in the Articles of Association. Where permitted by the Articles, the board may however delegate this responsibility to a committee, which might include the chief executive.

B.2.4   Shareholders should be invited specifically to approve all new long-term incentive schemes (as defined in the Listing Rules) and significant changes to existing schemes, save in the circumstances permitted by the Listing Rules.

C Accountability and audit

C.1 *Financial Reporting*

Main Principle

The board should present a balanced and understandable assessment of the company's position and prospects.

Supporting Principle

The board's responsibility to present a balanced and understandable assessment extends to interim and other price-sensitive public reports and reports to regulators as well as to information required to be presented by statutory requirements.

Code Provisions

C.1.1 The directors should explain in the annual report their responsibility for preparing the accounts and there should be a statement by the auditors about their reporting responsibilities.

C.1.2 The directors should report that the business is a going concern, with supporting assumptions or qualifications as necessary.

C.2 *Internal Control*

Main Principle

The board should maintain a sound system of internal control to safeguard shareholders' investment and the company's assets.

Code Provision

C.2.1 The board should, at least annually, conduct a review of the effectiveness of the group's system of internal controls and should report to shareholders that they have done so. The review should cover all material controls, including financial, operational and compliance controls and risk management systems.

C.3 *Audit Committee and Auditors*

Main Principle

The board should establish formal and transparent arrangements for considering how they should apply the financial reporting and internal control principles and for maintaining an appropriate relationship with the company's auditors.

Code provisions

C.3.1 The board should establish an audit committee of at least three, or in the case of smaller companies two, members, who should all be independent non-executive directors. The board should satisfy itself that at least one member of the audit committee has recent and relevant financial experience.

C.3.2 The main role and responsibilities of the audit committee should be set out in written terms of reference and should include:

- to monitor the integrity of the financial statements of the company, and any formal announcements relating to the company's financial performance, reviewing significant financial reporting judgements contained in them;
- to review the company's internal financial controls and, unless expressly addressed by a separate board risk committee composed of independent directors, or by the board itself, to review the company's internal control and risk management systems;
- to monitor and review the effectiveness of the company's internal audit function;
- to make recommendations to the board, for it to put to the shareholders for their approval in general meeting, in relation to the appointment, reappointment and removal of the external auditor and to approve the remuneration and terms of engagement of the external auditor;
- to review and monitor the external auditor's independence and objectivity and the effectiveness of the audit process, taking into consideration relevant UK professional and regulatory requirements;
- to develop and implement policy on the engagement of the external auditor to supply non-audit services, taking into account relevant ethical guidance regarding the provision of non-audit services by the external audit firm; and to report to the board, identifying any matters in respect of which it considers that action or improvement is needed and making recommendations as to the steps to be taken.

C.3.3 The terms of reference of the audit committee, including its role and the authority delegated to it by the board, should be made available. A separate section of the annual report should describe the work of the committee in discharging those responsibilities.

C.3.4 The audit committee should review arrangements by which staff of the company may, in confidence, raise concerns about possible improprieties in matters of financial reporting or other matters. The audit committee's objective should be to ensure that arrangements are in place for the proportionate and independent investigation of such matters and for appropriate follow-up action.

C.3.5 The audit committee should monitor and review the effectiveness of the internal audit activities. Where there is no internal audit function, the audit committee should consider annually whether there is a need for an internal audit function and make a recommendation to the board, and the reasons for the absence of such a function should be explained in the relevant section of the annual report.

C.3.6 The audit committee should have primary responsibility for making a recommendation on the appointment, reappointment and removal of the external auditors. If the board does not accept the audit committee's recommendation, it should include in the annual report, and in any papers recommending appointment or reappointment, a statement from the audit committee explaining the recommendation and should set out reasons why the board has taken a different position.

C.3.7 The annual report should explain to shareholders how, if the auditor provides non-audit services, auditor objectivity and independence is safeguarded.

D Relations with shareholders

D.1 Dialogue with Institutional Shareholders

Main Principle

There should be a dialogue with shareholders based on the mutual understanding of objectives. The board as a whole has responsibility for ensuring that a satisfactory dialogue with shareholders takes place.

Supporting Principles

Whilst recognising that most shareholder contact is with the chief executive and finance director, the chairman (and the senior independent director and other directors as appropriate) should maintain sufficient contact with major shareholders to understand their issues and concerns.

The board should keep in touch with shareholder opinion in whatever ways are most practical and efficient.

Code Provisions

D.1.1 The chairman should ensure that the views of shareholders are communicated to the board as a whole. The chairman should discuss governance and strategy with major shareholders. Non-executive directors should be offered the opportunity to attend meetings with major shareholders and should expect to attend them if requested by major shareholders. The senior independent director should attend sufficient meetings with a range of major shareholders to listen to their views in order to help develop a balanced understanding of the issues and concerns of major shareholders.

D.1.2 The board should state in the annual report the steps they have taken to ensure that the members of the board, and in particular the non-executive directors, develop an understanding of the views of major shareholders about their company, for example through direct face-to-face contact, analysts' or brokers' briefings and surveys of shareholder opinion.

D.2 Constructive Use of the AGM

Main Principle

The board should use the AGM to communicate with investors and to encourage their participation.

Code Provisions

D.2.1 At any general meeting, the company should propose a separate resolution on each substantially separate issue, and should in particular propose a resolution at the AGM relating to the report and accounts. For each resolution, proxy appointment forms should provide shareholders with the option to direct their proxy to vote either for or against the resolution or to withhold their vote. The proxy form and any announcement of the results of a vote should make it clear that a 'vote withheld' is not a vote in law and will not be counted in the calculation of the proportion of the votes for and against the resolution.

D.2.2 The company should ensure that all valid proxy appointments received for general meetings are properly recorded and counted. For each resolution, after a vote has been taken, except where taken on a poll, the company should ensure that the following information is given at the meeting and made available as soon as reasonably practicable on a website which is maintained by or on behalf of the company:

- the number of shares in respect of which proxy appointments have been validly made;
- the number of votes for the resolution;
- the number of votes against the resolution; and
- the number of shares in respect of which the vote was directed to be withheld.

D.2.3 The chairman should arrange for the chairmen of the audit, remuneration and nomination committees to be available to answer questions at the AGM and for all directors to attend.

D.2.4 The company should arrange for the Notice of the AGM and related papers to be sent to shareholders at least 20 working days before the meeting.

Section 2 Institutional shareholders

E Institutional shareholders

E.1 *Dialogue with companies*

Main Principle

Institutional shareholders should enter into a dialogue with companies based on the mutual understanding of objectives.

Supporting Principles

Institutional shareholders should apply the principles set out in the Institutional Shareholders' Committee's 'The Responsibilities of Institutional Shareholders and Agents – Statement of Principles', which should be reflected in fund manager contracts.

E.2 *Evaluation of Governance Disclosures*

Main Principle

When evaluating companies' governance arrangements, particularly those relating to board structure and composition, institutional shareholders should give due weight to all relevant factors drawn to their attention.

Supporting Principle

Institutional shareholders should consider carefully explanations given for departure from this Code and make reasoned judgements in each case. They should give an explanation to the company, in writing where appropriate, and be prepared to enter a dialogue if they do not accept the company's position. They should avoid a box-ticking approach to assessing a company's corporate governance. They should bear in mind in particular the size and complexity of the company and the nature of the risks and challenges it faces.

E.3 Shareholder Voting

Main Principle

Institutional shareholders have a responsibility to make considered use of their votes.

Supporting Principles

Institutional shareholders should take steps to ensure their voting intentions are being translated into practice.

Institutional shareholders should, on request, make available to their clients information on the proportion of resolutions on which votes were cast and non-discretionary proxies lodged.

Major shareholders should attend AGMs where appropriate and practicable. Companies and registrars should facilitate this.

Schedule A: Provisions on the design of performance related remuneration

1   The remuneration committee should consider whether the directors should be eligible for annual bonuses. If so, performance conditions should be relevant, stretching and designed to enhance shareholder value. Upper limits should be set and disclosed. There may be a case for part payment in shares to be held for a significant period.

2   The remuneration committee should consider whether the directors should be eligible for benefits under long-term incentive schemes. Traditional share option schemes should be weighed against other kinds of long-term incentive scheme. In normal circumstances, shares granted or other forms of deferred remuneration should not vest, and options should not be exercisable, in less than three years. Directors should be encouraged to hold their shares for a further period after vesting or exercise, subject to the need to finance any costs of acquisition and associated tax liabilities.

3   Any new long-term incentive schemes which are proposed should be approved by shareholders and should preferably replace any existing schemes or at least form part of a well considered overall plan, incorporating existing schemes. The total rewards potentially available should not be excessive.

4   Payouts or grants under all incentive schemes, including new grants under existing share option schemes, should be subject to challenging performance criteria reflecting the company's objectives. Consideration should be given to criteria which reflect the company's performance relative to a group of comparator companies in some key variables such as total shareholder return.

5   Grants under executive share option and other long-term incentive schemes should normally be phased rather than awarded in one large block.

6   In general, only basic salary should be pensionable.

7   The remuneration committee should consider the pension consequences and associated costs to the company of basic salary increases and any other changes in pensionable remuneration, especially for directors close to retirement.

Schedule B: Guidance on liability of non-executive directors: care, skill and diligence

1   Although non-executive directors and executive directors have as board members the same legal duties and objectives, the time devoted to the company's affairs is likely to be significantly less for a non-executive director than for an executive director and the detailed knowledge and experience of a company's affairs that could reasonably be expected of a non-executive director will generally be less than for an executive director. These matters may be relevant in assessing the knowledge, skill and experience which may reasonably be expected of a non-executive director and therefore the care, skill and diligence that a non-executive director may be expected to exercise.

2   In this context, the following elements of the Code may also be particularly relevant.

    (i)   In order to enable directors to fulfil their duties, the Code states that:

        –   The letter of appointment of the director should set out the expected time commitment (Code provision A.4.4); and

        –   The board should be supplied in a timely manner with information in a form and of a quality appropriate to enable it to discharge its duties. The chairman is responsible for ensuring that the directors are provided by management with accurate, timely and clear information (Code principle A.5).

    (ii)   Non-executive directors should themselves:

        –   Undertake appropriate induction and regularly update and refresh their skills, knowledge and familiarity with the company (Code principle A.5 and provision A.5.1).

        –   Seek appropriate clarification or amplification of information and, where necessary, take and follow appropriate professional advice (Code principle A.5 and provision A.5.2).

        –   Where they have concerns about the running of the company or a proposed action, ensure that these are addressed by the board and, to the extent that they are not resolved, ensure that they are recorded in the board minutes (Code provision A.1.4).

        –   Give a statement to the board if they have such unresolved concerns on resignation (Code provision A.1.4).

3   It is up to each non-executive director to reach a view as to what is necessary in particular circumstances to comply with the duty of care, skill and diligence they

owe as a director to the company. In considering whether or not a person is in breach of that duty, a court would take into account all relevant circumstances. These may include having regard to the above where relevant to the issue of liability of a non-executive director.

Schedule C: Disclosure of corporate governance arrangements

Paragraph 9.8.6 of the Listing Rules states that in the case of a listed company incorporated in the United Kingdom, the following items must be included in its annual report and accounts:

- a statement of how the listed company has applied the principles set out in Section 1 of the Combined Code, in a manner that would enable shareholders to evaluate how the principles have been applied;
- a statement as to whether the listed company has
  - complied throughout the accounting period with all relevant provisions set out in Section 1 of the Combined Code; or
  - not complied throughout the accounting period with all relevant provisions set out in Section 1 of the Combined Code and if so, setting out:
    (i)   those provisions, if any, it has not complied with;
    (ii) in the case of provisions whose requirements are of a continuing nature, the period within which, if any, it did not comply with some or all of those provisions; and
    (iii) the company's reasons for non-compliance.

In addition the Code includes specific requirements for disclosure which are set out below:

The annual report should record:

- a statement of how the board operates, including a high level statement of which types of decisions are to be taken by the board and which are to be delegated to management (A.1.1);
- the names of the chairman, the deputy chairman (where there is one), the chief executive, the senior independent director and the chairmen and members of the nomination, audit and remuneration committees (A.1.2);
- the number of meetings of the board and those committees and individual attendance by directors (A.1.2);
- the names of the non-executive directors whom the board determines to be independent, with reasons where necessary (A.3.1);
- the other significant commitments of the chairman and any changes to them during the year (A.4.3);
- how performance evaluation of the board, its committees and its directors has been conducted (A.6.1);

- the steps the board has taken to ensure that members of the board, and in particular the non-executive directors, develop an understanding of the views of major shareholders about their company (D.1.2).

The report should also include:

- a separate section describing the work of the nomination committee, including the process it has used in relation to board appointments and an explanation if neither external search consultancy nor open advertising has been used in the appointment of a chairman or a non-executive director (A.4.6);
- a description of the work of the remuneration committee as required under the Directors' Remuneration Report Regulations 2002, and including, where an executive director serves as a non-executive director elsewhere, whether or not the director will retain such earnings and, if so, what the remuneration is (B.1.4);
- an explanation from the directors of their responsibility for preparing the accounts and a statement by the auditors about their reporting responsibilities (C.1.1);
- a statement from the directors that the business is a going concern, with supporting assumptions or qualifications as necessary (C.1.2);
- a report that the board has conducted a review of the effectiveness of the group's system of internal controls (C.2.1);
- a separate section describing the work of the audit committee in discharging its responsibilities (C.3.3);
- where there is no internal audit function, the reasons for the absence of such a function (C.3.5);
- where the board does not accept the audit committee's recommendation on the appointment, reappointment or removal of an external auditor, a statement from the audit committee explaining the recommendation and the reasons why the board has taken a different position (C.3.6); and
- an explanation of how, if the auditor provides non-audit services, auditor objectivity and independence is safeguarded (C.3.7).

The following information should be made available (which may be met by placing the information on a website that is maintained by or on behalf of the company):

- the terms of reference of the nomination, remuneration and audit committees, explaining their role and the authority delegated to them by the board (A.4.1, B.2.1 and C.3.3);
- the terms and conditions of appointment of non-executive directors (A.4.4); and
- where remuneration consultants are appointed, a statement of whether they have any other connection with the company (B.2.1).

The board should set out to shareholders in the papers accompanying a resolution to elect or re-elect directors:

- sufficient biographical details to enable shareholders to take an informed decision on their election or re-election (A.7.1);
- why they believe an individual should be elected to a non-executive role (A.7.2); and

- on re-election of a non-executive director, confirmation from the chairman that, following formal performance evaluation, the individual's performance continues to be effective and to demonstrate commitment to the role, including commitment of time for board and committee meetings and any other duties (A.7.2).

The board should set out to shareholders in the papers recommending appointment or re-appointment of an external auditor:

- if the board does not accept the audit committee's recommendation, a statement from the audit committee explaining the recommendation and from the board setting out reasons why they have taken a different position (C.3.6).

June 2006

Appendix 2

Good Boardroom Practice: A Guide for Directors and Company Secretaries

The Institute of Chartered Secretaries and Administrators (ICSA) believes that reliance on unwritten boardroom procedures and practices is no longer acceptable in the modern business environment. Whilst it is acknowledged that company law should not attempt to prescribe any particular style of boardroom management, ICSA believes that certain basic principles of good boardroom practice can be considered to be universally applicable.

Accordingly, ICSA has formulated this Code for directors and company secretaries as a guide to the matters which it believes should be addressed and, wherever applicable, accepted formally by boards of directors in recognition of a commitment to adhere to an overall concept of best practice.

ICSA also recommends that boardroom procedures should be periodically reviewed to ensure both the satisfactory operation of the Code and the identification of matters which individual companies could advantageously bring within its scope.

The Code

1　The board should establish written procedures for the conduct of its business which should include the matters covered in this Code. A copy of these written procedures should be given to each director. Compliance should be monitored, preferably by an audit committee of the board, and breaches of the procedures should be reported to the board.

2　The board should ensure that each director is given on appointment sufficient information to enable him/her to perform his/her duties. In particular, guidance for non-executive directors should cover the procedures:
   * for obtaining information concerning the company; and
   * for requisitioning a meeting of the board.

3　In the conduct of board business, two fundamental concepts should be observed:
   * each director should receive the same information at the same time, and
   * each director should be given sufficient time in which to consider any such information.

4   The board should identify matters which require the prior approval of the board and lay down procedures[1] to be followed when, exceptionally, a decision is required before its next meeting on any matter not required by law to be considered at board level.

5   As a basic principle, all material contracts, and especially those not in the ordinary course of business, should be referred to the board for decision prior to the commitment of the company.

6   The board should approve definitions of the terms 'material'[2] and 'not in the ordinary course of business' and these definitions should be brought to the attention of all relevant persons.

7   Where there is any uncertainty regarding the materiality or nature of a contract, it should normally be assumed that the contract should be brought before the board.

8   Decisions regarding the content of the agenda for individual meetings of the board and concerning the presentation of agenda items should be taken by the chairman in consultation with the company secretary.

9   The company secretary should be responsible to the chairman for the proper administration of the meetings of the company, the board and any committees thereof. To carry out this responsibility the company secretary should be entitled to be present at (or represented at) and prepare (or arrange for the preparation of) minutes of the proceedings of all such meetings.

10 The minutes of meetings should record the decisions taken and provide sufficient background to those decisions. All papers presented at the meeting should be clearly identified in the minutes and retained for reference. Procedures for the approval and circulation of minutes should be established.

11 Where the articles of association allow the board to delegate any of its powers to a committee, the board should give its prior approval to:
    •   the membership and quorum of any such committee;
    •   its term of reference; and
    •   the extent of any powers delegated to it.

12 The minutes of all meetings of committees of the board (or a written summary thereof) should be circulated to the board prior to its next meeting and the opportunity should be given at that meeting for any member of the board to ask questions thereon.

13 Notwithstanding the absence of a formal agenda item, the chairman should permit any director or the company secretary to raise at any board meeting any matter concerning the company's compliance with this Code of Practice, with the company's memorandum and articles of association and with any other legal or regulatory requirement.

Notes

1   If it is practicable, the approval of all the directors should be obtained by means of a written resolution. In all cases, however, the procedures should balance the need for urgency with the overriding principle that each director should be given as much information as possible and have an opportunity to requisition an emergency meeting of the board to discuss the matter prior to the commitment of the company.

2   Different definitions of the term 'material' should be established for 'contracts not in the ordinary course of business' and 'contracts in the ordinary course of business'. Financial limits should be set where appropriate.

Appendix 3

ICSA Guidance Note: Matters Reserved for the Board

No matter how effective a board of directors may be it is not possible for it to have hands-on involvement in every area of the company's business. An effective board controls the business but delegates day-to-day responsibility to the executive management. That said, there are a number of matters which are required to be or, in the interests of the company, should only be decided by the board of directors as a whole. It is incumbent upon the board to make it clear what these Matters Reserved for the Board are. The Combined Code on Corporate Governance (the 'Combined Code') states that 'There should be a formal schedule of matters specifically reserved for [the board's] decision'[1] and that the annual report should contain a 'high-level statement of which types of decisions are to be taken by the board and which are to be delegated to management'.[2]

The Combined Code also states that 'The board's role is to provide entrepreneurial leadership of the company within a framework of prudent and effective controls which enables risk to be assessed and managed. The board should set the company's strategic aims, ensure that the necessary financial and human resources are in place for the company to meet its objectives and review management performance. The board should set the company's values and standards and ensure that its obligations to its shareholders and others are understood and met.'[3]

ICSA has produced this guidance note to aid directors and company secretaries in drawing up such a schedule of Matters Reserved for the Board. The original version of this document was first published in the February 1993 edition of The Company Secretary and has been adopted as a precedent by a number of writers on corporate governance. It has been updated to incorporate more recent developments in best practice.

The relative importance of some matters included in this guidance note will vary according to the size and nature of the company's business. For example, all companies will have a different view on the establishment of the financial limits for transactions which should be referred to the board. Equally, there may well be items not mentioned in the guidance note which some companies (for example, those subject to additional forms of external regulation) would wish to include in their own schedule.

Multiple signatures

In drawing up a schedule of Matters Reserved for the Board, companies should clarify which transactions require multiple board signatures on the relevant documentation.

Delegation

Certain of the matters included in this guidance note should, under the provisions of the Combined Code, be the subject of recommendations by the audit, nomination or remuneration committee. However, full delegation is not normally permitted in these cases as the final decision on the matter is required to be taken by the whole board.

Urgent matters

In drawing up a schedule of Matters Reserved for the Board it is important to establish procedures for dealing with matters that need to be dealt with urgently between regular board meetings. In these circumstances, it is recommended that a telephone or video-conference meeting should be held in which as many directors as possible participate. This allows directors the opportunity to discuss the matter and ask questions. Any director who cannot attend should still be sent the relevant papers and have the opportunity to give their views to the chairman, another director or the company secretary before the meeting. If the matter is routine and discussion is not necessary the approval of all the directors may be obtained by means of a written resolution. In all cases, however, the procedures should balance the need for urgency with the overriding principle that each director should be given as much information as possible, the time to consider it properly and an opportunity to discuss the matter prior to the commitment of the company.

Notes on the ICSA guidance

The following schedule has been produced to assist boards of directors and company secretaries in preparing a schedule of Matters Reserved for the Board in accordance with good corporate governance practice.

Items marked * are not considered suitable for delegation to a committee of the board, for example because of Companies Act requirements or because, under the recommendations of the Combined Code, they are the responsibility of an audit, nomination or remuneration committee, with the final decision required to be taken by the board as a whole.

CA06 refers to the Companies Act 2006

CA85 refers to the Companies Act 1985

CC refers to the Combined Code

DTR refers to the UKLA's Disclosure and Transparency Rules

LR refers to the UKLA's Listing Rules

References to Audit, Nomination or Remuneration refer to the board committee which will consider the item and make recommendations to the board for its final decision.

Schedule of matters reserved for the board

1. Strategy and management

1.1   Responsibility for the overall management of the group. CC A.1
1.2   Approval of the group's long-term objectives and commercial strategy. CC A.1
1.3   Approval of the annual operating and capital expenditure budgets and any material changes to them.
1.4   Oversight of the group's operations ensuring:
  •   competent and prudent management
  •   sound planning
  •   an adequate system of internal control
  •   adequate accounting and other records
  •   compliance with statutory and regulatory obligations.
1.5   Review of performance in the light of the group's strategy, objectives, business plans and budgets and ensuring that any necessary corrective action is taken. CC A.1
1.6   Extension of the group's activities into new business or geographic areas.
1.7   Any decision to cease to operate all or any material part of the group's business.

2. Structure and capital

2.1   Changes relating to the group's capital structure including reduction of capital, share issues (except under employee share plans), share buy-backs (including the use of treasury shares).
2.2   Major changes to the group's corporate structure.
2.3   Changes to the group's management and control structure.
2.4   Any changes to the company's listing or its status as a plc.

3. Financial reporting and controls

3.1   * Approval of the half-yearly report, interim management statements and any preliminary announcement of the final results. CC C.1 Audit DTR 5
3.2   * Approval of the annual report and accounts, [including the corporate governance statement and remuneration report].[4] CA85 s233, s234C DTR 5, LR 9.8 CC C.I Audit

3.3   * Approval of the dividend policy.
3.4   * Declaration of the interim dividend and recommendation of the final dividend.[4] LR 9.7A.2 DTR 6.1.13
3.5   * Approval of any significant changes in accounting policies or practices. Audit
3.6   Approval of treasury policies [including foreign currency exposure and the use of financial derivatives].

4. Internal controls

4.1   Ensuring maintenance of a sound system of internal control and risk management including:
- receiving reports on, and reviewing the effectiveness of, the group's risk and control processes to support its strategy and objectives
- undertaking an annual assessment of these processes
- approving an appropriate statement for inclusion in the annual report. CC C.2, C.2.1 Audit

5. Contracts

5.1   Major capital projects.

5.2   Contracts which are material strategically or by reason of size, entered into by the company [or any subsidiary] in the ordinary course of business, for example bank borrowings [above £xx million] and acquisitions or disposals of fixed assets [above £xx million].

5.3   Contracts of the company [or any subsidiary] not in the ordinary course of business, for example loans and repayments [above £xx million]; foreign currency transactions [above £xx million]; major acquisitions or disposals [above £xx million].

5.4   Major investments [including the acquisition or disposal of interests of more than (5) per cent in the voting shares of any company or the making of any takeover offer].

6. Communication

6.1   Approval of resolutions and corresponding documentation to be put forward to shareholders at a general meeting. LR 13

6.2   * Approval of all circulars, prospectuses and listing particulars [approval of routine documents such as periodic circulars about scrip dividend procedures or exercise of conversion rights could be delegated to a committee]. LR 13 PR 5.5

6.3   * Approval of press releases concerning matters decided by the board.

7. Board membership and other appointments

7.1   * Changes to the structure, size and composition of the board, following recommendations from the nomination committee. Nomination

7.2   * Ensuring adequate succession planning for the board and senior management. CC A.4, A.7

7.3   * Appointments to the board, following recommendations by the nomination committee. Nomination

7.4   * Selection of the chairman of the board and the chief executive. Nomination

7.5   * Appointment of the senior independent director. CC A.3.3 Nomination

7.6   * Membership and chairmanship of board committees. Nomination

7.7   * Continuation in office of directors at the end of their term of office, when they are due to be re-elected by shareholders at the AGM and otherwise as appropriate. Nomination

7.8   * Continuation in office of any director at any time, including the suspension or termination of service of an executive director as an employee of the company, subject to the law and their service contract. Nomination

7.9   * Appointment or removal of the company secretary. CA85 s283, s286 CC A.5.3

7.10 * Appointment, reappointment or removal of the external auditor to be put to shareholders for approval, following the recommendation of the audit committee. CA85 s384 CC C.3.2 Audit

7.11 Appointments to boards of subsidiaries.

8. Remuneration

8.1   * Determining the remuneration policy for the directors, company secretary and other senior executives. Remuneration

8.2   Determining the remuneration of the non-executive directors, subject to the articles of association and shareholder approval as appropriate. CC B.2.3

8.3   * The introduction of new share incentive plans or major changes to existing plans, to be put to shareholders for approval. Remuneration

9. Delegation of authority

9.1   * The division of responsibilities between the chairman, the chief executive [and other executive directors,] which should be in writing. CC A.2.1

9.2   * Approval of terms of reference of board committees. CC A.4.1, B.2.1, C.3.1

9.3   * Receiving reports from board committees on their activities.

10. Corporate governance matters

10.1 * Undertaking a formal and rigorous review [annually] of its own performance, that of its committees and individual directors. CC A.6

10.2 * Determining the independence of directors. CC A.3.1

10.3 * Considering the balance of interests between shareholders, employees, customers and the community.

10.4 Review of the group's overall corporate governance arrangements.

10.5 * Receiving reports on the views of the company's shareholders. CC D.1.1

11. Policies

11.1 Approval of policies, including:
- Code of Conduct
- Share dealing code
- Health and safety policy
- Environmental policy
- Communications policy [including procedures for the release of price sensitive information]
- Corporate social responsibility policy
- Charitable donations policy. CC A.1

12. Other

12.1 The making of political donations.

12.2 Approval of the appointment of the group's principal professional advisers.

12.3 Prosecution, defence or settlement of litigation [involving above £xx million or being otherwise material to the interests of the group].

12.4 Approval of the overall levels of insurance for the group including Directors' & Officers' liability insurance [and indemnification of directors].

12.5 Major changes to the rules of the group's pension scheme, or changes of trustees or [when this is subject to the approval of the company] changes in the fund management arrangements.

12.6 This schedule of matters reserved for board decisions.

Matters which the board considers suitable for delegation are contained in the terms of reference of its committees.

In addition, the board will receive reports and recommendations from time to time on any matter which it considers significant to the group.

Notes

1   The Combined Code on Corporate Governance is published by the Financial Reporting Council and can be found at www.frc.gov.uk. All references to the Combined Code in this guidance note are to the version published in June 2006.

2   The Combined Code, A.1.1.

3   The Combined Code, A.1, first supporting principle.

4   These items are often considered by the whole board but with the final formal decision being delegated to a committee (set up solely for that purpose). This allows time for any changes requested at the board meeting to be incorporated into the final document before publication.

Appendix 4

Higgs Guidance: Summary of the Principal Duties of the Nomination Committee

There should be a nomination committee which should lead the process for board appointments and make recommendations to the board.

A majority of members of the committee should be independent non-executive directors. The chairman or an independent non-executive director should chair the committee, but the chairman should not chair the nomination committee when it is dealing with the appointment of a successor to the chairmanship.

Duties

The committee should:

- be responsible for identifying and nominating for the approval of the board, candidates to fill board vacancies as and when they arise;
- before making an appointment, evaluate the balance of skills, knowledge and experience on the board and, in the light of this evaluation, prepare a description of the role and capabilities required for a particular appointment;
- review annually the time required from a non-executive director. Performance evaluation should be used to assess whether the non-executive director is spending enough time to fulfil their duties;
- consider candidates from a wide range of backgrounds and look beyond the 'usual suspects';
- give full consideration to succession planning in the course of its work, taking into account the challenges and opportunities facing the company and what skills and expertise are therefore needed on the board in the future;
- regularly review the structure, size and composition (including the skills, knowledge and experience) of the board and make recommendations to the board with regard to any changes;

- keep under review the leadership needs of the organisation, both executive and non-executive, with a view to ensuring the continued ability of the organisation to compete effectively in the marketplace;
- make a statement in the annual report about its activities; the process used for appointments and explain if external advice or open advertising has not been used; the membership of the committee, number of committee meetings and attendance over the course of the year;
- make available its terms of reference explaining clearly its role and the authority delegated to it by the board; and
- ensure that on appointment to the board, non-executive directors receive a formal letter of appointment setting out clearly what is expected of them in terms of time commitment, committee service and involvement outside board meetings.

The committee should make recommendations to the board:

- as regards plans for succession for both executive and non-executive directors;
- as regards the reappointment of any non-executive director at the conclusion of their specified term of office;
- concerning the re-election by shareholders of any director under the retirement by rotation provisions in the company's articles of association;
- concerning any matters relating to the continuation in office of any director at any time; and
- concerning the appointment of any director to executive or other office other than to the positions of chairman and chief executive, the recommendation for which would be considered at a meeting of the board.

This guidance has been compiled with the assistance of ICSA who have kindly agreed to produce updated guidance on their website www.icsa.org.uk in the future.

Appendix 5

Higgs Guidance on Performance Evaluation

The [Combined] Code provides that the board should undertake a formal and rigorous annual evaluation of its own performance and that of its committees and individual directors. Individual evaluation should aim to show whether each director continues to contribute effectively and to demonstrate commitment to the role (including commitment of time for board and committee meetings and any other duties). The chairman should act on the results of the performance evaluation by recognising the strengths and addressing the weaknesses of the board and, where appropriate, proposing new members be appointed to the board or seeking the resignation of directors. The board should state in the annual report how such performance evaluation has been conducted.

It is the responsibility of the chairman to select an effective process and to act on its outcome. The use of an external third party to conduct the evaluation will bring objectivity to the process.

The non-executive directors, led by the senior independent director, should be responsible for performance evaluation of the chairman, taking into account the views of executive directors.

The evaluation process will be used constructively as a mechanism to improve board effectiveness, maximise strengths and tackle weaknesses. The results of board evaluation should be shared with the board as a whole while the results of individual assessments should remain confidential between the chairman and the non-executive director concerned.

The following are some of the questions that should be considered in a performance evaluation. They are, however, by no means definitive or exhaustive and companies will wish to tailor the questions to suit their own needs and circumstances.

The responses to these questions and others should enable boards to assess how they are performing and to identify how certain elements of their performance areas might be improved.

Performance evaluation of the board

- How well has the board performed against any performance objectives that have been set?
- What has been the board's contribution to the testing and development of strategy?

- What has been the board's contribution to ensuring robust and effective risk management?
- Is the composition of the board and its committees appropriate, with the right mix of knowledge and skills to maximise performance in the light of future strategy? Are inside and outside the board relationships working effectively?
- How has the board responded to any problems or crises that have emerged and could or should these have been foreseen?
- Are the matters specifically reserved for the board the right ones?
- How well does the board communicate with the management team, company employees and others? How effectively does it use mechanisms such as the AGM and the annual report?
- Is the board as a whole up to date with latest developments in the regulatory environment and the market?
- How effective are the board's committees? [Specific questions on the performance of each committee should be included such as, for example, their role, their composition and their interaction with the board.]

The processes that help underpin the board's effectiveness should also be evaluated, e.g.:

- Is appropriate, timely information of the right length and quality provided to the board and is management responsive to requests for clarification or amplification?
- Does the board provide helpful feedback to management on its requirements?
- Are sufficient board and committee meetings of appropriate length held to enable proper consideration of issues? Is time used effectively?
- Are board procedures conducive to effective performance and flexible enough to deal with all eventualities?

In addition, there are some specific issues relating to the chairman which should be included as part of an evaluation of the board's performance, e.g.:

- Is the chairman demonstrating effective leadership of the board?
- Are relationships and communications with shareholders well managed?
- Are relationships and communications within the board constructive?
- Are the processes for setting the agenda working? Do they enable board members to raise issues and concerns?
- Is the company secretary being used appropriately and to maximum value?

Performance evaluation of the non-executive director

The chairman and other board members should consider the following issues and the individual concerned should also be asked to assess themselves. For each non-executive director:

- How well prepared and informed are they for board meetings and is their meeting attendance satisfactory?
- Do they demonstrate a willingness to devote time and effort to understand the company and its business and a readiness to participate in events outside the boardroom such as site visits?
- What has been the quality and value of their contributions at board meetings?
- What has been their contribution to development of strategy and to risk management?
- How successfully have they brought their knowledge and experience to bear in the consideration of strategy?
- How effectively have they probed to test information and assumptions? Where necessary, how resolute are they in maintaining their own views and resisting pressure from others?
- How effectively and proactively have they followed up their areas of concern?
- How effective and successful are their relationships with fellow board members, the company secretary and senior management? Does their performance and behaviour engender mutual trust and respect within the board?
- How actively and successfully do they refresh their knowledge and skills and are they up to date with:
  - the latest developments in areas such as corporate governance framework and financial reporting?
  - the industry and market conditions?
- How well do they communicate with fellow board members, senior management and others, for example shareholders? Are they able to present their views convincingly yet diplomatically and do they listen and take on board the views of others?

Guidance on Audit Committees (The Smith Guidance)

1 Introduction

1.1. This guidance is designed to assist company boards in making suitable arrangements for their audit committees, and to assist directors serving on audit committees in carrying out their role.

1.2. The paragraphs in bold are taken from the Combined Code (Section C3). Listed companies that do not comply with those provisions should include an explanation as to why they have not complied in the statement required by the Listing Rules.

1.3. Best practice requires that every board should consider in detail what arrangements for its audit committee are best suited for its particular circumstances. Audit committee arrangements need to be proportionate to the task, and will vary according to the size, complexity and risk profile of the company.

1.4. While all directors have a duty to act in the interests of the company the audit committee has a particular role, acting independently from the executive, to ensure that the interests of shareholders are properly protected in relation to financial reporting and internal control.

1.5. Nothing in the guidance should be interpreted as a departure from the principle of the unitary board. All directors remain equally responsible for the company's affairs as a matter of law. The audit committee, like other committees to which particular responsibilities are delegated (such as the remuneration committee), remains a committee of the board. Any disagreement within the board, including disagreement between the audit committee's members and the rest of the board, should be resolved at board level.

1.6. The Code provides that a separate section of the annual report should describe the work of the committee. This deliberately puts the spotlight on the audit committee and gives it an authority that it might otherwise lack. This is not incompatible with the principle of the unitary board.

1.7. The guidance contains recommendations about the conduct of the audit committee's relationship with the board, with the executive management and with internal and external auditors. However, the most important features of this relationship cannot be drafted as guidance or put into a code of practice: a frank, open working relationship and a high level of mutual respect are essential, particularly between the audit committee chairman and the board chairman, the chief executive and the finance director. The audit committee must be prepared to take a robust stand, and all parties must be prepared to make information freely available to the audit committee, to listen to their views and to talk through the issues openly.

1.8. In particular, the management is under an obligation to ensure the audit committee is kept properly informed, and should take the initiative in supplying information rather than waiting to be asked. The board should make it clear to all directors and staff that they must cooperate with the audit committee and provide it with any information it requires. In addition, executive board members will have regard to their common law duty to provide all directors, including those on the audit committee, with all the information they need to discharge their responsibilities as directors of the company.

1.9. Many of the core functions of audit committees set out in this guidance are expressed in terms of 'oversight', 'assessment' and 'review' of a particular function. It is not the duty of audit committees to carry out functions that properly belong to others, such as the company's management in the preparation of the financial statements or the auditors in the planning or conducting of audits. To do so could undermine the responsibility of management and auditors. Audit committees should, for example, satisfy themselves that there is a proper system and allocation of responsibilities for the day-to-day monitoring of financial controls but they should not seek to do the monitoring themselves.

1.10. However, the high-level oversight function may lead to detailed work. The audit committee must intervene if there are signs that something may be seriously amiss. For example, if the audit committee is uneasy about the explanations of management and auditors about a particular financial reporting policy decision, there may be no alternative but to grapple with the detail and perhaps to seek independent advice.

1.11. Under this guidance, audit committees have wide-ranging, time-consuming and sometimes intensive work to do. Companies need to make the necessary resources available. This includes suitable payment for the members of audit committees themselves. They – and particularly the audit committee chairman – bear a significant responsibility and they need to commit a significant extra amount of time to the job. Companies also need to make provision for induction and training for new audit committee members and continuing training as may be required.

1.12. This guidance applies to all companies to which the Code applies – i.e. UK listed companies. For groups, it will usually be necessary for the audit committee of the parent company to review issues that relate to particular subsidiaries or activities carried on by the group. Consequently, the board of a UK-listed parent company should ensure that there is adequate cooperation within the group (and with internal and external auditors of individual companies within the group) to enable the parent company audit committee to discharge its responsibilities effectively.

2 Establishment and role of the audit committee; membership, procedures and resources

Establishment and role

2.1   The board should establish an audit committee of at least three, or in the case of smaller companies two, members.

2.2   The main role and responsibilities of the audit committee should be set out in written terms of reference and should include:

- to monitor the integrity of the financial statements of the company and any formal announcements relating to the company's financial performance, reviewing significant financial reporting judgements contained in them;
- to review the company's internal financial controls and, unless expressly addressed by a separate board risk committee composed of independent directors or by the board itself, the company's internal control and risk management systems;
- to monitor and review the effectiveness of the company's internal audit function;
- to make recommendations to the board, for it to put to the shareholders for their approval in general meeting, in relation to the appointment of the external auditor and to approve the remuneration and terms of engagement of the external auditor;
- to review and monitor the external auditor's independence and objectivity and the effectiveness of the audit process, taking into consideration relevant UK professional and regulatory requirements;
- to develop and implement policy on the engagement of the external auditor to supply non-audit services, taking into account relevant ethical guidance regarding the provision of non-audit services by the external audit firm; and to report to the board, identifying any matters in respect of which it considers that action or improvement is needed, and making recommendations as to the steps to be taken.

Membership and appointment

2.3   All members of the committee should be independent non-executive directors. The board should satisfy itself that at least one member of the audit committee has recent and relevant financial experience.

2.4   The chairman of the company should not be an audit committee member.

2.5   Appointments to the audit committee should be made by the board on the recommendation of the nomination committee (where there is one), in consultation with the audit committee chairman.

2.6   Appointments should be for a period of up to three years, extendable by no more than two additional three-year periods, so long as members continue to be independent.

Meetings of the audit committee

2.7   It is for the audit committee chairman, in consultation with the company secretary, to decide the frequency and timing of its meetings. There should be as many meetings as the audit committee's role and responsibilities require. It is recommended there should be not fewer than three meetings during the year, held to coincide with key dates within the financial reporting and audit cycle. However, most audit committee chairmen will wish to call more frequent meetings.

2.8   No one other than the audit committee's chairman and members is entitled to be present at a meeting of the audit committee. It is for the audit committee to decide if non-members should attend for a particular meeting or a particular agenda item. It is to be expected that the external audit lead partner will be invited regularly to attend meetings as well as the finance director. Others may be invited to attend.

2.9   Sufficient time should be allowed to enable the audit committee to undertake as full a discussion as may be required. A sufficient interval should be allowed between audit committee meetings and main board meetings to allow any work arising from the audit committee meeting to be carried out and reported to the board as appropriate.

2.10   The audit committee should, at least annually, meet the external and internal auditors, without management, to discuss matters relating to its remit and any issues arising from the audit.

2.11   Formal meetings of the audit committee are the heart of its work. However, they will rarely be sufficient. It is expected that the audit committee chairman, and to a lesser extent the other members, will wish to keep in touch on a continuing basis with the key people involved in the company's governance, including the board chairman, the chief executive, the finance director, the external audit lead partner and the head of internal audit.

Resources

2.12   The audit committee should be provided with sufficient resources to undertake its duties.

2.13   The audit committee should have access to the services of the company secretariat on all audit committee matters including: assisting the chairman in planning the audit committee's work, drawing up meeting agendas, maintenance of minutes, drafting of material about its activities for the annual report, collection and distribution of information and provision of any necessary practical support.

2.14   The company secretary should ensure that the audit committee receives information and papers in a timely manner to enable full and proper consideration to be given to the issues.

2.15   The board should make funds available to the audit committee to enable it to take independent legal, accounting or other advice when the audit committee reasonably believes it necessary to do so.

Remuneration

2.16   In addition to the remuneration paid to all non-executive directors, each company should consider the further remuneration that should be paid to members of the audit committee to recompense them for the additional responsibilities of membership. Consideration should be given to the time members are required to give to audit committee business, the skills they bring to bear and the onerous duties they take on, as well as the value of their work to the company. The level of remuneration paid to the members of the audit committee should take into account the level of fees paid to other members of the board. The chairman's responsibilities and time demands will generally be heavier than the other members of the audit committee and this should be reflected in his or her remuneration.

Skills, experience and training

2.17   It is desirable that the committee member whom the board considers to have recent and relevant financial experience should have a professional qualification from one of the professional accountancy bodies. The need for a degree of financial literacy among the other members will vary according to the nature of the company, but experience of corporate financial matters will normally be required. The availability of appropriate financial expertise will be particularly important where the company's activities involve specialised financial activities.

2.18   The company should provide an induction programme for new audit committee members. This should cover the role of the audit committee, including its terms of reference and expected time commitment by members; and an overview of the company's business, identifying the main business and financial dynamics and risks. It could also include meeting some of the company staff.

2.19   Training should also be provided to members of the audit committee on an ongoing and timely basis and should include an understanding of the principles of and developments in financial reporting and related company law. In appropriate cases, it may also include, for example, understanding financial statements, applicable accounting standards and recommended practice; the regulatory framework for the company's business; the role of internal and external auditing and risk management.

2.20   The induction programme and ongoing training may take various forms, including attendance at formal courses and conferences, internal company talks and seminars, and briefings by external advisers.

3   Relationship with the board

3.1   The role of the audit committee is for the board to decide and to the extent that the audit committee undertakes tasks on behalf of the board, the results should be reported to, and considered by, the board. In doing so it should identify any matters in respect of which it considers that action or improvement is needed, and make recommendations as to the steps to be taken.

3.2   The terms of reference should be tailored to the particular circumstances of the company.

3.3   The audit committee should review annually its terms of reference and its own effectiveness and recommend any necessary changes to the board.

3.4   The board should review the audit committee's effectiveness annually.

3.5   Where there is disagreement between the audit committee and the board, adequate time should be made available for discussion of the issue with a view to resolving the disagreement. Where any such disagreements cannot be resolved, the audit committee should have the right to report the issue to the shareholders as part of the report on its activities in the annual report.

4   Role and responsibilities

Financial reporting

4.1   The audit committee should review the significant financial reporting issues and judgements made in connection with the preparation of the company's financial statements, interim reports, preliminary announcements and related formal statements.

4.2   It is management's, not the audit committee's, responsibility to prepare complete and accurate financial statements and disclosures in accordance with financial reporting standards and applicable rules and regulations. However the audit committee should consider significant accounting policies, any changes to them and any significant estimates and judgements. The management should inform the audit committee of the methods used to account for significant or unusual transactions where the accounting treatment is open to different approaches. Taking into account the external auditor's view, the audit committee should consider whether the company has adopted appropriate accounting policies and, where necessary, made appropriate estimates and judgements. The audit committee should review the clarity and completeness of disclosures in the financial statements and consider whether the disclosures made are set properly in context.

4.3   Where, following its review, the audit committee is not satisfied with any aspect of the proposed financial reporting by the company, it shall report its views to the board.

4.4   The audit committee should review related information presented with the financial statements, including the operating and financial review, and corporate governance statements relating to the audit and to risk management. Similarly, where board approval is required for other statements containing financial information (for example, summary financial statements, significant financial returns to regulators and release of price sensitive information), whenever practicable (without being inconsistent with any requirement for prompt reporting under the Listing Rules) the audit committee should review such statements first.

Internal controls and risk management systems

4.5   The audit committee should review the company's internal financial controls (that is, the systems established to identify, assess, manage and monitor financial risks); and unless expressly addressed by a separate board risk committee comprised of independent directors or by the board itself, the company's internal control and risk management systems.

4.6   The company's management is responsible for the identification, assessment, management and monitoring of risk, for developing, operating and monitoring the system of internal control and for providing assurance to the board that it has done so. Except where the board or a risk committee is expressly responsible for reviewing the effectiveness of the internal control and risk management systems, the audit committee should receive reports from management on the effectiveness of the systems they have established and the conclusions of any testing carried out by internal and external auditors.

4.7   Except to the extent that this is expressly dealt with by the board or risk committee, the audit committee should review and approve the statements included in the annual report in relation to internal control and the management of risk.

Whistleblowing

4.8   The audit committee should review arrangements by which staff of the company may, in confidence, raise concerns about possible improprieties in matters of financial reporting or other matters. The audit committee's objective should be to ensure that arrangements are in place for the proportionate and independent investigation of such matters and for appropriate follow-up action.

The internal audit process

4.9   The audit committee should monitor and review the effectiveness of the company's internal audit function. Where there is no internal audit function, the audit committee should consider annually whether there is a need for an internal audit function and make a recommendation to the board, and the reasons for the absence of such a function should be explained in the relevant section of the annual report.

4.10   The need for an internal audit function will vary depending on company specific factors including the scale, diversity and complexity of the company's activities and the number of employees, as well as cost/benefit considerations. Senior management and the board may desire objective assurance and advice on risk and control. An adequately resourced internal audit function (or its equivalent where, for example, a third party is contracted to perform some or all of the work concerned) may provide such assurance and advice. There may be other functions within the company that also provide assurance and advice covering specialist areas such as health and safety, regulatory and legal compliance and environmental issues.

4.11   When undertaking its assessment of the need for an internal audit function, the audit committee should also consider whether there are any trends or current factors relevant to the company's activities, markets or other aspects of its external environment, that have increased, or are expected to increase, the risks faced by the company. Such an increase in risk may also arise from internal factors such as organisational restructuring or from changes in reporting processes or underlying information systems. Other matters to be taken into account may include adverse trends evident from the monitoring of internal control systems or an increased incidence of unexpected occurrences.

4.12 In the absence of an internal audit function, management needs to apply other monitoring processes in order to assure itself, the audit committee and the board that the system of internal control is functioning as intended. In these circumstances, the audit committee will need to assess whether such processes provide sufficient and objective assurance.

4.13 The audit committee should review and approve the internal audit function's remit, having regard to the complementary roles of the internal and external audit functions. The audit committee should ensure that the function has the necessary resources and access to information to enable it to fulfil its mandate, and is equipped to perform in accordance with appropriate professional standards for internal auditors.

4.14 The audit committee should approve the appointment or termination of appointment of the head of internal audit.

4.15 In its review of the work of the internal audit function, the audit committee should, inter alia:

- ensure that the internal auditor has direct access to the board chairman and to the audit committee and is accountable to the audit committee;
- review and assess the annual internal audit work plan;
- receive a report on the results of the internal auditors' work on a periodic basis;
- review and monitor management's responsiveness to the internal auditor's findings and recommendations;
- meet with the head of internal audit at least once a year without the presence of management; and
- monitor and assess the role and effectiveness of the internal audit function in the overall context of the company's risk management system.

The external audit process

4.16 The audit committee is the body responsible for overseeing the company's relations with the external auditor.

Appointment

4.17 The audit committee should have primary responsibility for making a recommendation on the appointment, reappointment and removal of the external auditors. If the board does not accept the audit committee's recommendation, it should include in the annual report, and in any papers recommending appointment or reappointment, a statement from the audit committee explaining its recommendation and should set out reasons why the board has taken a different position.

4.18 The audit committee's recommendation to the board should be based on the assessments referred to below. If the audit committee recommends considering the selection of possible new appointees as external auditors, it should oversee the selection process.

4.19 The audit committee should assess annually the qualification, expertise and resources, and independence (see below) of the external auditors and the effectiveness of the audit process. The assessment should cover all aspects of the audit service provided by the audit firm, and include obtaining a report on the audit firm's own internal quality control procedures.

4.20   If the external auditor resigns, the audit committee should investigate the issues giving rise to such resignation and consider whether any action is required.

Terms and Remuneration

4.21   The audit committee should approve the terms of engagement and the remuneration to be paid to the external auditor in respect of audit services provided.

4.22   The audit committee should review and agree the engagement letter issued by the external auditor at the start of each audit, ensuring that it has been updated to reflect changes in circumstances arising since the previous year. The scope of the external audit should be reviewed by the audit committee with the auditor. If the audit committee is not satisfied as to its adequacy it should arrange for additional work to be undertaken.

4.23   The audit committee should satisfy itself that the level of fee payable in respect of the audit services provided is appropriate and that an effective audit can be conducted for such a fee.

Independence, including the provision of non-audit services

4.24   The audit committee should have procedures to ensure the independence and objectivity of the external auditor annually, taking into consideration relevant UK professional and regulatory requirements. This assessment should involve a consideration of all relationships between the company and the audit firm (including the provision of non-audit services). The audit committee should consider whether, taken as a whole and having regard to the views, as appropriate, of the external auditor, management and internal audit, those relationships appear to impair the auditor's judgement or independence.

4.25   The audit committee should seek reassurance that the auditors and their staff have no family, financial, employment, investment or business relationship with the company (other than in the normal course of business). The audit committee should seek from the audit firm, on an annual basis, information about policies and processes for maintaining independence and monitoring compliance with relevant requirements, including current requirements regarding the rotation of audit partners and staff.

4.26   The audit committee should agree with the board the company's policy for the employment of former employees of the external auditor, paying particular attention to the policy regarding former employees of the audit firm who were part of the audit team and moved directly to the company. This should be drafted taking into account the relevant ethical guidelines governing the accounting profession. The audit committee should monitor application of the policy, including the number of former employees of the external auditor currently employed in senior positions in the company, and consider whether in the light of this there has been any impairment, or appearance of impairment, of the auditor's judgement or independence in respect of the audit.

4.27   The audit committee should monitor the external audit firm's compliance with applicable United Kingdom ethical guidance relating to the rotation of audit partners, the level of fees that the company pays in proportion to the overall fee income of the firm, office and partner, and other related regulatory requirements.

4.28 The audit committee should develop and recommend to the board the company's policy in relation to the provision of non-audit services by the auditor. The audit committee's objective should be to ensure that the provision of such services does not impair the external auditor's independence or objectivity. In this context, the audit committee should consider:

- whether the skills and experience of the audit firm make it a suitable supplier of the non audit service;
- whether there are safeguards in place to ensure that there is no threat to objectivity and independence in the conduct of the audit resulting from the provision of such services by the external auditor;
- the nature of the non-audit services, the related fee levels and the fee levels individually and in aggregate relative to the audit fee; and
- the criteria which govern the compensation of the individuals performing the audit.

4.29 The audit committee should set and apply a formal policy specifying the types of non-audit work:

- from which the external auditors are excluded;
- for which the external auditors can be engaged without referral to the audit committee; and
- for which a case-by-case decision is necessary.

In addition, the policy may set fee limits generally or for particular classes of work.

4.30 In the third category, if it is not practicable to give approval to individual items in advance, it may be appropriate to give a general pre-approval for certain classes for work, subject to a fee limit determined by the audit committee and ratified by the board. The subsequent provision of any service by the auditor should be ratified at the next meeting of the audit committee.

4.31 In determining the policy, the audit committee should take into account relevant ethical guidance regarding the provision of non-audit services by the external audit firm, and in principle should not agree to the auditor providing a service if, having regard to the ethical guidance, the result is that:

- the external auditor audits its own firm's work;
- the external auditor makes management decisions for the company;
- a mutuality of interest is created; or
- the external auditor is put in the role of advocate for the company.

The audit committee should satisfy itself that any safeguards required by ethical guidance are implemented.

4.32 The annual report should explain to shareholders how, if the auditor provides non-audit services, auditor objectivity and independence is safeguarded.

Annual audit cycle

4.33 At the start of each annual audit cycle, the audit committee should ensure that appropriate plans are in place for the audit.

4.34 The audit committee should consider whether the auditor's overall work plan, including planned levels of materiality, and proposed resources to execute the audit plan appears consistent with the scope of the audit engagement, having regard also to the seniority, expertise and experience of the audit team.

4.35   The audit committee should review, with the external auditors, the findings of their work. In the course of its review, the audit committee should:

- discuss with the external auditor major issues that arose during the course of the audit and have subsequently been resolved and those issues that have been left unresolved;

- review key accounting and audit judgements; and review levels of errors identified during the audit, obtaining explanations from management and, where necessary the external auditors, as to why certain errors might remain unadjusted.

4.36   The audit committee should also review the audit representation letters before signature by management and give particular consideration to matters where representation has been requested that relate to non-standard issues. The audit committee should consider whether the information provided is complete and appropriate based on its own knowledge.

4.37   As part of the ongoing monitoring process, the audit committee should review the management letter (or equivalent). The audit committee should review and monitor management's responsiveness to the external auditor's findings and recommendations.

4.38   At the end of the annual audit cycle, the audit committee should assess the effectiveness of the audit process. In the course of doing so, the audit committee should:

- review whether the auditor has met the agreed audit plan and understand the reasons for any changes, including changes in perceived audit risks and the work undertaken by the external auditors to address those risks;

- consider the robustness and perceptiveness of the auditors in their handling of the key accounting and audit judgements identified and in responding to questions from the audit committees, and in their commentary where appropriate on the systems of internal control;

- obtain feedback about the conduct of the audit from key people involved, e.g. the finance director and the head of internal audit; and

- review and monitor the content of the external auditor's management letter, in order to assess whether it is based on a good understanding of the company's business and establish whether recommendations have been acted upon and, if not, the reasons why they have not been acted upon.

5   Communication with shareholders

5.1   The terms of reference of the audit committee, including its role and the authority delegated to it by the board, should be made available. A separate section in the annual report should describe the work of the committee in discharging those responsibilities.

5.2   The audit committee section should include, inter alia:

- a summary of the role of the audit committee;

- the names and qualifications of all members of the audit committee during the period;

- the number of audit committee meetings;
- a report on the way the audit committee has discharged its responsibilities; and
- the explanation provided for in paragraph 4.29 above.

October 2005

Appendix 7

ICSA Guidance Note: Terms of Reference – Audit Committee

Introduction

This guidance note proposes model terms of reference for the audit committee of a company seeking to comply fully with the requirements of the Combined Code on Corporate Governance. It draws on the experience of senior company secretaries and is based on best practice as carried out in some of the UK's top listed companies. Companies with a US listing may need to amend the terms of reference in light of US requirements introduced pursuant to the Sarbanes–Oxley Act.

Although the guidance note is aimed primarily at the corporate sector, the doctrine of good governance, including the adoption of audit committees, is increasingly being embraced by other organisations, particularly in the public and not-for-profit sectors. The principles underlying the content of this guidance note are likely to be applicable regardless of the size or type of organisation and should be useful across all sectors.

The Combined Code

The Combined Code on Corporate Governance (the Combined Code) states as a principle that:

> 'The board should establish formal and transparent arrangements for considering how they should apply the financial reporting and internal control principles and for maintaining an appropriate relationship with the company's auditors.'[1]

It goes on to clarify that, in practical terms, this means that: 'The board should establish an audit committee ...'.[2] Listed companies throughout Europe will soon be required by EU legislation to establish an audit committee.[3] Other influential organisations, such as the Commonwealth Association for Corporate Governance and the International Corporate Governance Network, also support the establishment of audit committees.

The Combined Code recommends that the main role and responsibilities of the audit committee should be 'set out in written terms of reference'[4] and be made 'available'[5] (e.g. by including them on a website maintained by or on behalf of the company).[6]

In addition, it recommends that the work of the committee should be described in a separate section of the annual report[7] and that the committee chairman should attend the AGM prepared to respond to any questions on the committee's area of responsibility.[8] So, as with most aspects of corporate governance, companies are not only required to go through a formal process of considering their internal audit and control procedures and evaluating their relationship with their external auditor, but must also be seen to be doing so in a fair and thorough manner. As part of this process it is essential that the audit committee is properly constituted with a clear remit and identified authority.

Notes on the terms of reference

The Smith Guidance[9] recognises that 'audit committee arrangements need to be proportionate to the task, and will vary according to the size, complexity and risk profile of the company'.[10]

As regards the make-up of the committee, we have followed the Combined Code and recommend a minimum of three independent non-executive directors (although two is permissible for smaller companies).[11] The board should satisfy itself that at least one member of the committee has recent and relevant financial experience. We have made specific recommendations that others may be required to assist the committee from time to time, according to the particular items being considered and discussed.

Although not a provision in the Code, the Higgs Review states as good practice, in its non-code recommendations, that the company secretary, or their designee, should act as secretary to the committee.[12] The Smith Guidance states that the audit committee should have access to the services of the company secretariat on all audit committee matters including: assisting the chairman in planning the audit committee's work, drawing up meeting agendas, maintenance of minutes, drafting of material about its activities for the annual report, collection and distribution of information and provision of any necessary practical support. It also states that the company secretary should ensure that the audit committee receives information and papers in a timely manner to enable full and proper consideration to be given to the issues.[13]

The frequency with which the committee needs to meet will vary from company to company and may change from time to time. As a general rule, most audit committees would be expected to meet quarterly – the Combined Code provides that the committee should meet at least three times a year.

The list of duties we have proposed are those which we believe all audit committees should consider. Some companies may wish to add to this list[14] and some smaller companies may need to modify it in other ways.

The Combined Code includes a provision for a report on the audit committee to be included in the company's annual report.[15] Such report will need to disclose the following:

- Role and main responsibilities of the audit committee.
- Composition of committee, including relevant qualifications and experience; the appointment process; and any fees paid in respect of membership.
- Number of meetings and attendance levels.
- A description of the main activities of the year to:
  - monitor the integrity of the financial statements;

- review the integrity of the internal financial control and risk management systems;
- review the independence of the external auditors, and the provision of non-audit services;
- describe the oversight of the external audit process, and how its effectiveness was assessed;
- explain the recommendation to the board on the appointment of auditors.
- References to 'the committee' are to 'the audit committee'.
- References to 'the board' are to 'the board of directors'.

The square brackets contain recommendations which are in line with best practice but which may need to be changed to suit the circumstances of the particular organisation.

I. Membership

1.1 Members of the committee shall be appointed by the board, on the recommendation of the nomination committee in consultation with the chairman of the audit committee. The committee shall be made up of at least [3] members.

1.2 All members of the committee shall be independent non-executive directors,[16] at least one of whom shall have recent and relevant financial experience. The chairman of the board shall not be a member of the committee.[17]

1.3 Only members of the committee have the right to attend committee meetings. However, other individuals, such as the chairman of the board, chief executive, finance director, other directors, the heads of risk, compliance and internal audit and representatives from the finance function, may be invited to attend all or part of any meeting as and when appropriate.

1.4 The external auditors will be invited to attend meetings of the committee on a regular basis.

1.5 Appointments to the committee shall be for a period of up to three years, which may be extended for two further three-year periods, provided the director remains independent.

1.6 The board shall appoint the committee chairman who shall be an independent non-executive director. In the absence of the committee chairman and/or an appointed deputy, the remaining members present shall elect one of themselves to chair the meeting.

2. Secretary

2.1 The company secretary or their nominee shall act as the secretary of the committee.

3. Quorum

3.1 The quorum necessary for the transaction of business shall be [2] members. A duly convened meeting of the committee at which a quorum is present shall be competent to exercise all or any of the authorities, powers and discretions vested in or exercisable by the committee.

4. Frequency of meetings

4.1   The committee shall meet [at least three times a year at appropriate times in the reporting and audit cycle] [quarterly on the first Wednesday in each of January, April, July and October] and otherwise as required.[18]

5. Notice of meetings

5.1   Meetings of the committee shall be called by the secretary of the committee at the request of any of its members or at the request of external or internal auditors if they consider it necessary.

5.2   Unless otherwise agreed, notice of each meeting confirming the venue, time and date together with an agenda of items to be discussed, shall be forwarded to each member of the committee, any other person required to attend and all other non-executive directors, no later than [5] working days before the date of the meeting. Supporting papers shall be sent to committee members and to other attendees as appropriate, at the same time.

6. Minutes of meetings

6.1   The secretary shall minute the proceedings and resolutions of all meetings of the committee, including recording the names of those present and in attendance.

6.2   The secretary shall ascertain, at the beginning of each meeting, the existence of any conflicts of interest and minute them accordingly.

6.3   Minutes of committee meetings shall be circulated promptly to all members of the committee and, once agreed, to all members of the board, unless a conflict of interest exists.

7. Annual General Meeting

7.1   The chairman of the committee shall attend the Annual General Meeting prepared to respond to any shareholder questions on the committee's activities.

8. Duties

The committee should carry out the duties below for the parent company, major subsidiary undertakings and the group as a whole, as appropriate.

8.1 Financial reporting

8.1.1   The committee shall monitor the integrity of the financial statements of the company, including its annual and half-yearly reports, interim management statements, [preliminary results' announcements] and any other formal announcement relating to its financial performance, reviewing significant financial reporting issues and judgements which they contain. The committee shall also review summary financial statements, significant financial returns to regulators and any financial information contained in certain other documents, such as announcements of a price sensitive nature.

8.1.2   The committee shall review and challenge where necessary:

    8.1.2.1   the consistency of, and any changes to, accounting policies both on a year on year basis and across the company/group

    8.1.2.2   the methods used to account for significant or unusual transactions where different approaches are possible

    8.1.2.3   whether the company has followed appropriate accounting standards and made appropriate estimates and judgements, taking into account the views of the external auditor

    8.1.2.4   the clarity of disclosure in the company's financial reports and the context in which statements are made; and

    8.1.2.5   all material information presented with the financial statements, such as the operating and financial review and the corporate governance statement (insofar as it relates to the audit and risk management).

8.1.3   The committee shall review the annual financial statements of the pension funds where not reviewed by the board as a whole.

8.2 Internal controls and risk management systems

The committee shall:

8.2.1   keep under review the effectiveness of the company's internal controls and risk management systems; and

8.2.2   review and approve the statements to be included in the annual report concerning internal controls and risk management.[19]

8.3 Whistleblowing and fraud

The committee shall:

8.3.1   review the company's arrangements for its employees to raise concerns, in confidence, about possible wrongdoing in financial reporting or other matters. The committee shall ensure that these arrangements allow proportionate and independent investigation of such matters and appropriate follow up action; and

8.3.2.   review the company's procedures for detecting fraud.

8.4 Internal audit

The committee shall:

8.4.1   monitor and review the effectiveness of the company's internal audit function in the context of the company's overall risk management system;[20]

8.4.2   approve the appointment and removal of the head of the internal audit function;

8.4.3   consider and approve the remit of the internal audit function and ensure it has adequate resources and appropriate access to information to enable it to perform its function effectively and in accordance with the relevant professional standards. The committee shall also ensure the function has adequate standing and is free from management or other restrictions;

8.4.4   review and assess the annual internal audit plan;

8.4.5   review promptly all reports on the company from the internal auditors;

8.4.6   review and monitor management's responsiveness to the findings and recommendations of the internal auditor; and

8.4.7   meet the head of internal audit at least once a year, without management being present, to discuss their remit and any issues arising from the internal audits carried out. In addition, the head of internal audit shall be given the right of direct access to the chairman of the board and to the committee.

8.5 External audit

The committee shall:

8.5.1   consider and make recommendations to the board, to be put to shareholders for approval at the AGM, in relation to the appointment, reappointment and removal of the company's external auditor. The committee shall oversee the selection process for new auditors and if an auditor resigns the committee shall investigate the issues leading to this and decide whether any action is required;

8.5.2   oversee the relationship with the external auditor including (but not limited to):

8.5.2.1   approval of their remuneration, whether fees for audit or non-audit services and that the level of fees is appropriate to enable an adequate audit to be conducted;

8.5.2.2   approval of their terms of engagement, including any engagement letter issued at the start of each audit and the scope of the audit;

8.5.2.3   assessing annually their independence and objectivity taking into account relevant [UK] professional and regulatory requirements and the relationship with the auditor as a whole, including the provision of any non-audit services;

8.5.2.4   satisfying itself that there are no relationships (such as family, employment, investment, financial or business) between the auditor and the company (other than in the ordinary course of business);

8.5.2.5   agreeing with the board a policy on the employment of former employees of the company's auditor, then monitoring the implementation of this policy;

8.5.2.6   monitoring the auditor's compliance with relevant ethical and professional guidance on the rotation of audit partners, the level of fees paid by the company compared to the overall fee income of the firm, office and partner and other related requirements;

8.5.2.7   assessing annually their qualifications, expertise and resources and the effectiveness of the audit process which shall include a report from the external auditor on their own internal quality procedures;

8.5.2.8   seeking to ensure coordination with the activities of the internal audit function;

8.5.3   meet regularly with the external auditor, including once at the planning stage before the audit and once after the audit at the reporting stage. The committee shall meet the external auditor at least once a year, without management being present, to discuss their remit and any issues arising from the audit;

8.5.4   review and approve the annual audit plan and ensure that it is consistent with the scope of the audit engagement;

8.5.5   review the findings of the audit with the external auditor. This shall include but not be limited to, the following:

8.5.5.1   a discussion of any major issues which arose during the audit;

8.5.5.2   any accounting and audit judgements;

8.5.5.3   levels of errors identified during the audit.

The committee shall also review the effectiveness of the audit;

8.5.6   review any representation letter(s) requested by the external auditor before they are signed by management;

8.5.7   review the management letter and management's response to the auditor's findings and recommendations;

8.5.8   develop and implement a policy on the supply of non-audit services by the external auditor, taking into account any relevant ethical guidance on the matter.

8.6 Reporting responsibilities

8.6.1   The committee chairman shall report formally to the board on its proceedings after each meeting on all matters within its duties and responsibilities.

8.6.2   The committee shall make whatever recommendations to the board it deems appropriate on any area within its remit where action or improvement is needed.

8.6.3   The committee shall compile a report to shareholders on its activities to be included in the company's annual report.

8.7 Other matters

The committee shall:

8.7.1   have access to sufficient resources in order to carry out its duties, including access to the company secretariat for assistance as required;

8.7.2   be provided with appropriate and timely training, both in the form of an induction programme for new members and on an ongoing basis for all members;

8.7.3   give due consideration to laws and regulations, the provisions of the Combined Code and the requirements of the UK Listing Authority's Listing, Prospectus and Disclosure and Transparency Rules as appropriate;

8.7.4   be responsible for coordination of the internal and external auditors;

8.7.5   oversee any investigation of activities which are within its terms of reference and act for internal purposes as a court of the last resort;

8.7.6   at least once a year, review its own performance, constitution and terms of reference to ensure it is operating at maximum effectiveness and recommend any changes it considers necessary to the board for approval.

9. Authority

The committee is authorized:

9.1   to seek any information it requires from any employee of the company in order to perform its duties;

9.2   to obtain, at the company's expense, outside legal or other professional advice on any matter within its terms of reference;

9.3   to call any employee to be questioned at a meeting of the committee as and when required.

Notes

1 The Combined Code June 2006, C.3.
2 The Combined Code June 2006, C.3.1.
3 Directive 2006/43/EC on Statutory Audits of Annual and Consolidated Accounts must be implemented by 29 June 2008.
4 The Combined Code June 2006, C.3.2.
5 The Combined Code June 2006, C.3.3.
6 See footnote 4 to the Combined Code June 2006.
7 The Combined Code June 2006, C.3.3.
8 The Combined Code June 2006 D.2.3
9 Guidance on Audit Committees (The Smith Guidance), January 2003. This report was originally included as an appendix in the Combined Code but can now be obtained separately from the FRC website (www.frc.org.uk/).
10 Guidance on Audit Committees (The Smith Guidance), January 2003, para. 1.3.
11 A smaller company is defined in footnote 3 to the Combined Code as one which is below the FTSE 350 throughout the year immediately prior to the reporting year.
12 Higgs Review of the role and effectiveness of non-executive directors, January 2003, para. 11.30.
13 Guidance on Audit Committees (The Smith Guidance) – January 2003, paras 2.13 and 2.14.
14 For example, some companies also require the committee to monitor/make recommendations on the potential implications of legal actions being taken against the company, the adequacy of arrangements for managing conflicts of interest, the expenses incurred by the chairman and treasury management policies.
15 The Combined Code, June 2006 C.3.3 and Guidance on Audit Committees (The Smith Guidance), January 2003, para. 5.2.
16 An independent non-executive director is defined in Combined Code provision A.3.1.
17 Except on appointment, the chairman of the company is not considered to meet the test of independence. Combined Code provision A.3.1.
18 The frequency and timing of meetings will differ according to the needs of the company. Meetings should be organised so that attendance is maximised (for example, by timetabling them to coincide with board meetings).
19 Unless this is done by the board as a whole.
20 If the company does not have an internal audit function, the Committee should consider annually whether there should be one and make a recommendation to the board accordingly. The absence of such a function should be explained in the annual report.

Higgs Guidance: Summary of the Principal Duties of the Remuneration Committee

The Code provides that the remuneration committee should consist exclusively of independent non-executive directors and should comprise at least three or, in the case of smaller companies,[1] two such directors.

Duties

The committee should:

- determine and agree with the board the framework or broad policy for the remuneration of the chief executive, the chairman of the company and such other members of the executive management as it is designated to consider.[2] At a minimum, the committee should have delegated responsibility for setting remuneration for all executive directors, the chairman and, to maintain and assure their independence, the company secretary. The remuneration of non-executive directors shall be a matter for the chairman and executive members of the board. No director or manager should be involved in any decisions as to their own remuneration;
- determine targets for any performance-related pay schemes operated by the company;
- determine the policy for and scope of pension arrangements for each executive director;
- ensure that contractual terms on termination, and any payments made, are fair to the individual and the company, that failure is not rewarded and that the duty to mitigate loss is fully recognised;[3]
- within the terms of the agreed policy, determine the total individual remuneration package of each executive director including, where appropriate, bonuses, incentive payments and share options;
- in determining such packages and arrangements, give due regard to the contents of the Code as well as the UK Listing Authority's Listing Rules and associated guidance;
- be aware of and advise on any major changes in employee benefit structures throughout the company or group;

- agree the policy for authorising claims for expenses from the chief executive and chairman;
- ensure that provisions regarding disclosure of remuneration, including pensions, as set out in the Directors' Remuneration Report Regulations 2002 and the Code, are fulfilled;
- be exclusively responsible for establishing the selection criteria, selecting, appointing and setting the terms of reference for any remuneration consultants who advise the committee;
- report the frequency of, and attendance by members at, remuneration committee meetings in the annual reports; and
- make available the committee's terms of reference. These should set out the committee's delegated responsibilities and be reviewed and, where necessary, updated annually.

This guidance has been compiled with the assistance of ICSA who have kindly agreed to produce updated guidance on their website www.icsa.org.uk in the future.

Notes

1   A smaller company is one that is below the FTSE 350 throughout the year immediately prior to the reporting year.
2   Some companies require the remuneration committee to consider the packages of all executives at or above a specified level such as those reporting to a main board director whilst others require the committee to deal with all packages above a certain figure.
3   Remuneration committees should consider reviewing and agreeing a standard form of contract for their executive directors, and ensuring that new appointees are offered and accept terms within the previously agreed level.

Guidance on Internal Control (The Turnbull Guidance)

Preface

Internal Control: Guidance for Directors on the Combined Code (The Turnbull Guidance) was first issued in 1999.

In 2004, the Financial Reporting Council established the Turnbull Review Group to consider the impact of the guidance and the related disclosures and to determine whether the guidance needed to be updated.

In reviewing the impact of the guidance, our consultations revealed that it has very successfully gone a long way to meeting its original objectives. Boards and investors alike indicated that the guidance has contributed to a marked improvement in the overall standard of risk management and internal control since 1999.

Notably, the evidence gathered by the Review Group demonstrated that respondents considered that the substantial improvements in internal control instigated by application of the Turnbull Guidance have been achieved without the need for detailed prescription as to how to implement the guidance.

The principles-based approach has required boards to think seriously about control issues and enabled them to apply the principles in a way that appropriately dealt with the circumstances of their business.

The evidence also supported the proposition that the companies which have derived most benefit from application of the guidance were those whose boards saw embedded risk management and internal control as an integral part of running the business.

Accordingly, the Review Group strongly endorsed retention of the flexible, principles-based approach of the original guidance and has made only a small number of changes.

This however does not mean that there is nothing new for boards to do or that some companies could not make more effective use of the guidance. Establishing an effective system of internal control is not a one-off exercise. No such system remains effective unless it develops to take account of new and emerging risks, control failures, market expectations or changes in the company's circumstances or business objectives. The Review Group reiterates the view of the vast majority of respondents in emphasising the importance of regular and systematic assessment of the risks facing the business and the value of embedding risk management and internal control systems within business processes. It is the board's responsibility to make sure this happens.

Boards should review whether they can make more of the communication opportunity of the internal control statement in the annual report. Investors consider the board's attitude towards risk management and internal control to be an important factor when making investment decisions about a company. Taken together with the Operating and Financial Review, the internal control statement provides an opportunity for the board to help shareholders understand the risk and control issues facing the company, and to explain how the company maintains a framework of internal controls to address these issues and how the board has reviewed the effectiveness of that framework.

It is in this spirit that directors need to exercise their responsibility to review on a continuing basis their application of the revised guidance.

Turnbull Review Group
October 2005

Introduction

The importance of internal control and risk management

1   A company's system of internal control has a key role in the management of risks that are significant to the fulfilment of its business objectives. A sound system of internal control contributes to safeguarding the shareholders' investment and the company's assets.

2   Internal control (as referred to in paragraph 19) facilitates the effectiveness and efficiency of operations, helps ensure the reliability of internal and external reporting and assists compliance with laws and regulations.

3   Effective financial controls, including the maintenance of proper accounting records, are an important element of internal control. They help ensure that the company is not unnecessarily exposed to avoidable financial risks and that financial information used within the business and for publication is reliable. They also contribute to the safeguarding of assets, including the prevention and detection of fraud.

4   A company's objectives, its internal organisation and the environment in which it operates are continually evolving and, as a result, the risks it faces are continually changing. A sound system of internal control therefore depends on a thorough and regular evaluation of the nature and extent of the risks to which the company is exposed. Since profits are, in part, the reward for successful risk-taking in business, the purpose of internal control is to help manage and control risk appropriately rather than to eliminate it.

Objectives of the guidance

5   This guidance is intended to:
   - reflect sound business practice whereby internal control is embedded in the business processes by which a company pursues its objectives;

- remain relevant over time in the continually evolving business environment; and
- enable each company to apply it in a manner which takes account of its particular circumstances.

The guidance requires directors to exercise judgement in reviewing how the company has implemented the requirements of the Combined Code relating to internal control and reporting to shareholders thereon.

6   The guidance is based on the adoption by a company's board of a risk-based approach to establishing a sound system of internal control and reviewing its effectiveness. This should be incorporated by the company within its normal management and governance processes. It should not be treated as a separate exercise undertaken to meet regulatory requirements.

Internal control requirements of the Combined Code

7   Principle C.2 of the Code states that 'The board should maintain a sound system of internal control to safeguard shareholders' investment and the company's assets'.

8   Provision C.2.1 states that 'The directors should, at least annually, conduct a review of the effectiveness of the group's system of internal control and should report to shareholders that they have done so. The review should cover all material controls, including financial, operational and compliance controls and risk management systems'.

9   Paragraph 9.8.6 of the UK Listing Authority's Listing Rules states that in the case of a listed company incorporated in the United Kingdom, the following items must be included in its annual report and accounts:

- a statement of how the listed company has applied the principles set out in Section 1 of the Combined Code, in a manner that would enable shareholders to evaluate how the principles have been applied;
- a statement as to whether the listed company has:
    - Complied throughout the accounting period with all relevant provisions set out in Section 1 of the Combined Code; or
    - not complied throughout the accounting period with all relevant provisions set out in Section 1 of the Combined Code and if so, setting out:
        - (i)   those provisions, if any, it has not complied with;
        - (ii) in the case of provisions whose requirements are of a continuing nature, the period within which, if any, it did not comply with some or all of those provisions; and
        - (iii) the company's reasons for non-compliance.

10 The Preamble to the Code makes it clear that there is no prescribed form or content for the statement setting out how the various principles in the Code have been applied. The intention is that companies should have a free hand to explain their governance policies in the light of the principles, including any special circumstances which have led to them adopting a particular approach.

11 The guidance in this document applies for accounting periods beginning on or after 1 January 2006, and should be followed by boards of listed companies in:

- assessing how the company has applied Code Principle C.2;
- implementing the requirements of Code Provision C.2.1; and
- reporting on these matters to shareholders in the annual report and accounts.

12 For the purposes of this guidance, internal controls considered by the board should include all types of controls including those of an operational and compliance nature, as well as internal financial controls.

Groups of companies

13 Throughout this guidance, where reference is made to 'company' it should be taken, where applicable, as referring to the group of which the reporting company is the parent company. For groups of companies, the review of effectiveness of internal control and the report to the shareholders should be from the perspective of the group as a whole.

The Appendix

14 The Appendix to this document contains questions which boards may wish to consider in applying this guidance.

Maintaining a sound system of internal control

Responsibilities

15 The board of directors is responsible for the company's system of internal control. It should set appropriate policies on internal control and seek regular assurance that will enable it to satisfy itself that the system is functioning effectively. The board must further ensure that the system of internal control is effective in managing those risks in the manner which it has approved.

16 In determining its policies with regard to internal control, and thereby assessing what constitutes a sound system of internal control in the particular circumstances of the company, the board's deliberations should include consideration of the following factors:
- the nature and extent of the risks facing the company;
- the extent and categories of risk which it regards as acceptable for the company to bear;
- the likelihood of the risks concerned materialising;
- the company's ability to reduce the incidence and impact on the business of risks that do materialise; and
- the costs of operating particular controls relative to the benefit thereby obtained in managing the related risks.

17 It is the role of management to implement board policies on risk and control. In fulfilling its responsibilities management should identify and evaluate the risks faced by the company for consideration by the board and design, operate and monitor

a suitable system of internal control which implements the policies adopted by the board.

18 All employees have some responsibility for internal control as part of their accountability for achieving objectives. They, collectively, should have the necessary knowledge, skills, information, and authority to establish, operate and monitor the system of internal control. This will require an understanding of the company, its objectives, the industries and markets in which it operates, and the risks it faces.

Elements of a sound system of internal control

19 An internal control system encompasses the policies, processes, tasks, behaviours and other aspects of a company that, taken together:
  • facilitate its effective and efficient operation by enabling it to respond appropriately to significant business, operational, financial, compliance and other risks to achieving the company's objectives. This includes the safeguarding of assets from inappropriate use or from loss and fraud and ensuring that liabilities are identified and managed;
  • help ensure the quality of internal and external reporting. This requires the maintenance of proper records and processes that generate a flow of timely, relevant and reliable information from within and outside the organisation;
  • help ensure compliance with applicable laws and regulations, and also with internal policies with respect to the conduct of business.

20 A company's system of internal control will reflect its control environment which encompasses its organisational structure. The system will include:
  • control activities;
  • information and communications processes; and
  • processes for monitoring the continuing effectiveness of the system of internal control.

21 The system of internal control should:
  • be embedded in the operations of the company and form part of its culture;
  • be capable of responding quickly to evolving risks to the business arising from factors within the company and to changes in the business environment; and
  • include procedures for reporting immediately to appropriate levels of management any significant control failings or weaknesses that are identified together with details of corrective action being undertaken.

22 A sound system of internal control reduces, but cannot eliminate, the possibility of poor judgement in decision-making; human error; control processes being deliberately circumvented by employees and others; management overriding controls; and the occurrence of unforeseeable circumstances.

23 A sound system of internal control therefore provides reasonable, but not absolute, assurance that a company will not be hindered in achieving its business objectives, or in the orderly and legitimate conduct of its business, by circumstances which may reasonably be foreseen. A system of internal control cannot, however, provide protection with certainty against a company failing to meet its business objectives or all material errors, losses, fraud, or breaches of laws or regulations.

Reviewing the effectiveness of internal control responsibilities

24 Reviewing the effectiveness of internal control is an essential part of the board's responsibilities. The board will need to form its own view on effectiveness based on the information and assurances provided to it, exercising the standard of care generally applicable to directors in the exercise of their duties. Management is accountable to the board for monitoring the system of internal control and for providing assurance to the board that it has done so.

25 The role of board committees in the review process, including that of the audit committee, is for the board to decide and will depend upon factors such as the size and composition of the board; the scale, diversity and complexity of the company's operations; and the nature of the significant risks that the company faces. To the extent that designated board committees carry out, on behalf of the board, tasks that are attributed in this guidance document to the board, the results of the relevant committees' work should be reported to, and considered by, the board. The board takes responsibility for the disclosures on internal control in the annual report and accounts.

The process for reviewing effectiveness

26 Effective monitoring on a continuous basis is an essential component of a sound system of internal control. The board cannot, however, rely solely on the embedded monitoring processes within the company to discharge its responsibilities. It should regularly receive and review reports on internal control. In addition, the board should undertake an annual assessment for the purposes of making its public statement on internal control to ensure that it has considered all significant aspects of internal control for the company for the year under review and up to the date of approval of the annual report and accounts.

27 The board should define the process to be adopted for its review of the effectiveness of internal control. This should encompass both the scope and frequency of the reports it receives and reviews during the year, and also the process for its annual assessment, such that it will be provided with sound, appropriately documented, support for its statement on internal control in the company's annual report and accounts.

28 The reports from management to the board should, in relation to the areas covered by them, provide a balanced assessment of the significant risks and the effectiveness of the system of internal control in managing those risks. Any significant control failings or weaknesses identified should be discussed in the reports, including the impact that they have had, or may have, on the company and the actions being taken to rectify them. It is essential that there be openness of communication by management with the board on matters relating to risk and control.

29 When reviewing reports during the year, the board should:
- consider what are the significant risks and assess how they have been identified, evaluated and managed;

- assess the effectiveness of the related system of internal control in managing the significant risks, having regard in particular to any significant failings or weaknesses in internal control that have been reported;
- consider whether necessary actions are being taken promptly to remedy any significant failings or weaknesses; and
- consider whether the findings indicate a need for more extensive monitoring of the system of internal control.

30 Additionally, the board should undertake an annual assessment for the purpose of making its public statement on internal control. The assessment should consider issues dealt with in reports reviewed by it during the year together with any additional information necessary to ensure that the board has taken account of all significant aspects of internal control for the company for the year under review and up to the date of approval of the annual report and accounts.

31 The board's annual assessment should, in particular, consider:
- the changes since the last annual assessment in the nature and extent of significant risks, and the company's ability to respond to changes in its business and the external environment;
- the scope and quality of management's ongoing monitoring of risks and of the system of internal control, and, where applicable, the work of its internal audit function and other providers of assurance;
- the extent and frequency of the communication of the results of the monitoring to the board (or board committee(s)) which enables it to build up a cumulative assessment of the state of control in the company and the effectiveness with which risk is being managed;
- the incidence of significant control failings or weaknesses that have been identified at any time during the period and the extent to which they have resulted in unforeseen outcomes or contingencies that have had, could have had, or may in the future have, a material impact on the company's financial performance or condition; and
- the effectiveness of the company's public reporting processes.

32 Should the board become aware at any time of a significant failing or weakness in internal control, it should determine how the failing or weakness arose and reassess the effectiveness of management's ongoing processes for designing, operating and monitoring the system of internal control.

The board's statement on internal control

33 The annual report and accounts should include such meaningful, high-level information as the board considers necessary to assist shareholders' understanding of the main features of the company's risk management processes and system of internal control, and should not give a misleading impression.

34 In its narrative statement of how the company has applied Code Principle C.2, the board should, as a minimum, disclose that there is an ongoing process for identifying, evaluating and managing the significant risks faced by the company, that it

has been in place for the year under review and up to the date of approval of the annual report and accounts, that it is regularly reviewed by the board and accords with the guidance in this document.

35 The disclosures relating to the application of Principle C.2 should include an acknowledgement by the board that it is responsible for the company's system of internal control and for reviewing its effectiveness. It should also explain that such a system is designed to manage rather than eliminate the risk of failure to achieve business objectives, and can only provide reasonable and not absolute assurance against material misstatement or loss.

36 In relation to Code Provision C.2.1, the board should summarise the process it (where applicable, through its committees) has applied in reviewing the effectiveness of the system of internal control and confirm that necessary actions have been or are being taken to remedy any significant failings or weaknesses identified from that review. It should also disclose the process it has applied to deal with material internal control aspects of any significant problems disclosed in the annual report and accounts.

37 Where a board cannot make one or more of the disclosures in paragraphs 34 and 36, it should state this fact and provide an explanation. The Listing Rules require the board to disclose if it has failed to conduct a review of the effectiveness of the company's system of internal control.

38 Where material joint ventures and associates have not been dealt with as part of the group for the purposes of applying this guidance, this should be disclosed.

Appendix

Assessing the effectiveness of the company's risk and control processes

Some questions which the board may wish to consider and discuss with management when regularly reviewing reports on internal control and when carrying out its annual assessment are set out below. The questions are not intended to be exhaustive and will need to be tailored to the particular circumstances of the company.

This Appendix should be read in conjunction with the guidance set out in this document.

Risk assessment

- Does the company have clear objectives and have they been communicated so as to provide effective direction to employees on risk assessment and control issues? For example, do objectives and related plans include measurable performance targets and indicators?
- Are the significant internal and external operational, financial, compliance and other risks identified and assessed on an ongoing basis? These are likely to include the principal risks identified in the Operating and Financial Review.
- Is there a clear understanding by management and others within the company of what risks are acceptable to the board?

Control environment and control activities

- Does the board have clear strategies for dealing with the significant risks that have been identified? Is there a policy on how to manage these risks?
- Do the company's culture, code of conduct, human resource policies and performance reward systems support the business objectives and risk management and internal control system?
- Does senior management demonstrate, through its actions as well as its policies, the necessary commitment to competence, integrity and fostering a climate of trust within the company?
- Are authority, responsibility and accountability defined clearly such that decisions are made and actions taken by the appropriate people? Are the decisions and actions of different parts of the company appropriately coordinated?
- Does the company communicate to its employees what is expected of them and the scope of their freedom to act? This may apply to areas such as customer relations; service levels for both internal and outsourced activities; health, safety and environmental protection; security of tangible and intangible assets; business continuity issues; expenditure matters; accounting; and financial and other reporting.
- Do people in the company (and in its providers of outsourced services) have the knowledge, skills and tools to support the achievement of the company's objectives and to manage effectively risks to their achievement?
- How are processes/controls adjusted to reflect new or changing risks, or operational deficiencies?

Information and communication

- Do management and the board receive timely, relevant and reliable reports on progress against business objectives and the related risks that provide them with the information, from inside and outside the company, needed for decision-making and management review purposes? This could include performance reports and indicators of change, together with qualitative information such as on customer satisfaction, employee attitudes, etc.
- Are information needs and related information systems reassessed as objectives and related risks change or as reporting deficiencies are identified?
- Are periodic reporting procedures, including half-yearly and annual reporting, effective in communicating a balanced and understandable account of the company's position and prospects?
- Are there established channels of communication for individuals to report suspected breaches of law or regulations or other improprieties?

Monitoring

- Are there ongoing processes embedded within the company's overall business operations, and addressed by senior management, which monitor the effective application of the policies, processes and activities related to internal control and risk management? (Such processes may include control self-assessment, confirmation by personnel of compliance with policies and codes of conduct, internal audit reviews or other management reviews.)

- Do these processes monitor the company's ability to re-evaluate risks and adjust controls effectively in response to changes in its objectives, its business, and its external environment?
- Are there effective follow-up procedures to ensure that appropriate change or action occurs in response to changes in risk and control assessments?
- Is there appropriate communication to the board (or board committees) on the effectiveness of the ongoing monitoring processes on risk and control matters? This should include reporting any significant failings or weaknesses on a timely basis.
- Are there specific arrangements for management monitoring and reporting to the board on risk and control matters of particular importance? These could include, for example, actual or suspected fraud and other illegal or irregular acts, or matters that could adversely affect the company's reputation or financial position.

Glossary

accountability The requirement for a person in a position of responsibility to justify, explain or account for the exercise of his/her authority and his/her performance or actions. Accountability is to the person or persons from whom the authority is derived.

aggressive accounting Accounting policies by a company that are just within accepted accounting practice, but which have the effect of making the company's performance seem better than it would if more conservative accounting policies were used. For example, accounting policies might be used that recognise income at an early stage in a transaction process, or defer the recognition of expenses.

AGM Annual general meeting of a company.

audit committee A committee of the board of directors, with responsibility for a range of audit-related issues, and in particular the conduct of the external audit and the company's relationship with its auditors.

audit report Report for shareholders produced by the external auditors on completion of the annual audit, and included in the company's published annual report and accounts.

auditor independence Relationship between the external auditors and a client company, whereby the auditors are able to exercise their independent professional judgement, and where their judgement will not be influenced by the closeness of the relationship with the client company or by matters of self-interest.

balance of power A situation in which power is shared out more or less evenly between a number of different individuals or groups, so that no single individual or group is in a position to dominate.

board committee A committee established by the board of directors, with responsibility for a particular aspect of the board's affairs. For example, audit committee, remuneration/compensation committee and nomination committee.

board succession The replacement of a senior executive when he or she retires or resigns. A board of directors should consider the succession to top positions on the board, in particular those of the chief executive officer and the chairman.

bond credit ratings Ratings given to issues of bonds by agencies such as Standard & Poor's and Moody's, that give an assessment of the credit risk for investors in the bonds, i.e. the risk of default by the bond issuer.

box ticking A term that refers to a process of complying with the detailed requirements of a set of regulations (i.e. ticking the boxes against a list of things that have to be done), rather than complying with the spirit and purpose of the regulations.

business risks Risks in the operations of a business that actual results could be worse (or better) than anticipated. Businesses must be entrepreneurial to succeed, and entrepreneurship means having to take business risks. Companies should, however, avoid unnecessary business risks or risks where the losses could not be afforded if an adverse outcome were to occur.

Cadbury Code A code of corporate governance, published by the Cadbury Committee in the UK in 1992 (and since superseded).

CEO (chief executive officer) The head of the executive management team in an organisation.

chairman Leader of the board of directors. Often referred to as the 'company chairman'.

Class 1 transactions A large transaction, such as an acquisition or the disposal of a business that meets the specifications for this type of transaction as set out in the Listing Rules. Class 1 transactions by a listed company, unlike smaller Class 2 and Class 3 transactions, must be approved by the shareholders before they can go ahead.

code of ethics A comprehensive set of rules or guidelines for moral behaviour; rules of conduct recognised as appropriate. A code of ethics can be written or unwritten.

Combined Code The UK code on corporate governance, which applies to UK listed companies. It is a voluntary code rather than a regulatory requirement. However, the UK Listing Rules require listed companies to disclose in their annual report the extent of their compliance or non-compliance with the Code. The Code was revised in 2003.

compliance statement A statement by a listed company of whether it has complied with the requirements of the national code of corporate governance and, if not, in what ways has it failed to do so. In the UK, listed companies are required by the Combined Code to include a compliance statement in their annual report and accounts.

corporate accountability legislation Legislation requiring companies to be accountable to their shareholders.

corporate shareholders Shareholders in a company that are themselves companies. Companies, as legal persons, may own shares in other companies.

corporate social responsibility Responsibility shown by a company (or other organisations) for matters of general concern to the society in which it operates, such as protection of the environment, health and safety, and social welfare.

Cromme Code Code of corporate governance introduced in Germany.

cross-shareholdings Mutual shareholdings in each other. A cross-shareholding occurs when company A owns shares in company B, and company B also owns shares in company A.

deferred annual bonus scheme An element in a remuneration package for directors or senior executives whereby the individuals are allowed to use some or all of their annual cash bonus entitlement to acquire shares in the company, which are then matched after several years (typically three years) by the award of additional free shares.

directors' report A report by the board of directors to the shareholders, contained in the annual report and accounts of the company and containing mainly statutory disclosures of information.

disaster recovery plans Contingency plans to be implemented, in the event of a disaster that puts normal operational systems out of action, to restore operational capability as quickly as possible. The need for many companies to have a disaster recovery plan was highlighted by the terrorist attack on the US on 11 September 2001.

disclosure Making something known. Revealing information.

dominant personality An individual who is able, through force of character or other means, to impose his or her way of thinking on others, so that the others will normally agree with or accept that individual's point of view. Where a board of directors has a dominant personality (for example, a forceful individual who is both chairman and CEO) there is a risk of poor corporate governance.

downside risk A risk that actual events will turn out worse than expected. Downside risk can be measured in terms of the amount by which profits could be worse than expected. The expected outcome is the forecast or budget expectation.

duty of skill and care A duty owed by a director to the company. In the UK, this is currently a common law duty, but might be made a statutory duty. A question can be raised, however, about what level of skill and care should be expected from a director.

electronic communications Communication between a company and its shareholders by electronic means, i.e. by email or via the company's website.

electronic voting Voting by an electronic method, via email or the company's website.

enlightened shareholder approach View on corporate governance that the directors should run the company in the interests of the equity shareholders, but taking into consideration the interests of other stakeholder groups.

equity shareholders Shareholders with an interest in the ownership of a company. In the UK, these are the ordinary shareholders. In the US, they are referred to as 'common stockholders'.

ESG risks Environmental, social and governance risks. These are risks of adverse consequences to a company from circumstances or events relating to environmental, social or corporate governance issues.

ethical conduct Behaviour that is in accordance with a written or unwritten code of ethics and set of moral values. In the context of corporate governance, ethical conduct applies to individuals and also to organisations.

executive director A director who also has responsibilities as an executive manager.

external audit Statutory annual audit of a company by independent external auditors.

fair dealing Unbiased and equitable dealing, possibly in accordance with established rules or guidelines.

fairness Impartiality, a lack of bias. In the context of corporate governance, the quality of fairness refers to things that are done or decided in a reasonable manner, and with a sense of justice, and avoiding bias.

fiduciary duty A duty of a trustee. The directors of a company are given their powers in trust by the company, and have fiduciary duties towards the company.

financial statement A statement containing financial information. The main financial statements by a company are the balance sheet and profit and loss account in the annual report and accounts. Other financial statements include a cash flow statement, and the balance sheet and profit and loss account in a company's published interim or quarterly accounts.

fraudulent trading A term used in insolvency law. It occurs when an individual, including a director of a company, allows the company to continue trading when insolvent. It is a criminal offence, unlike wrongful trading, and fraud has to be proved for a person's guilt to be established. A director found guilty of fraudulent trading might be disqualified from being a director, and might also be held personally liable. Personal liability is more likely to be established for wrongful trading, which is easier to prove.

gagging clause A clause in a contract or agreement that forbids a person from speaking out, typically to the public or the press.

general meeting A meeting of the equity shareholders of a company, either an Annual General Meeting (AGM) or an Extraordinary General Meeting. Public companies are required to hold an AGM.

going concern statement A requirement of some corporate governance codes, such as the Combined Code. A statement by the board of directors that in their view the company will remain as a going concern for the next financial year.

Greenbury Report Report in the UK in 1995 by the Greenbury Committee, focusing mainly on corporate governance issues related to directors' remuneration.

Hampel Committee Committee set up in the UK to continue the review of corporate governance practices in the UK, following the Cadbury and Greenbury Committee Reports. The Hampel Committee suggested that the recommendations of all three committees should be integrated into a single code of corporate governance, which was published in 1998 as the Combined Code.

Higgs Report The 2003 UK-government commissioned review into the role and effectiveness of non-executive directors.

independence Free from the influence of another individual (or individuals) and free from conflicts of interest.

independent NED A non-executive director who is also independent.

insider dealing Dealing in the shares of a company by an individual who has knowledge of undisclosed 'insider information' (price-sensitive information) that comes from an 'inside source'. In the UK, insider dealing is a criminal offence under Part V of the Criminal Justice Act 1993.

institutional investor An organisation or institution that invests funds of clients, savers or depositors. The main institutional investors are pension funds, insurance/life assurance companies, investment trust companies and organisations such as unit trusts and open-ended investment companies ('OEICs'). Institutional investors are the main investors in shares in the leading stock markets of the world. In the UK, most institutional investors are members of an 'industry association', such as the Association of British Insurers and the National Association of Pension Funds. These make best practice recommendations to their members.

internal audit Investigations and checks carried out by internal auditors of an organisation. Internal audit is a function rather than a specific activity. However, the work programme of the internal audit team might reduce the amount of work the external auditors need to carry out in their annual audit, provided the internal and external auditors collaborate properly.

internal control report A statement by the board of directors of a listed company to the shareholders on internal control, and contained in the company's annual report and accounts. This statement is a requirement of the combined Code in the UK.

internal control system A system of internal controls within an organisation. In the UK, the board of directors of a listed company has responsibility for the system of risk management, including the system of internal control.

internal controls Control measures within an organisation that are intended to ensure the safeguarding of the organisation's assets and the prevention or detection of fraud or error.

key performance indicators A factor by which the development, performance or position of the company can be measured and assessed. The business review in the directors' report should include financial key performance indicators and (except for medium-sized companies) other non-financial key performance indicators where appropriate, including measurements relating to environmental and employee factors.

Listing Rules Rules that must be complied with in order for shares of a company to be accepted on to (and retained on) the Official List. In the UK, shares must be admitted to the Official List ('listed') by the UK Listing Authority before they can be admitted to trading on the main market of the London Stock Exchange. Listed Companies are required to comply with the continuing obligations in the Listing Rules. In the UK, this includes making certain disclosures about directors' remuneration, and disclosing in its annual report the extent to which the company has/has not complied with the Combined Code.

majority shareholder A shareholder holding a majority of the equity shares in a company and so having a controlling interest in the company. (A majority shareholder has the voting power to remove directors from the board, and so can control the board.)

management board A board of executive managers, chaired by the chief executive officer, within a two-tier board structure. The chairman of the management board reports to the chairman of the supervisory board. The management board has responsibility for the operational performance of the business.

market abuse A civil offence under the Financial Services and Markets Act 2000, for which an individual can be fined by the Financial Services Authority. Market abuse occurs when an individual distorts a market in investments, creates a false or misleading impression of the value or price of an investment or misuses relevant information before it is published. (In effect, this is similar to insider trading, but it is a civil offence, rather than a criminal offence, and the burden of proof is lower.)

minority shareholders Shareholders whose combined shareholdings are insufficient to affect resolutions by the company in general meeting. The term is often used when a majority of the shareholders (and possibly a single majority shareholder) favours one course of action whilst a minority opposes it. Company law provides some safeguards for minority shareholders, to protect them from unfair or discriminatory actions by the majority.

Model Articles of Association In the context of UK company law, a company may adopt standard articles of association (company constitution) and amend these as necessary to meet the requirements and particular circumstances of the individual company. In practice, the articles of association of most UK companies formed under the Companies Act 1985 are based on the Table A Articles. Different model articles apply to companies formed under the Companies Act 2006.

Model Code A Code that applies restrictions on share dealings that go beyond the restrictions imposed by law, for example the insider dealing legislation. Its aim is to ensure that directors, relevant employees and 'connected persons' do not abuse price-sensitive information, especially in a period leading up to the announcement of results by the company (a 'close period'). Listed companies must apply a code of conduct that is at least as stringent as the Model Code.

Myners Report A UK report into the role and responsibilities of institutional investors.

nomination/nominating committee A committee of the board of directors, with responsibility for identifying potential new members for the board of directors. Suitable candidates are recommended to the main board, which then makes a decision about their appointment.

nominee shareholders A shareholder holding the shares as a nominee for the beneficial shareholder. The nominee's name appears on the register of shareholders. It might be possible for an investor to use nominee shareholdings to hide the size of his or her shareholdings from the company.

non-audit work Work done by a firm of auditors for a client company, other than work on the annual audit. In the context of corporate governance, the independence of the auditors might be questionable when they earn high fees for non-audit work. The annual audit might be used to maintain a close relationship with the company in the hope of winning more non-audit work in the future.

non-executive director A director who does not have any responsibilities for executive management in the company.

Operating and Financial Review (OFR) A report by a company, written in simple English and contained in the company's annual report and accounts, giving a description of the company's operations and financial performance and position for the year under review. Operating and financial reviews are voluntary statements.

ordinary resolution A decision reached by the shareholders in a general meeting, voting for or against a proposal, where a simple majority is required to carry the resolution for or against the proposal.

performance-based incentives Incentives to an individual, typically to an executive director and in the form of a cash bonus, that are payable if certain performance targets are achieved. Performance targets might be related to a rise in the share price, growth in sales or profits, growth in earnings per share, or to non-financial performance criteria.

pluralist approach See stakeholder approach.

poison pills An arrangement that provides for something that will occur in the event of a successful takeover, making the acquisition less attractive to the buyer. Poison pills are designed to deter hostile takeovers, and are considered detrimental to good corporate governance.

pre-emption rights Rights given in UK law to shareholders, whereby a company cannot issue new shares to raise cash without first offering them to the existing shareholders in proportion to their current shareholdings. The shareholders might agree to disapply their pre-emption rights, and allow the directors to issue new shares to other investors, but only up to a maximum limit of new shares. In listed companies, shareholders typically pass a special resolution each year to allow the disapplication of their pre-emption rights, so that the company can issue some shares for cash (for example, under the arrangements of a share option scheme).

price-sensitive information Undisclosed information that, if made generally known, would be likely to have an effect on the share price of the company concerned.

private shareholders Individual shareholders in a company. The term 'private' distinguishes individual shareholders from corporate shareholders and investment institutions holding shares.

proxy vote A vote delivered by an individual (a proxy) on behalf of a shareholder, in the shareholder's absence. The absent shareholder gives instructions to the proxy on how to vote (although might give the proxy discretion in deciding how to vote).

qualified opinion Audit report in which the auditors express some reservations about the financial statements of the company.

quasi-loan Something in the nature of a loan without actually being a loan as such, for example, a company making a payment to a third party on a director's behalf, without the director undertaking to pay the money back at a future time.

remuneration/compensation committee A committee of the board of directors, with responsibility for deciding remuneration policy for top executives and the individual remuneration packages of certain senior executives, for example all the executive directors.

remuneration policy The policy of a company on the remuneration of its senior executives, including basic salary and all incentive-related elements and severance payment terms. The remuneration policy might be formulated by the remuneration committee, and shareholders might be invited to vote to approve the policy at the company AGM.

reputational risk Risk to the reputation of a company or other organisation in the mind of the public (including customers and suppliers) when a particular matter becomes public knowledge.

responsibility Having authority over something, and so liable to be held accountable for the exercise of that authority.

responsible voting Voting by a shareholder in a way that fulfils the shareholder's responsibilities to another group, typically the shareholder's clients. The term is used in connection with voting by institutional shareholders. It is increasingly accepted that institutional shareholders should vote responsibly in the interests of their clients. Responsible voting is associated with upholding best practice in corporate governance.

risk assessment An assessment of risks faced by an organisation. Typically, risks are assessed according to how probable or how frequent an adverse outcome is likely to be in the planning period and the potential size of the losses if an adverse outcome occurs. The greatest risks are those with a high probability of an adverse outcome combined with the likelihood of a large loss if this were to happen.

risk management The process of identifying and assessing potential risks facing an organisation, and taking measures to avoid or control the risk. Many risks are controlled through a system of internal controls. In listed companies, the board of directors has overall responsibility for risk management.

rotation of audit partners A system whereby a company might keep the same firm of external auditors for as long as it wishes, but the partner in charge of the annual audit must be changed at regular intervals. Rotation of audit partners has been suggested as a method of protecting auditor independence, which could be put at risk by the personal relationships between the audit partner and the company's senior management.

rotation of auditors A system whereby a company changes its external auditors at regular intervals, say every five years. Rotation of auditors has been suggested as a method of protecting auditor independence, because the auditors have less to lose if they apply their professional judgement with greater rigour.

secret profit A profit that is not revealed. In the context of corporate governance, a director should not make a secret profit for his/her personal benefit and at the expense of the company.

senior independent director An independent non-executive director, recognised as the senior individual amongst the non-executives.

service contract Contract of service between a director and the company. A service contract should ideally be in writing, but could be verbal.

severance payment Payment to a director (or other employee) on being required to resign (or otherwise leave the company).

share options Instruments giving their holder the right (but not the obligation) to subscribe for shares in a company at a predetermined price (the exercise price). When issued, share options are usually exercisable at any time after a given future date, up to a final date when they eventually lapse. If the company share price rises, an option holder stands to make an immediate profit by exercising share options and buying shares at the exercise price and selling them at the current market price.

shareholder A person holding shares in a company. Shares may be held by the share owner or by a nominee acting on behalf of the share owner. (The US term for shares is 'stock'.)

shareholder activism (engagement) A term that refers to (1) the considered use by institutional investors of their rights as shareholders, by voting against the board of directors at general meetings (or threatening to vote against the board); and (2) active dialogue with the boards of companies, to influence decisions by the board.

shareholder engagement See shareholder activism.

shareholder property rights As defined in the OECD Principles, the property rights of shareholders include: the right to secure methods of registering their ownership of the shares, the right to transfer their shares, the right to receive relevant information about the company on a 'timely and regular' basis, the right to participate and vote in general meetings of the company and elect members of the board of directors, and a right to share in the profits of the company.

shareholder value approach View on corporate governance that the directors should run the company with the objective of maximising the wealth of its owners, the equity shareholders.

Smith Report The 2003 Report by an FRC-appointed group into the role and responsibilities of audit committees.

special resolution A decision reached by the shareholders in a general meeting, voting for or against a proposal, where a majority of at least 75 per cent is required to carry the resolution for or against the proposal.

stakeholder A stakeholder group is an identifiable group of individuals or organisations with a vested interest. Stakeholder groups in a company include the shareholders, the directors, senior executive management and other employees, customers, suppliers, the general public and (in the case of many companies) the government. The nature of their interests differs between stakeholder groups. Issues in corporate governance are which stakeholder group interests should predominate and to what extent can the interests of the different groups be met or reconciled.

stakeholder approach View on corporate governance that the directors should be permitted or required to run the company in a way that balances the interests of the equity shareholders with those of other stakeholders, particularly the employees. Also called the 'pluralist approach'.

statutory duties Duties imposed by statute.

supervisory board A board of non-executive directors, found in a company with a two-tier board structure. The supervisory board reserves some responsibilities to itself. These include oversight of the management board.

sustainability reporting A report by a socially responsible company on its social, ethical, health and safety and environmental policies and procedures. It might also refer more specifically to environmental reporting, with a focus on how the company is following the business options with the least-damaging effect on the environment.

total shareholder return The total returns in a period earned by the company's shareholders, consisting normally of the dividends received and the gain (or minus the fall) in the share price during the period. The returns might be expressed as a percentage of the share value, e.g. the share price at the start of the period.

transparency/visibility In the context of corporate governance, it refers to outcomes that are reached or decisions that are made as a result of clear and visible procedures/ processes. In the context of company reporting, it refers to information that makes clear the position and performance of the company, and the way in which the information has been derived.

Turnbull Report A report of the Turnbull Committee in the UK, giving listed companies guidance on how the directors should carry out their responsibility for the internal control system, as required by the Combined Code.

two-tier board A board structure with two boards, a supervisory board of non-executive directors and beneath it a management board of executive directors. The CEO heads the management board and reports to the chairman of the supervisory board. Responsibilities for governance are divided between the two boards. A two-tier board is the norm in some countries, notably Germany. (See also unitary board.)

unitary (one-tier) board A board structure where the organisation has just a single board of directors. This consists of executive directors and (in the case of listed companies and also many other public companies and some private companies) non-executive directors. A unitary board structure is used by companies in many countries, including the US and UK. (See also two-tier board.)

upside risk A risk that actual events will turn out better than expected and will provide unexpected profits. Some risks, such as the risk of a change in foreign exchange rates, or a change in interest rates, or a change in consumer buying patterns, could be 'two-way', with both upside and downside potential.

VFM audit/value for money audit This is an investigation into an activity or operation, to assess whether costs are under proper control, whether resources are being used efficiently, and whether the activity or operation is achieving its purpose. A VFM audit is therefore sometimes referred to as an audit of the '3 Es' – economy, efficiency and effectiveness.

voting cap A limit on the voting power of any shareholder, regardless of the number of shares that the shareholder owns. Considered detrimental to good corporate governance.

whistleblower An individual, usually an employee, who reports concerns about misconduct or misdemeanours by someone in an organisation. A whistleblower does not use normal lines of reporting, but instead goes to a senior individual within the organisation or to someone outside the organisation, such as the press or a regulatory body.

whistleblowing procedure A procedure that encourages or allows whistleblowers to report genuine (non-malicious) concerns about suspected misconduct or misdemeanours, and that gives the whistleblower protection against retaliatory/punitive action by the employer. Procedures might be established by an employer that provide for reporting to someone within the organisation (internal procedure) or to an external body. Alternatively, external whistleblowing procedures might be established by an external body, such as a financial markets regulator.

wrongful trading A term used in insolvency law. Wrongful trading occurs when a company continues to trade when the directors are aware that the company had gone into (or would soon go into) insolvent liquidation. It is a civil offence. A liquidator of the company can apply to the court for a director or shadow director to be held liable to make a contribution to the assets of the company.

Directory of web resources

ICSA Guidance Notes

The ICSA Policy Unit produces a range of Guidance Notes on Corporate Governance topics, including electronic communications and committee terms of reference. These are available at www.icsa.org.uk/news/guidance.php

ABI remuneration guidelines www.ivis.co.uk

Accounting Standards Board www.frc.org.uk/asb

Asian Corporate Governance Association www.acga-asia.org

Association of British Insurers www.abi.org.uk

Australian Stock Exchange www.asx.com.au

Business for Social Responsibility www.bsr.org

Business in the Community www.bitc.org.uk

Calpers www.calpers.org

Combined Code www.frc.co.uk

Committee on Standards in Public Life, UK www.public-standards.gov.uk

Council of Institutional Investors, USA www.cii.org

Davis Global Advisors www.davisglobal.com

Deminor (scorecards) www.deminor.com

Department for Business Enterprise and Regulatory Reform (BERR) (formerly the DTI) www.berr.gov.uk

EIRIS (Ethical Investment Research Service) www.eiris.org

European Corporate Governance Institute www.ecgi.org

Financial Reporting Council www.frc.org.uk

Financial Services Authority www.fsa.gov.uk

Global Corporate Governance Forum www.gcgf.org

Hermes www.hermes.co.uk

Institutional Shareholder Services (ISS) www.issproxy.com

International Corporate Governance Network www.icgn.org

International Organization of Securities Commissions www.iosco.org

Investor Relations Society www.ir-soc.org.uk

ISC Principles www.institutionalshareholdercommittee.org.uk

Kuala Lumpur Stock Exchange www.klse.com.my

London Stock Exchange www.stockex.com

National Association of Pension Funds (NAPF) www.napf.co.uk

New York Stock Exchange www.nyse.com

OECD Principles of Corporate Governance www.oecd.org

Pensions & Investment Research Consultants Limited www.pirc.co.uk

Pre-emption Group www.pre-emptiongroup.org.uk

Public Concern at Work (Whistleblowing) www.pcaw.co.uk

Quoted Companies Alliance (QCA) www.qcanet.co.uk

Standard and Poors (ratings) www.standardandpoors.com

Stock Exchange of Hong Kong www.hkex.hk

Stock Exchange of Singapore www.ses.com.sg

The Corporate Library www.thecorporatelibrary.com

The Institute of Business Ethics www.ibe.org.uk

The Institute of Chartered Accountants in England and Wales www.icaew.co.uk

The Institute of Chartered Secretaries and Administrators(ICSA) www.icsa.org.uk

The Institute of Directors www.iod.co.uk

The Investor Responsibility Research Centre www.irrc.org

The National Association of Corporate Directors, USA www.nacdonline.org

Toronto Stock Exchange www.tse.com

UK Company Law Review www.dti.gov.uk/cld/

US Securities and Exchange Commission www.sec.gov

Index